Nighthogs

Other *Pearls Before Swine* Books

BLTs Taste So Darn Good
This Little Piggy Stayed Home
Sgt. Piggy's Lonely Hearts Club Comic

Nighthogs

A *Pearls Before Swine* Collection

by Stephan Pastis

**Andrews McMeel
Publishing, LLC**

Kansas City

Pearls Before Swine is distributed internationally by United Feature Syndicate.

08 09 BBG 10 9 8
ISBN-13: 978-0-7407-5009-0
ISBN-10: 0-7407-5009-7

Library of Congress Control Number: 200411445

www.andrewsmcmeel.com

Pearls Before Swine can be viewed on the Internet at
www.comics.com/comics/pearls.

These strips appeared in newspapers from July 14, 2003 to April 18, 2004.

With apologies to Edward Hopper

For Penny and Parisa, the two smartest
and most beautiful sisters I have.

Introduction

When I was a little kid, I used to stay up very late every Saturday night to watch what almost always seemed to be the last segment on *Saturday Night Live*. That segment involved a six-inch-high piece of Play-Doh named Mr. Bill. In a very brief animated short, the yellow-haired, clownish looking Mr. Bill and his faithful dog, Spot, happily went about their adventures around the streets of New York City. And every Saturday, without fail, Mr. Bill met a tragic end. He was stepped on, eaten, burned, shot, sawed in half, punched in the head, or pushed off the Empire State Building. And every time it happened, a high-pitched voice would wail, "Ohhhhh noooooo, Mr. Bill!"

This, I knew, was comedy.

When I look at *Pearls* today, I can see the obvious influence that Mr. Bill had on the ten-year-old kid that was me. Pig is punched, barbecued, buried alive, and shot through the head with an arrow. Every inanimate object he befriends (be it a piece of fruit, gingerbread cookie, or piggy bank) faces a catastrophic end. Every character with a sunny disposition and positive outlook invariably meets his doom. And then there is Angry Bob, Rat's literary creation, who week after week dies in an endless array of bizarre scenarios.

Anyone who writes comedy can't help but be influenced by the stuff that has made them laugh. For me, it was a lot of things.

Before all else, almost before I could read, my biggest influence was far and away the comic strip *Peanuts*. To this day, I have trouble identifying exactly what it was about those *Peanuts* books that affected me so. But it obviously did, as I read those same books over and over again. I think those endless readings unconsciously taught me the structure and timing of a comic strip, as well as the importance of strong characters.

The other big influence that I can see sometimes when I'm drawing the strip are the thousands of Bugs Bunny and Road Runner and Tom and Jerry cartoons I must have watched as a kid. When I break what they call the "fourth wall" of my comic strip and have Rat and Pig realize that they are really just pen and ink in a comic strip, I can see Bugs Bunny popping out of his cartoon and talking to the hand that was animating him. When I draw Zebra being pursued by crocodiles, I can see Wile E. Coyote laying traps for the Road Runner, and when I have Pig punched in the head or Rat crushing people with the Mallet O' Understanding, I can see the countless head punches and hammer blows delivered by Tom and Jerry upon each other.

But it was more than just comic strips and cartoons. There were *The Little Rascals*, the old Abbott and Costello movies, the *I Love Lucy* reruns, and as I got older, Steve Martin albums, the first *Airplane* movie, *Caddyshack*, *Animal House*, and pretty much anything John Belushi did on *Saturday Night Live*. Whether he was dressed up as that oversized bee or playing the Samurai guy or being the Greek hamburger stand owner ("Cheeseburger! Cheeseburger! Cheeseburger . . . Pepsi! Pepsi! Pepsi!"), Belushi always made me laugh.

In my teens, the biggest influence was again comic strips. Only this time it was the Big Three of the '80s and early '90s: *Calvin and Hobbes*, *Bloom County*, and *The Far Side*. To this day, I think Gary Larson is the all-time undeniable champion of Comicdom. I will never understand how he achieved that level of humor that consistently. Perhaps he's an alien.

When I got serious about developing a comic strip and wanted to learn how to write funny sentences, my two biggest sources of inspiration were the novel *A Confederacy of Dunces* by John Kennedy Toole and the comic strip *Dilbert*. If you've never read *A Confederacy of Dunces*, you should. It is sheer comedic brilliance. *Dilbert* also had a tremendous effect on me. Scott Adams' economy of impactful words is a model of how to write comedy in the confines of a three-panel comic strip.

Nowadays, when I'm not doing the strip and just want to find something to laugh at, I frequently find it in any TV show that shows real-life tragic moments happening to stupid people who are not me. Whether it's the twentysomething kid who decides to skateboard off his two-story roof into the pool (well, missing the pool, actually, whereupon his smart friend asks, "Duuude, you okay?"), or the guy who uses the bungee cord that is ten feet longer than the height of the bridge, or the woman who decides it's a good idea to pet the polar bear, I just can't stop laughing.

It was on one of these shows that I saw what must surely be the single greatest moment of comedy ever. A parachutist jumped from an airplane, only to find that his airplane had been too low to the ground, giving him too little time to fully open his parachute. After he hit the ground, a fellow parachutist ran to his aid. Finding him unconscious, the fellow parachutist yelled to a group of onlookers, "Can we get a hand?"

And the onlookers responded.

By clapping.

And in my head, as I watched, I could hear that high-pitched wail . . .
"Ohhhhh noooooo, Mr. Bill!"

—Stephan Pastis
March, 2005

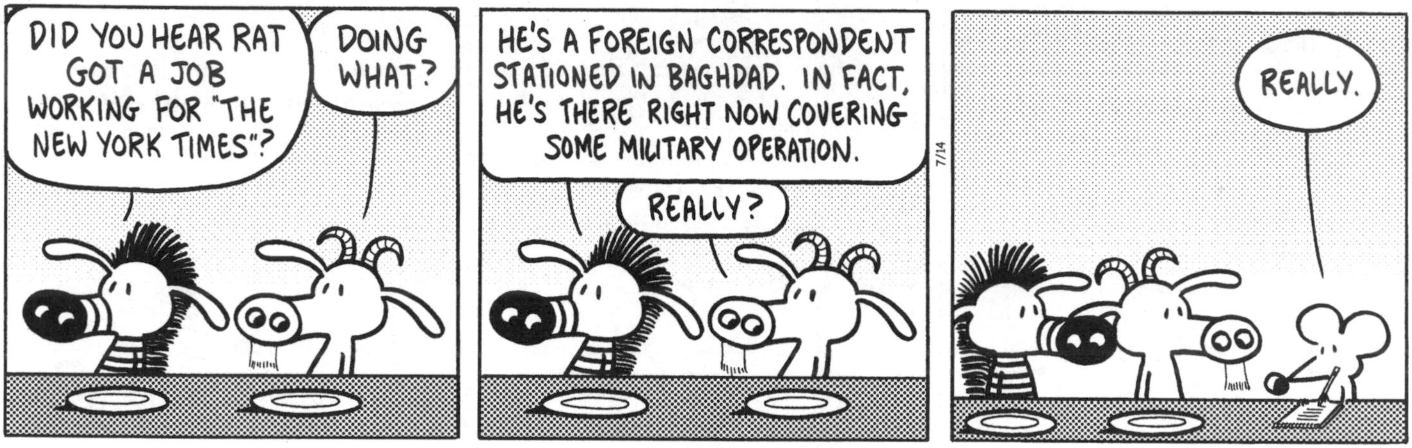
DID YOU HEAR RAT GOT A JOB WORKING FOR "THE NEW YORK TIMES"?
DOING WHAT?
HE'S A FOREIGN CORRESPONDENT STATIONED IN BAGHDAD. IN FACT, HE'S THERE RIGHT NOW COVERING SOME MILITARY OPERATION.
REALLY?
7/14
REALLY.

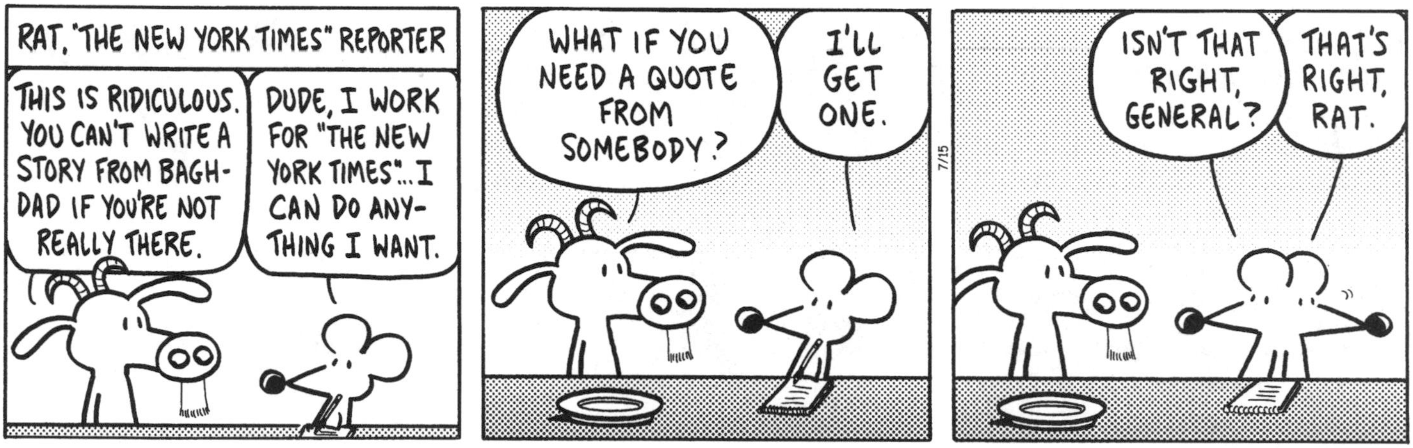
RAT, "THE NEW YORK TIMES" REPORTER
THIS IS RIDICULOUS. YOU CAN'T WRITE A STORY FROM BAGHDAD IF YOU'RE NOT REALLY THERE.
DUDE, I WORK FOR "THE NEW YORK TIMES"... I CAN DO ANYTHING I WANT.
WHAT IF YOU NEED A QUOTE FROM SOMEBODY?
I'LL GET ONE.
7/15
ISN'T THAT RIGHT, GENERAL?
THAT'S RIGHT, RAT.

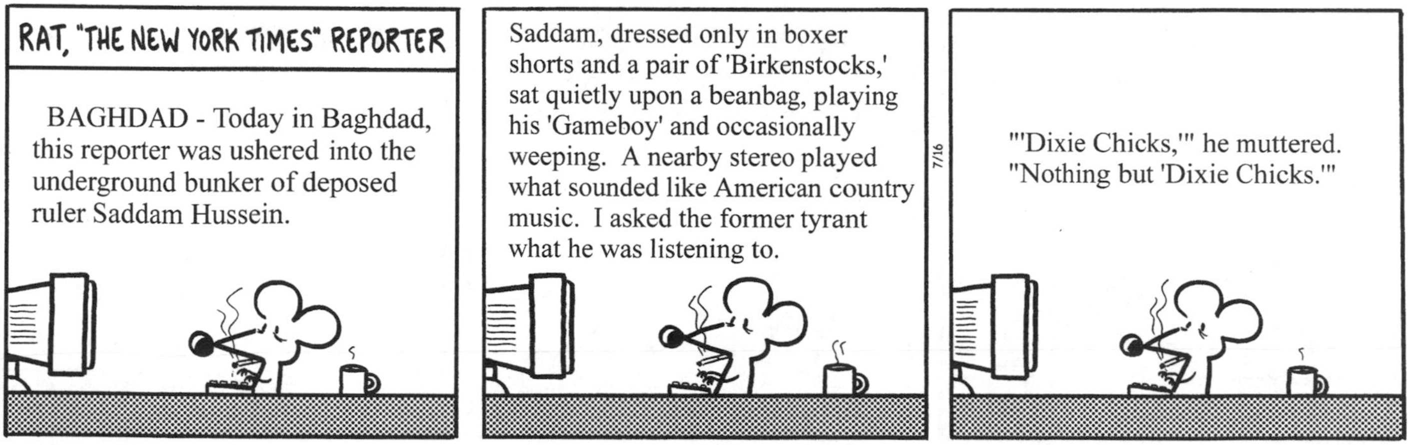
RAT, "THE NEW YORK TIMES" REPORTER
BAGHDAD - Today in Baghdad, this reporter was ushered into the underground bunker of deposed ruler Saddam Hussein.
Saddam, dressed only in boxer shorts and a pair of 'Birkenstocks,' sat quietly upon a beanbag, playing his 'Gameboy' and occasionally weeping. A nearby stereo played what sounded like American country music. I asked the former tyrant what he was listening to.
7/16
"'Dixie Chicks,'" he muttered. "Nothing but 'Dixie Chicks.'"

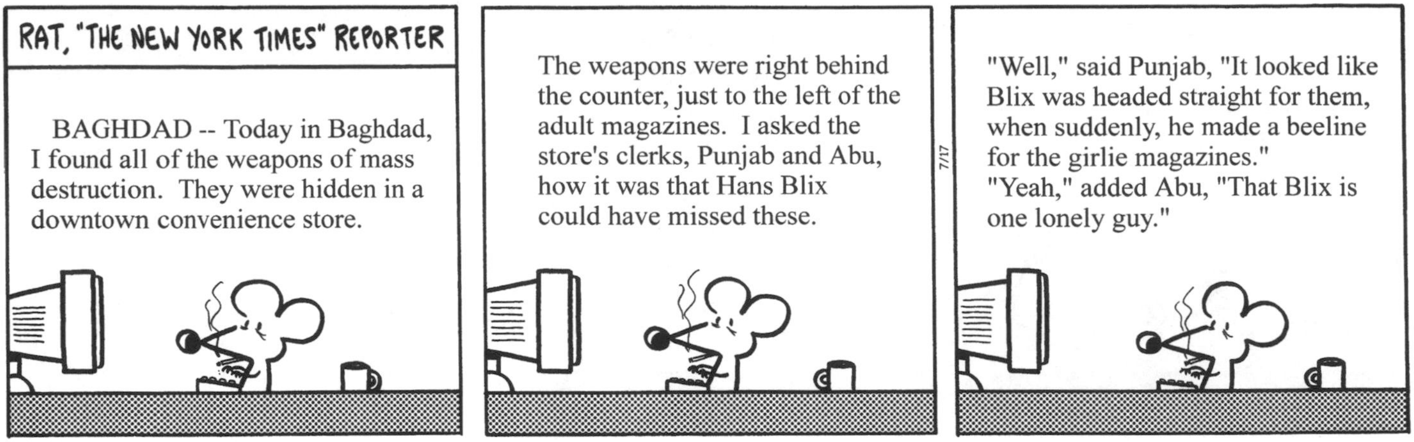
RAT, "THE NEW YORK TIMES" REPORTER
BAGHDAD -- Today in Baghdad, I found all of the weapons of mass destruction. They were hidden in a downtown convenience store.
The weapons were right behind the counter, just to the left of the adult magazines. I asked the store's clerks, Punjab and Abu, how it was that Hans Blix could have missed these.
7/17
"Well," said Punjab, "It looked like Blix was headed straight for them, when suddenly, he made a beeline for the girlie magazines."
"Yeah," added Abu, "That Blix is one lonely guy."

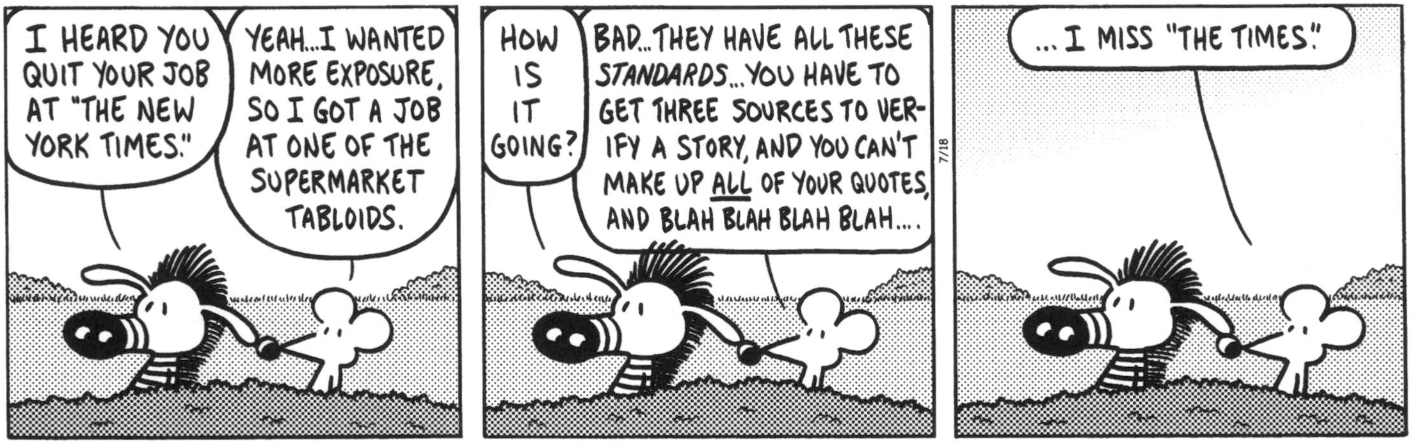
I HEARD YOU QUIT YOUR JOB AT "THE NEW YORK TIMES."
YEAH...I WANTED MORE EXPOSURE, SO I GOT A JOB AT ONE OF THE SUPERMARKET TABLOIDS.
HOW IS IT GOING?
BAD...THEY HAVE ALL THESE STANDARDS...YOU HAVE TO GET THREE SOURCES TO VERIFY A STORY, AND YOU CAN'T MAKE UP ALL OF YOUR QUOTES, AND BLAH BLAH BLAH BLAH....
7/18
...I MISS "THE TIMES."

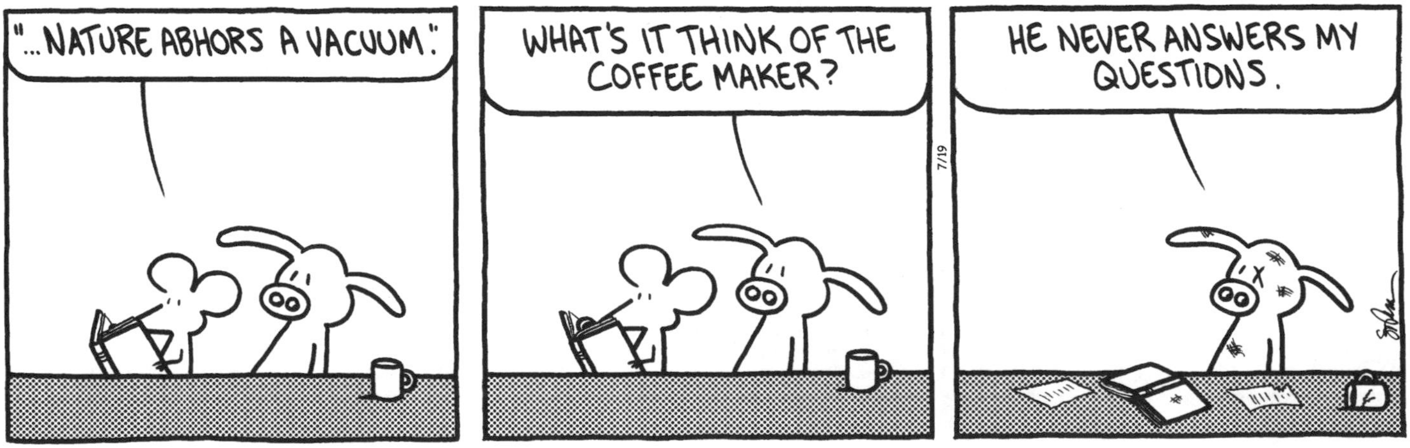
"...NATURE ABHORS A VACUUM."
WHAT'S IT THINK OF THE COFFEE MAKER?
7/19
HE NEVER ANSWERS MY QUESTIONS.

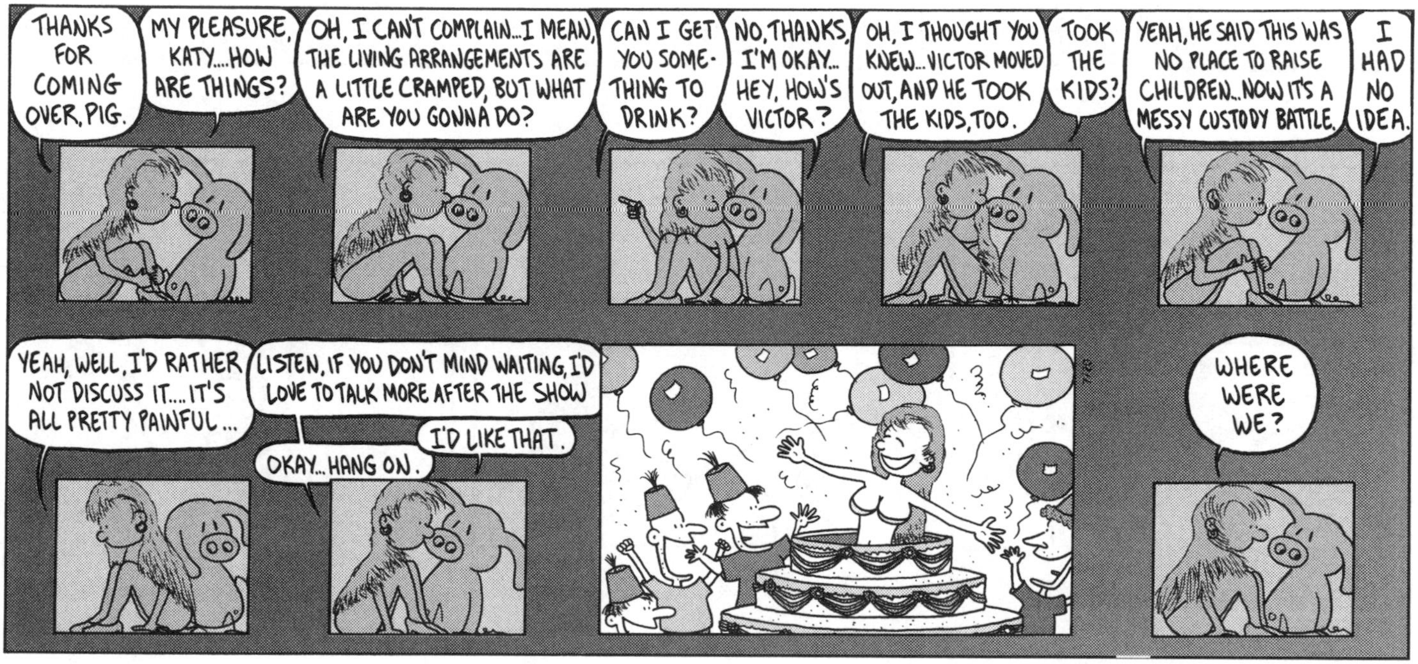
THANKS FOR COMING OVER, PIG.
MY PLEASURE, KATY....HOW ARE THINGS?
OH, I CAN'T COMPLAIN...I MEAN, THE LIVING ARRANGEMENTS ARE A LITTLE CRAMPED, BUT WHAT ARE YOU GONNA DO?
CAN I GET YOU SOME-THING TO DRINK?
NO, THANKS, I'M OKAY... HEY, HOW'S VICTOR?
OH, I THOUGHT YOU KNEW...VICTOR MOVED OUT, AND HE TOOK THE KIDS, TOO.
TOOK THE KIDS?
YEAH, HE SAID THIS WAS NO PLACE TO RAISE CHILDREN...NOW IT'S A MESSY CUSTODY BATTLE.
I HAD NO IDEA.
YEAH, WELL, I'D RATHER NOT DISCUSS IT....IT'S ALL PRETTY PAINFUL...
LISTEN, IF YOU DON'T MIND WAITING, I'D LOVE TO TALK MORE AFTER THE SHOW
I'D LIKE THAT.
OKAY...HANG ON.
WHERE WERE WE?

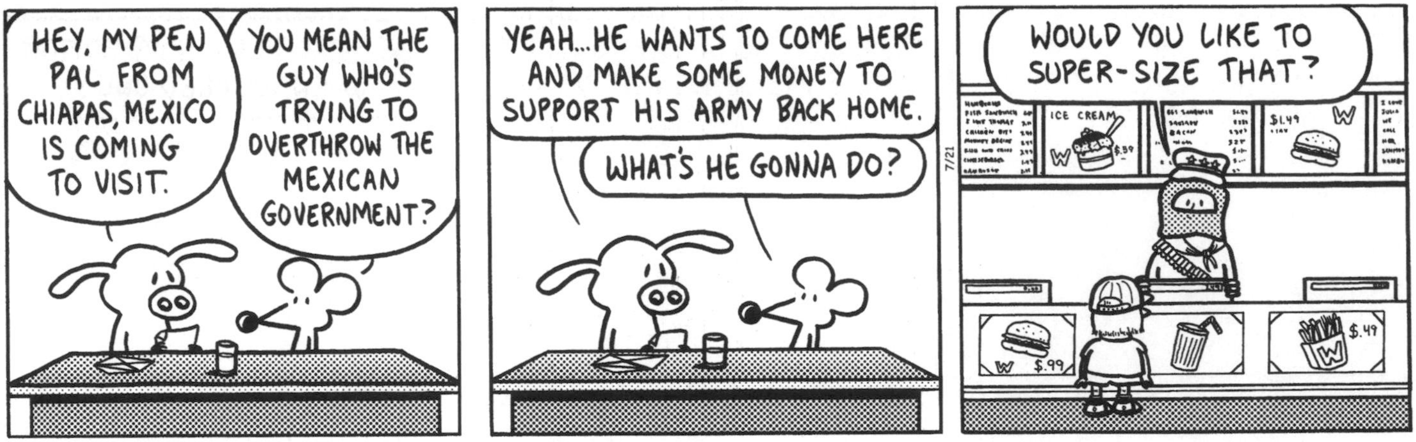
HEY, MY PEN PAL FROM CHIAPAS, MEXICO IS COMING TO VISIT.
YOU MEAN THE GUY WHO'S TRYING TO OVERTHROW THE MEXICAN GOVERNMENT?
YEAH...HE WANTS TO COME HERE AND MAKE SOME MONEY TO SUPPORT HIS ARMY BACK HOME.
WHAT'S HE GONNA DO?
7/21
WOULD YOU LIKE TO SUPER-SIZE THAT?
ICE CREAM
$1.49
$.99
$.49

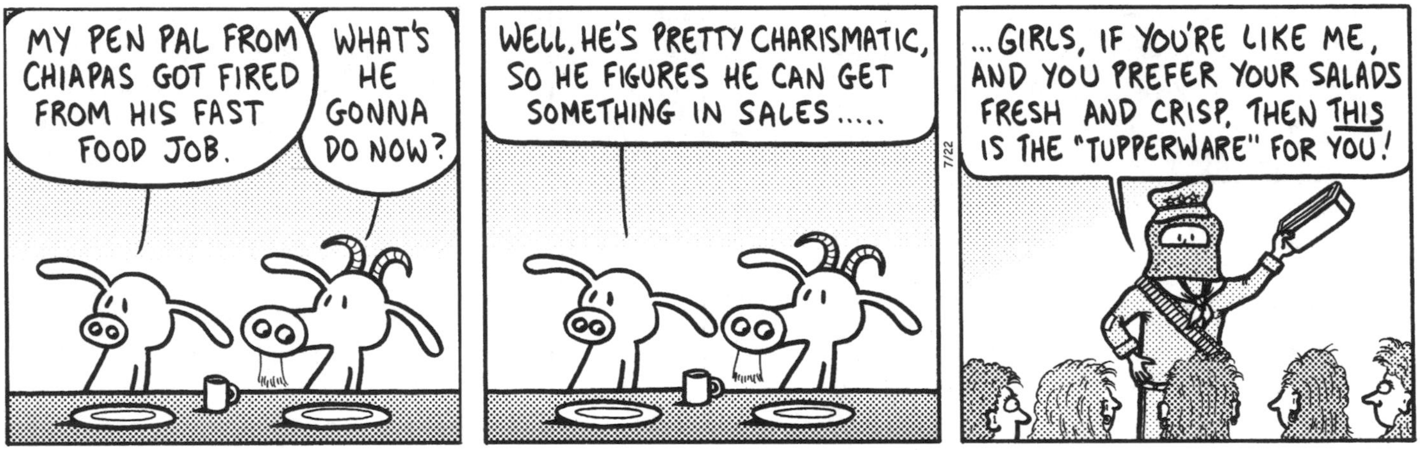
MY PEN PAL FROM CHIAPAS GOT FIRED FROM HIS FAST FOOD JOB.
WHAT'S HE GONNA DO NOW?
WELL, HE'S PRETTY CHARISMATIC, SO HE FIGURES HE CAN GET SOMETHING IN SALES.....
7/22
...GIRLS, IF YOU'RE LIKE ME, AND YOU PREFER YOUR SALADS FRESH AND CRISP, THEN THIS IS THE "TUPPERWARE" FOR YOU!

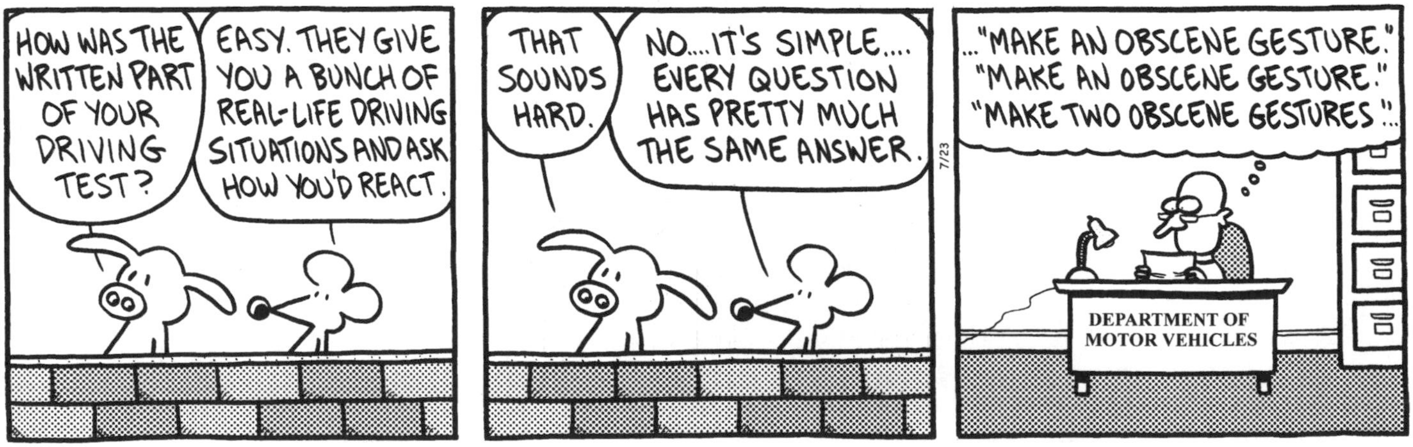
HOW WAS THE WRITTEN PART OF YOUR DRIVING TEST?
EASY. THEY GIVE YOU A BUNCH OF REAL-LIFE DRIVING SITUATIONS AND ASK HOW YOU'D REACT.
THAT SOUNDS HARD.
NO....IT'S SIMPLE.... EVERY QUESTION HAS PRETTY MUCH THE SAME ANSWER.
7/23
..."MAKE AN OBSCENE GESTURE." "MAKE AN OBSCENE GESTURE." "MAKE TWO OBSCENE GESTURES."...
DEPARTMENT OF MOTOR VEHICLES

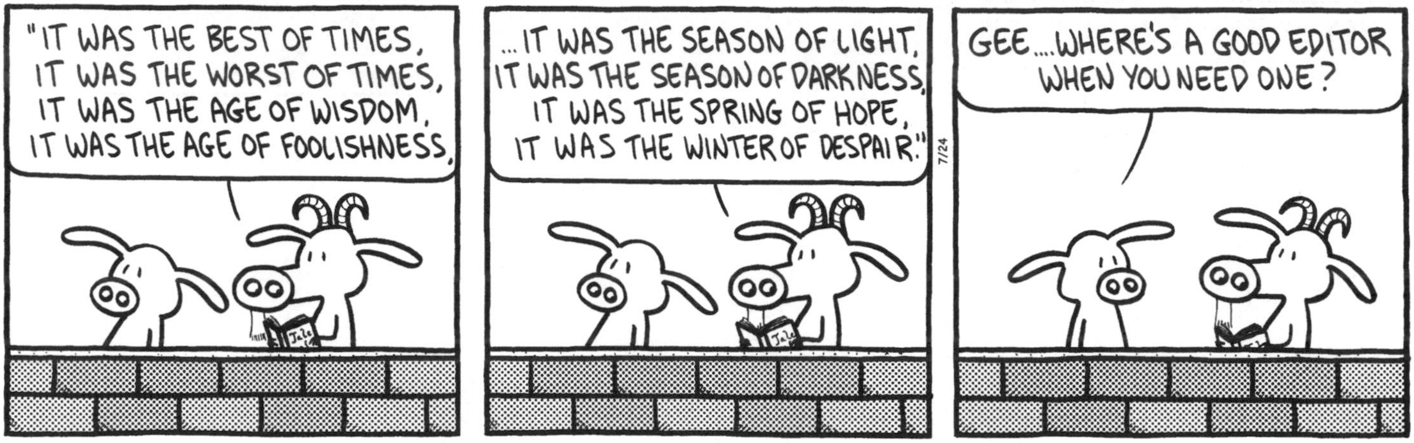
"IT WAS THE BEST OF TIMES, IT WAS THE WORST OF TIMES, IT WAS THE AGE OF WISDOM, IT WAS THE AGE OF FOOLISHNESS,
...IT WAS THE SEASON OF LIGHT, IT WAS THE SEASON OF DARKNESS, IT WAS THE SPRING OF HOPE, IT WAS THE WINTER OF DESPAIR."
7/24
GEE....WHERE'S A GOOD EDITOR WHEN YOU NEED ONE?

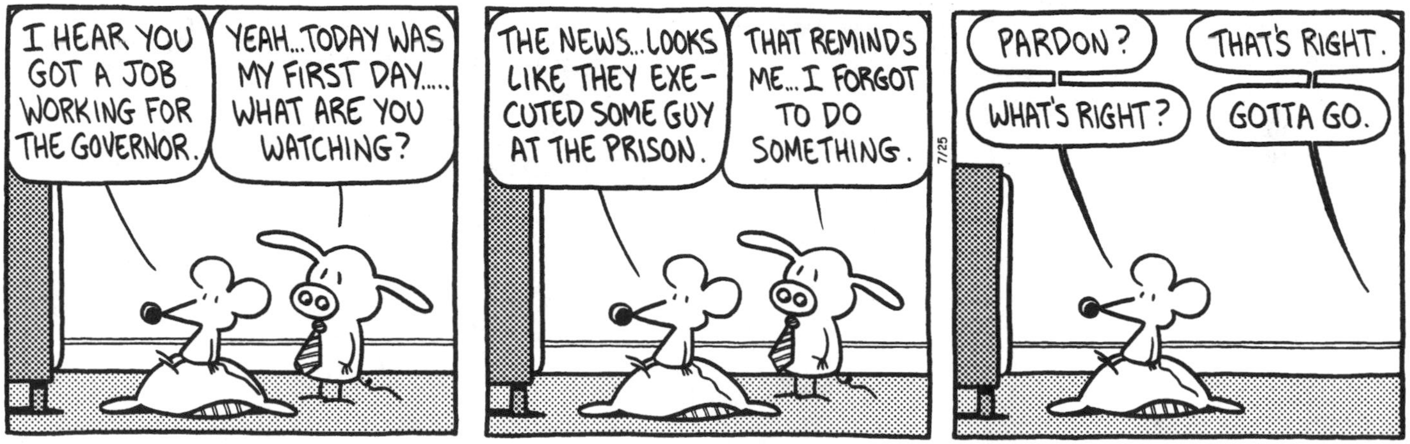
I HEAR YOU GOT A JOB WORKING FOR THE GOVERNOR.
YEAH...TODAY WAS MY FIRST DAY..... WHAT ARE YOU WATCHING?
THE NEWS...LOOKS LIKE THEY EXECUTED SOME GUY AT THE PRISON.
THAT REMINDS ME...I FORGOT TO DO SOMETHING.
7/25
PARDON?
WHAT'S RIGHT?
THAT'S RIGHT.
GOTTA GO.

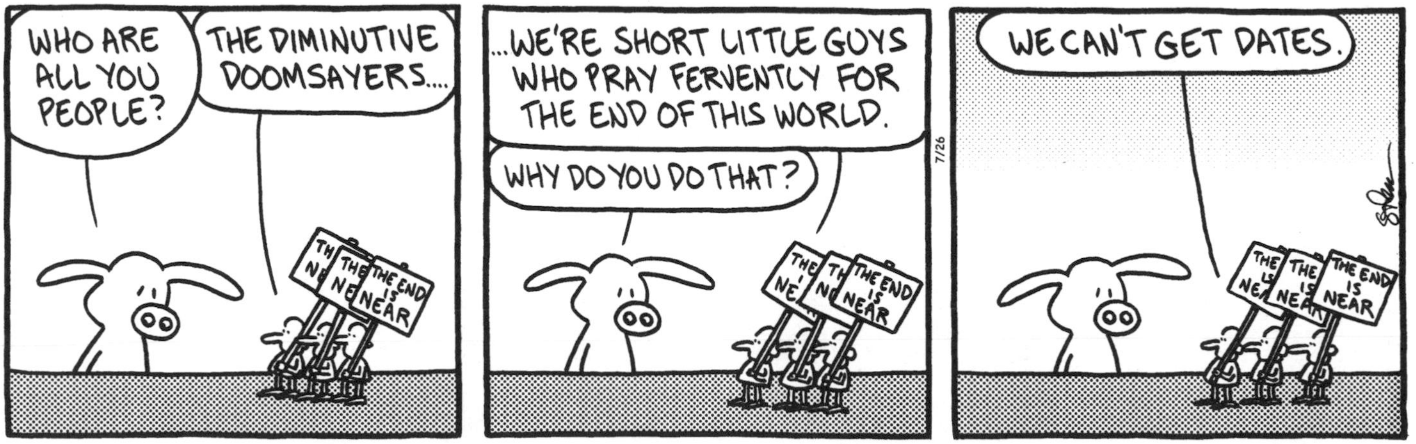
WHO ARE ALL YOU PEOPLE?
THE DIMINUTIVE DOOMSAYERS....
THE END IS NEAR
...WE'RE SHORT LITTLE GUYS WHO PRAY FERVENTLY FOR THE END OF THIS WORLD.
WHY DO YOU DO THAT?
7/26
WE CAN'T GET DATES.

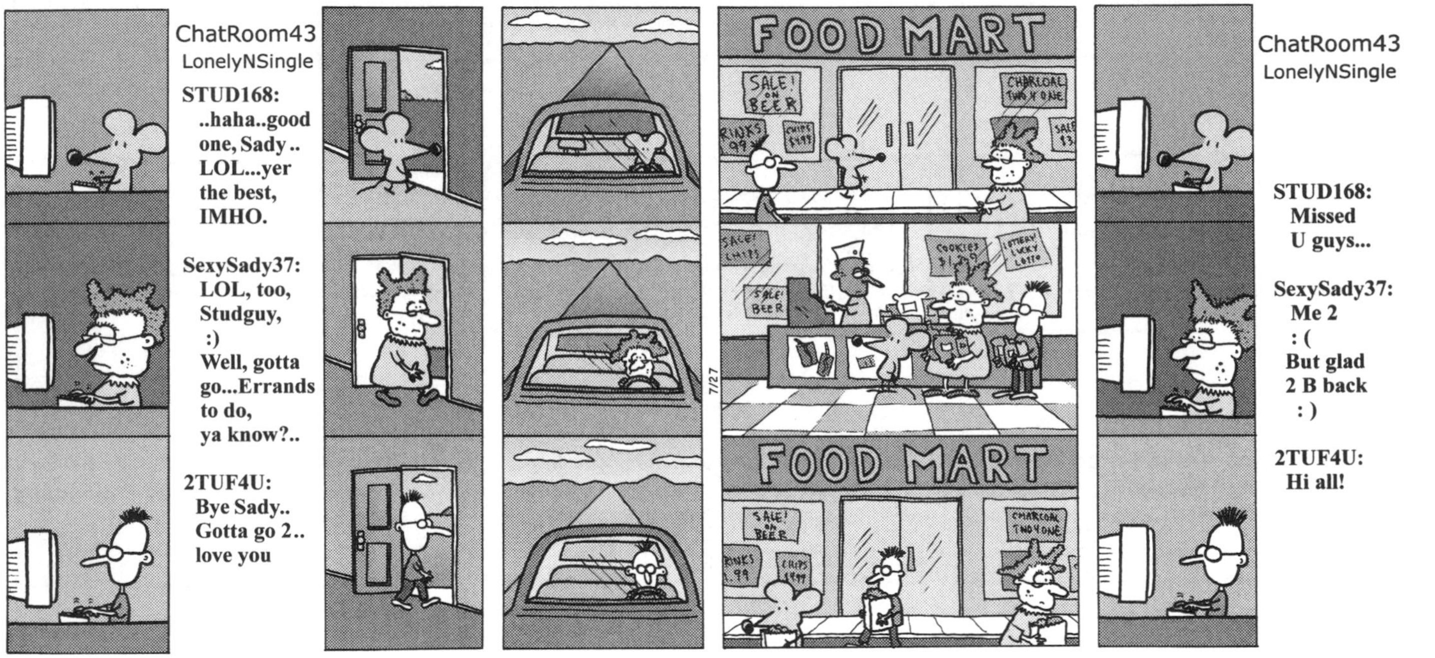

ChatRoom43
LonelyNSingle
STUD168: ..haha..good one, Sady .. LOL...yer the best, IMHO.
SexySady37: LOL, too, Studguy, :) Well, gotta go...Errands to do, ya know?..
2TUF4U: Bye Sady.. Gotta go 2.. love you
FOOD MART
SALE! ON BEER
FOOD MART
ChatRoom43
LonelyNSingle
STUD168: Missed U guys...
SexySady37: Me 2 : (But glad 2 B back :)
2TUF4U: Hi all!

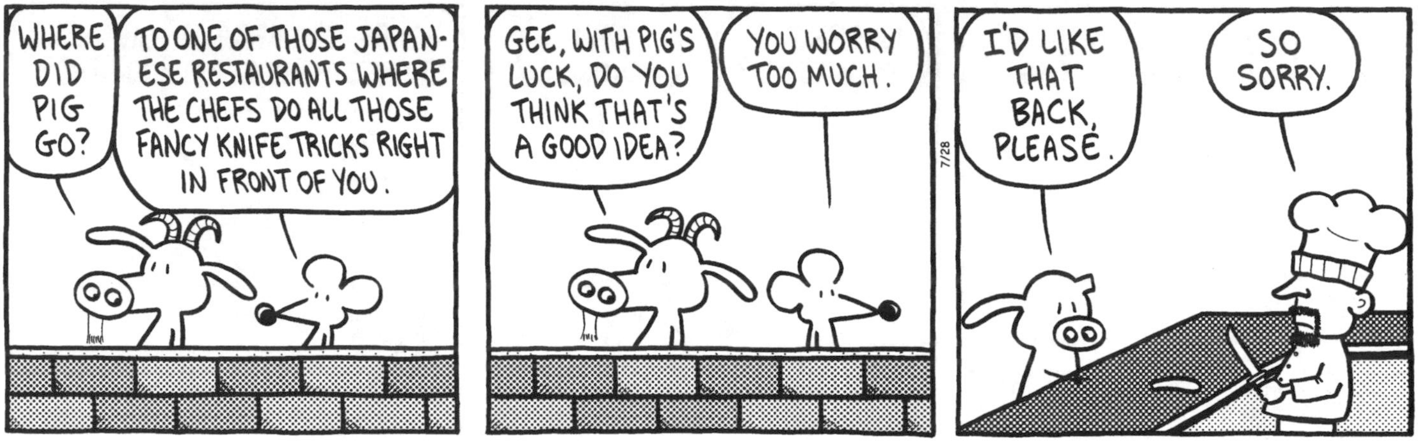
WHERE DID PIG GO?
TO ONE OF THOSE JAPANESE RESTAURANTS WHERE THE CHEFS DO ALL THOSE FANCY KNIFE TRICKS RIGHT IN FRONT OF YOU.
GEE, WITH PIG'S LUCK, DO YOU THINK THAT'S A GOOD IDEA?
YOU WORRY TOO MUCH.
7/28
I'D LIKE THAT BACK, PLEASE.
SO SORRY.

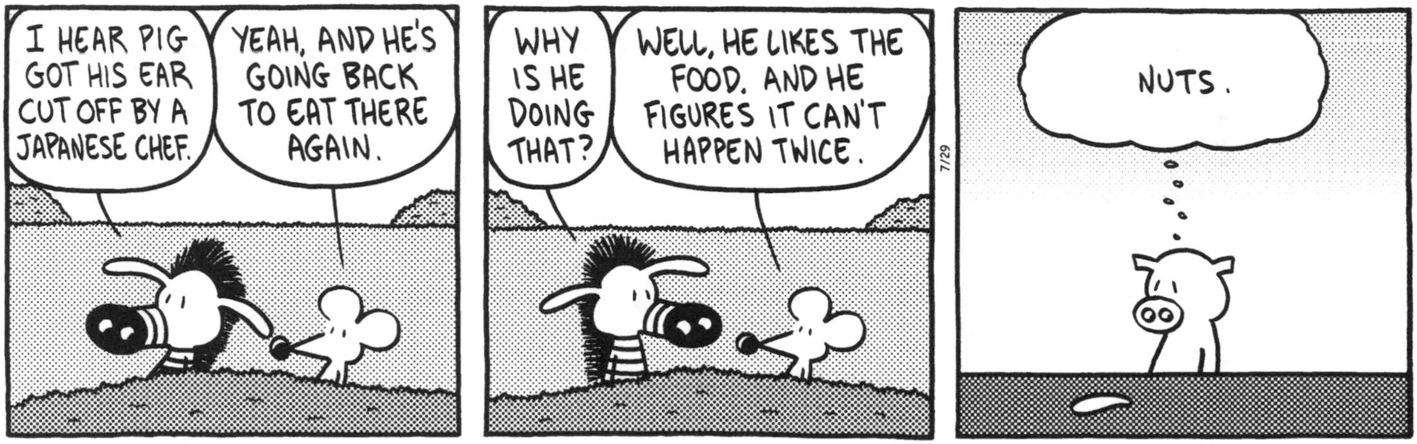
I HEAR PIG GOT HIS EAR CUT OFF BY A JAPANESE CHEF.
YEAH, AND HE'S GOING BACK TO EAT THERE AGAIN.
WHY IS HE DOING THAT?
WELL, HE LIKES THE FOOD. AND HE FIGURES IT CAN'T HAPPEN TWICE.
7/29
NUTS.

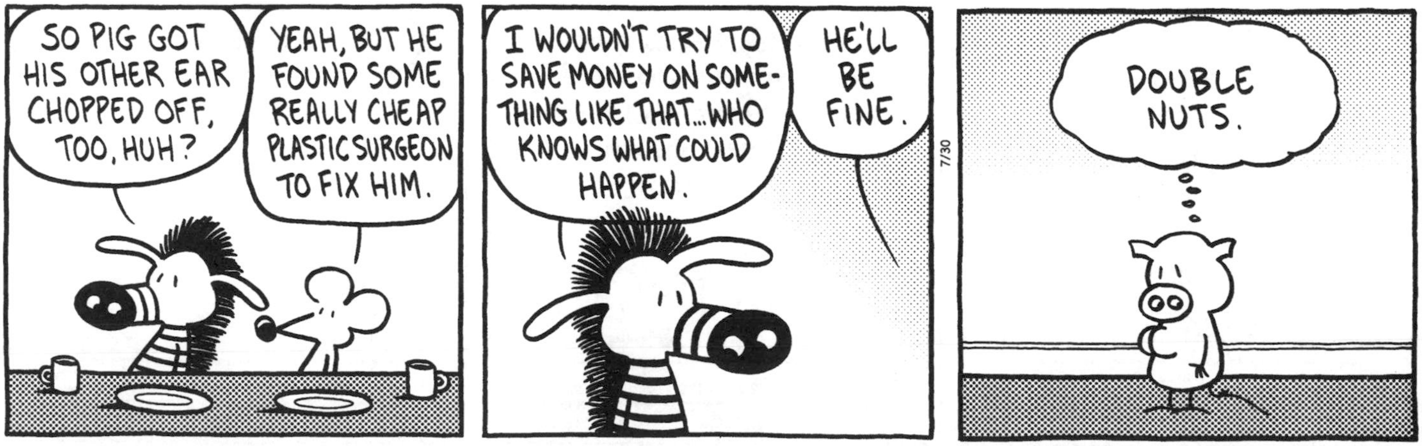
SO PIG GOT HIS OTHER EAR CHOPPED OFF, TOO, HUH?
YEAH, BUT HE FOUND SOME REALLY CHEAP PLASTIC SURGEON TO FIX HIM.
I WOULDN'T TRY TO SAVE MONEY ON SOMETHING LIKE THAT...WHO KNOWS WHAT COULD HAPPEN.
HE'LL BE FINE.
7/30
DOUBLE NUTS.

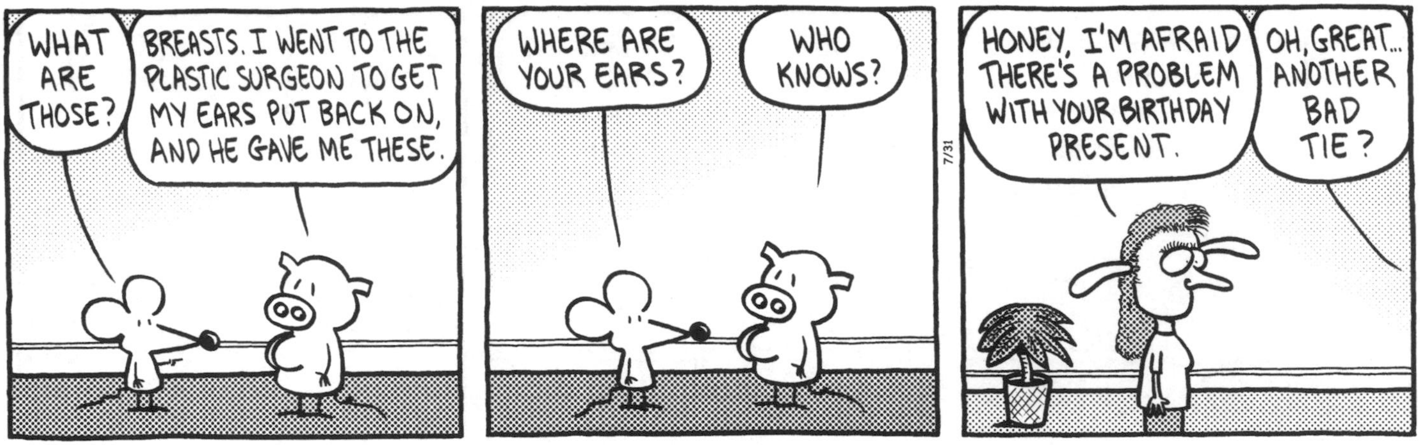
WHAT ARE THOSE?
BREASTS. I WENT TO THE PLASTIC SURGEON TO GET MY EARS PUT BACK ON, AND HE GAVE ME THESE.
WHERE ARE YOUR EARS?
WHO KNOWS?
7/31
HONEY, I'M AFRAID THERE'S A PROBLEM WITH YOUR BIRTHDAY PRESENT.
OH, GREAT... ANOTHER BAD TIE?

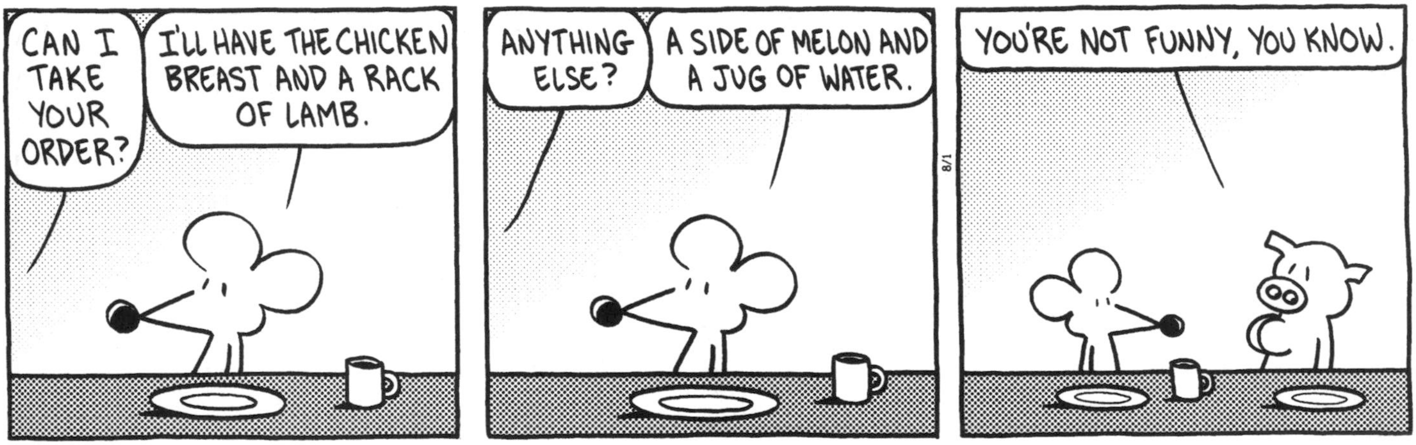
CAN I TAKE YOUR ORDER?
I'LL HAVE THE CHICKEN BREAST AND A RACK OF LAMB.
ANYTHING ELSE?
A SIDE OF MELON AND A JUG OF WATER.
8/1
YOU'RE NOT FUNNY, YOU KNOW.

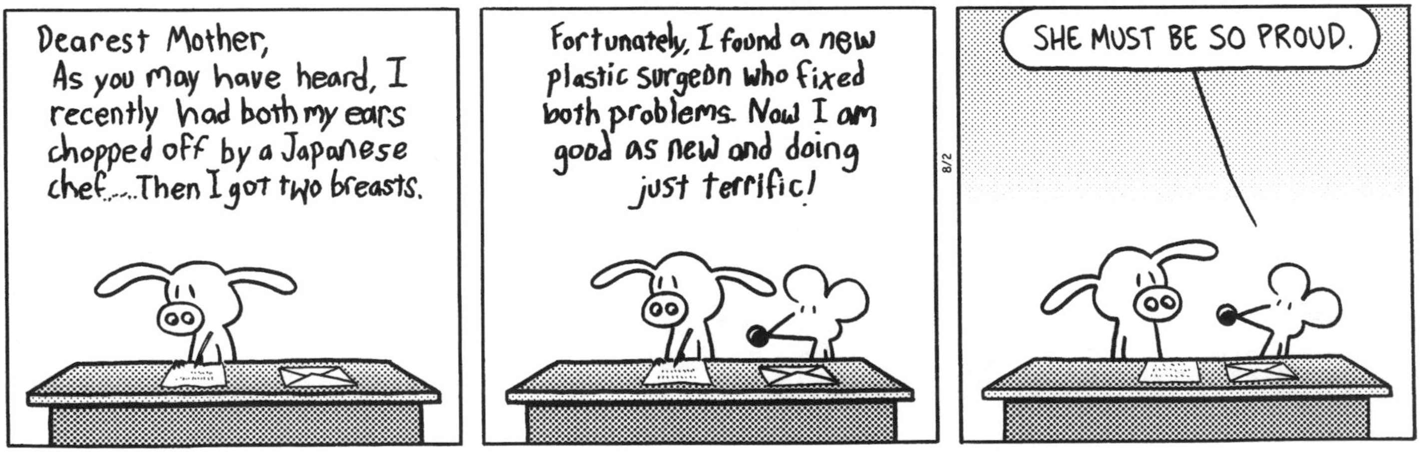
Dearest Mother,
As you may have heard, I recently had both my ears chopped off by a Japanese chef.....Then I got two breasts.
Fortunately, I found a new plastic surgeon who fixed both problems. Now I am good as new and doing just terrific!
8/2
SHE MUST BE SO PROUD.

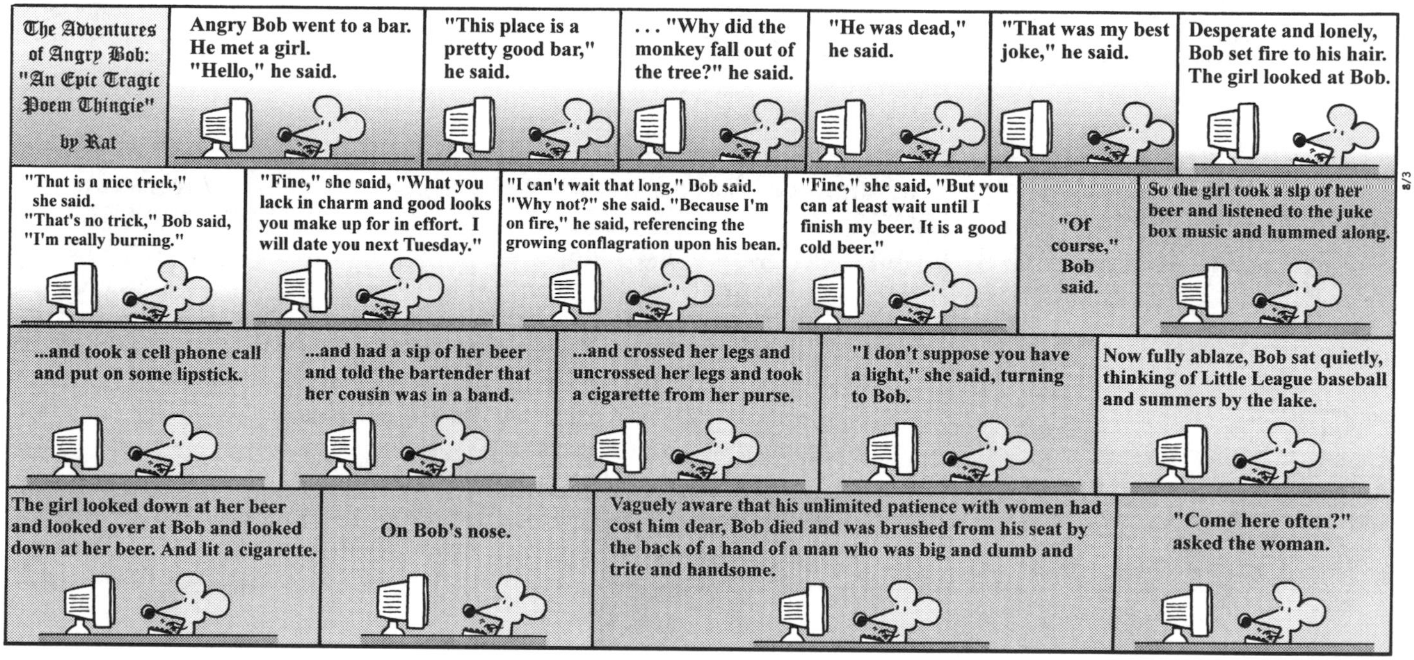

The Adventures of Angry Bob: "An Epic Tragic Poem Thingie" by Rat
Angry Bob went to a bar. He met a girl. "Hello," he said.
"This place is a pretty good bar," he said.
. . . "Why did the monkey fall out of the tree?" he said.
"He was dead," he said.
"That was my best joke," he said.
Desperate and lonely, Bob set fire to his hair. The girl looked at Bob.
"That is a nice trick," she said. "That's no trick," Bob said, "I'm really burning."
"Fine," she said, "What you lack in charm and good looks you make up for in effort. I will date you next Tuesday."
"I can't wait that long," Bob said. "Why not?" she said. "Because I'm on fire," he said, referencing the growing conflagration upon his bean.
"Fine," she said, "But you can at least wait until I finish my beer. It is a good cold beer."
"Of course," Bob said.
So the girl took a sip of her beer and listened to the juke box music and hummed along.
...and took a cell phone call and put on some lipstick.
...and had a sip of her beer and told the bartender that her cousin was in a band.
...and crossed her legs and uncrossed her legs and took a cigarette from her purse.
"I don't suppose you have a light," she said, turning to Bob.
Now fully ablaze, Bob sat quietly, thinking of Little League baseball and summers by the lake.
The girl looked down at her beer and looked over at Bob and looked down at her beer. And lit a cigarette.
On Bob's nose.
Vaguely aware that his unlimited patience with women had cost him dear, Bob died and was brushed from his seat by the back of a hand of a man who was big and dumb and trite and handsome.
"Come here often?" asked the woman.
8/3

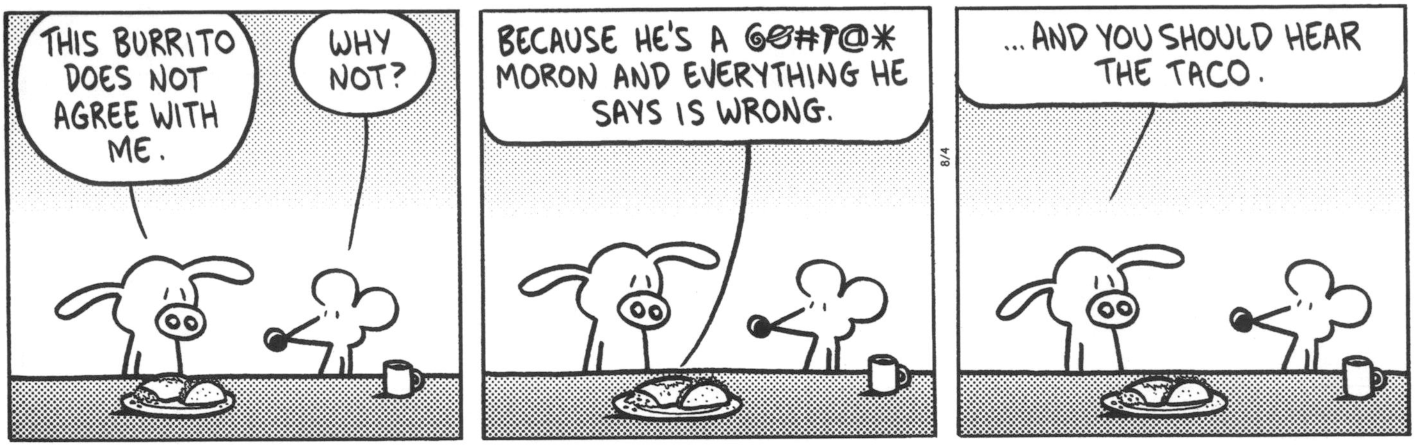
THIS BURRITO DOES NOT AGREE WITH ME.
WHY NOT?
BECAUSE HE'S A @@#?@* MORON AND EVERYTHING HE SAYS IS WRONG.
8/4
...AND YOU SHOULD HEAR THE TACO.

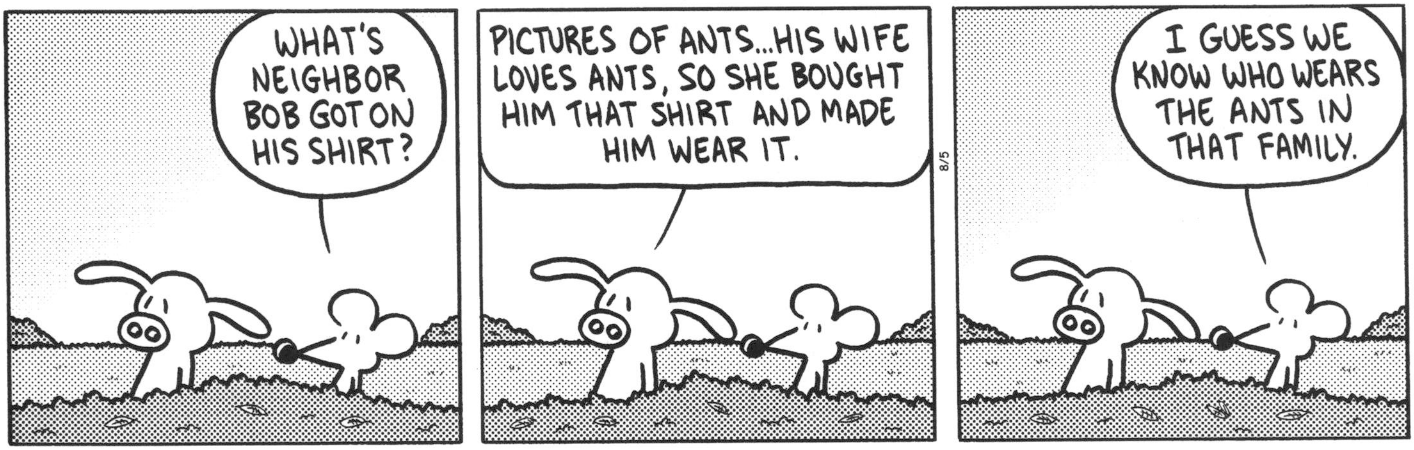
WHAT'S NEIGHBOR BOB GOT ON HIS SHIRT?
PICTURES OF ANTS...HIS WIFE LOVES ANTS, SO SHE BOUGHT HIM THAT SHIRT AND MADE HIM WEAR IT.
8/5
I GUESS WE KNOW WHO WEARS THE ANTS IN THAT FAMILY.

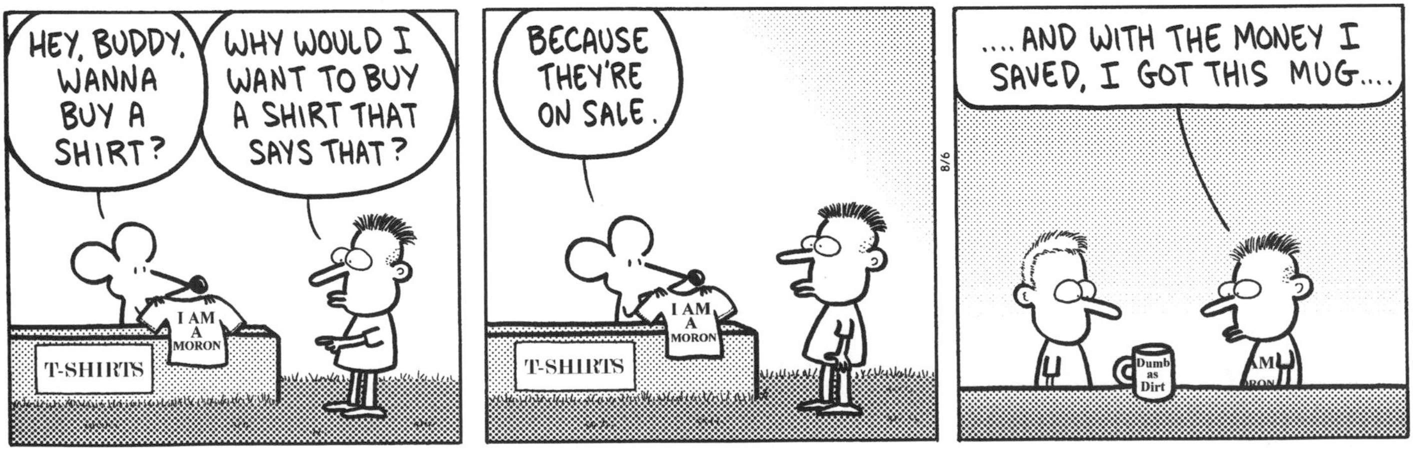
HEY, BUDDY. WANNA BUY A SHIRT?
WHY WOULD I WANT TO BUY A SHIRT THAT SAYS THAT?
I AM A MORON
T-SHIRTS
BECAUSE THEY'RE ON SALE.
I AM A MORON
T-SHIRTS
8/6
....AND WITH THE MONEY I SAVED, I GOT THIS MUG....
Dumb as Dirt

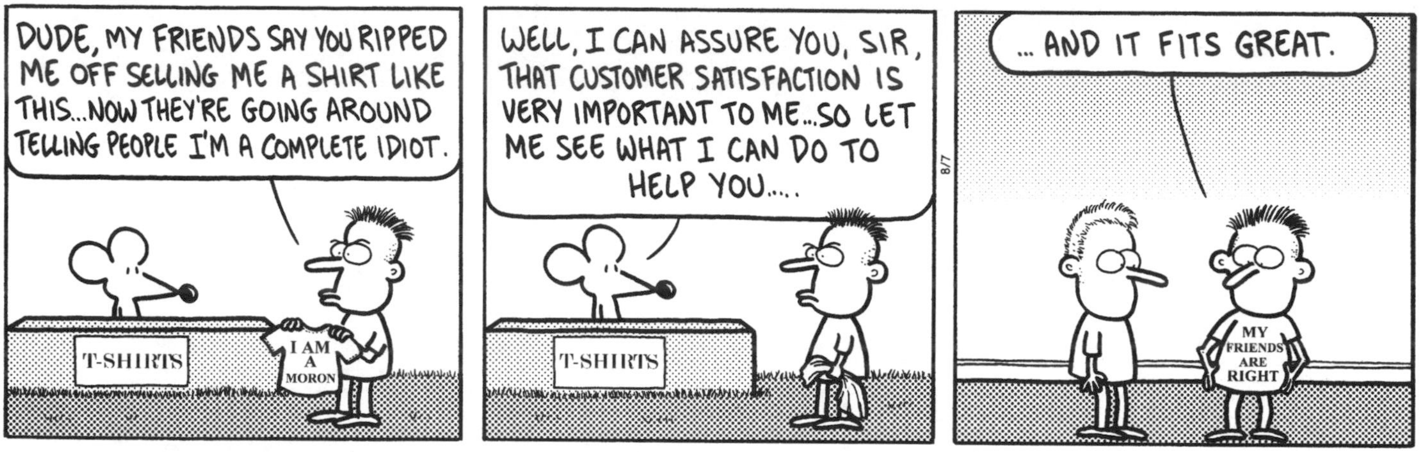
DUDE, MY FRIENDS SAY YOU RIPPED ME OFF SELLING ME A SHIRT LIKE THIS...NOW THEY'RE GOING AROUND TELLING PEOPLE I'M A COMPLETE IDIOT.
T-SHIRTS
I AM A MORON
WELL, I CAN ASSURE YOU, SIR, THAT CUSTOMER SATISFACTION IS VERY IMPORTANT TO ME...SO LET ME SEE WHAT I CAN DO TO HELP YOU....
T-SHIRTS
8/7
... AND IT FITS GREAT.
MY FRIENDS ARE RIGHT

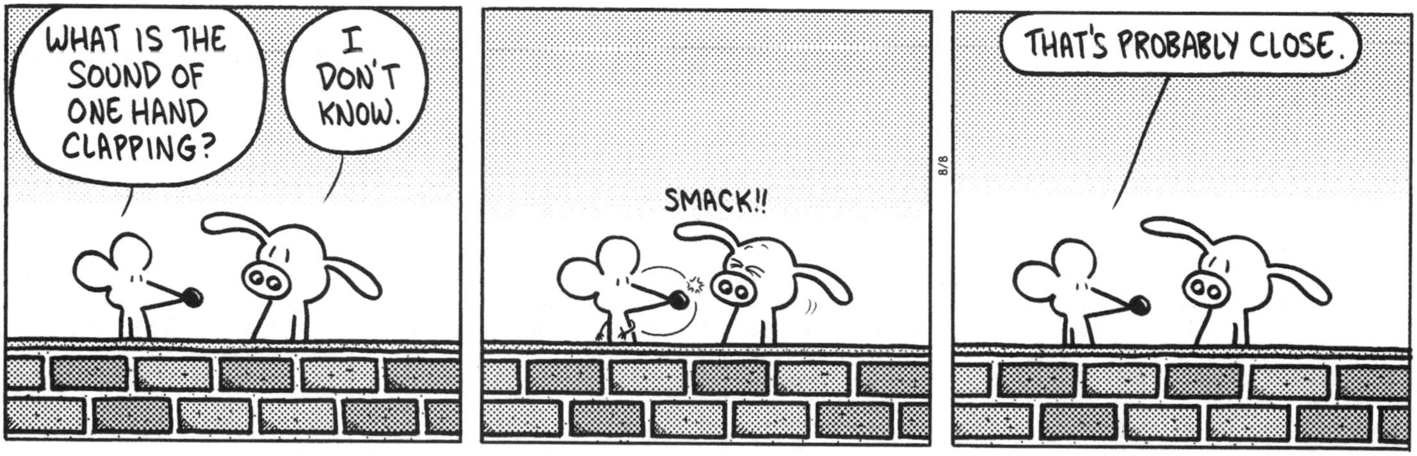
WHAT IS THE SOUND OF ONE HAND CLAPPING?
I DON'T KNOW.
SMACK!!
8/8
THAT'S PROBABLY CLOSE.

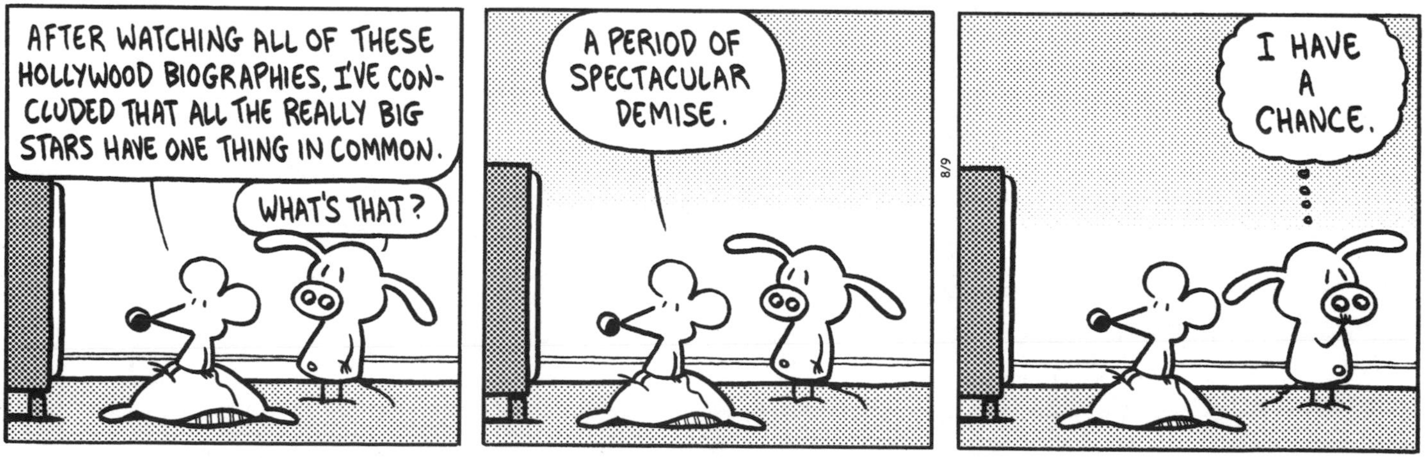
AFTER WATCHING ALL OF THESE HOLLYWOOD BIOGRAPHIES, I'VE CONCLUDED THAT ALL THE REALLY BIG STARS HAVE ONE THING IN COMMON.
WHAT'S THAT?
A PERIOD OF SPECTACULAR DEMISE.
8/9
I HAVE A CHANCE.

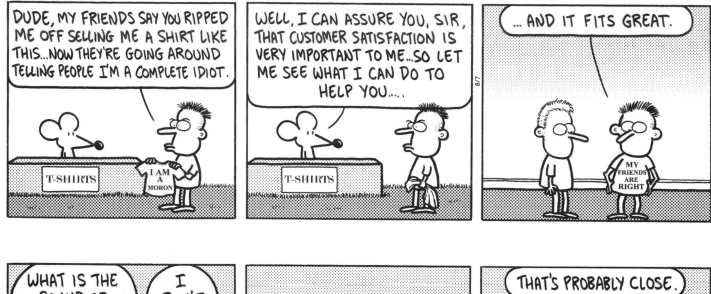

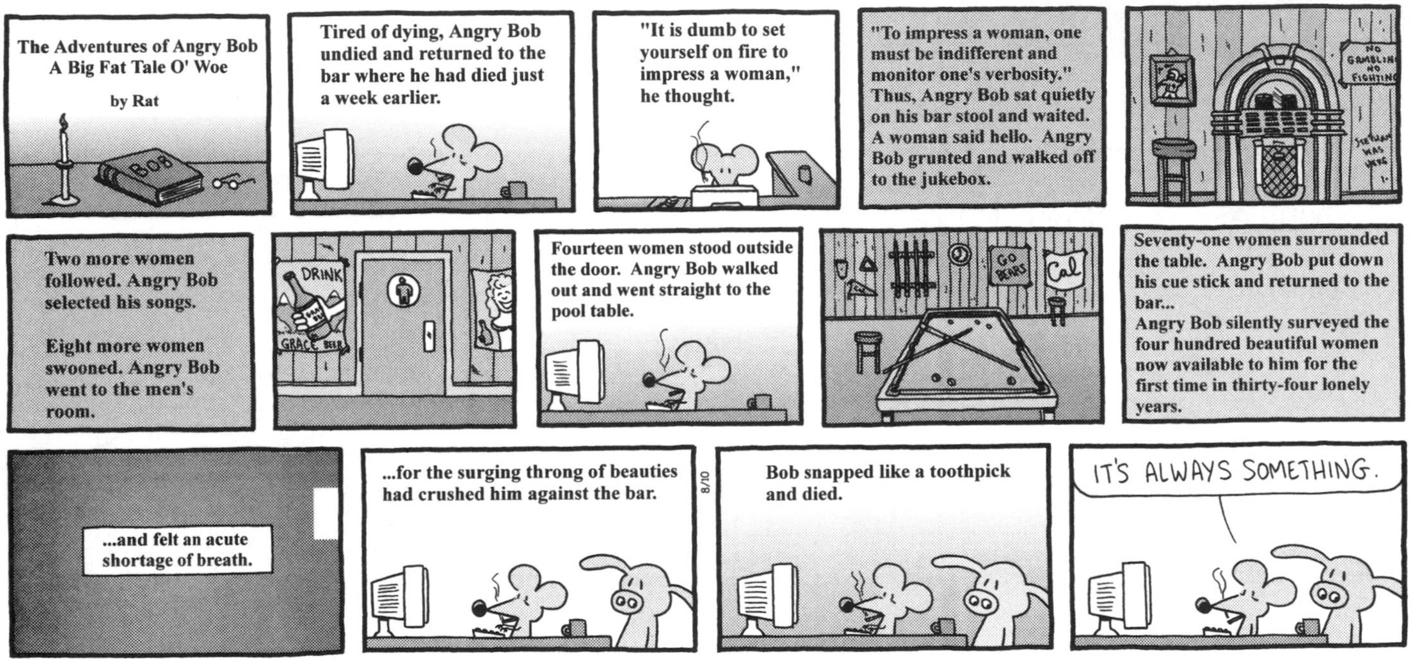

The Adventures of Angry Bob
A Big Fat Tale O' Woe
by Rat
BOB
Tired of dying, Angry Bob undied and returned to the bar where he had died just a week earlier.
"It is dumb to set yourself on fire to impress a woman," he thought.
"To impress a woman, one must be indifferent and monitor one's verbosity." Thus, Angry Bob sat quietly on his bar stool and waited. A woman said hello. Angry Bob grunted and walked off to the jukebox.
Two more women followed. Angry Bob selected his songs.
Eight more women swooned. Angry Bob went to the men's room.
DRINK
GRACE BEER
Fourteen women stood outside the door. Angry Bob walked out and went straight to the pool table.
GO BEARS
Cal
Seventy-one women surrounded the table. Angry Bob put down his cue stick and returned to the bar...
Angry Bob silently surveyed the four hundred beautiful women now available to him for the first time in thirty-four lonely years.
...and felt an acute shortage of breath.
...for the surging throng of beauties had crushed him against the bar.
8/10
Bob snapped like a toothpick and died.
IT'S ALWAYS SOMETHING.

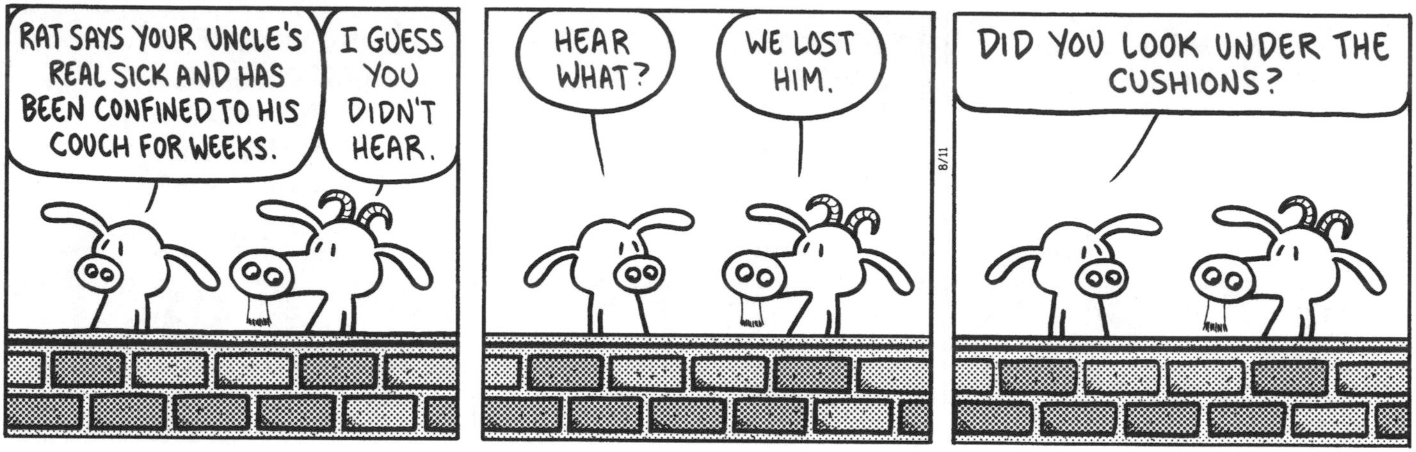
RAT SAYS YOUR UNCLE'S REAL SICK AND HAS BEEN CONFINED TO HIS COUCH FOR WEEKS.
I GUESS YOU DIDN'T HEAR.
HEAR WHAT?
WE LOST HIM.
8/11
DID YOU LOOK UNDER THE CUSHIONS?

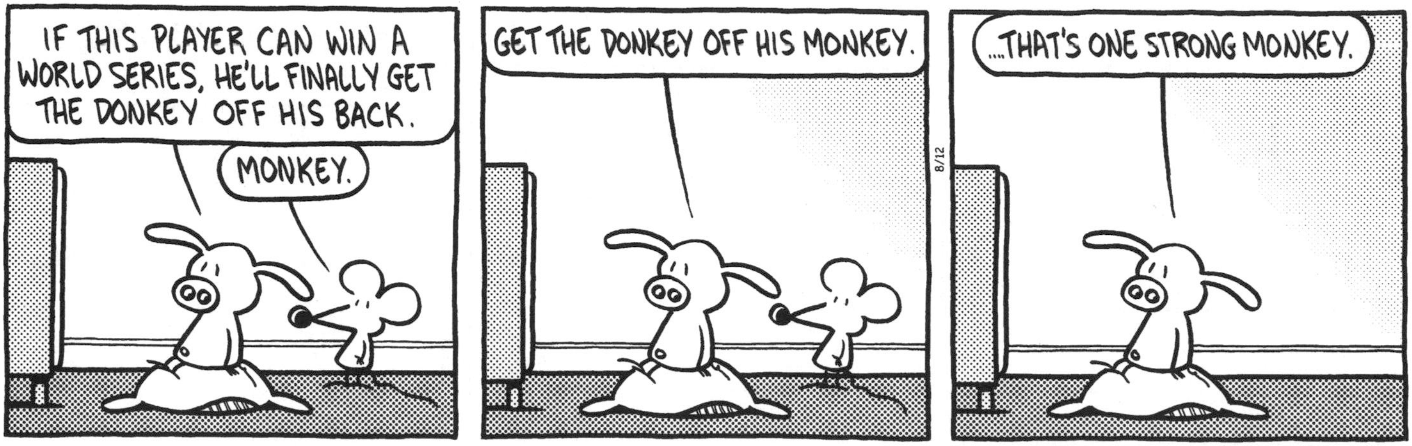
IF THIS PLAYER CAN WIN A WORLD SERIES, HE'LL FINALLY GET THE DONKEY OFF HIS BACK.
MONKEY.
GET THE DONKEY OFF HIS MONKEY.
8/12
....THAT'S ONE STRONG MONKEY.

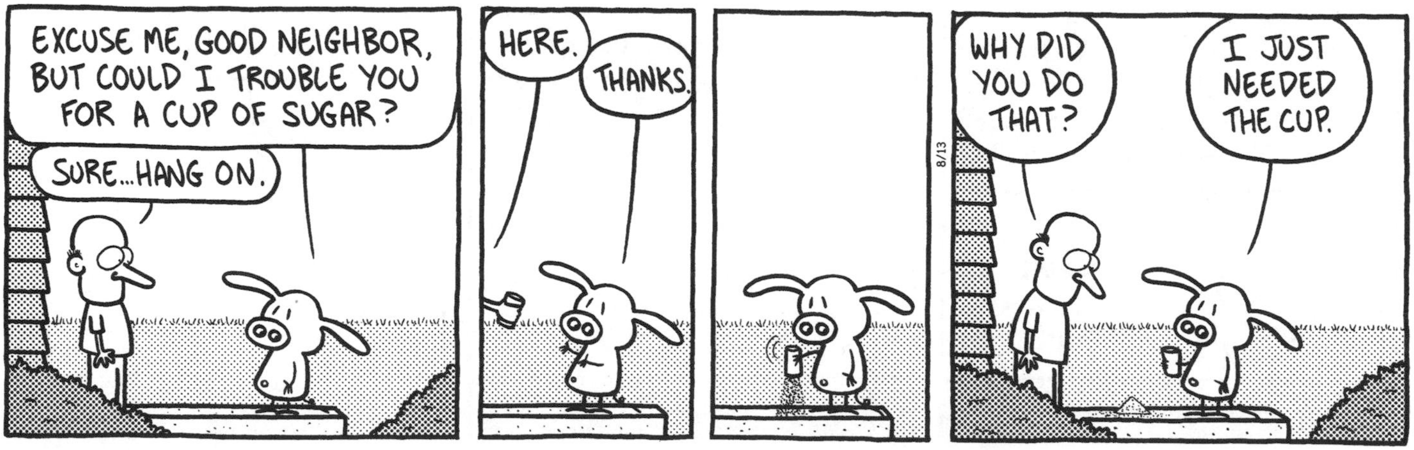
EXCUSE ME, GOOD NEIGHBOR, BUT COULD I TROUBLE YOU FOR A CUP OF SUGAR?
SURE...HANG ON.
HERE.
THANKS.
8/13
WHY DID YOU DO THAT?
I JUST NEEDED THE CUP.

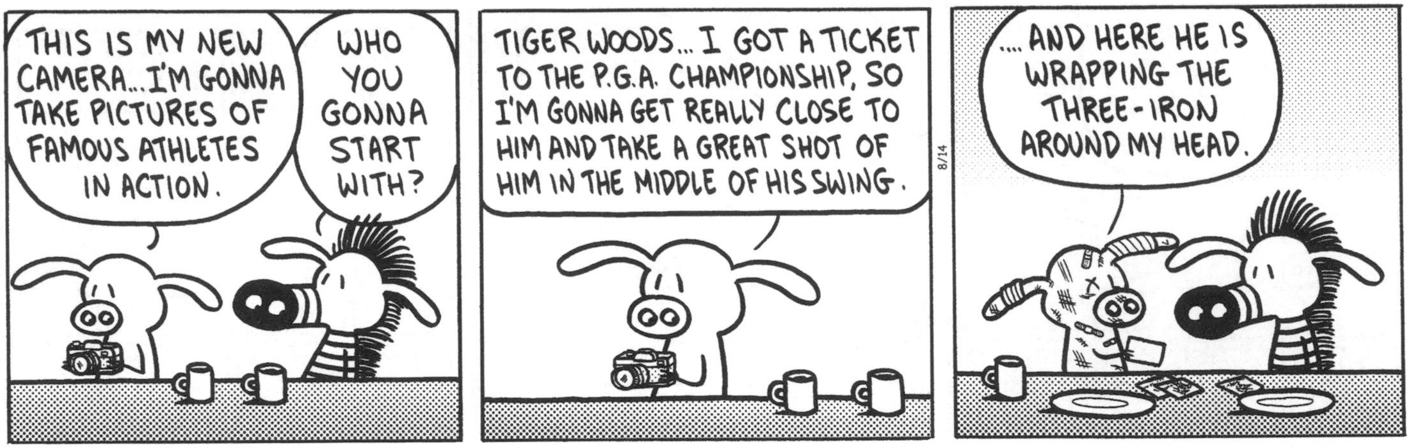
THIS IS MY NEW CAMERA...I'M GONNA TAKE PICTURES OF FAMOUS ATHLETES IN ACTION.
WHO YOU GONNA START WITH?
TIGER WOODS... I GOT A TICKET TO THE P.G.A. CHAMPIONSHIP, SO I'M GONNA GET REALLY CLOSE TO HIM AND TAKE A GREAT SHOT OF HIM IN THE MIDDLE OF HIS SWING.
8/14
.... AND HERE HE IS WRAPPING THE THREE-IRON AROUND MY HEAD.

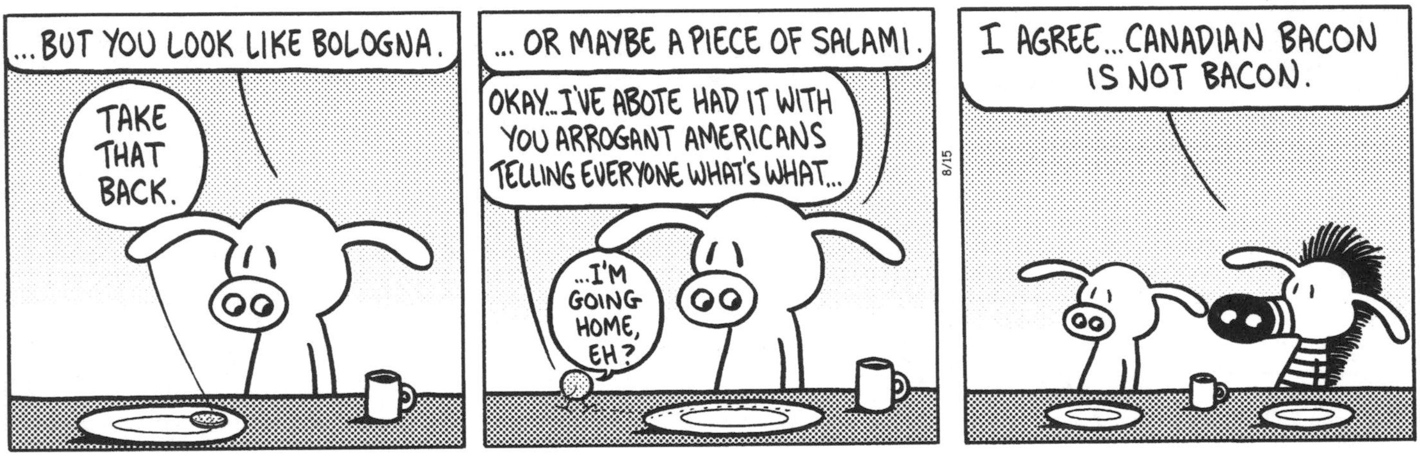
... BUT YOU LOOK LIKE BOLOGNA.
TAKE THAT BACK.
... OR MAYBE A PIECE OF SALAMI.
OKAY... I'VE ABOTE HAD IT WITH YOU ARROGANT AMERICANS TELLING EVERYONE WHAT'S WHAT...
...I'M GOING HOME, EH?
8/15
I AGREE... CANADIAN BACON IS NOT BACON.

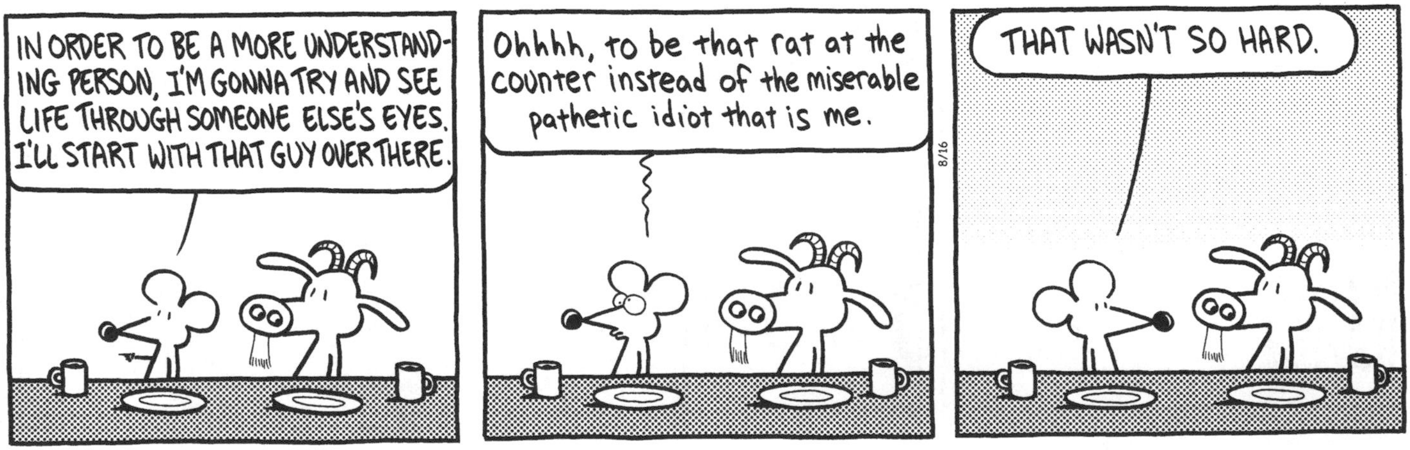
IN ORDER TO BE A MORE UNDERSTANDING PERSON, I'M GONNA TRY AND SEE LIFE THROUGH SOMEONE ELSE'S EYES. I'LL START WITH THAT GUY OVER THERE.
Ohhhh, to be that rat at the counter instead of the miserable pathetic idiot that is me.
8/16
THAT WASN'T SO HARD.

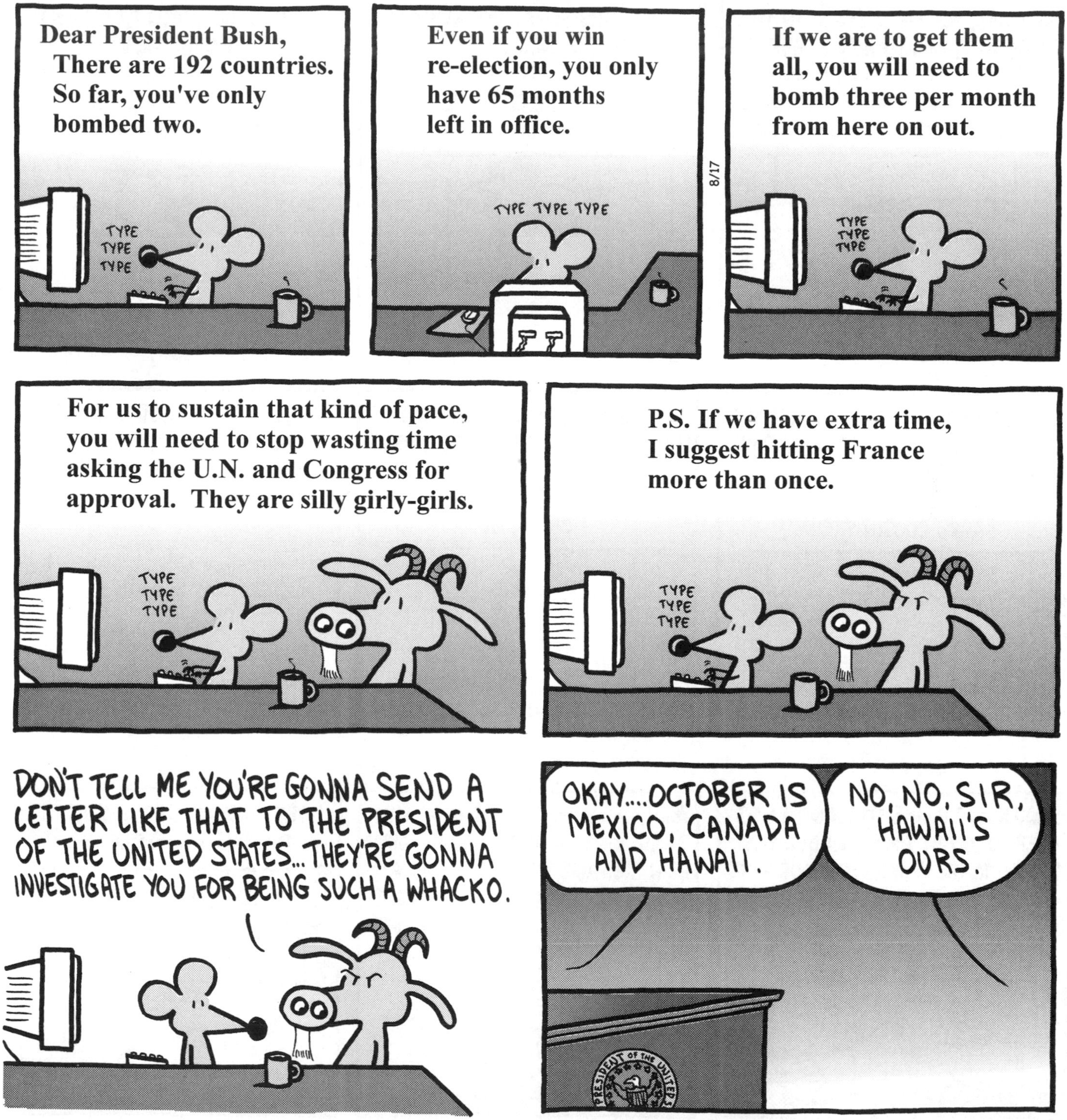
Dear President Bush,
There are 192 countries.
So far, you've only
bombed two.
TYPE
TYPE
TYPE
Even if you win
re-election, you only
have 65 months
left in office.
TYPE TYPE TYPE
8/17
If we are to get them
all, you will need to
bomb three per month
from here on out.
TYPE
TYPE
TYPE
For us to sustain that kind of pace,
you will need to stop wasting time
asking the U.N. and Congress for
approval. They are silly girly-girls.
TYPE
TYPE
TYPE
P.S. If we have extra time,
I suggest hitting France
more than once.
TYPE
TYPE
TYPE
DON'T TELL ME YOU'RE GONNA SEND A LETTER LIKE THAT TO THE PRESIDENT OF THE UNITED STATES...THEY'RE GONNA INVESTIGATE YOU FOR BEING SUCH A WHACKO.
OKAY....OCTOBER IS MEXICO, CANADA AND HAWAII.
NO, NO, SIR, HAWAII'S OURS.

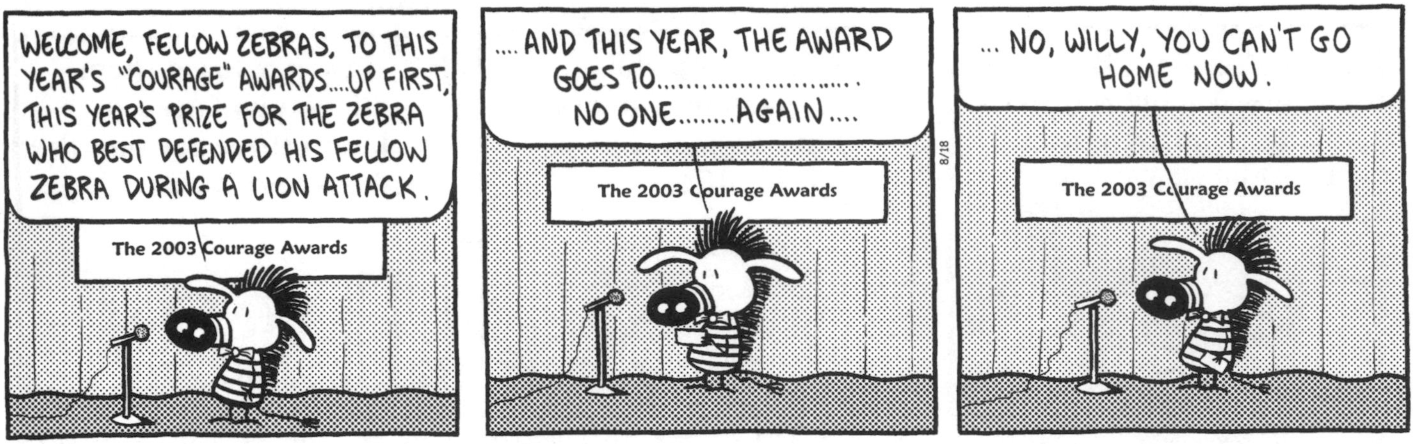
WELCOME, FELLOW ZEBRAS, TO THIS YEAR'S "COURAGE" AWARDS....UP FIRST, THIS YEAR'S PRIZE FOR THE ZEBRA WHO BEST DEFENDED HIS FELLOW ZEBRA DURING A LION ATTACK.
The 2003 Courage Awards
....AND THIS YEAR, THE AWARD GOES TO........................ NO ONE........AGAIN....
8/18
... NO, WILLY, YOU CAN'T GO HOME NOW.

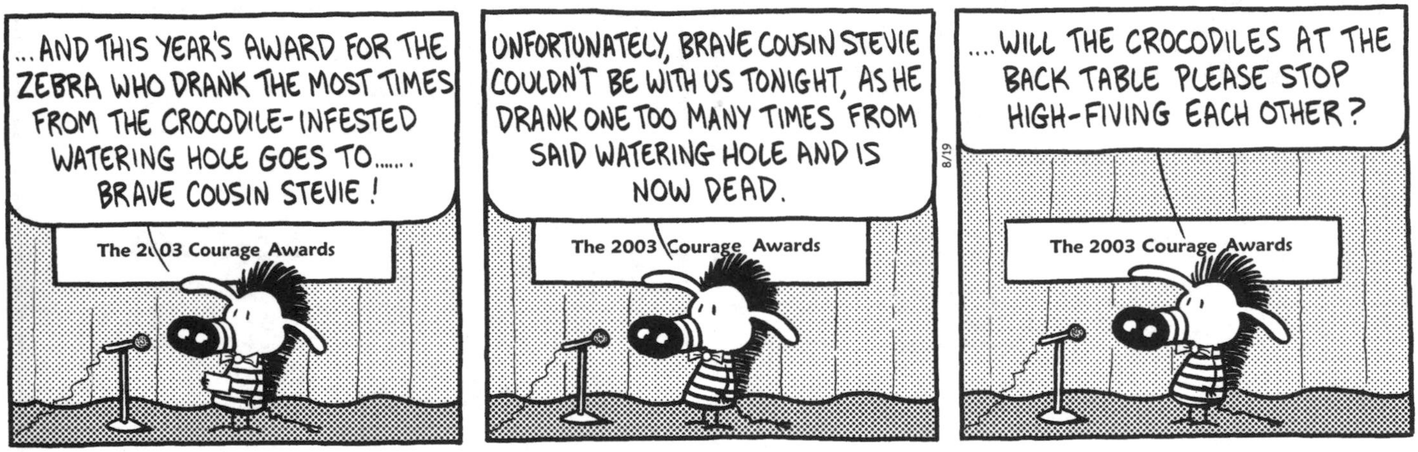
...AND THIS YEAR'S AWARD FOR THE ZEBRA WHO DRANK THE MOST TIMES FROM THE CROCODILE-INFESTED WATERING HOLE GOES TO....... BRAVE COUSIN STEVIE!
The 2003 Courage Awards
UNFORTUNATELY, BRAVE COUSIN STEVIE COULDN'T BE WITH US TONIGHT, AS HE DRANK ONE TOO MANY TIMES FROM SAID WATERING HOLE AND IS NOW DEAD.
8/19
....WILL THE CROCODILES AT THE BACK TABLE PLEASE STOP HIGH-FIVING EACH OTHER?

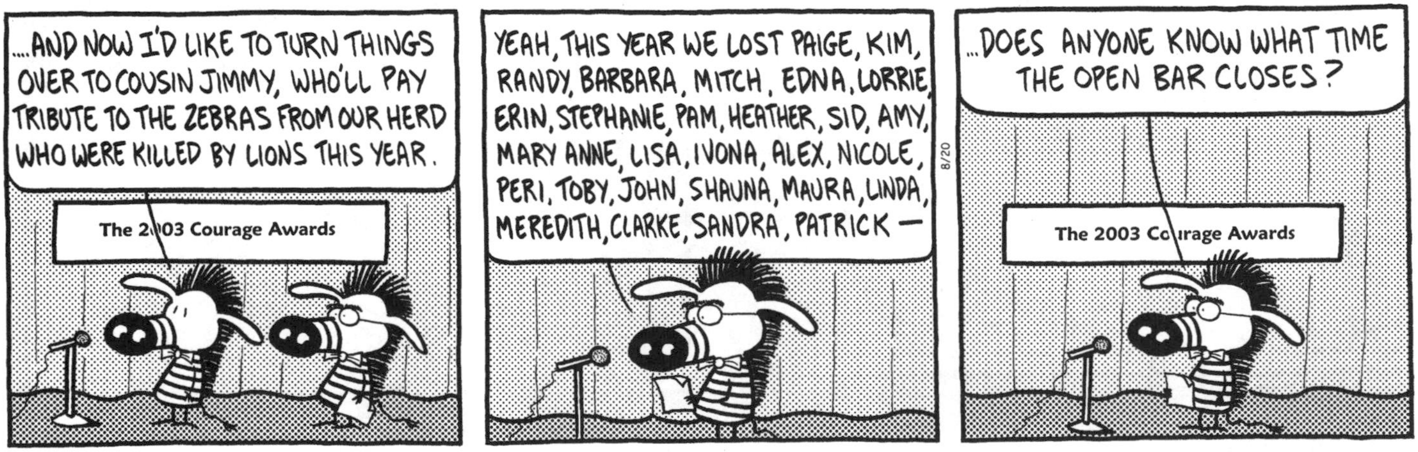
....AND NOW I'D LIKE TO TURN THINGS OVER TO COUSIN JIMMY, WHO'LL PAY TRIBUTE TO THE ZEBRAS FROM OUR HERD WHO WERE KILLED BY LIONS THIS YEAR.
The 2003 Courage Awards
YEAH, THIS YEAR WE LOST PAIGE, KIM, RANDY, BARBARA, MITCH, EDNA, LORRIE, ERIN, STEPHANIE, PAM, HEATHER, SID, AMY, MARY ANNE, LISA, IVONA, ALEX, NICOLE, PERI, TOBY, JOHN, SHAUNA, MAURA, LINDA, MEREDITH, CLARKE, SANDRA, PATRICK —
8/20
...DOES ANYONE KNOW WHAT TIME THE OPEN BAR CLOSES?

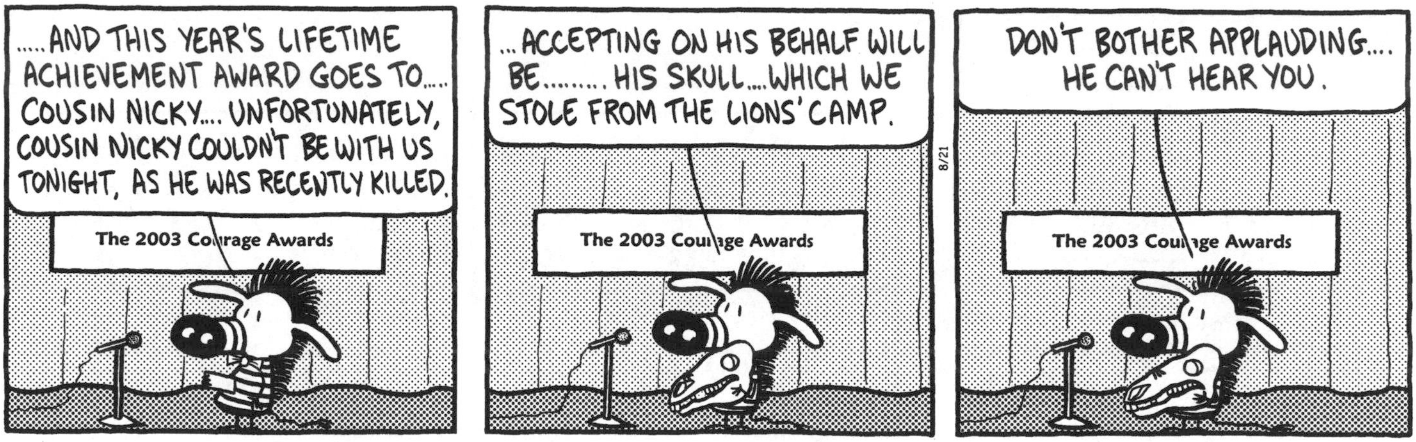
.....AND THIS YEAR'S LIFETIME ACHIEVEMENT AWARD GOES TO..... COUSIN NICKY.... UNFORTUNATELY, COUSIN NICKY COULDN'T BE WITH US TONIGHT, AS HE WAS RECENTLY KILLED.
The 2003 Courage Awards
...ACCEPTING ON HIS BEHALF WILL BE......... HIS SKULL....WHICH WE STOLE FROM THE LIONS' CAMP.
The 2003 Courage Awards
8/21
DON'T BOTHER APPLAUDING.... HE CAN'T HEAR YOU.
The 2003 Courage Awards

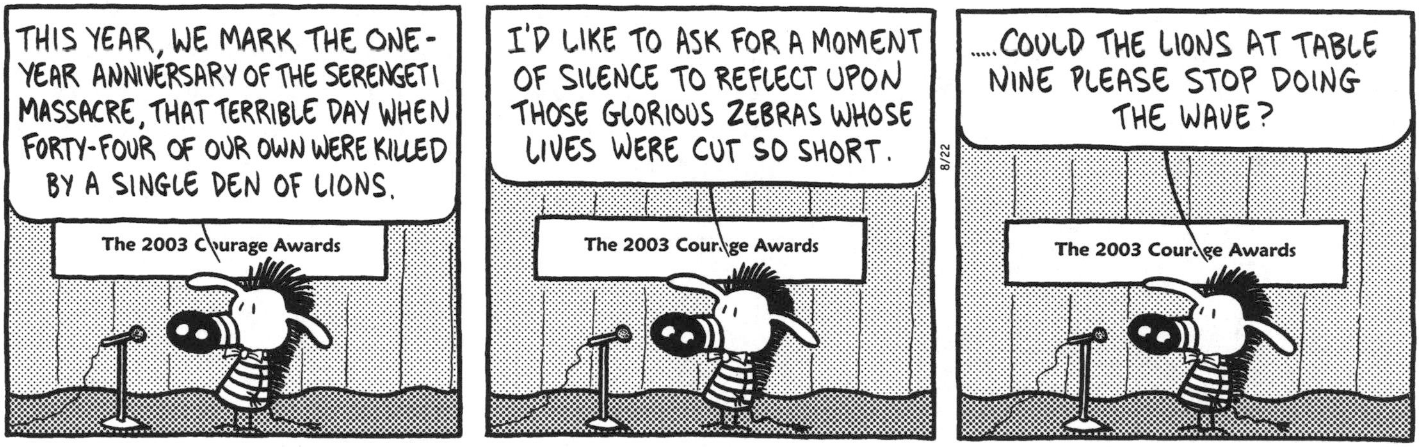
THIS YEAR, WE MARK THE ONE-YEAR ANNIVERSARY OF THE SERENGETI MASSACRE, THAT TERRIBLE DAY WHEN FORTY-FOUR OF OUR OWN WERE KILLED BY A SINGLE DEN OF LIONS.
The 2003 Courage Awards
I'D LIKE TO ASK FOR A MOMENT OF SILENCE TO REFLECT UPON THOSE GLORIOUS ZEBRAS WHOSE LIVES WERE CUT SO SHORT.
The 2003 Courage Awards
8/22
.....COULD THE LIONS AT TABLE NINE PLEASE STOP DOING THE WAVE?
The 2003 Courage Awards

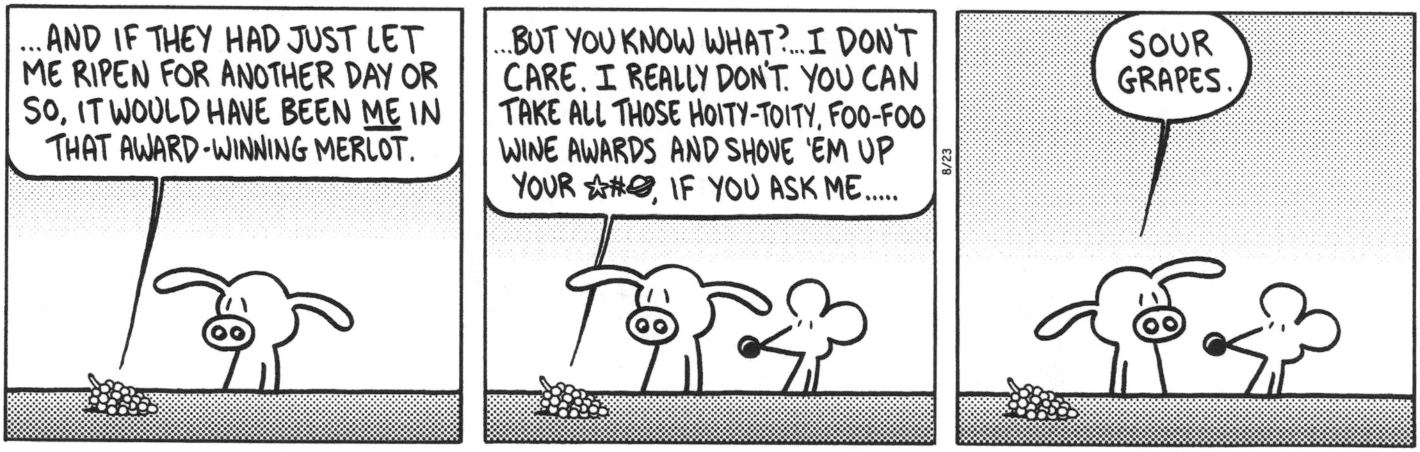
...AND IF THEY HAD JUST LET ME RIPEN FOR ANOTHER DAY OR SO, IT WOULD HAVE BEEN ME IN THAT AWARD-WINNING MERLOT.
...BUT YOU KNOW WHAT?...I DON'T CARE. I REALLY DON'T. YOU CAN TAKE ALL THOSE HOITY-TOITY, FOO-FOO WINE AWARDS AND SHOVE 'EM UP YOUR ☆#@, IF YOU ASK ME.....
8/23
SOUR GRAPES.

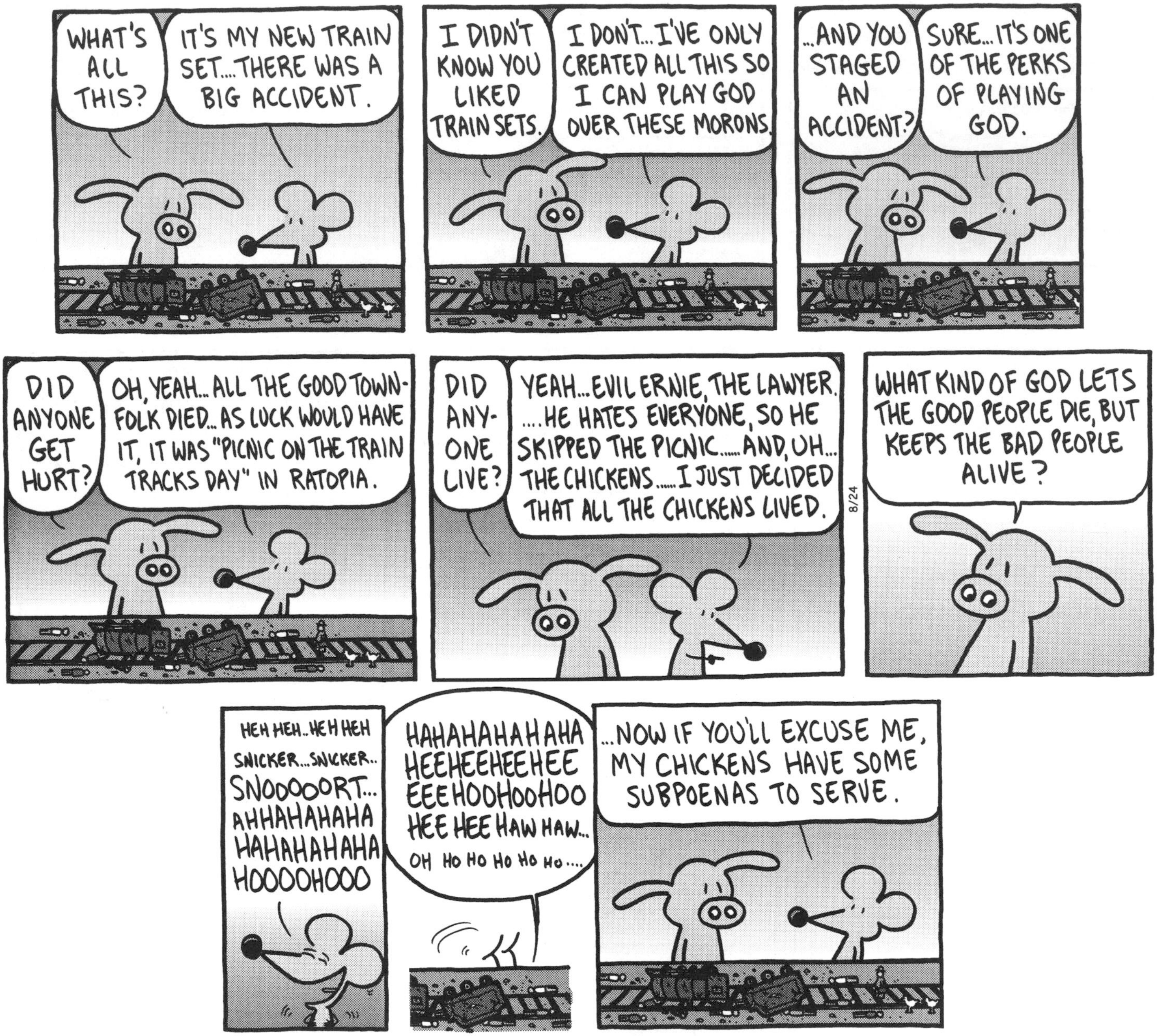
WHAT'S ALL THIS?
IT'S MY NEW TRAIN SET.... THERE WAS A BIG ACCIDENT.
I DIDN'T KNOW YOU LIKED TRAIN SETS.
I DON'T... I'VE ONLY CREATED ALL THIS SO I CAN PLAY GOD OVER THESE MORONS.
...AND YOU STAGED AN ACCIDENT?
SURE... IT'S ONE OF THE PERKS OF PLAYING GOD.
DID ANYONE GET HURT?
OH, YEAH... ALL THE GOOD TOWNFOLK DIED... AS LUCK WOULD HAVE IT, IT WAS "PICNIC ON THE TRAIN TRACKS DAY" IN RATOPIA.
DID ANY-ONE LIVE?
YEAH... EVIL ERNIE, THE LAWYER. ....HE HATES EVERYONE, SO HE SKIPPED THE PICNIC...... AND, UH... THE CHICKENS...... I JUST DECIDED THAT ALL THE CHICKENS LIVED.
8/24
WHAT KIND OF GOD LETS THE GOOD PEOPLE DIE, BUT KEEPS THE BAD PEOPLE ALIVE?
HEH HEH.. HEH HEH
SNICKER... SNICKER..
SNOOOOORT...
AHHAHAHAHA
HAHAHAHAHA
HOOOOHOOO
HAHAHAHAHAHA
HEEHEEHEEHEE
EEEHOOHooHOO
HEE HEE HAW HAW...
OH HO HO HO HO HO....
...NOW IF YOU'LL EXCUSE ME, MY CHICKENS HAVE SOME SUBPOENAS TO SERVE.

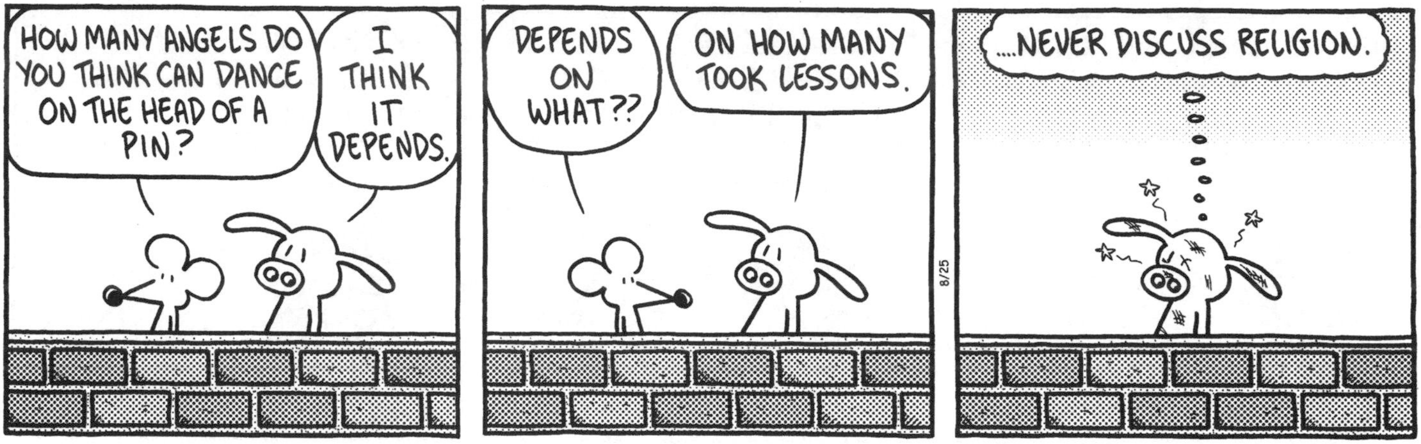
HOW MANY ANGELS DO YOU THINK CAN DANCE ON THE HEAD OF A PIN?
I THINK IT DEPENDS.
DEPENDS ON WHAT??
ON HOW MANY TOOK LESSONS.
8/25
....NEVER DISCUSS RELIGION.

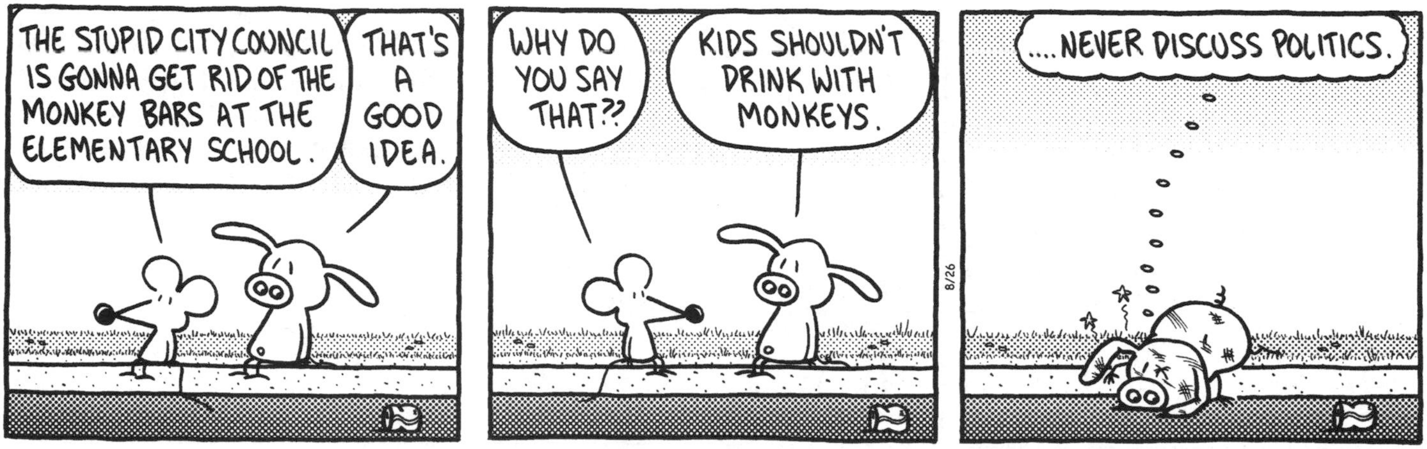
THE STUPID CITY COUNCIL IS GONNA GET RID OF THE MONKEY BARS AT THE ELEMENTARY SCHOOL.
THAT'S A GOOD IDEA.
WHY DO YOU SAY THAT??
KIDS SHOULDN'T DRINK WITH MONKEYS.
8/26
....NEVER DISCUSS POLITICS.

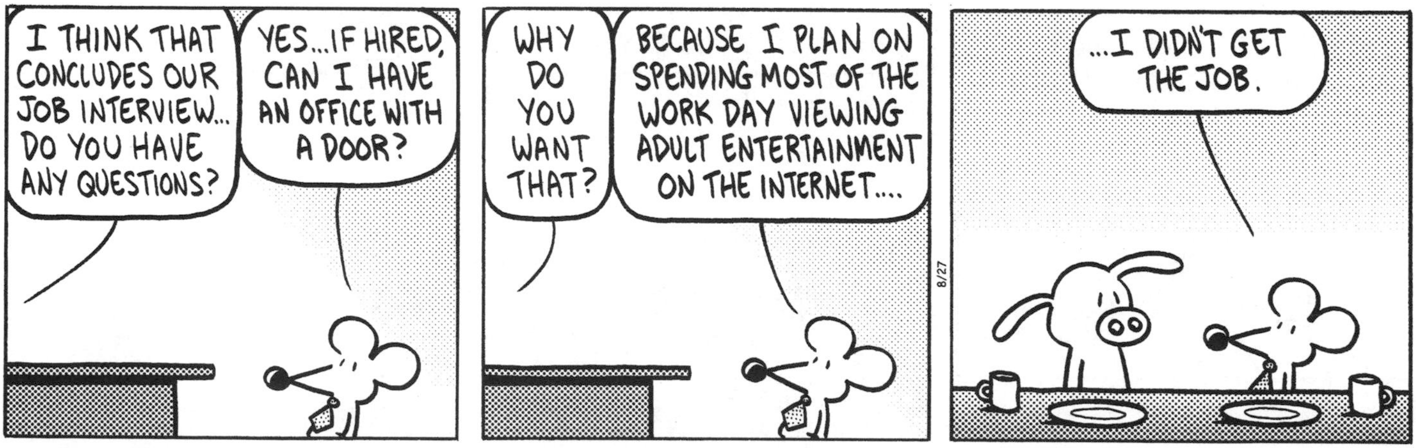
I THINK THAT CONCLUDES OUR JOB INTERVIEW... DO YOU HAVE ANY QUESTIONS?
YES...IF HIRED, CAN I HAVE AN OFFICE WITH A DOOR?
WHY DO YOU WANT THAT?
BECAUSE I PLAN ON SPENDING MOST OF THE WORK DAY VIEWING ADULT ENTERTAINMENT ON THE INTERNET....
8/27
...I DIDN'T GET THE JOB.

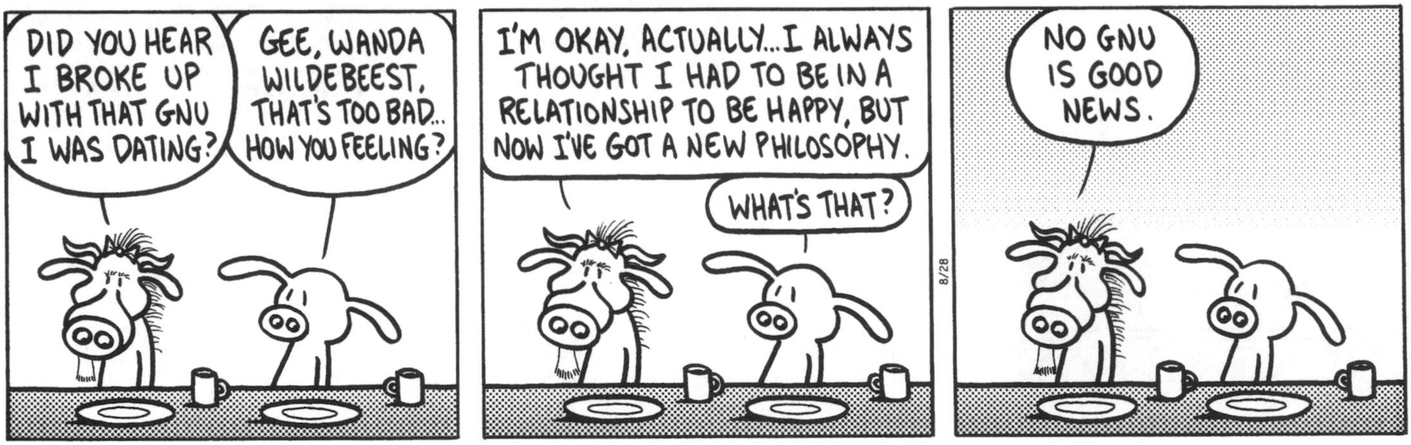
DID YOU HEAR I BROKE UP WITH THAT GNU I WAS DATING?
GEE, WANDA WILDEBEEST, THAT'S TOO BAD... HOW YOU FEELING?
I'M OKAY, ACTUALLY...I ALWAYS THOUGHT I HAD TO BE IN A RELATIONSHIP TO BE HAPPY, BUT NOW I'VE GOT A NEW PHILOSOPHY.
WHAT'S THAT?
NO GNU IS GOOD NEWS.
8/28

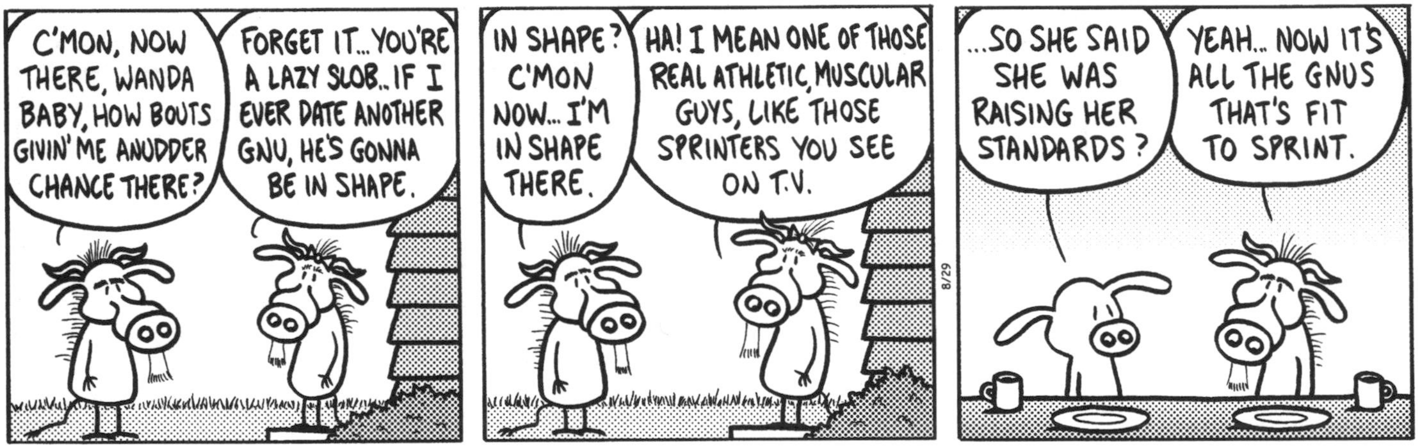
C'MON, NOW THERE, WANDA BABY, HOW BOUTS GIVIN' ME ANUDDER CHANCE THERE?
FORGET IT... YOU'RE A LAZY SLOB.. IF I EVER DATE ANOTHER GNU, HE'S GONNA BE IN SHAPE.
IN SHAPE? C'MON NOW... I'M IN SHAPE THERE.
HA! I MEAN ONE OF THOSE REAL ATHLETIC, MUSCULAR GUYS, LIKE THOSE SPRINTERS YOU SEE ON T.V.
...SO SHE SAID SHE WAS RAISING HER STANDARDS?
YEAH... NOW IT'S ALL THE GNUS THAT'S FIT TO SPRINT.
8/29

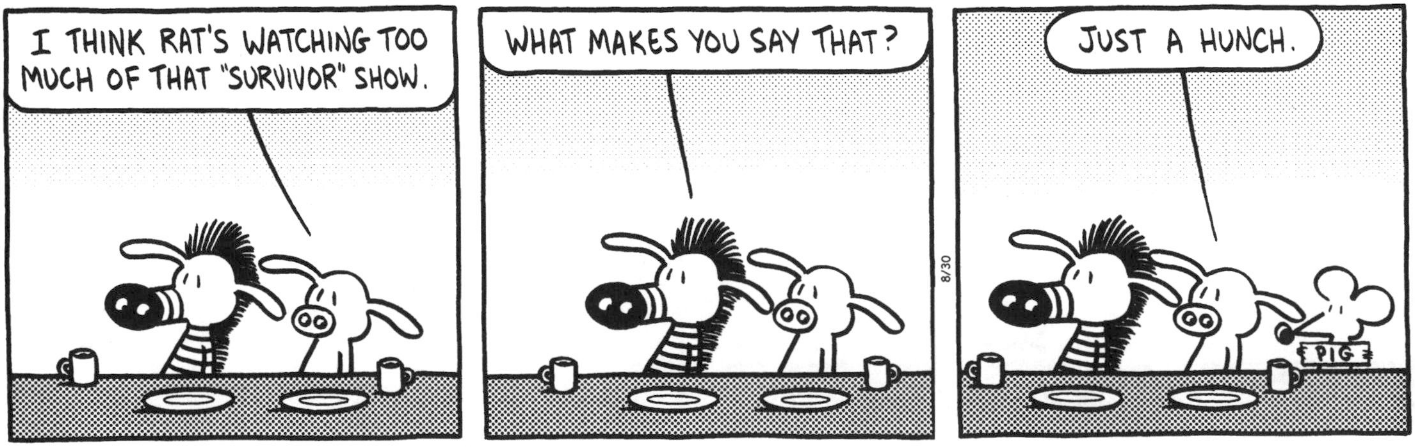
I THINK RAT'S WATCHING TOO MUCH OF THAT "SURVIVOR" SHOW.
WHAT MAKES YOU SAY THAT?
JUST A HUNCH.
PIG
8/30

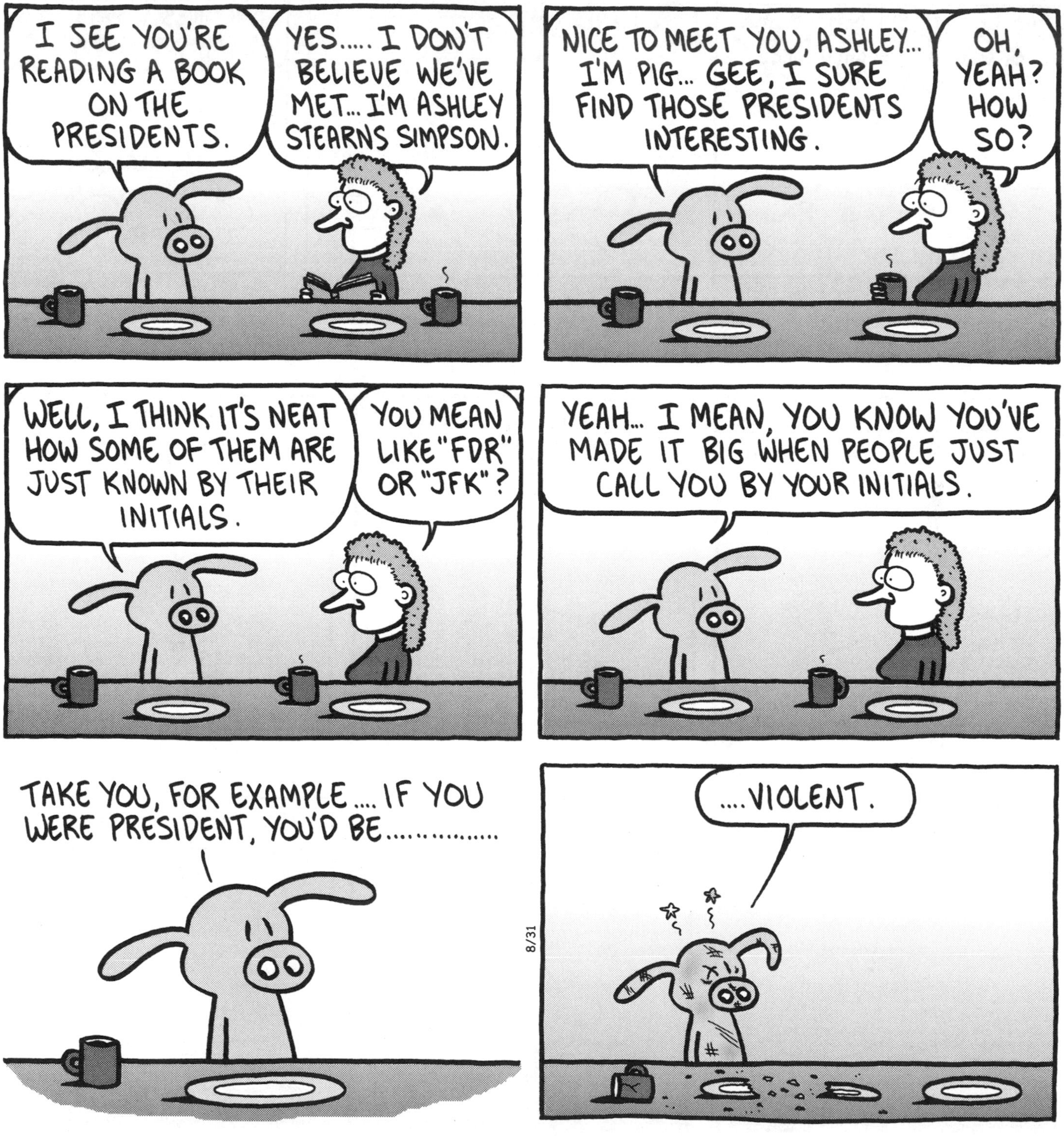
I SEE YOU'RE READING A BOOK ON THE PRESIDENTS.
YES..... I DON'T BELIEVE WE'VE MET... I'M ASHLEY STEARNS SIMPSON.
NICE TO MEET YOU, ASHLEY... I'M PIG... GEE, I SURE FIND THOSE PRESIDENTS INTERESTING.
OH, YEAH? HOW SO?
WELL, I THINK IT'S NEAT HOW SOME OF THEM ARE JUST KNOWN BY THEIR INITIALS.
YOU MEAN LIKE "FDR" OR "JFK"?
YEAH... I MEAN, YOU KNOW YOU'VE MADE IT BIG WHEN PEOPLE JUST CALL YOU BY YOUR INITIALS.
TAKE YOU, FOR EXAMPLE.... IF YOU WERE PRESIDENT, YOU'D BE...............
8/31
....VIOLENT.

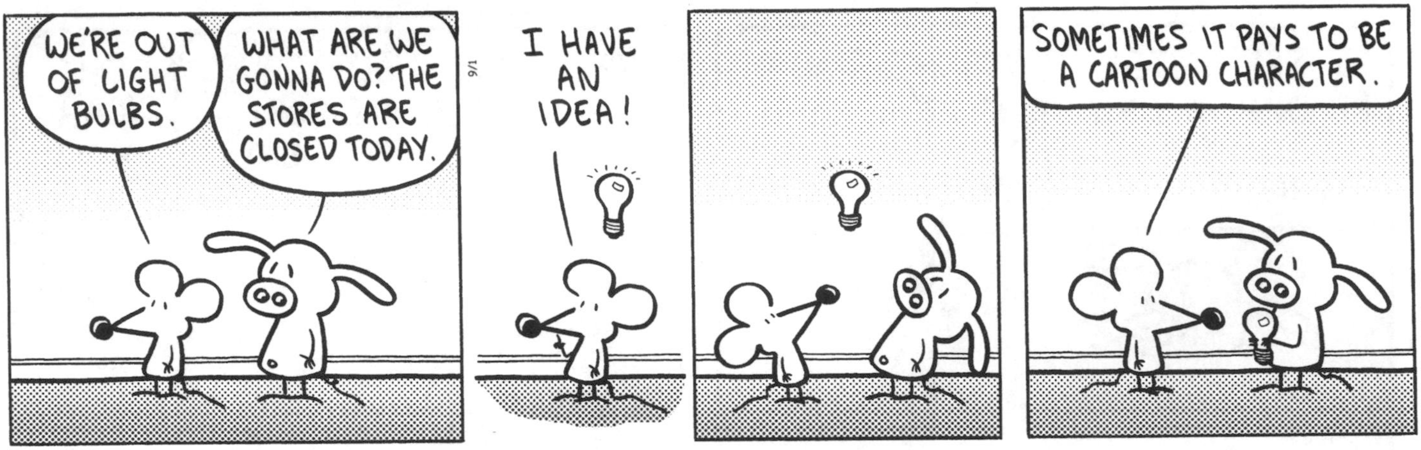
WE'RE OUT OF LIGHT BULBS.
WHAT ARE WE GONNA DO? THE STORES ARE CLOSED TODAY.
9/1
I HAVE AN IDEA!
SOMETIMES IT PAYS TO BE A CARTOON CHARACTER.

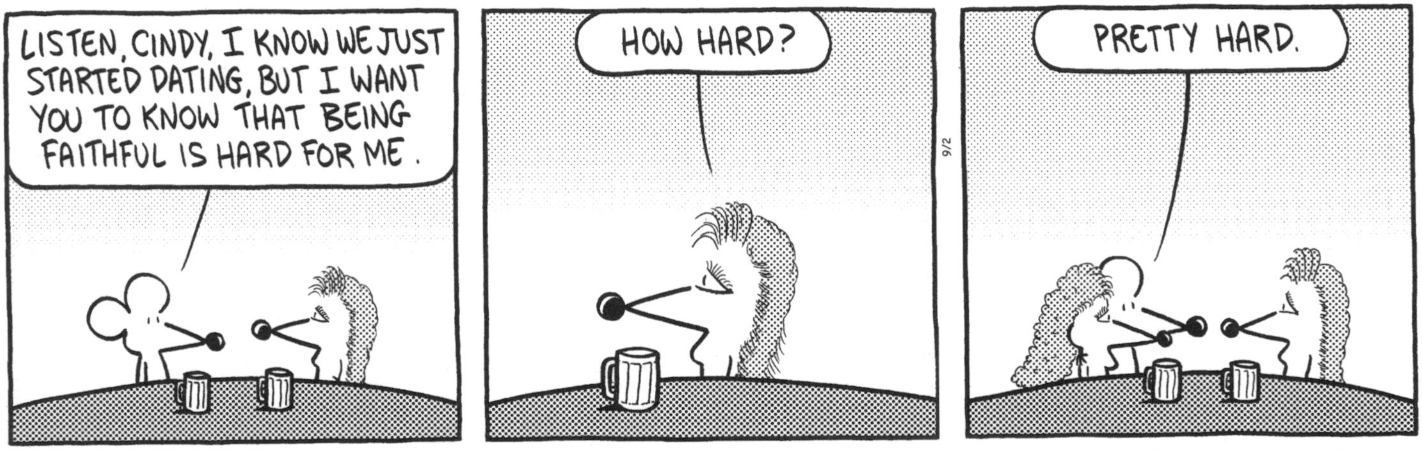
LISTEN, CINDY, I KNOW WE JUST STARTED DATING, BUT I WANT YOU TO KNOW THAT BEING FAITHFUL IS HARD FOR ME.
HOW HARD?
9/2
PRETTY HARD.

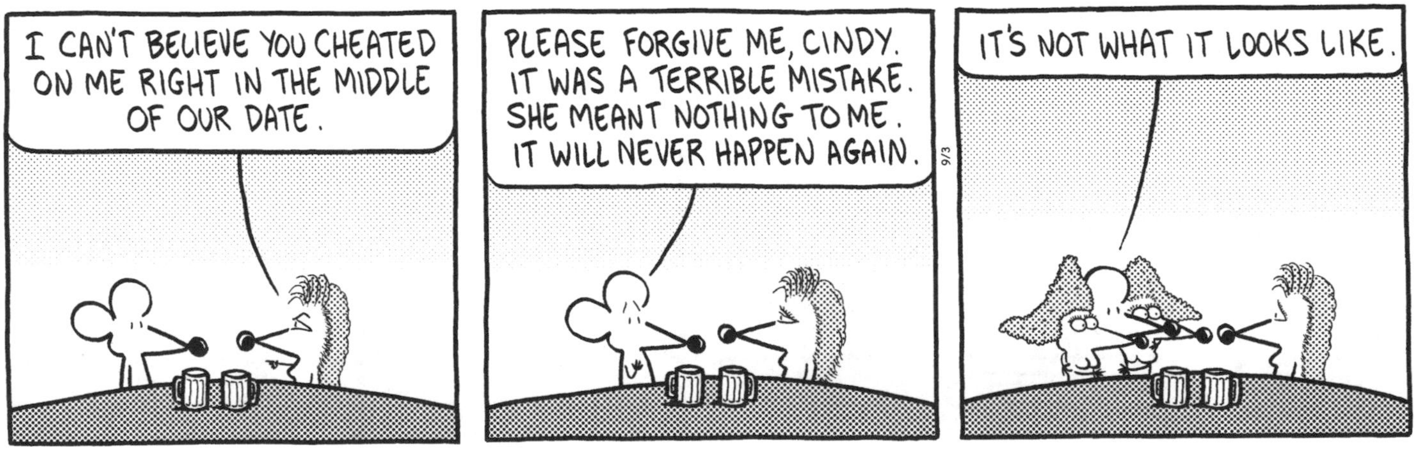
I CAN'T BELIEVE YOU CHEATED ON ME RIGHT IN THE MIDDLE OF OUR DATE.
PLEASE FORGIVE ME, CINDY. IT WAS A TERRIBLE MISTAKE. SHE MEANT NOTHING TO ME. IT WILL NEVER HAPPEN AGAIN.
9/3
IT'S NOT WHAT IT LOOKS LIKE.

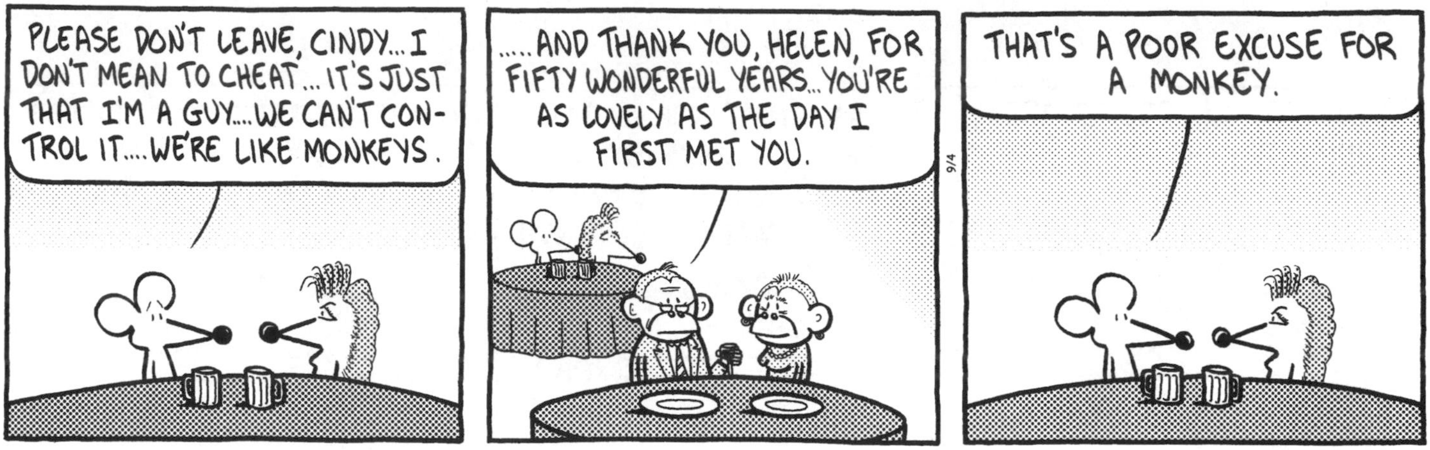
PLEASE DON'T LEAVE, CINDY... I DON'T MEAN TO CHEAT... IT'S JUST THAT I'M A GUY.... WE CAN'T CONTROL IT.... WE'RE LIKE MONKEYS.
..... AND THANK YOU, HELEN, FOR FIFTY WONDERFUL YEARS... YOU'RE AS LOVELY AS THE DAY I FIRST MET YOU.
9/4
THAT'S A POOR EXCUSE FOR A MONKEY.

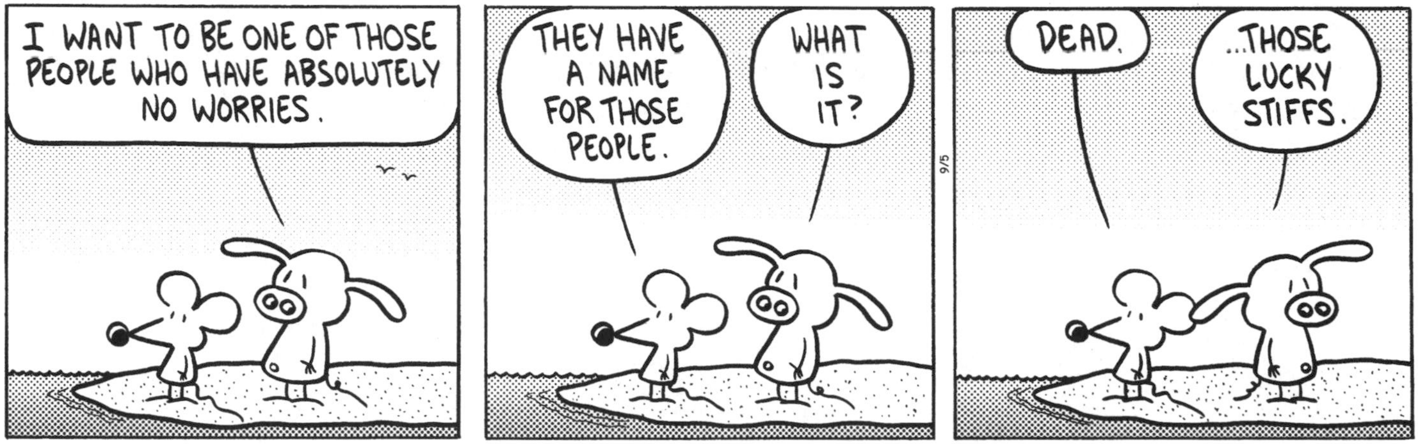
I WANT TO BE ONE OF THOSE PEOPLE WHO HAVE ABSOLUTELY NO WORRIES.
THEY HAVE A NAME FOR THOSE PEOPLE.
WHAT IS IT?
9/5
DEAD.
...THOSE LUCKY STIFFS.

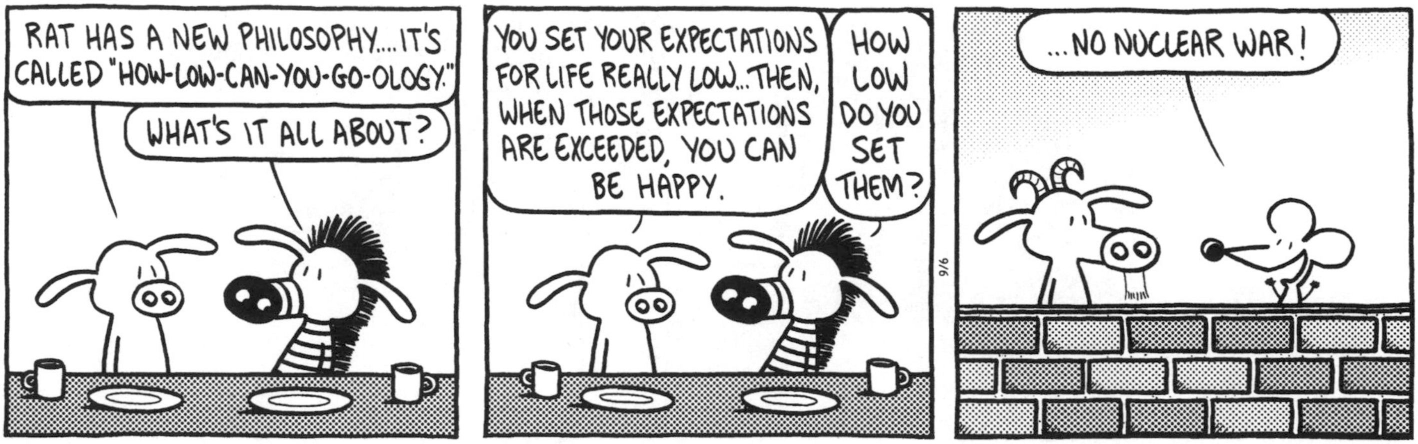
RAT HAS A NEW PHILOSOPHY.... IT'S CALLED "HOW-LOW-CAN-YOU-GO-OLOGY."
WHAT'S IT ALL ABOUT?
YOU SET YOUR EXPECTATIONS FOR LIFE REALLY LOW... THEN, WHEN THOSE EXPECTATIONS ARE EXCEEDED, YOU CAN BE HAPPY.
HOW LOW DO YOU SET THEM?
9/6
... NO NUCLEAR WAR!

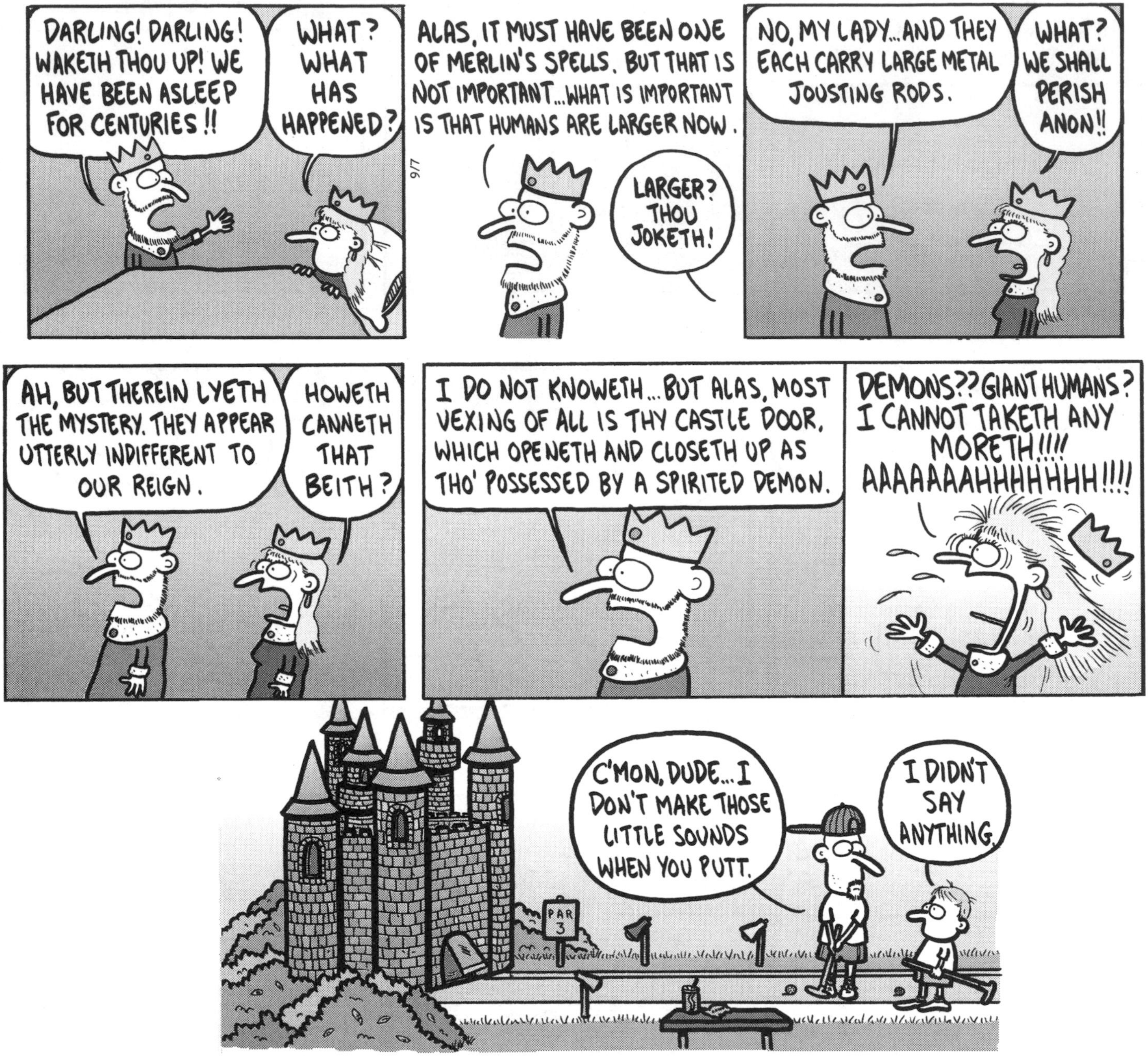

DARLING! DARLING! WAKETH THOU UP! WE HAVE BEEN ASLEEP FOR CENTURIES!!
WHAT? WHAT HAS HAPPENED?
ALAS, IT MUST HAVE BEEN ONE OF MERLIN'S SPELLS. BUT THAT IS NOT IMPORTANT...WHAT IS IMPORTANT IS THAT HUMANS ARE LARGER NOW.
9/7
LARGER? THOU JOKETH!
NO, MY LADY...AND THEY EACH CARRY LARGE METAL JOUSTING RODS.
WHAT? WE SHALL PERISH ANON!!
AH, BUT THEREIN LYETH THE MYSTERY. THEY APPEAR UTTERLY INDIFFERENT TO OUR REIGN.
HOWETH CANNETH THAT BEITH?
I DO NOT KNOWETH...BUT ALAS, MOST VEXING OF ALL IS THY CASTLE DOOR, WHICH OPENETH AND CLOSETH UP AS THO' POSSESSED BY A SPIRITED DEMON.
DEMONS?? GIANT HUMANS? I CANNOT TAKETH ANY MORETH!!!! AAAAAAAHHHHHHH!!!!
PAR 3
C'MON, DUDE...I DON'T MAKE THOSE LITTLE SOUNDS WHEN YOU PUTT.
I DIDN'T SAY ANYTHING.

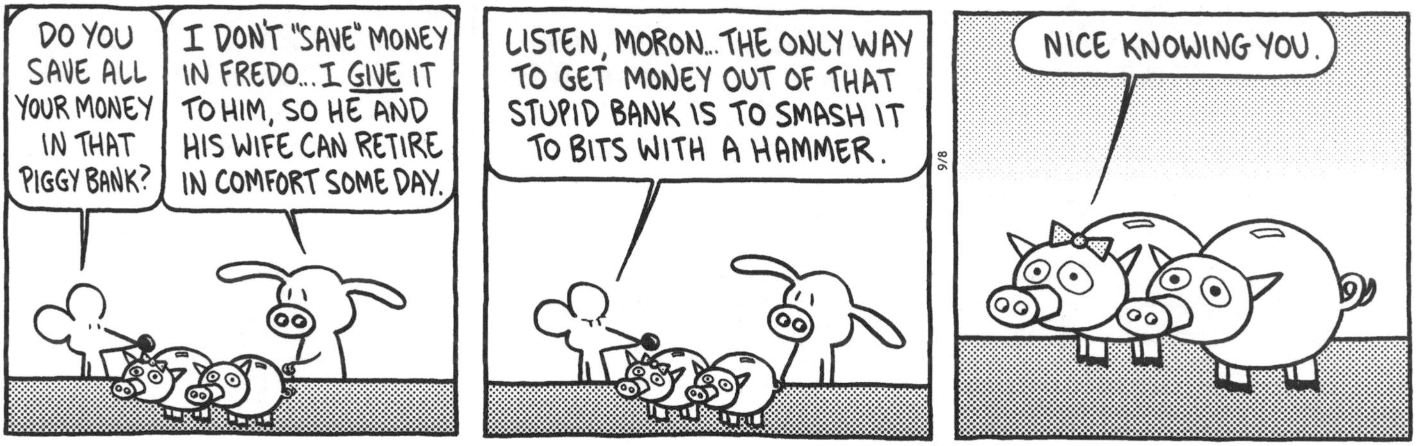
DO YOU SAVE ALL YOUR MONEY IN THAT PIGGY BANK?
I DON'T "SAVE" MONEY IN FREDO... I GIVE IT TO HIM, SO HE AND HIS WIFE CAN RETIRE IN COMFORT SOME DAY.
LISTEN, MORON... THE ONLY WAY TO GET MONEY OUT OF THAT STUPID BANK IS TO SMASH IT TO BITS WITH A HAMMER.
9/8
NICE KNOWING YOU.

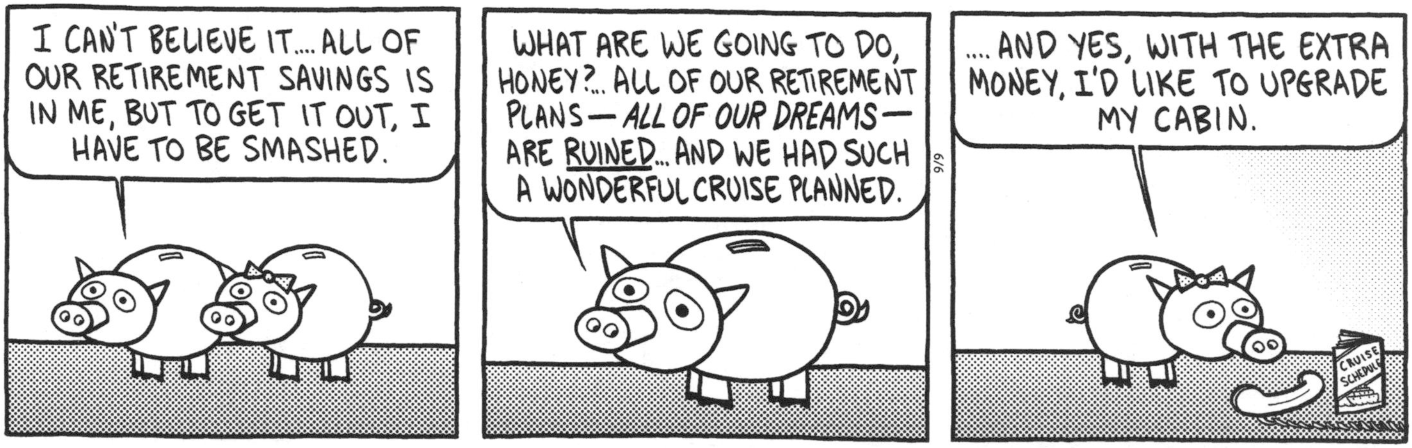
I CAN'T BELIEVE IT.... ALL OF OUR RETIREMENT SAVINGS IS IN ME, BUT TO GET IT OUT, I HAVE TO BE SMASHED.
WHAT ARE WE GOING TO DO, HONEY?... ALL OF OUR RETIREMENT PLANS — ALL OF OUR DREAMS — ARE RUINED... AND WE HAD SUCH A WONDERFUL CRUISE PLANNED.
9/9
.... AND YES, WITH THE EXTRA MONEY, I'D LIKE TO UPGRADE MY CABIN.
CRUISE SCHEDULE

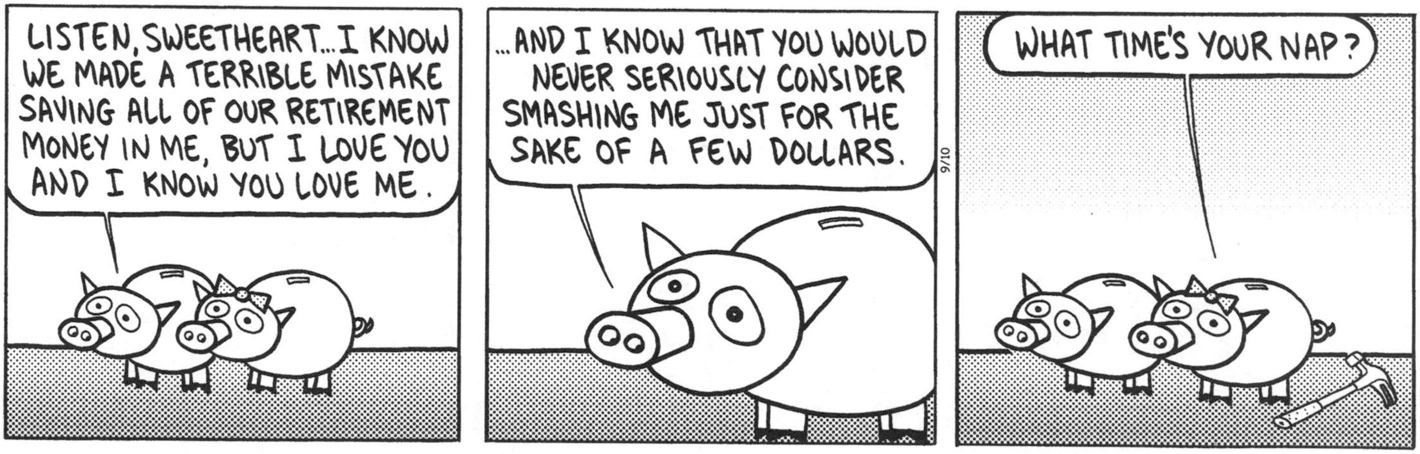
LISTEN, SWEETHEART... I KNOW WE MADE A TERRIBLE MISTAKE SAVING ALL OF OUR RETIREMENT MONEY IN ME, BUT I LOVE YOU AND I KNOW YOU LOVE ME.
... AND I KNOW THAT YOU WOULD NEVER SERIOUSLY CONSIDER SMASHING ME JUST FOR THE SAKE OF A FEW DOLLARS.
9/10
WHAT TIME'S YOUR NAP?

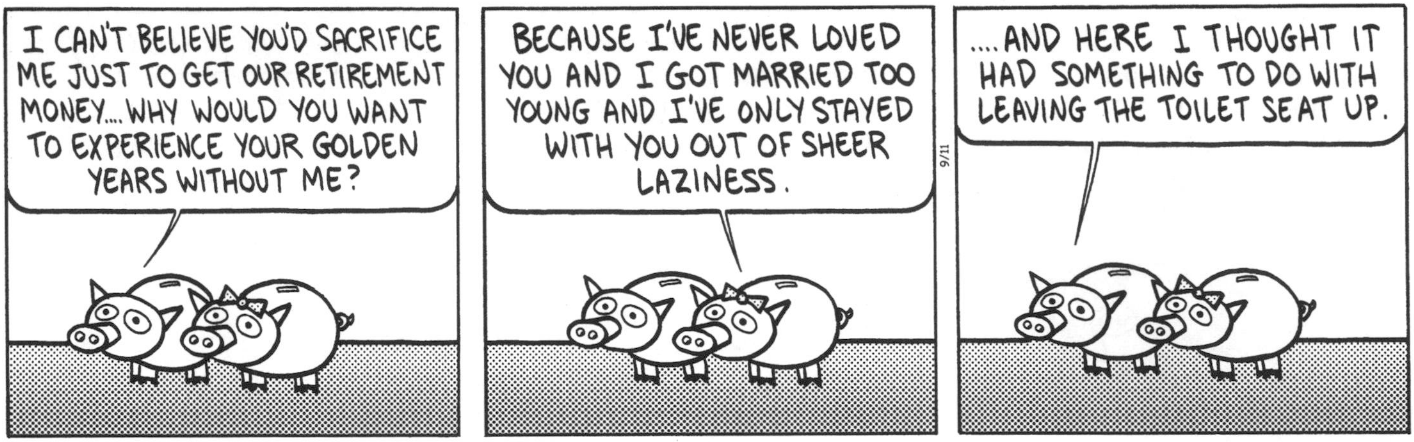
I CAN'T BELIEVE YOU'D SACRIFICE ME JUST TO GET OUR RETIREMENT MONEY.... WHY WOULD YOU WANT TO EXPERIENCE YOUR GOLDEN YEARS WITHOUT ME?
BECAUSE I'VE NEVER LOVED YOU AND I GOT MARRIED TOO YOUNG AND I'VE ONLY STAYED WITH YOU OUT OF SHEER LAZINESS.
9/11
....AND HERE I THOUGHT IT HAD SOMETHING TO DO WITH LEAVING THE TOILET SEAT UP.

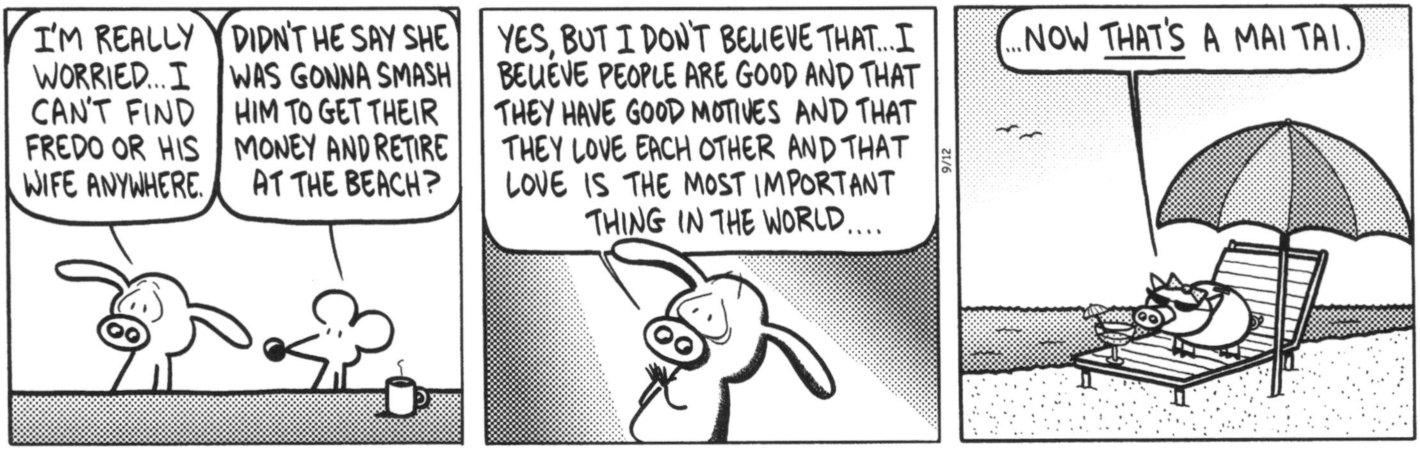
I'M REALLY WORRIED... I CAN'T FIND FREDO OR HIS WIFE ANYWHERE.
DIDN'T HE SAY SHE WAS GONNA SMASH HIM TO GET THEIR MONEY AND RETIRE AT THE BEACH?
YES, BUT I DON'T BELIEVE THAT... I BELIEVE PEOPLE ARE GOOD AND THAT THEY HAVE GOOD MOTIVES AND THAT THEY LOVE EACH OTHER AND THAT LOVE IS THE MOST IMPORTANT THING IN THE WORLD....
9/12
...NOW THAT'S A MAI TAI.

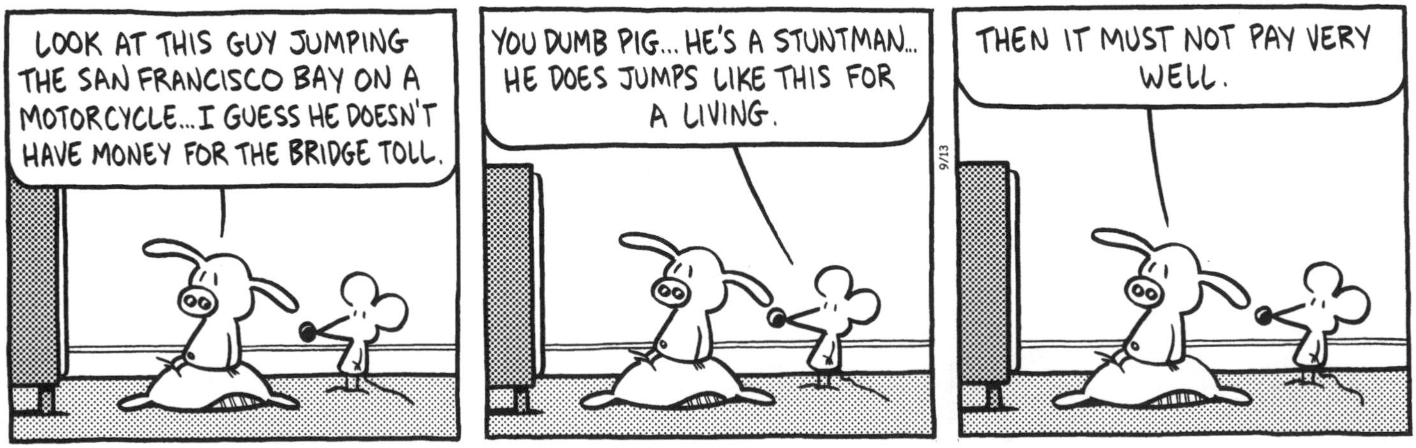
LOOK AT THIS GUY JUMPING THE SAN FRANCISCO BAY ON A MOTORCYCLE... I GUESS HE DOESN'T HAVE MONEY FOR THE BRIDGE TOLL.
YOU DUMB PIG... HE'S A STUNTMAN... HE DOES JUMPS LIKE THIS FOR A LIVING.
9/13
THEN IT MUST NOT PAY VERY WELL.

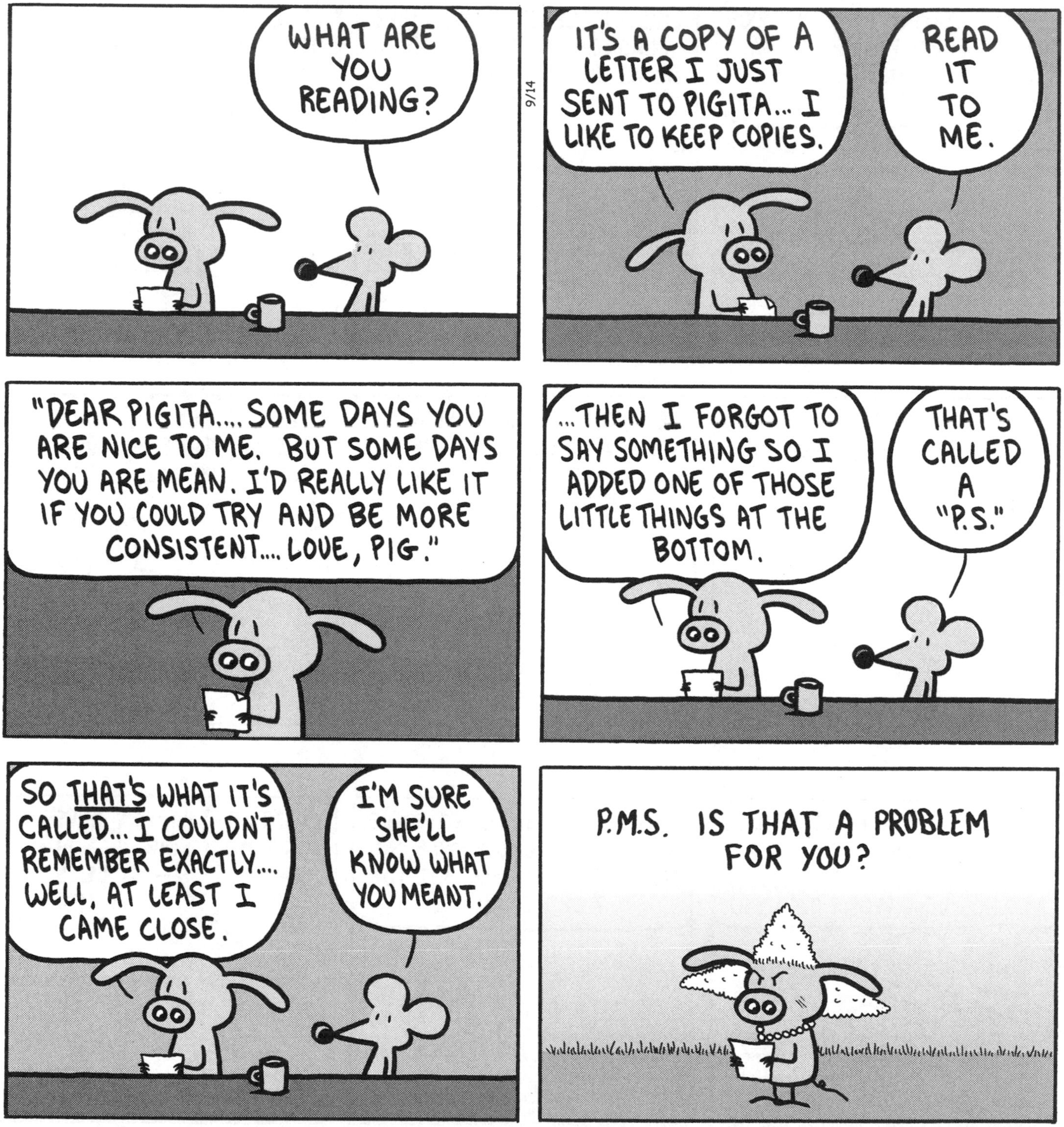
WHAT ARE YOU READING?
9/14
IT'S A COPY OF A LETTER I JUST SENT TO PIGITA... I LIKE TO KEEP COPIES.
READ IT TO ME.
"DEAR PIGITA.... SOME DAYS YOU ARE NICE TO ME. BUT SOME DAYS YOU ARE MEAN. I'D REALLY LIKE IT IF YOU COULD TRY AND BE MORE CONSISTENT.... LOVE, PIG."
...THEN I FORGOT TO SAY SOMETHING SO I ADDED ONE OF THOSE LITTLE THINGS AT THE BOTTOM.
THAT'S CALLED A "P.S."
SO THAT'S WHAT IT'S CALLED... I COULDN'T REMEMBER EXACTLY.... WELL, AT LEAST I CAME CLOSE.
I'M SURE SHE'LL KNOW WHAT YOU MEANT.
P.M.S. IS THAT A PROBLEM FOR YOU?

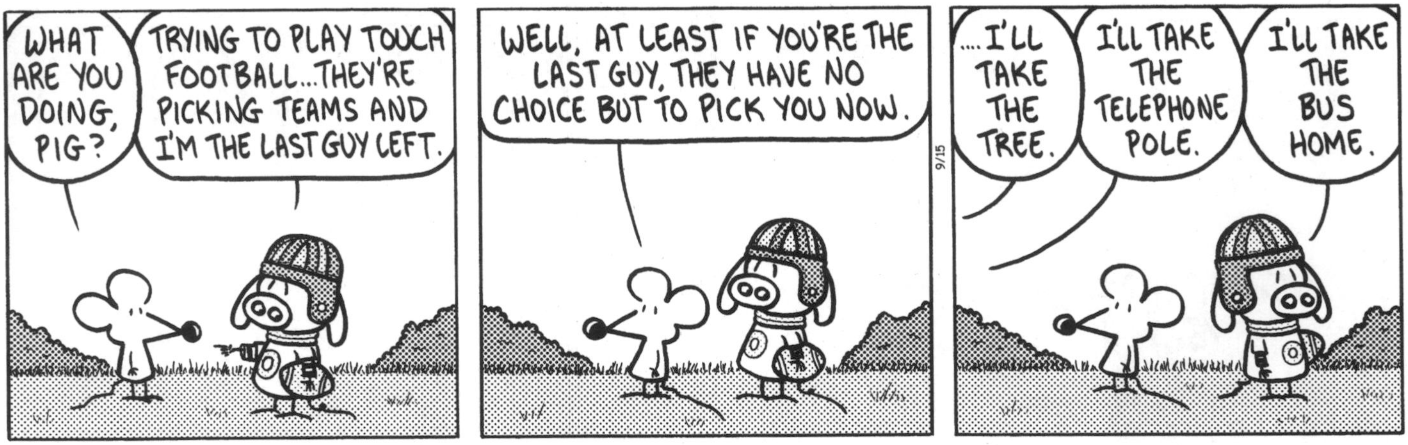
WHAT ARE YOU DOING, PIG?
TRYING TO PLAY TOUCH FOOTBALL...THEY'RE PICKING TEAMS AND I'M THE LAST GUY LEFT.
WELL, AT LEAST IF YOU'RE THE LAST GUY, THEY HAVE NO CHOICE BUT TO PICK YOU NOW.
9/15
....I'LL TAKE THE TREE.
I'LL TAKE THE TELEPHONE POLE.
I'LL TAKE THE BUS HOME.

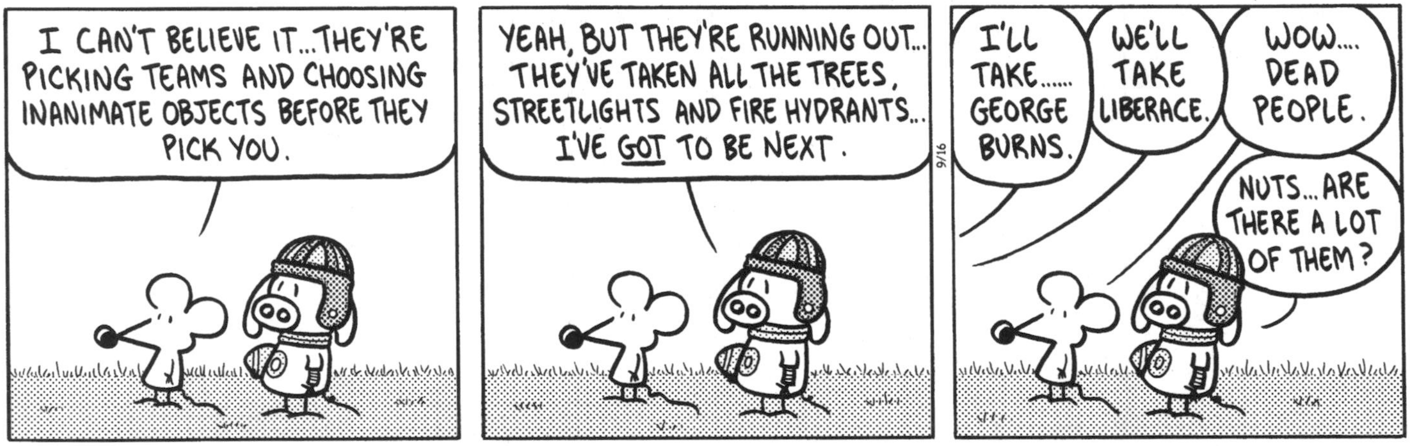
I CAN'T BELIEVE IT...THEY'RE PICKING TEAMS AND CHOOSING INANIMATE OBJECTS BEFORE THEY PICK YOU.
YEAH, BUT THEY'RE RUNNING OUT... THEY'VE TAKEN ALL THE TREES, STREETLIGHTS AND FIRE HYDRANTS... I'VE GOT TO BE NEXT.
9/16
I'LL TAKE...... GEORGE BURNS.
WE'LL TAKE LIBERACE.
WOW.... DEAD PEOPLE.
NUTS...ARE THERE A LOT OF THEM?

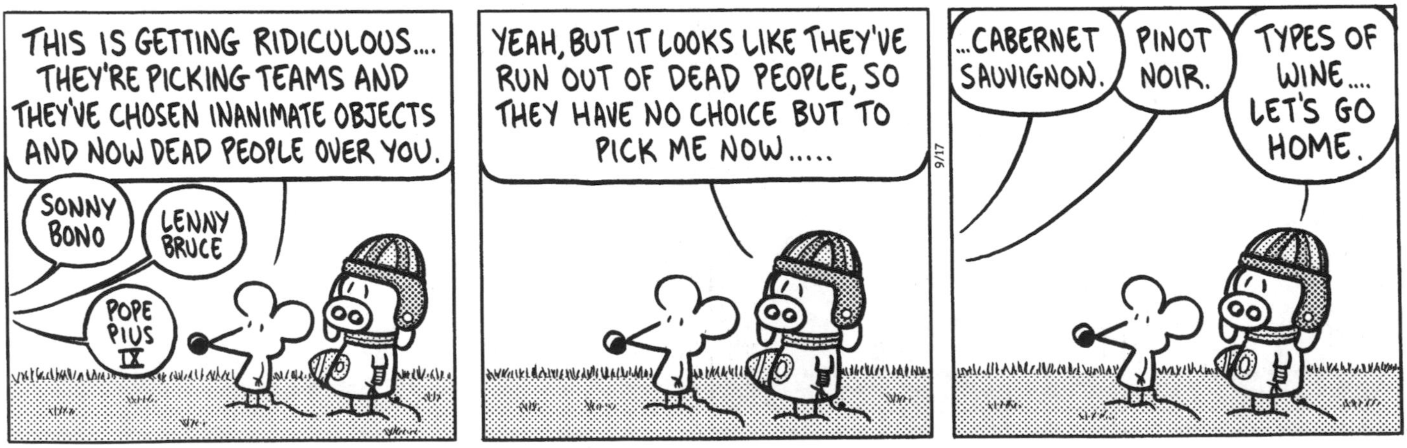
THIS IS GETTING RIDICULOUS.... THEY'RE PICKING TEAMS AND THEY'VE CHOSEN INANIMATE OBJECTS AND NOW DEAD PEOPLE OVER YOU.
SONNY BONO
LENNY BRUCE
POPE PIUS IX
YEAH, BUT IT LOOKS LIKE THEY'VE RUN OUT OF DEAD PEOPLE, SO THEY HAVE NO CHOICE BUT TO PICK ME NOW.....
9/17
...CABERNET SAUVIGNON.
PINOT NOIR.
TYPES OF WINE.... LET'S GO HOME.

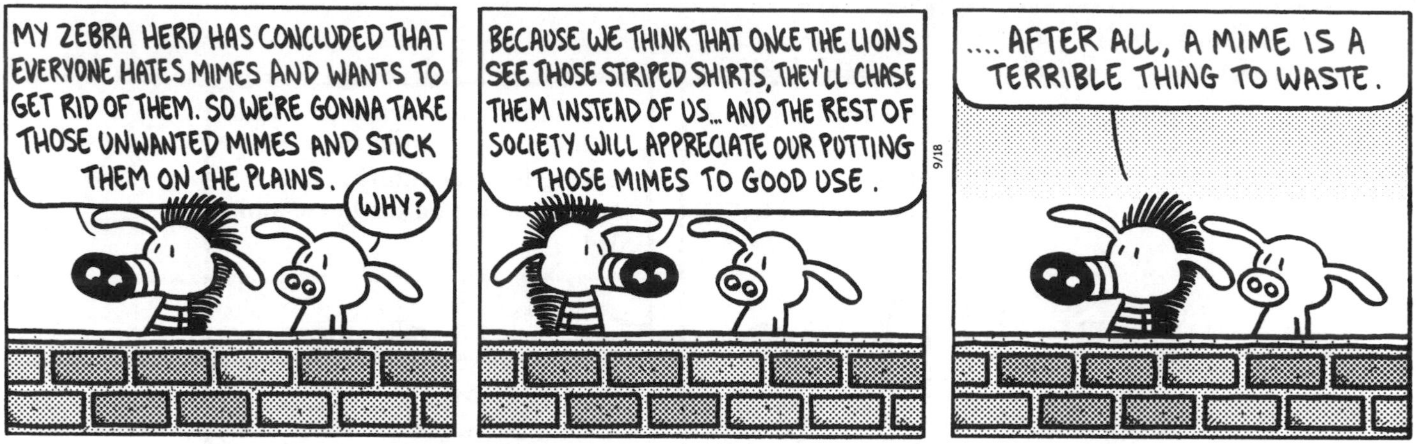
MY ZEBRA HERD HAS CONCLUDED THAT EVERYONE HATES MIMES AND WANTS TO GET RID OF THEM. SO WE'RE GONNA TAKE THOSE UNWANTED MIMES AND STICK THEM ON THE PLAINS.
WHY?
BECAUSE WE THINK THAT ONCE THE LIONS SEE THOSE STRIPED SHIRTS, THEY'LL CHASE THEM INSTEAD OF US... AND THE REST OF SOCIETY WILL APPRECIATE OUR PUTTING THOSE MIMES TO GOOD USE.
9/18
.... AFTER ALL, A MIME IS A TERRIBLE THING TO WASTE.

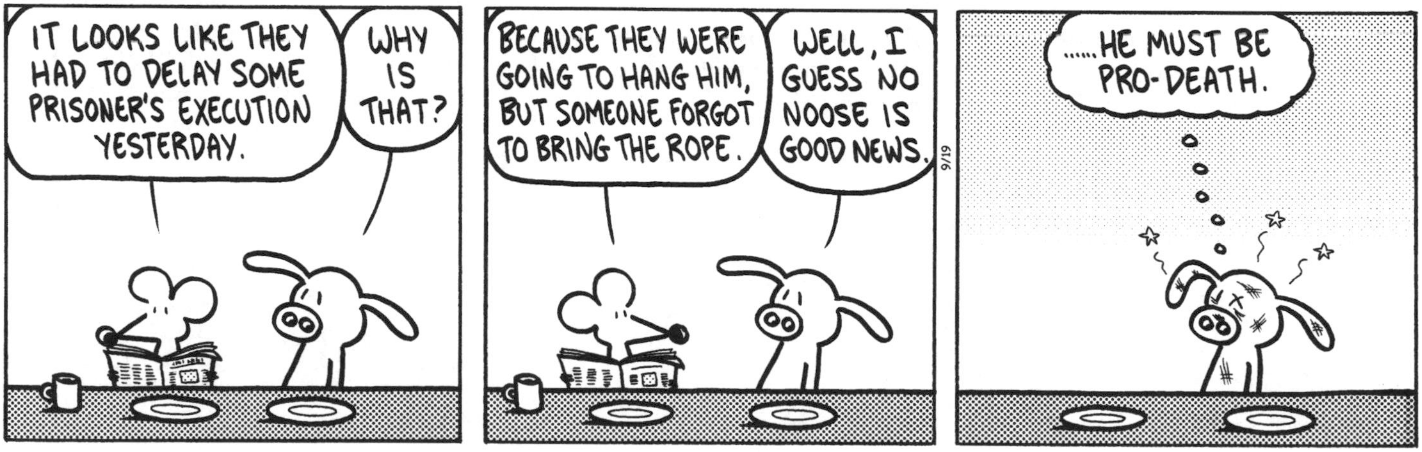
IT LOOKS LIKE THEY HAD TO DELAY SOME PRISONER'S EXECUTION YESTERDAY.
WHY IS THAT?
BECAUSE THEY WERE GOING TO HANG HIM, BUT SOMEONE FORGOT TO BRING THE ROPE.
WELL, I GUESS NO NOOSE IS GOOD NEWS.
9/19
......HE MUST BE PRO-DEATH.

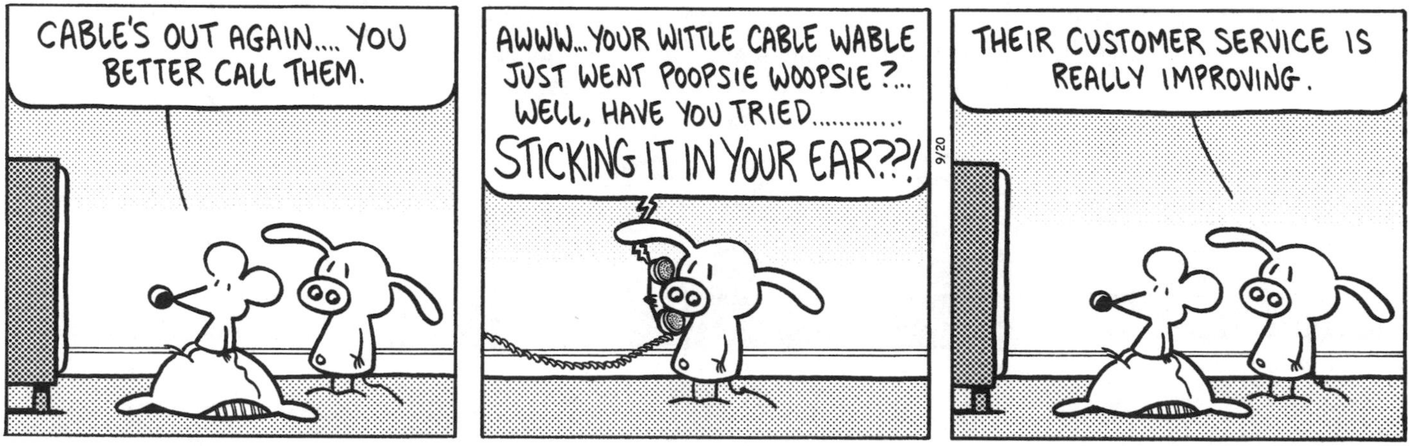
CABLE'S OUT AGAIN.... YOU BETTER CALL THEM.
AWWW...YOUR WITTLE CABLE WABLE JUST WENT POOPSIE WOOPSIE ?... WELL, HAVE YOU TRIED............
STICKING IT IN YOUR EAR??!
9/20
THEIR CUSTOMER SERVICE IS REALLY IMPROVING.

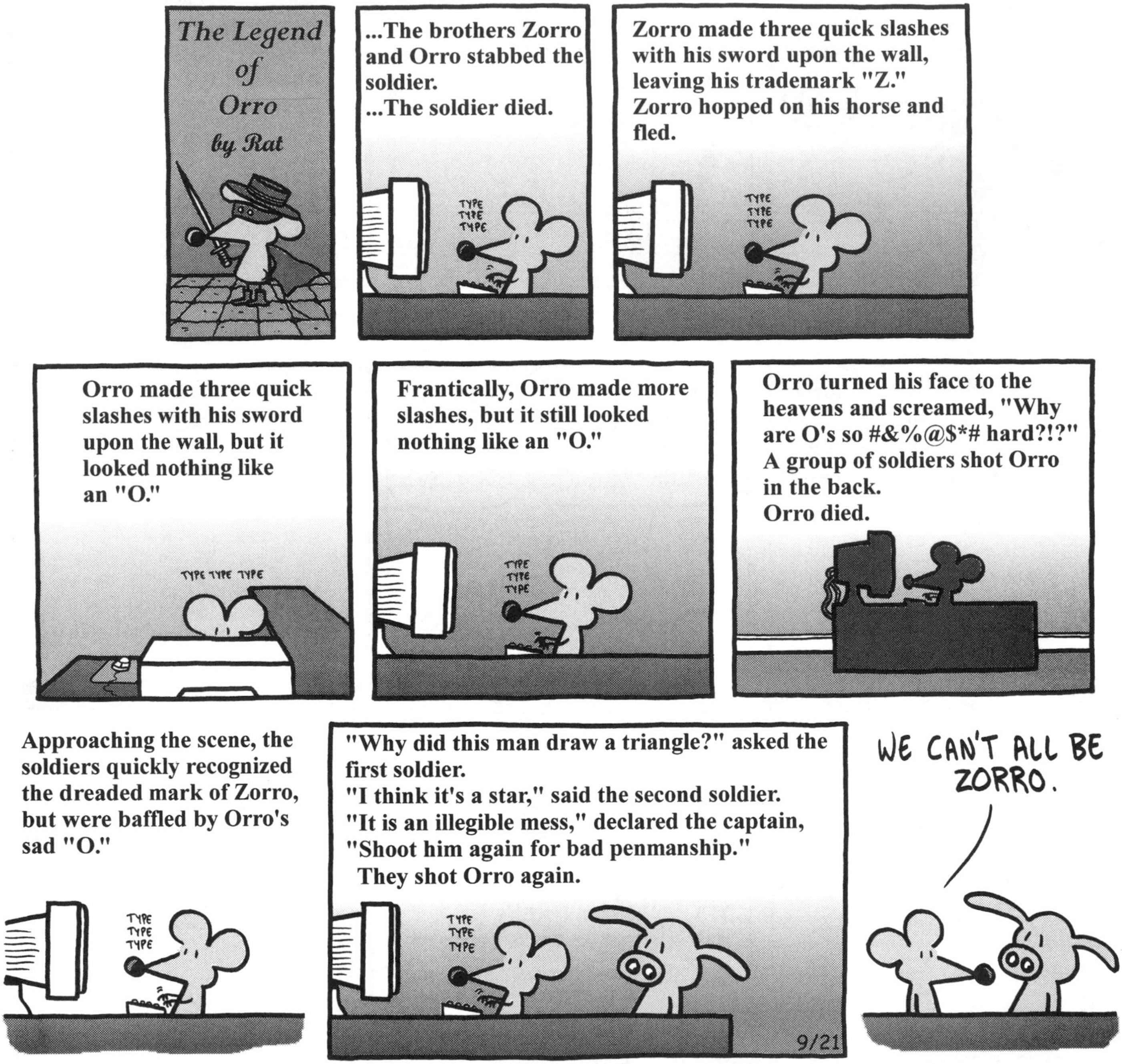
The Legend of Orro
by Rat
...The brothers Zorro and Orro stabbed the soldier.
...The soldier died.
TYPE TYPE TYPE
Zorro made three quick slashes with his sword upon the wall, leaving his trademark "Z."
Zorro hopped on his horse and fled.
TYPE TYPE TYPE
Orro made three quick slashes with his sword upon the wall, but it looked nothing like an "O."
TYPE TYPE TYPE
Frantically, Orro made more slashes, but it still looked nothing like an "O."
TYPE TYPE TYPE
Orro turned his face to the heavens and screamed, "Why are O's so #&%@$*# hard?!?"
A group of soldiers shot Orro in the back.
Orro died.
Approaching the scene, the soldiers quickly recognized the dreaded mark of Zorro, but were baffled by Orro's sad "O."
TYPE TYPE TYPE
"Why did this man draw a triangle?" asked the first soldier.
"I think it's a star," said the second soldier.
"It is an illegible mess," declared the captain, "Shoot him again for bad penmanship."
They shot Orro again.
TYPE TYPE TYPE
9/21
WE CAN'T ALL BE ZORRO.

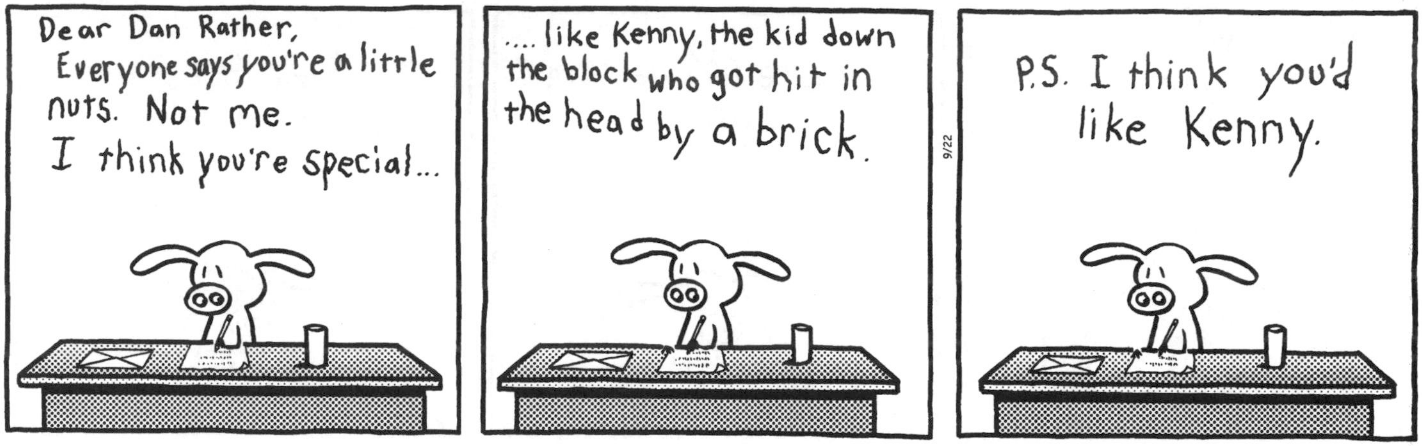
Dear Dan Rather,
Everyone says you're a little nuts. Not me.
I think you're special...
....like Kenny, the kid down the block who got hit in the head by a brick.
9/22
P.S. I think you'd like Kenny.

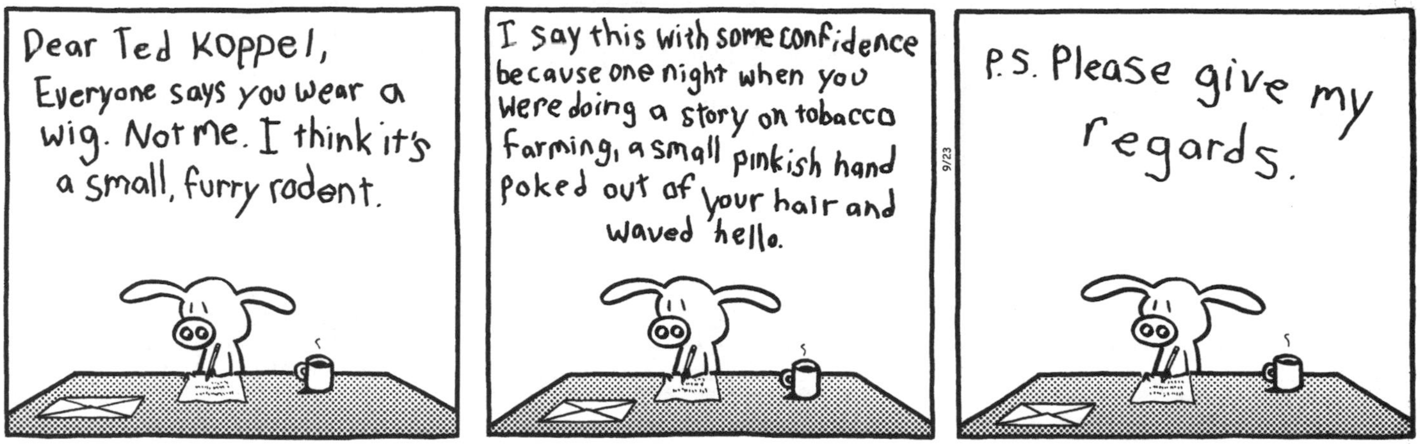
Dear Ted Koppel,
Everyone says you wear a wig. Not me. I think it's a small, furry rodent.
I say this with some confidence because one night when you were doing a story on tobacco farming, a small pinkish hand poked out of your hair and waved hello.
9/23
P.S. Please give my regards.

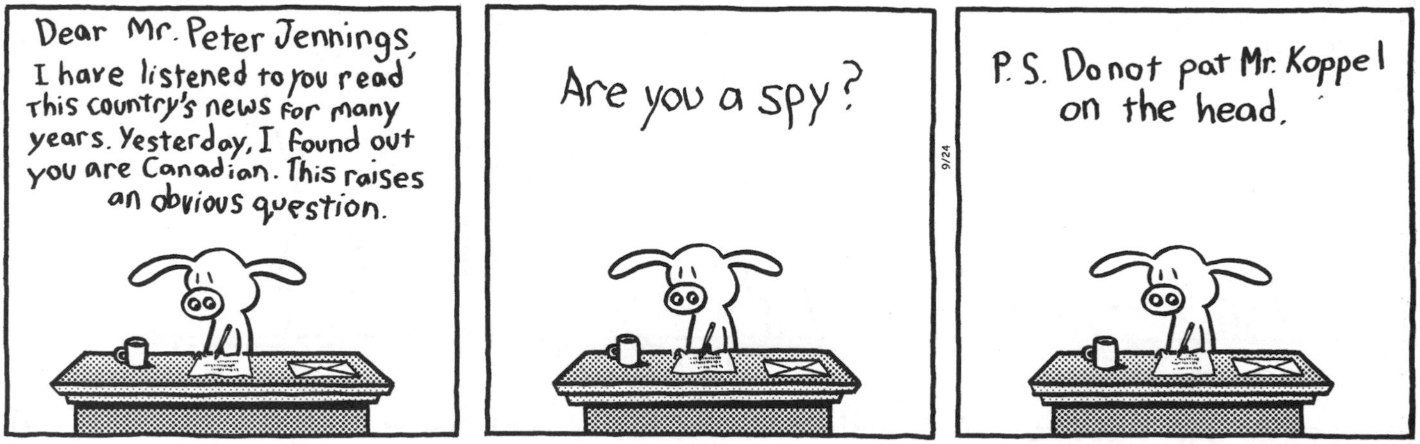
Dear Mr. Peter Jennings,
I have listened to you read this country's news for many years. Yesterday, I found out you are Canadian. This raises an obvious question.
Are you a spy?
9/24
P.S. Do not pat Mr. Koppel on the head.

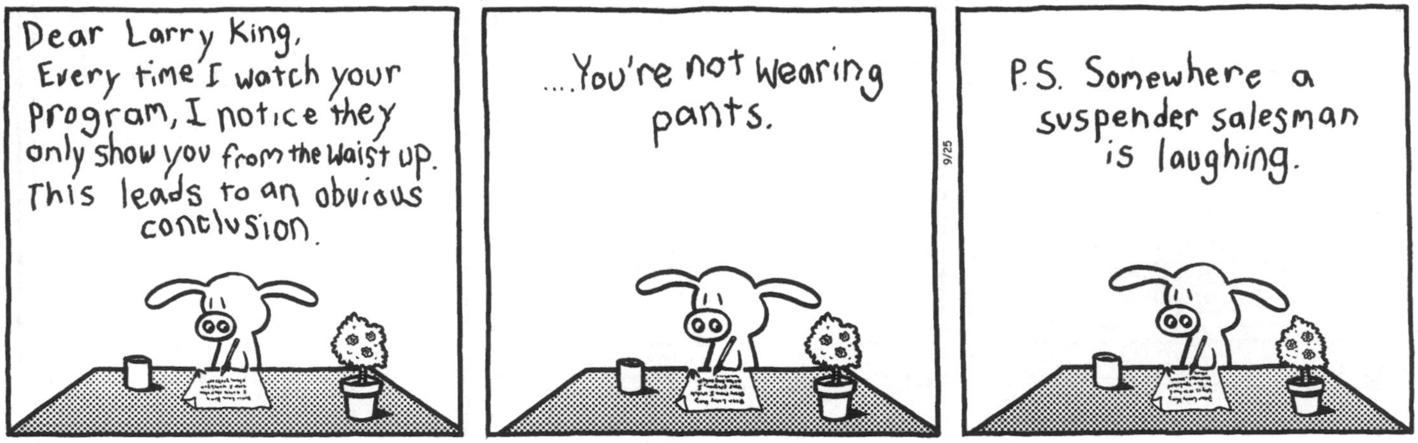
Dear Larry King,
Every time I watch your program, I notice they only show you from the waist up. This leads to an obvious conclusion.
....You're not wearing pants.
9/25
P.S. Somewhere a suspender salesman is laughing.

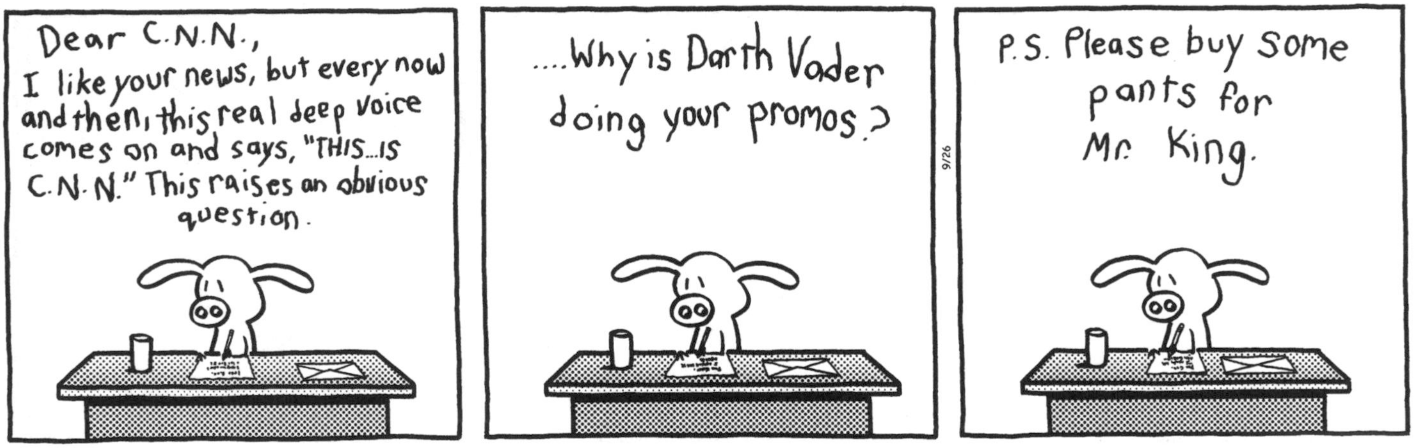
Dear C.N.N.,
I like your news, but every now and then, this real deep voice comes on and says, "THIS...IS C.N.N." This raises an obvious question.
....Why is Darth Vader doing your promos?
9/26
P.S. Please buy some pants for Mr. King.

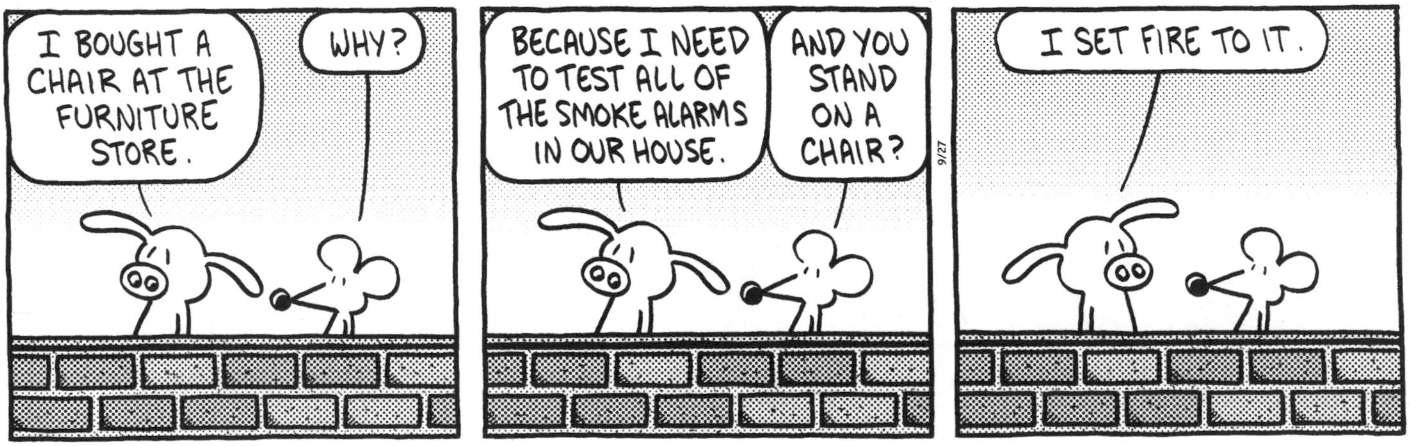
I BOUGHT A CHAIR AT THE FURNITURE STORE.
WHY?
BECAUSE I NEED TO TEST ALL OF THE SMOKE ALARMS IN OUR HOUSE.
AND YOU STAND ON A CHAIR?
9/27
I SET FIRE TO IT.

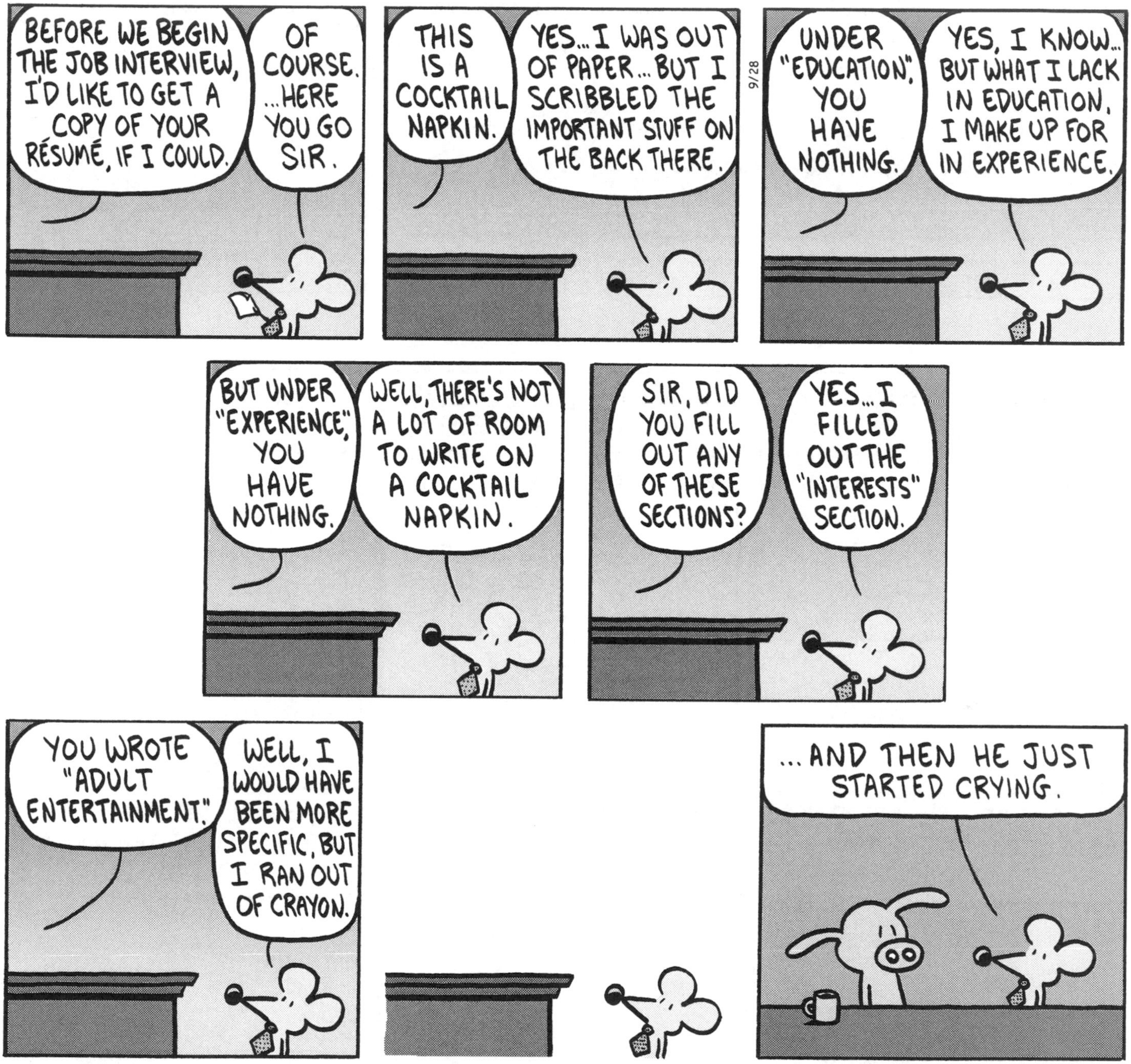
BEFORE WE BEGIN THE JOB INTERVIEW, I'D LIKE TO GET A COPY OF YOUR RÉSUMÉ, IF I COULD.
OF COURSE. ...HERE YOU GO SIR.
THIS IS A COCKTAIL NAPKIN.
YES... I WAS OUT OF PAPER... BUT I SCRIBBLED THE IMPORTANT STUFF ON THE BACK THERE.
9/28
UNDER "EDUCATION", YOU HAVE NOTHING.
YES, I KNOW... BUT WHAT I LACK IN EDUCATION, I MAKE UP FOR IN EXPERIENCE.
BUT UNDER "EXPERIENCE", YOU HAVE NOTHING.
WELL, THERE'S NOT A LOT OF ROOM TO WRITE ON A COCKTAIL NAPKIN.
SIR, DID YOU FILL OUT ANY OF THESE SECTIONS?
YES... I FILLED OUT THE "INTERESTS" SECTION.
YOU WROTE "ADULT ENTERTAINMENT."
WELL, I WOULD HAVE BEEN MORE SPECIFIC, BUT I RAN OUT OF CRAYON.
...AND THEN HE JUST STARTED CRYING.

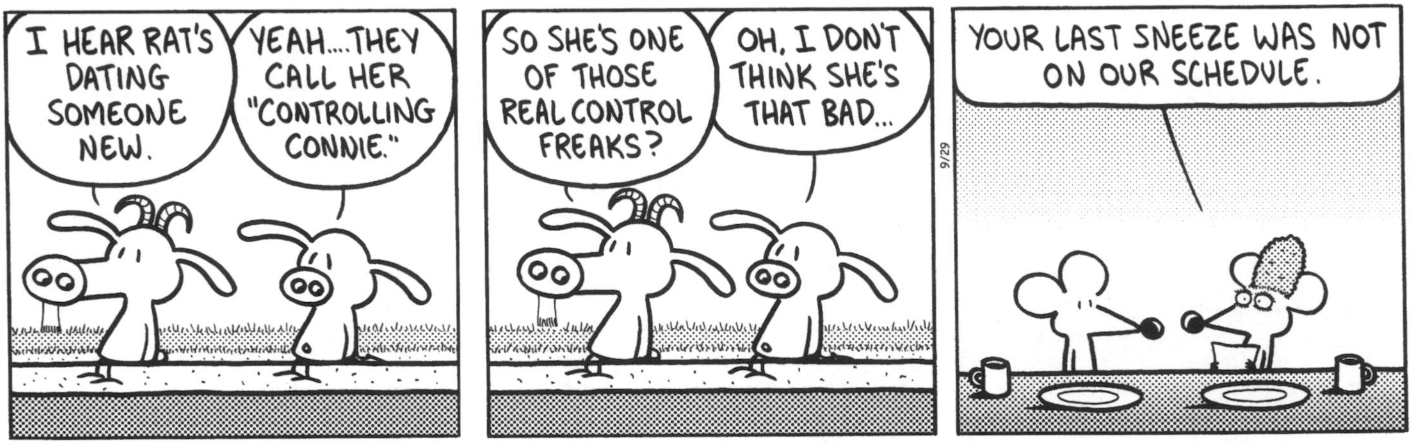
I HEAR RAT'S DATING SOMEONE NEW.
YEAH....THEY CALL HER "CONTROLLING CONNIE."
SO SHE'S ONE OF THOSE REAL CONTROL FREAKS?
OH, I DON'T THINK SHE'S THAT BAD...
9/29
YOUR LAST SNEEZE WAS NOT ON OUR SCHEDULE.

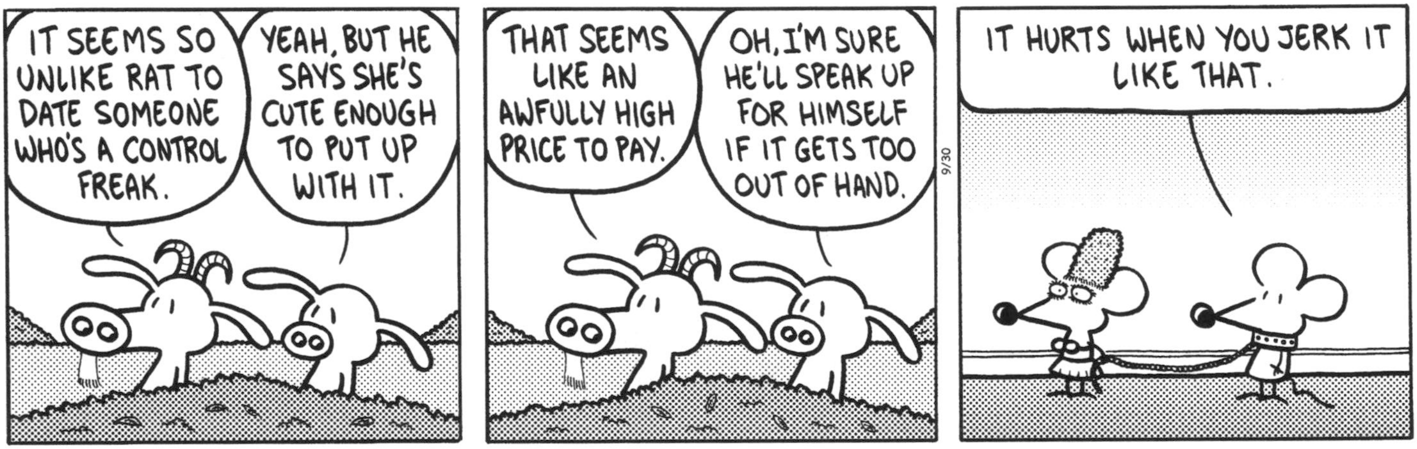
IT SEEMS SO UNLIKE RAT TO DATE SOMEONE WHO'S A CONTROL FREAK.
YEAH, BUT HE SAYS SHE'S CUTE ENOUGH TO PUT UP WITH IT.
THAT SEEMS LIKE AN AWFULLY HIGH PRICE TO PAY.
OH, I'M SURE HE'LL SPEAK UP FOR HIMSELF IF IT GETS TOO OUT OF HAND.
9/30
IT HURTS WHEN YOU JERK IT LIKE THAT.

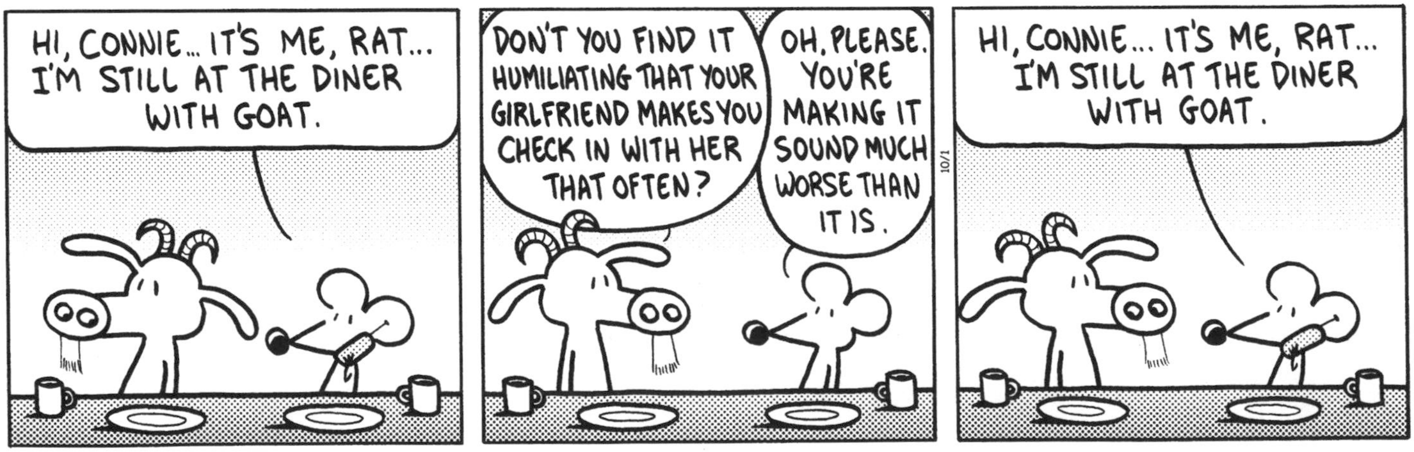
HI, CONNIE... IT'S ME, RAT... I'M STILL AT THE DINER WITH GOAT.
DON'T YOU FIND IT HUMILIATING THAT YOUR GIRLFRIEND MAKES YOU CHECK IN WITH HER THAT OFTEN?
OH, PLEASE. YOU'RE MAKING IT SOUND MUCH WORSE THAN IT IS.
10/1
HI, CONNIE... IT'S ME, RAT... I'M STILL AT THE DINER WITH GOAT.

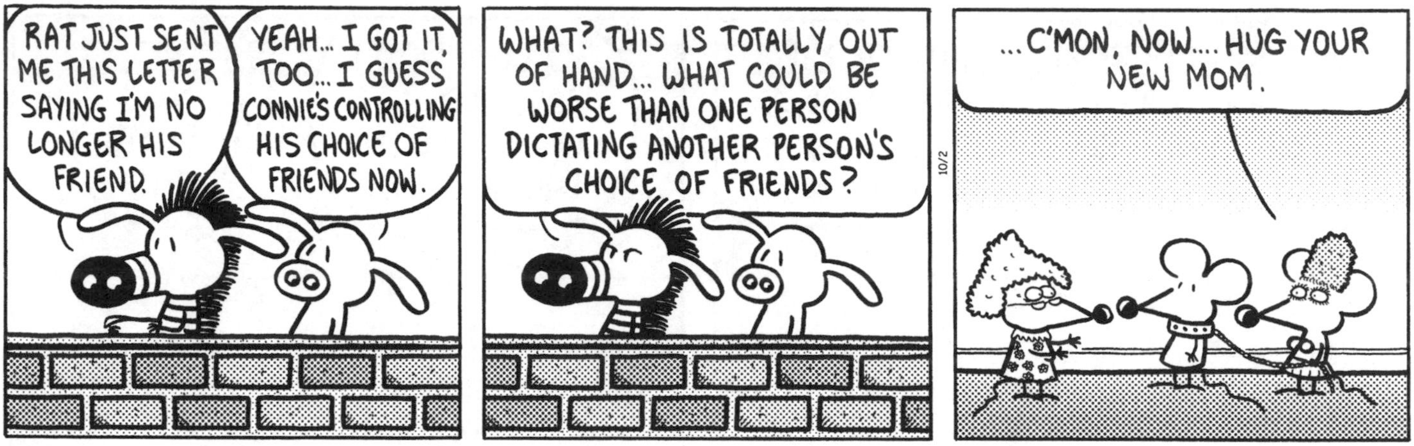
RAT JUST SENT ME THIS LETTER SAYING I'M NO LONGER HIS FRIEND.
YEAH... I GOT IT, TOO... I GUESS CONNIE'S CONTROLLING HIS CHOICE OF FRIENDS NOW.
WHAT? THIS IS TOTALLY OUT OF HAND... WHAT COULD BE WORSE THAN ONE PERSON DICTATING ANOTHER PERSON'S CHOICE OF FRIENDS?
10/2
... C'MON, NOW.... HUG YOUR NEW MOM.

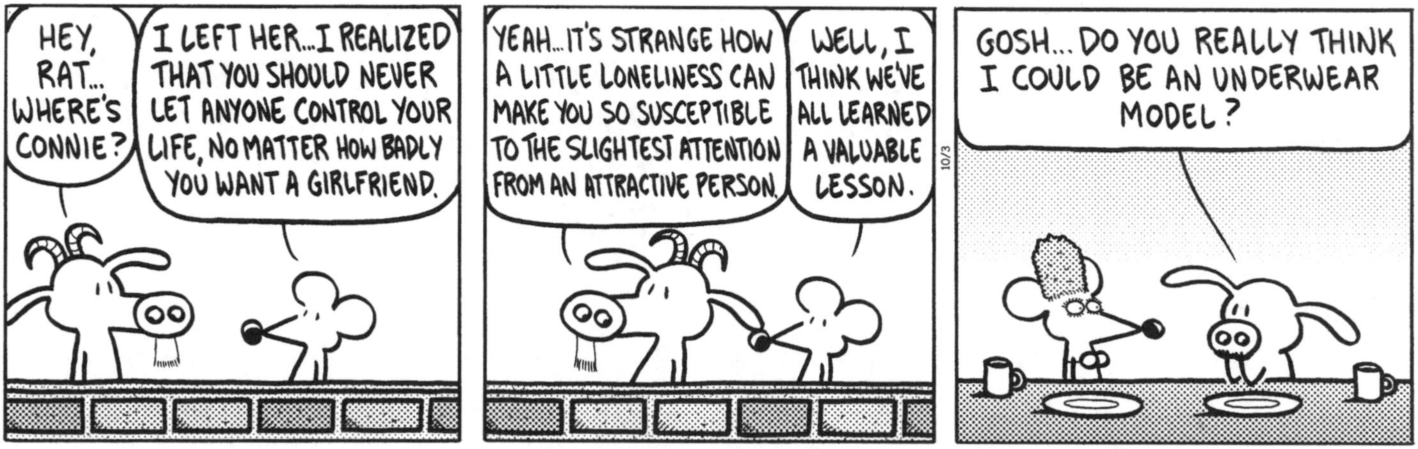
HEY, RAT... WHERE'S CONNIE?
I LEFT HER...I REALIZED THAT YOU SHOULD NEVER LET ANYONE CONTROL YOUR LIFE, NO MATTER HOW BADLY YOU WANT A GIRLFRIEND.
YEAH...IT'S STRANGE HOW A LITTLE LONELINESS CAN MAKE YOU SO SUSCEPTIBLE TO THE SLIGHTEST ATTENTION FROM AN ATTRACTIVE PERSON.
WELL, I THINK WE'VE ALL LEARNED A VALUABLE LESSON.
10/3
GOSH... DO YOU REALLY THINK I COULD BE AN UNDERWEAR MODEL?

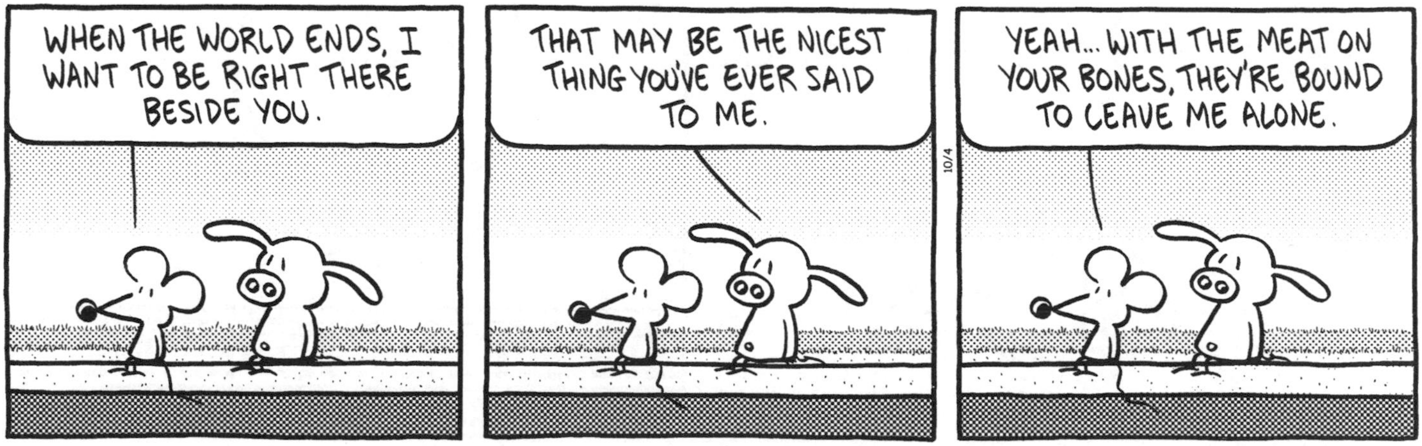
WHEN THE WORLD ENDS, I WANT TO BE RIGHT THERE BESIDE YOU.
THAT MAY BE THE NICEST THING YOU'VE EVER SAID TO ME.
10/4
YEAH... WITH THE MEAT ON YOUR BONES, THEY'RE BOUND TO LEAVE ME ALONE.

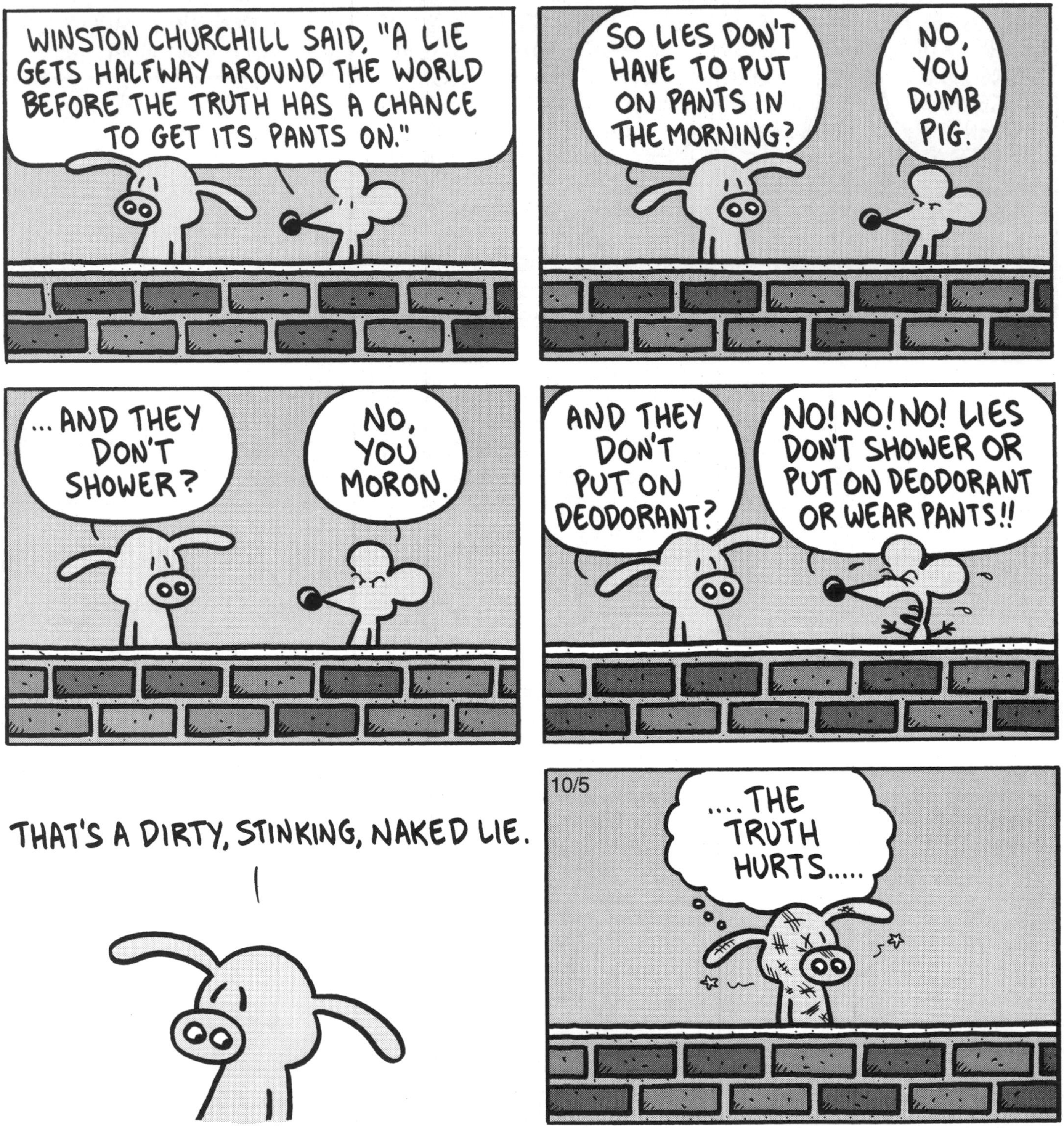
WINSTON CHURCHILL SAID, "A LIE GETS HALFWAY AROUND THE WORLD BEFORE THE TRUTH HAS A CHANCE TO GET ITS PANTS ON."
SO LIES DON'T HAVE TO PUT ON PANTS IN THE MORNING?
NO, YOU DUMB PIG.
... AND THEY DON'T SHOWER?
NO, YOU MORON.
AND THEY DON'T PUT ON DEODORANT?
NO! NO! NO! LIES DON'T SHOWER OR PUT ON DEODORANT OR WEAR PANTS!!
THAT'S A DIRTY, STINKING, NAKED LIE.
10/5
.... THE TRUTH HURTS.....

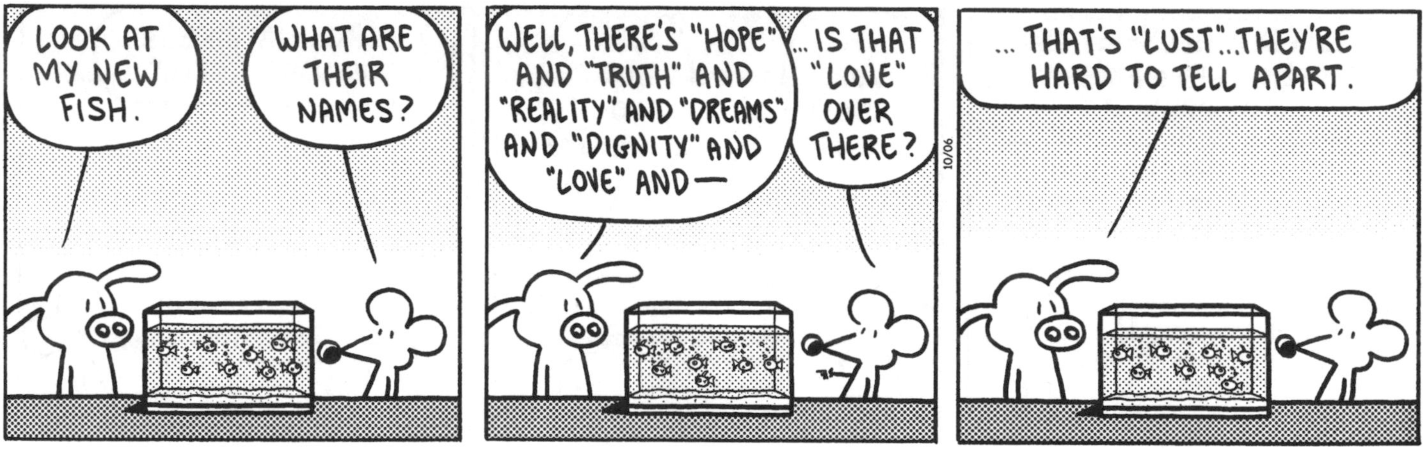
LOOK AT MY NEW FISH.
WHAT ARE THEIR NAMES?
WELL, THERE'S "HOPE" AND "TRUTH" AND "REALITY" AND "DREAMS" AND "DIGNITY" AND "LOVE" AND—
... IS THAT "LOVE" OVER THERE?
10/06
... THAT'S "LUST"... THEY'RE HARD TO TELL APART.

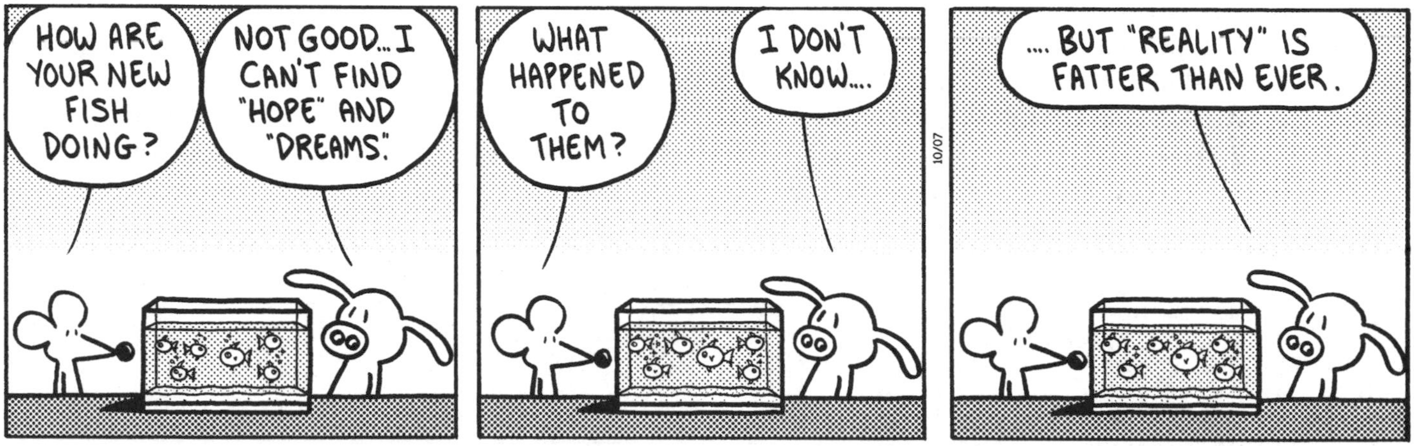
HOW ARE YOUR NEW FISH DOING?
NOT GOOD... I CAN'T FIND "HOPE" AND "DREAMS."
WHAT HAPPENED TO THEM?
I DON'T KNOW....
10/07
.... BUT "REALITY" IS FATTER THAN EVER.

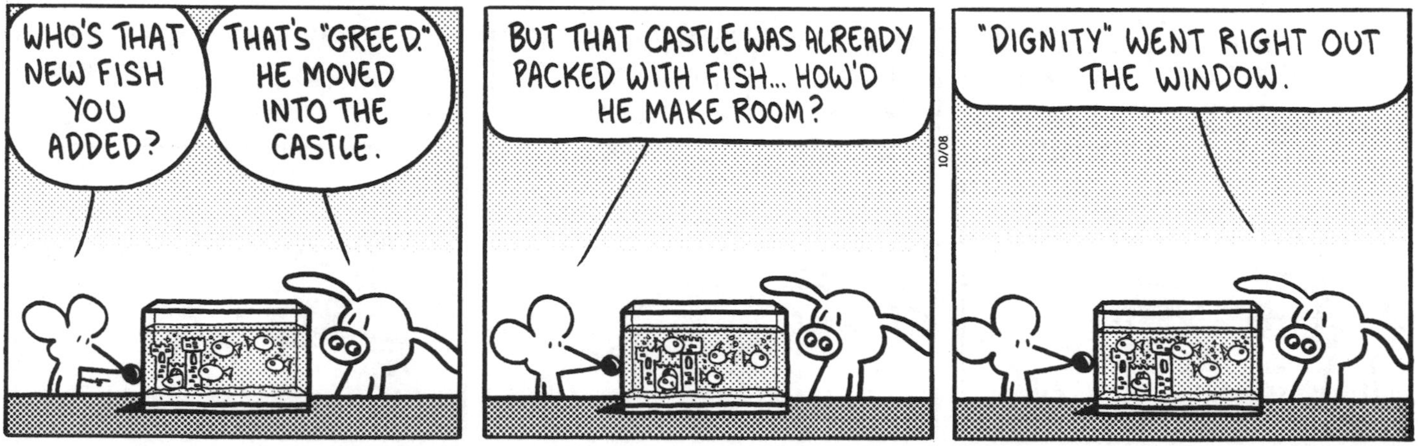
WHO'S THAT NEW FISH YOU ADDED?
THAT'S "GREED." HE MOVED INTO THE CASTLE.
BUT THAT CASTLE WAS ALREADY PACKED WITH FISH... HOW'D HE MAKE ROOM?
10/08
"DIGNITY" WENT RIGHT OUT THE WINDOW.

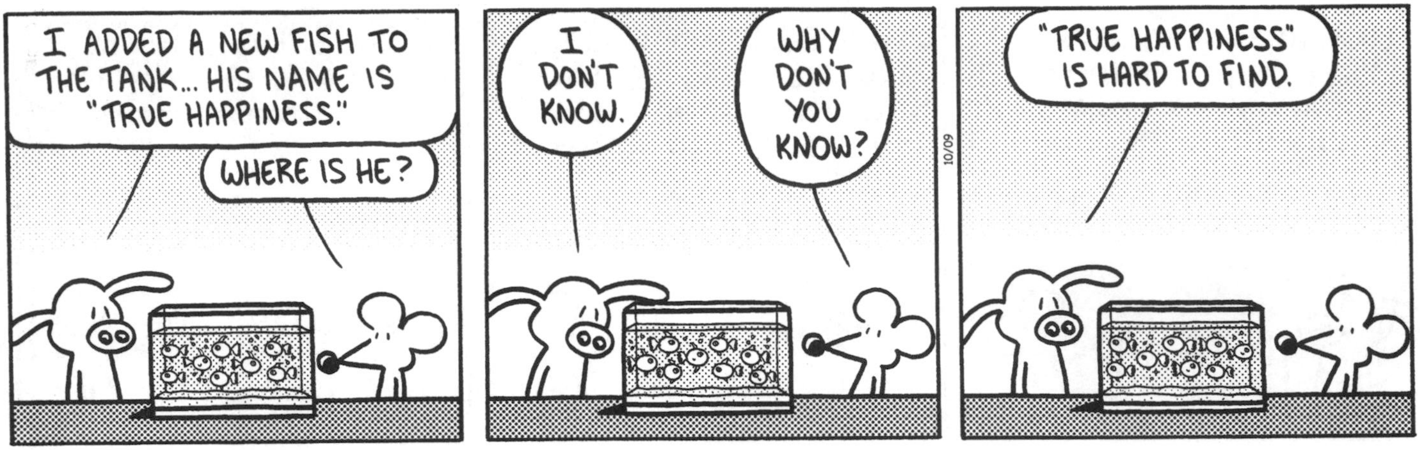
I ADDED A NEW FISH TO THE TANK... HIS NAME IS "TRUE HAPPINESS."
WHERE IS HE?
I DON'T KNOW.
WHY DON'T YOU KNOW?
10/09
"TRUE HAPPINESS" IS HARD TO FIND.

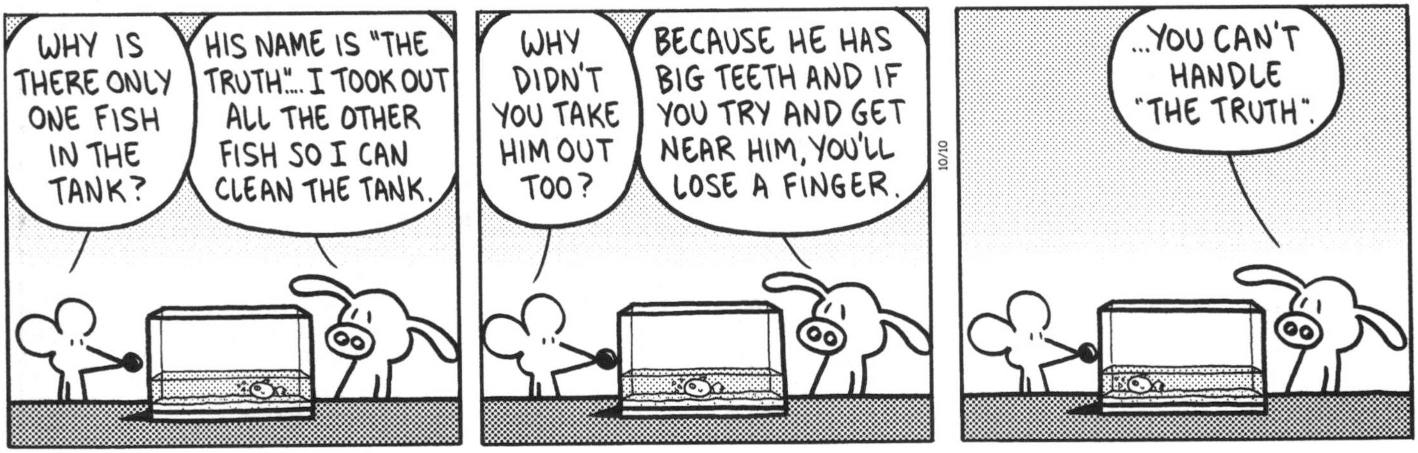
WHY IS THERE ONLY ONE FISH IN THE TANK?
HIS NAME IS "THE TRUTH"... I TOOK OUT ALL THE OTHER FISH SO I CAN CLEAN THE TANK.
WHY DIDN'T YOU TAKE HIM OUT TOO?
BECAUSE HE HAS BIG TEETH AND IF YOU TRY AND GET NEAR HIM, YOU'LL LOSE A FINGER.
10/10
...YOU CAN'T HANDLE "THE TRUTH".

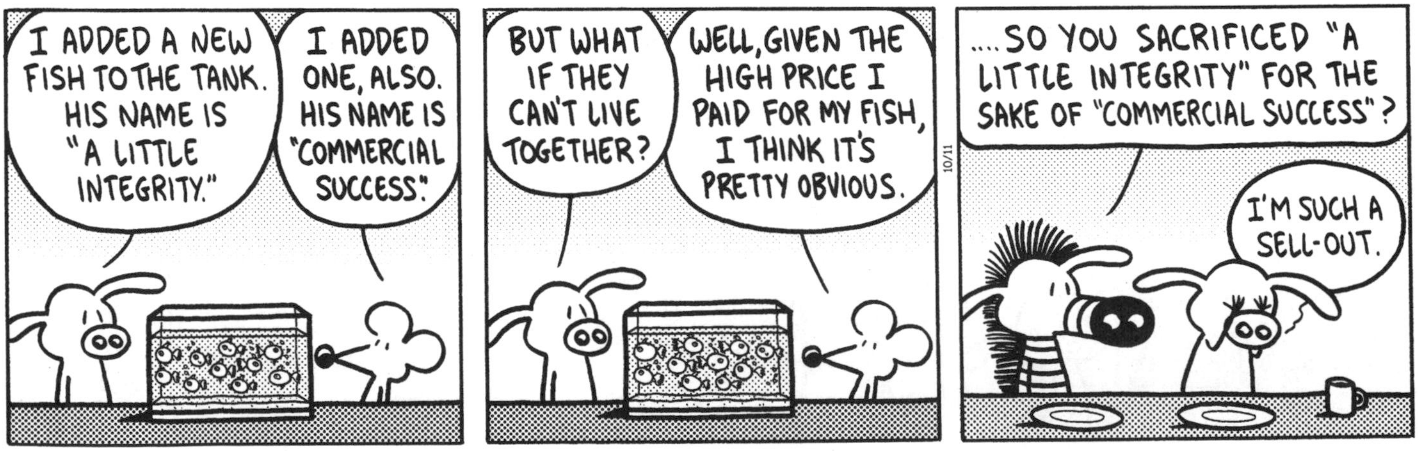
I ADDED A NEW FISH TO THE TANK. HIS NAME IS "A LITTLE INTEGRITY."
I ADDED ONE, ALSO. HIS NAME IS "COMMERCIAL SUCCESS."
BUT WHAT IF THEY CAN'T LIVE TOGETHER?
WELL, GIVEN THE HIGH PRICE I PAID FOR MY FISH, I THINK IT'S PRETTY OBVIOUS.
10/11
....SO YOU SACRIFICED "A LITTLE INTEGRITY" FOR THE SAKE OF "COMMERCIAL SUCCESS"?
I'M SUCH A SELL-OUT.

Dear Comics Reader:

We here at "Pearls" feel that the format of Sunday strips is a waste of your time. Why should you, the reader, have to read through numerous panels of dialogue when all you really want is the punchline?

Thus, in order to maximize your comic enjoyment, we here at "Pearls" have taken the actual punchlines from four other popular strips and given those lines to your favorite "Pearls" characters.

No wasted panels. No boring set-up dialogue. Just pure comic pleasure. . . We hope you enjoy.

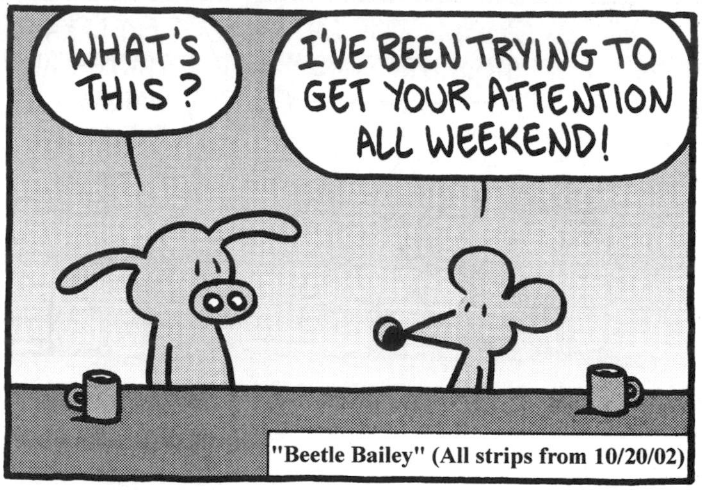
WHAT'S THIS?
I'VE BEEN TRYING TO GET YOUR ATTENTION ALL WEEKEND!
"Beetle Bailey" (All strips from 10/20/02)

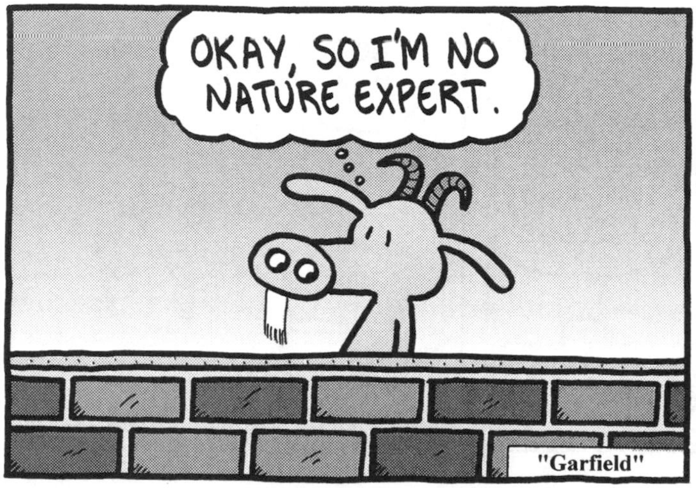
OKAY, SO I'M NO NATURE EXPERT.
"Garfield"

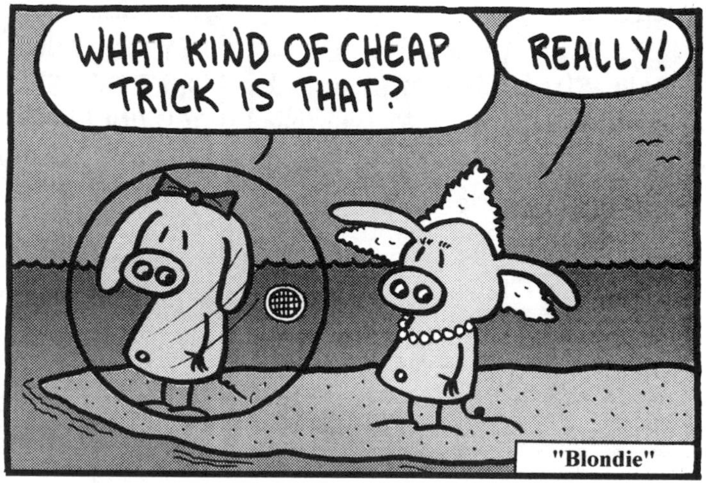
WHAT KIND OF CHEAP TRICK IS THAT?
REALLY!
"Blondie"

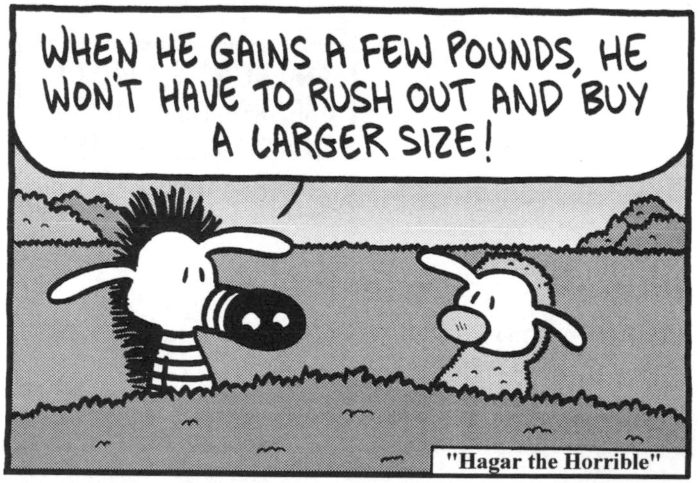
WHEN HE GAINS A FEW POUNDS, HE WON'T HAVE TO RUSH OUT AND BUY A LARGER SIZE!
"Hagar the Horrible"

pearls

...Four Times the Humor, at One-Fourth the Price

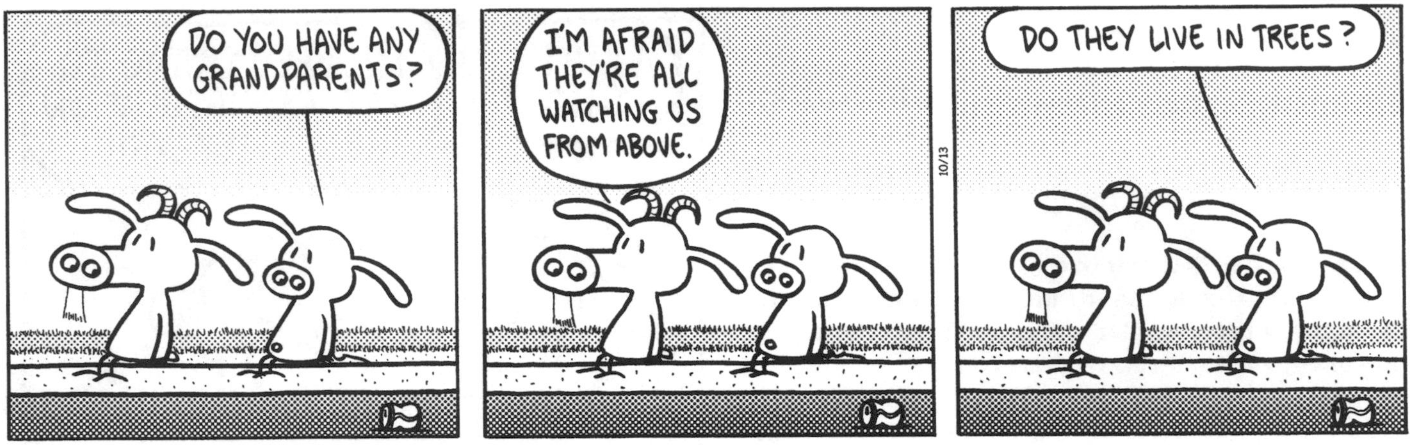
DO YOU HAVE ANY GRANDPARENTS?
I'M AFRAID THEY'RE ALL WATCHING US FROM ABOVE.
10/13
DO THEY LIVE IN TREES?

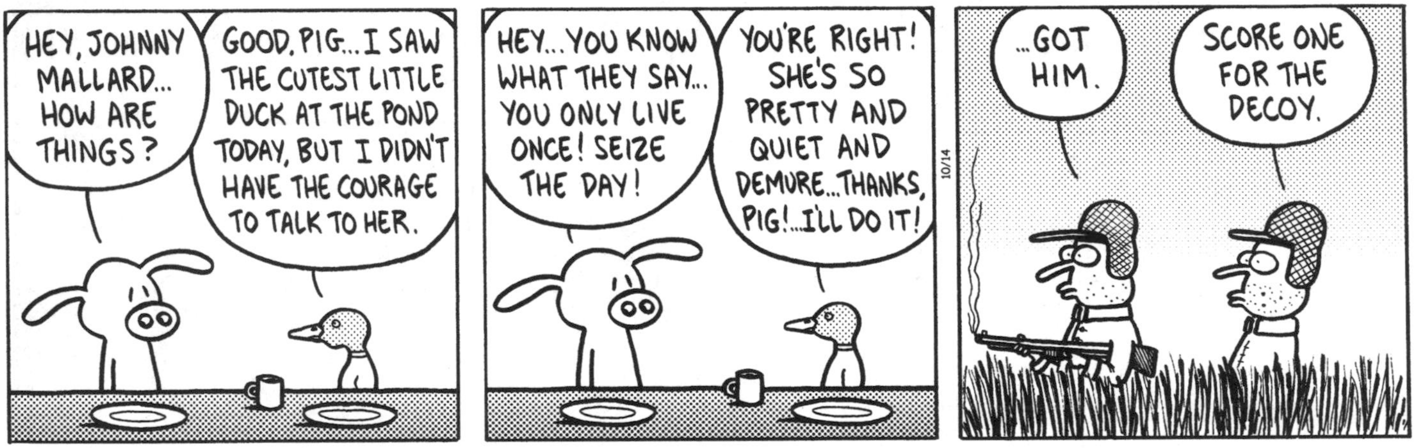
HEY, JOHNNY MALLARD... HOW ARE THINGS?
GOOD, PIG... I SAW THE CUTEST LITTLE DUCK AT THE POND TODAY, BUT I DIDN'T HAVE THE COURAGE TO TALK TO HER.
HEY... YOU KNOW WHAT THEY SAY... YOU ONLY LIVE ONCE! SEIZE THE DAY!
YOU'RE RIGHT! SHE'S SO PRETTY AND QUIET AND DEMURE... THANKS, PIG!... I'LL DO IT!
10/14
...GOT HIM.
SCORE ONE FOR THE DECOY.

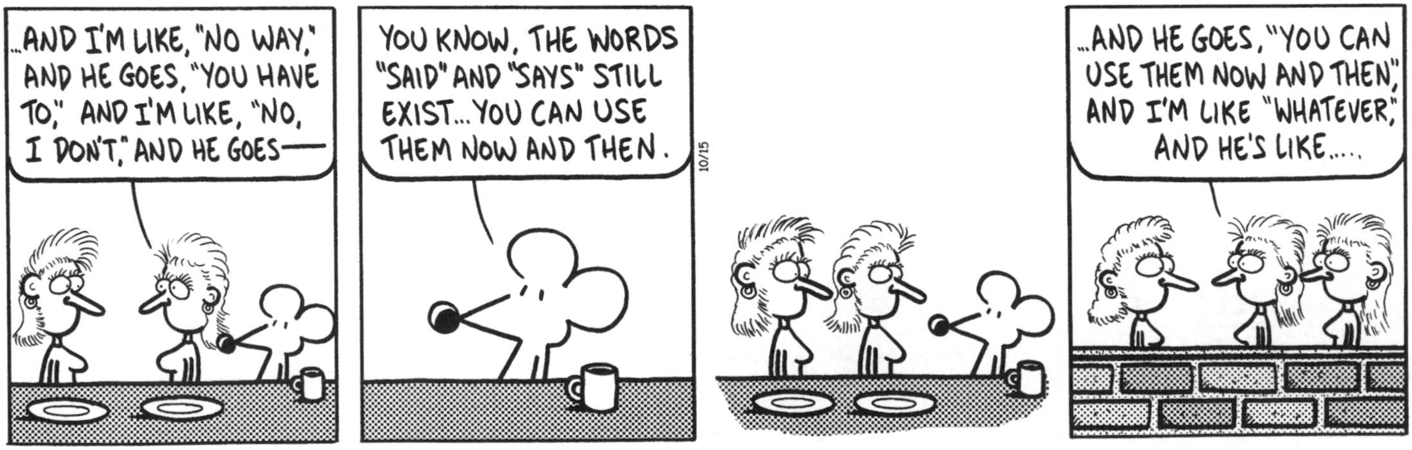
...AND I'M LIKE, "NO WAY," AND HE GOES, "YOU HAVE TO," AND I'M LIKE, "NO, I DON'T," AND HE GOES—
YOU KNOW, THE WORDS "SAID" AND "SAYS" STILL EXIST... YOU CAN USE THEM NOW AND THEN.
10/15
...AND HE GOES, "YOU CAN USE THEM NOW AND THEN," AND I'M LIKE "WHATEVER," AND HE'S LIKE....

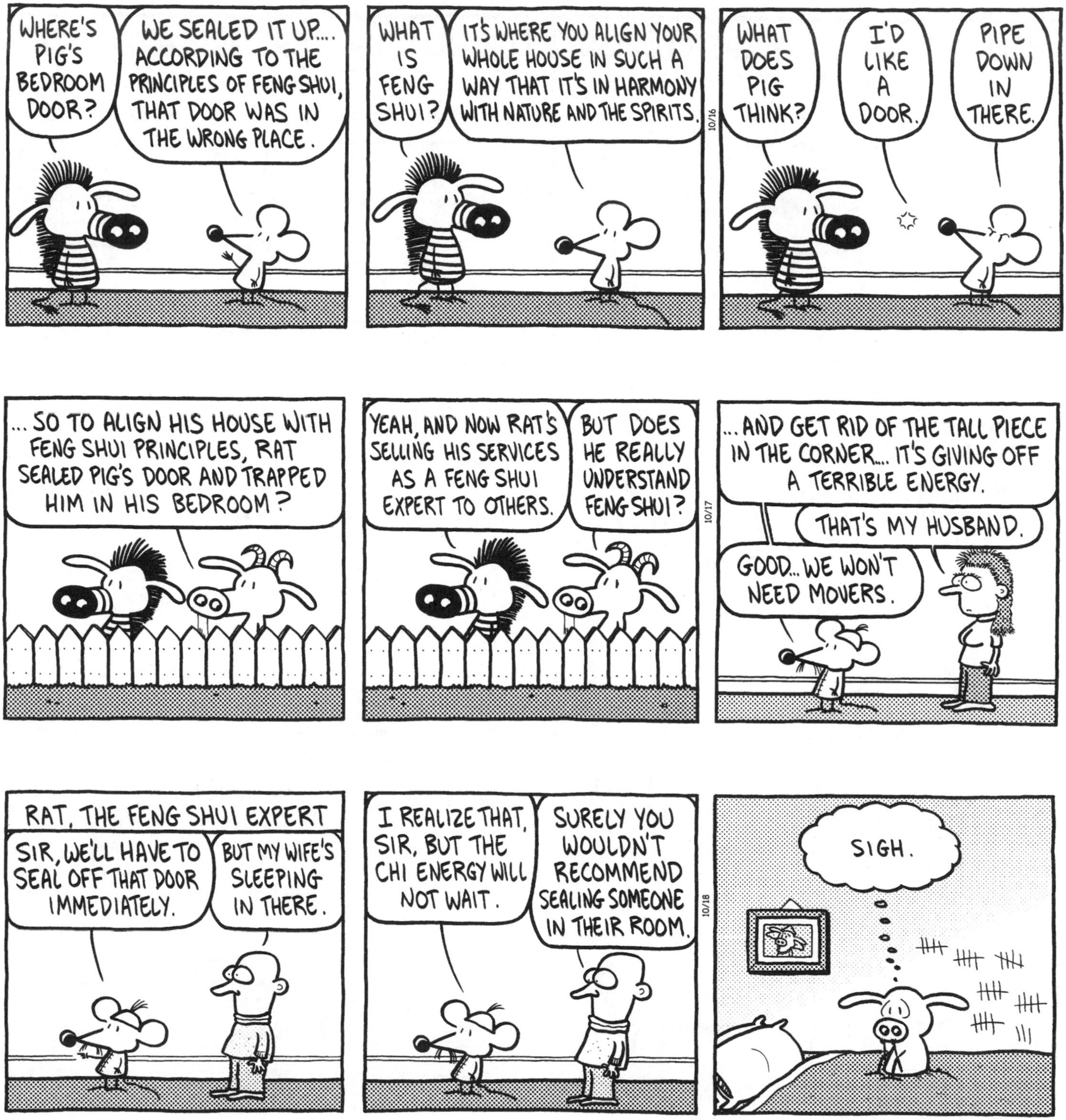
WHERE'S PIG'S BEDROOM DOOR?
WE SEALED IT UP.... ACCORDING TO THE PRINCIPLES OF FENG SHUI, THAT DOOR WAS IN THE WRONG PLACE.
WHAT IS FENG SHUI?
IT'S WHERE YOU ALIGN YOUR WHOLE HOUSE IN SUCH A WAY THAT IT'S IN HARMONY WITH NATURE AND THE SPIRITS.
10/16
WHAT DOES PIG THINK?
I'D LIKE A DOOR.
PIPE DOWN IN THERE.
... SO TO ALIGN HIS HOUSE WITH FENG SHUI PRINCIPLES, RAT SEALED PIG'S DOOR AND TRAPPED HIM IN HIS BEDROOM?
YEAH, AND NOW RAT'S SELLING HIS SERVICES AS A FENG SHUI EXPERT TO OTHERS.
BUT DOES HE REALLY UNDERSTAND FENG SHUI?
10/17
... AND GET RID OF THE TALL PIECE IN THE CORNER.... IT'S GIVING OFF A TERRIBLE ENERGY.
THAT'S MY HUSBAND.
GOOD... WE WON'T NEED MOVERS.
RAT, THE FENG SHUI EXPERT
SIR, WE'LL HAVE TO SEAL OFF THAT DOOR IMMEDIATELY.
BUT MY WIFE'S SLEEPING IN THERE.
I REALIZE THAT, SIR, BUT THE CHI ENERGY WILL NOT WAIT.
SURELY YOU WOULDN'T RECOMMEND SEALING SOMEONE IN THEIR ROOM.
10/18
SIGH.

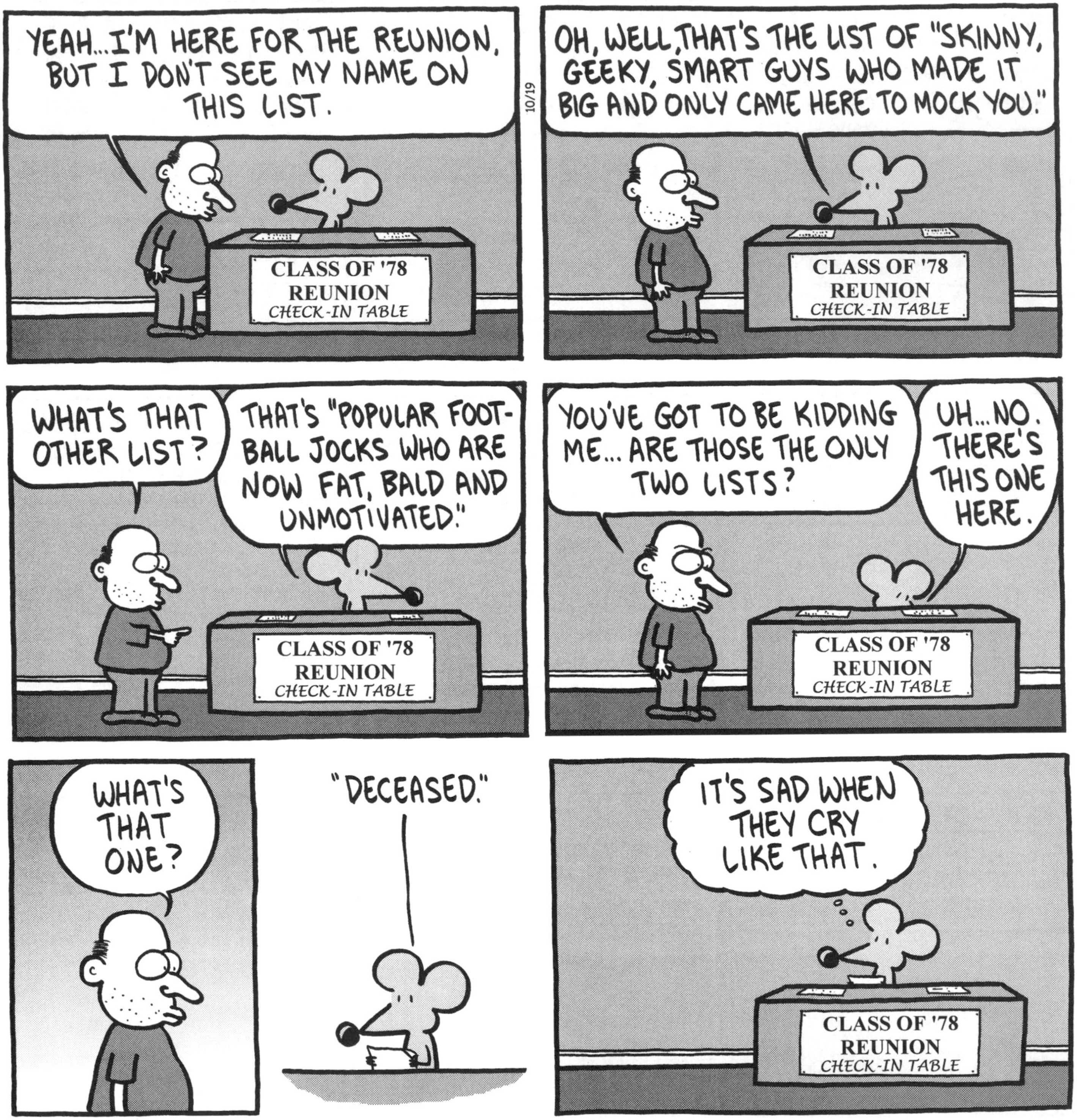
YEAH...I'M HERE FOR THE REUNION, BUT I DON'T SEE MY NAME ON THIS LIST.
CLASS OF '78 REUNION CHECK-IN TABLE
10/19
OH, WELL, THAT'S THE LIST OF "SKINNY, GEEKY, SMART GUYS WHO MADE IT BIG AND ONLY CAME HERE TO MOCK YOU."
CLASS OF '78 REUNION CHECK-IN TABLE
WHAT'S THAT OTHER LIST?
THAT'S "POPULAR FOOTBALL JOCKS WHO ARE NOW FAT, BALD AND UNMOTIVATED."
CLASS OF '78 REUNION CHECK-IN TABLE
YOU'VE GOT TO BE KIDDING ME... ARE THOSE THE ONLY TWO LISTS?
UH...NO. THERE'S THIS ONE HERE.
CLASS OF '78 REUNION CHECK-IN TABLE
WHAT'S THAT ONE?
"DECEASED."
IT'S SAD WHEN THEY CRY LIKE THAT.
CLASS OF '78 REUNION CHECK-IN TABLE

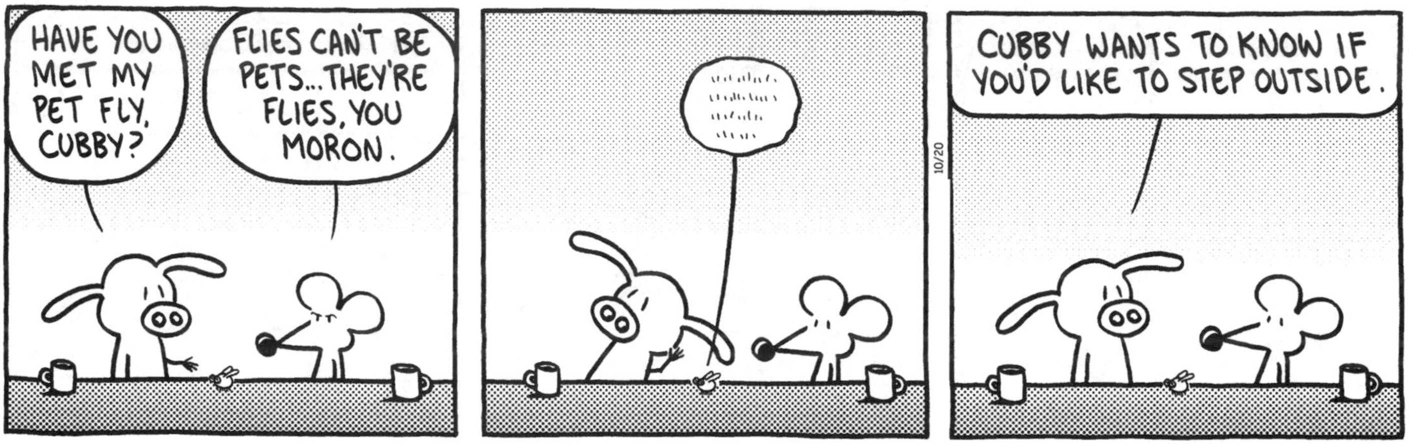
HAVE YOU MET MY PET FLY, CUBBY?
FLIES CAN'T BE PETS... THEY'RE FLIES, YOU MORON.
10/20
CUBBY WANTS TO KNOW IF YOU'D LIKE TO STEP OUTSIDE.

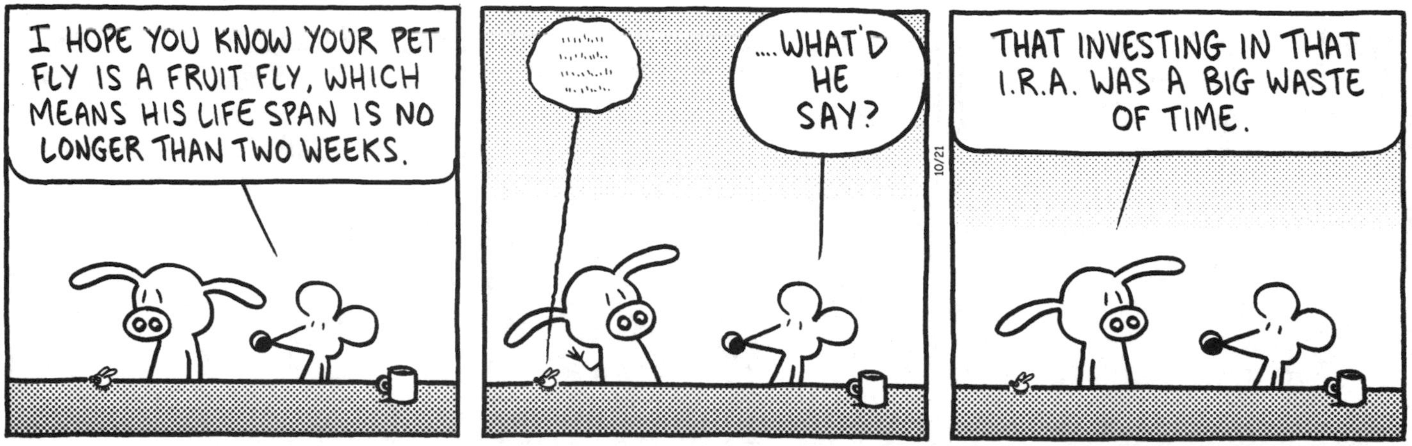
I HOPE YOU KNOW YOUR PET FLY IS A FRUIT FLY, WHICH MEANS HIS LIFE SPAN IS NO LONGER THAN TWO WEEKS.
....WHAT'D HE SAY?
10/21
THAT INVESTING IN THAT I.R.A. WAS A BIG WASTE OF TIME.

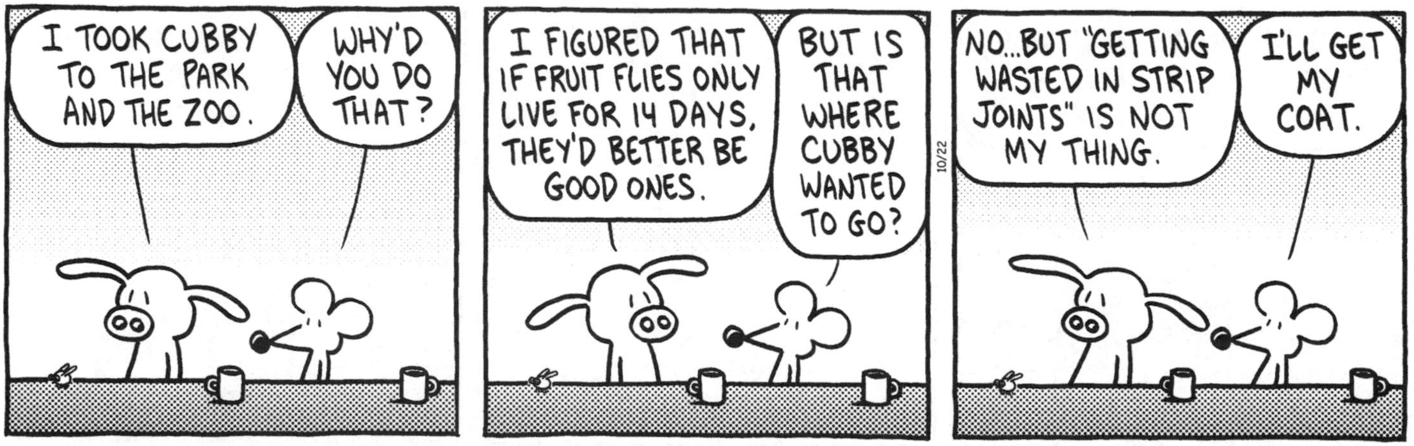
I TOOK CUBBY TO THE PARK AND THE ZOO.
WHY'D YOU DO THAT?
I FIGURED THAT IF FRUIT FLIES ONLY LIVE FOR 14 DAYS, THEY'D BETTER BE GOOD ONES.
BUT IS THAT WHERE CUBBY WANTED TO GO?
10/22
NO...BUT "GETTING WASTED IN STRIP JOINTS" IS NOT MY THING.
I'LL GET MY COAT.

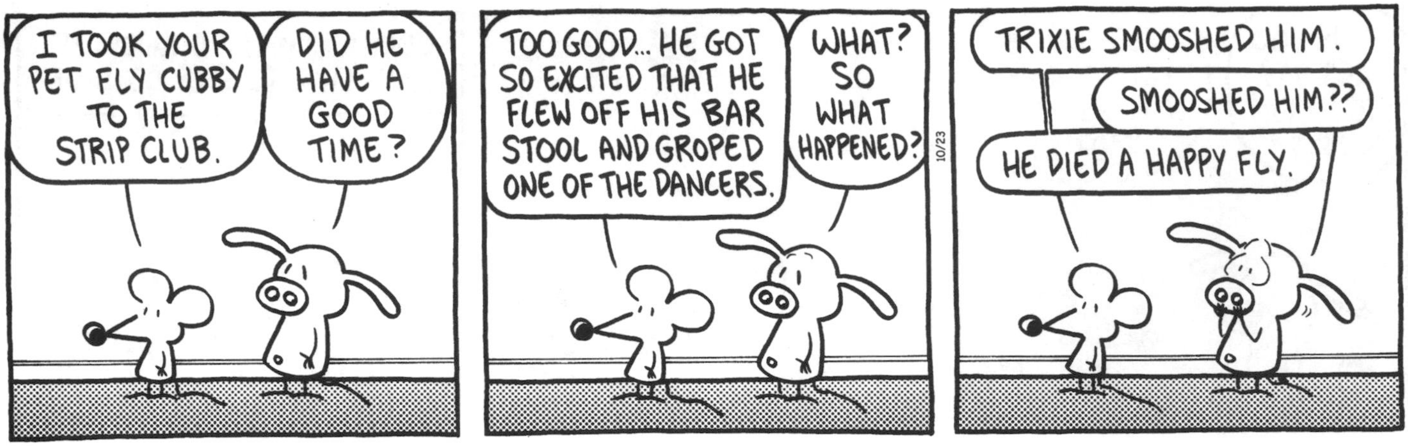
I TOOK YOUR PET FLY CUBBY TO THE STRIP CLUB.
DID HE HAVE A GOOD TIME?
TOO GOOD... HE GOT SO EXCITED THAT HE FLEW OFF HIS BAR STOOL AND GROPED ONE OF THE DANCERS.
WHAT? SO WHAT HAPPENED?
10/23
TRIXIE SMOOSHED HIM.
SMOOSHED HIM??
HE DIED A HAPPY FLY.

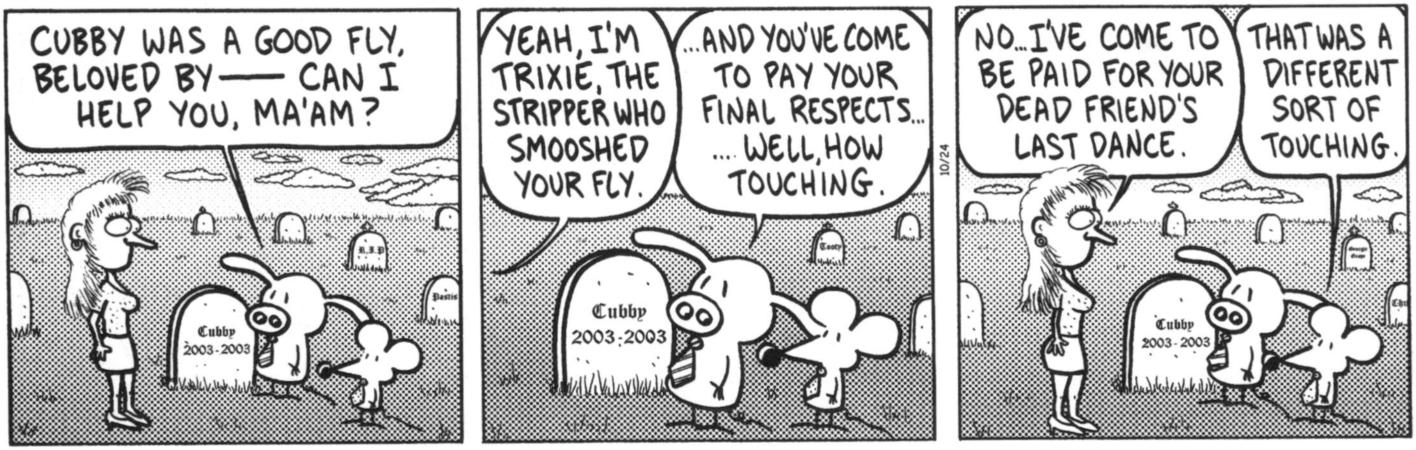
CUBBY WAS A GOOD FLY, BELOVED BY—— CAN I HELP YOU, MA'AM?
Cubby 2003-2003
YEAH, I'M TRIXIE, THE STRIPPER WHO SMOOSHED YOUR FLY.
...AND YOU'VE COME TO PAY YOUR FINAL RESPECTS... ...WELL, HOW TOUCHING.
10/24
NO...I'VE COME TO BE PAID FOR YOUR DEAD FRIEND'S LAST DANCE.
THAT WAS A DIFFERENT SORT OF TOUCHING.

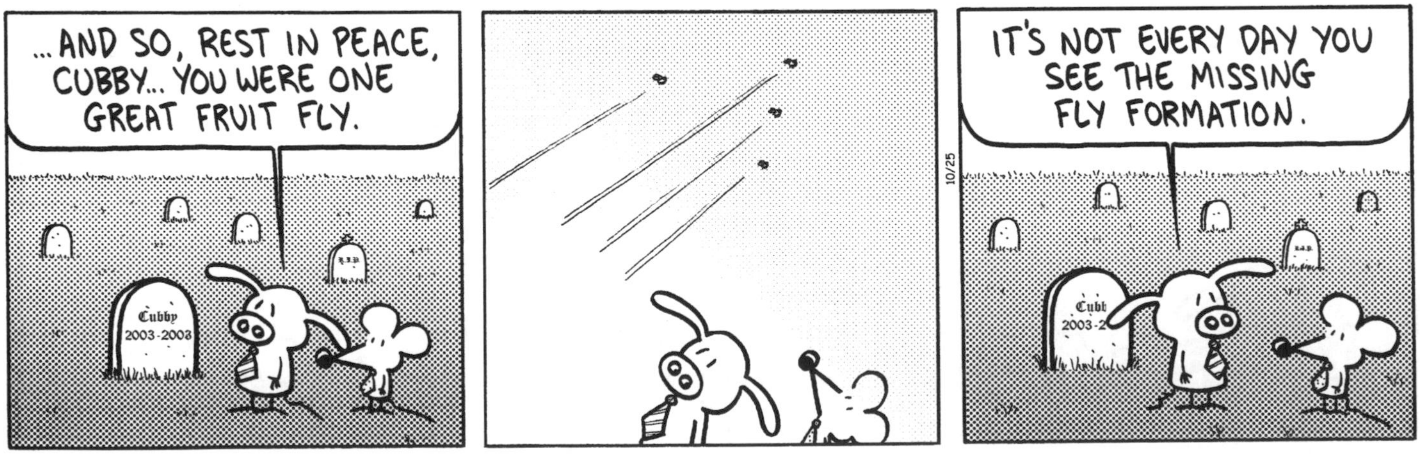
...AND SO, REST IN PEACE, CUBBY... YOU WERE ONE GREAT FRUIT FLY.
Cubby 2003-2003
10/25
IT'S NOT EVERY DAY YOU SEE THE MISSING FLY FORMATION.

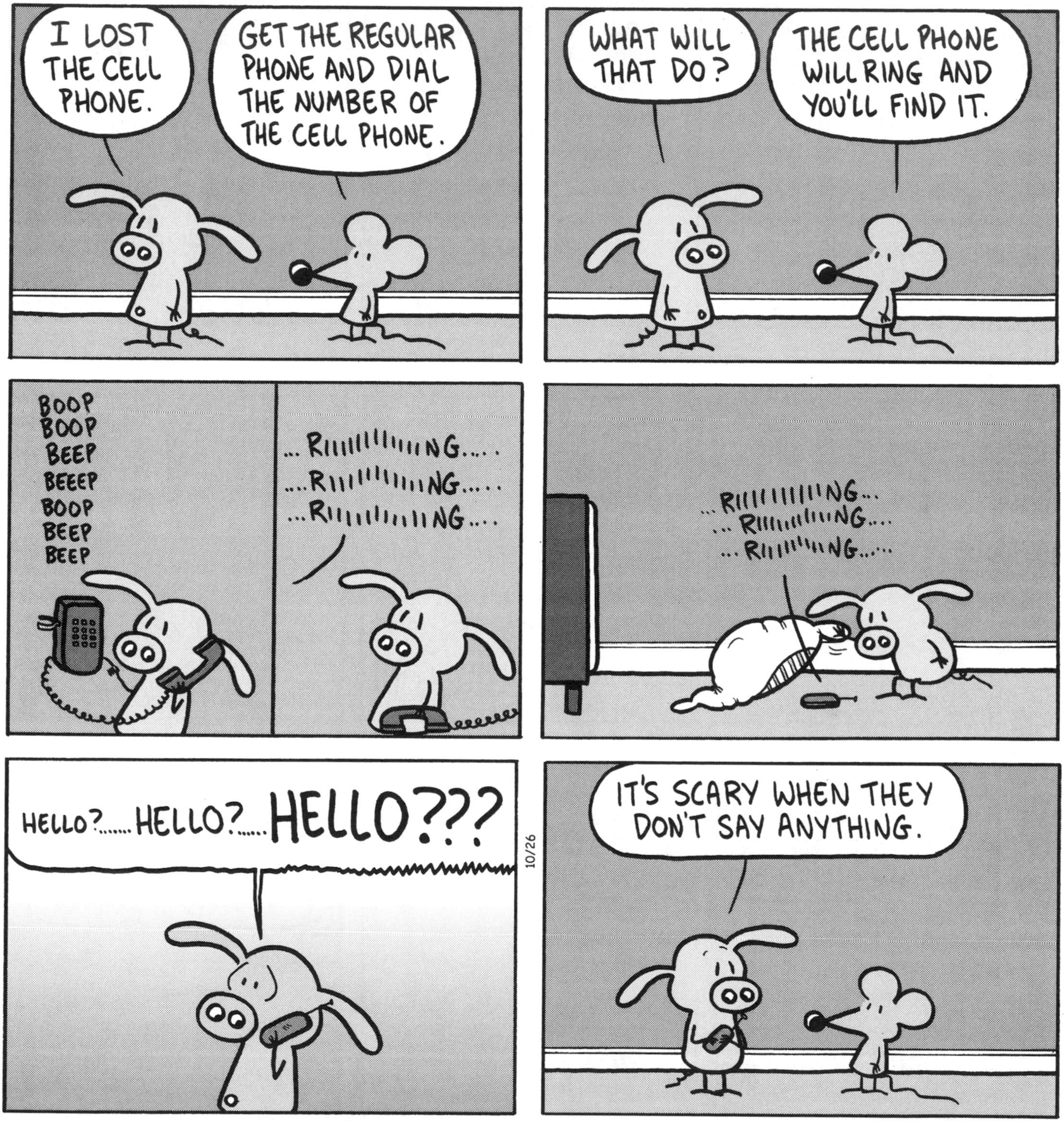
I LOST THE CELL PHONE.
GET THE REGULAR PHONE AND DIAL THE NUMBER OF THE CELL PHONE.
WHAT WILL THAT DO?
THE CELL PHONE WILL RING AND YOU'LL FIND IT.
BOOP BOOP BEEP BEEEP BOOP BEEP BEEP
...RIIIIIIIIING.....
....RIIIIIIIIING.....
...RIIIIIIIIING....
...RIIIIIIIING...
...RIIIIIIIING....
...RIIIIIIING.....
HELLO?....... HELLO?....... HELLO???
10/26
IT'S SCARY WHEN THEY DON'T SAY ANYTHING.

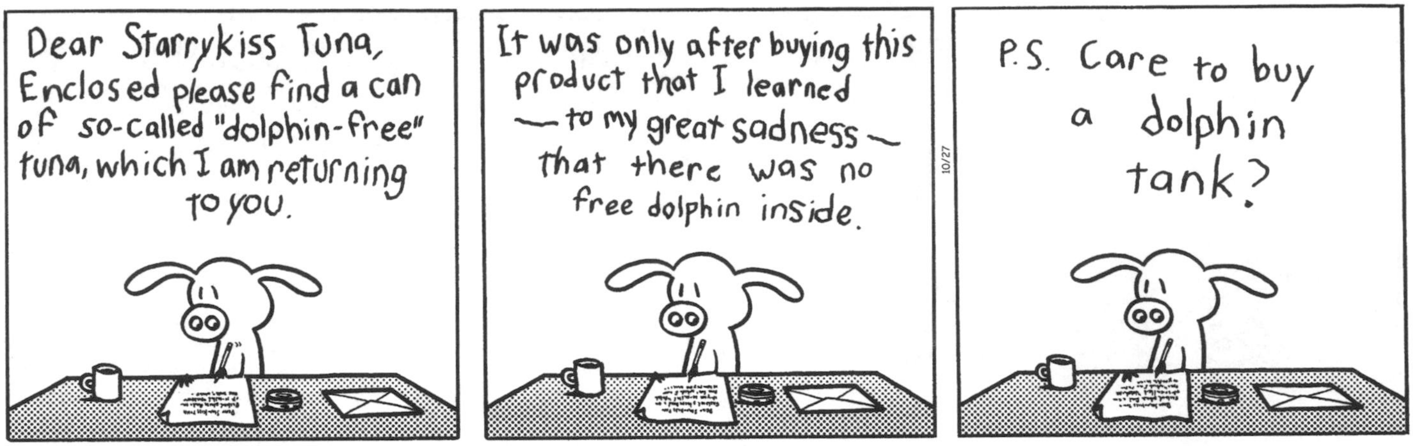
Dear Starrykiss Tuna, Enclosed please find a can of so-called "dolphin-free" tuna, which I am returning to you.
It was only after buying this product that I learned — to my great sadness — that there was no free dolphin inside.
10/27
P.S. Care to buy a dolphin tank?

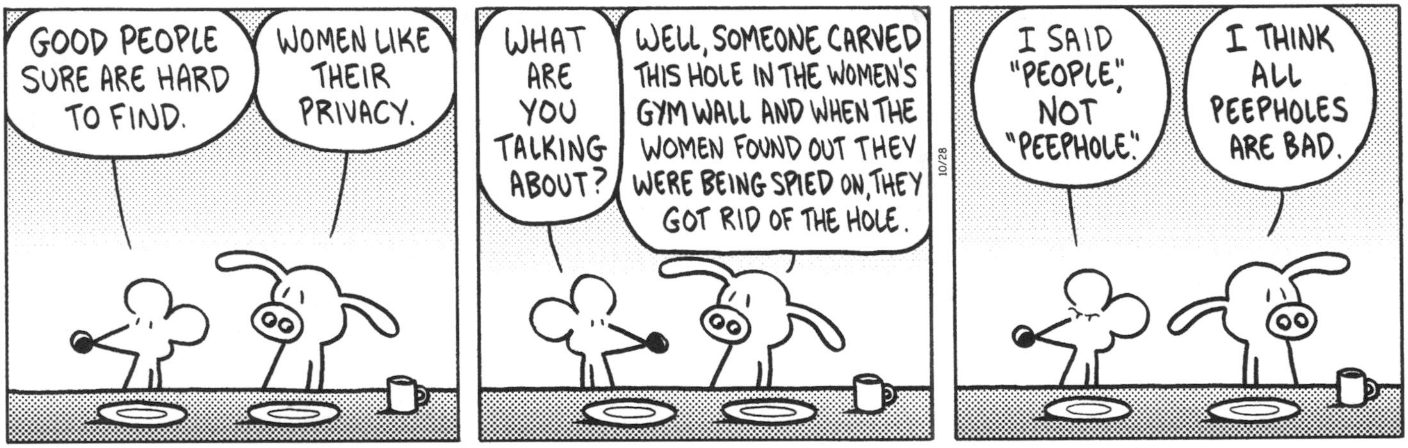
GOOD PEOPLE SURE ARE HARD TO FIND.
WOMEN LIKE THEIR PRIVACY.
WHAT ARE YOU TALKING ABOUT?
WELL, SOMEONE CARVED THIS HOLE IN THE WOMEN'S GYM WALL AND WHEN THE WOMEN FOUND OUT THEY WERE BEING SPIED ON, THEY GOT RID OF THE HOLE.
10/28
I SAID "PEOPLE," NOT "PEEPHOLE."
I THINK ALL PEEPHOLES ARE BAD.

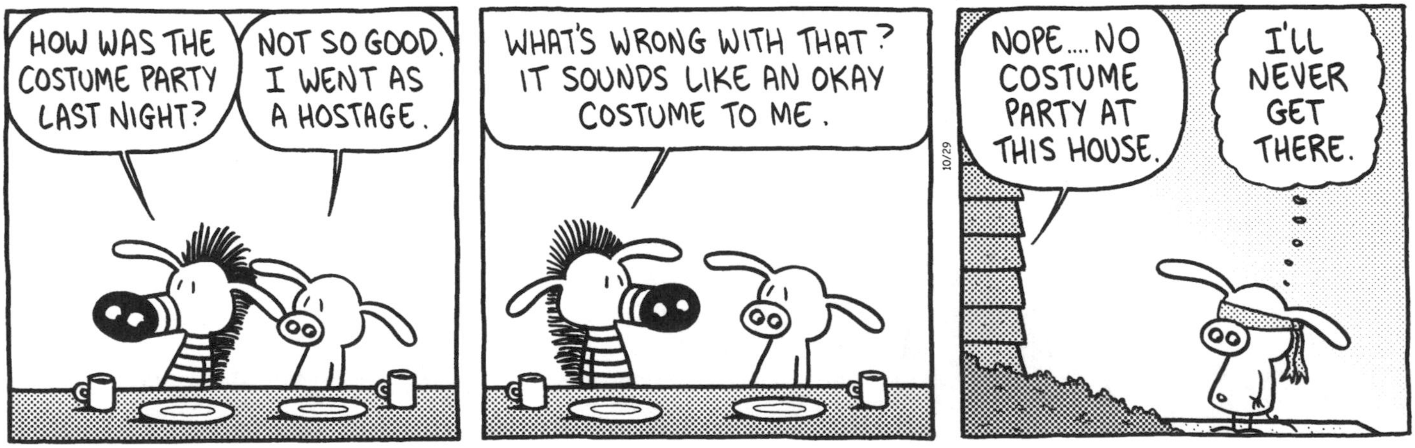
HOW WAS THE COSTUME PARTY LAST NIGHT?
NOT SO GOOD. I WENT AS A HOSTAGE.
WHAT'S WRONG WITH THAT? IT SOUNDS LIKE AN OKAY COSTUME TO ME.
10/29
NOPE.... NO COSTUME PARTY AT THIS HOUSE.
I'LL NEVER GET THERE.

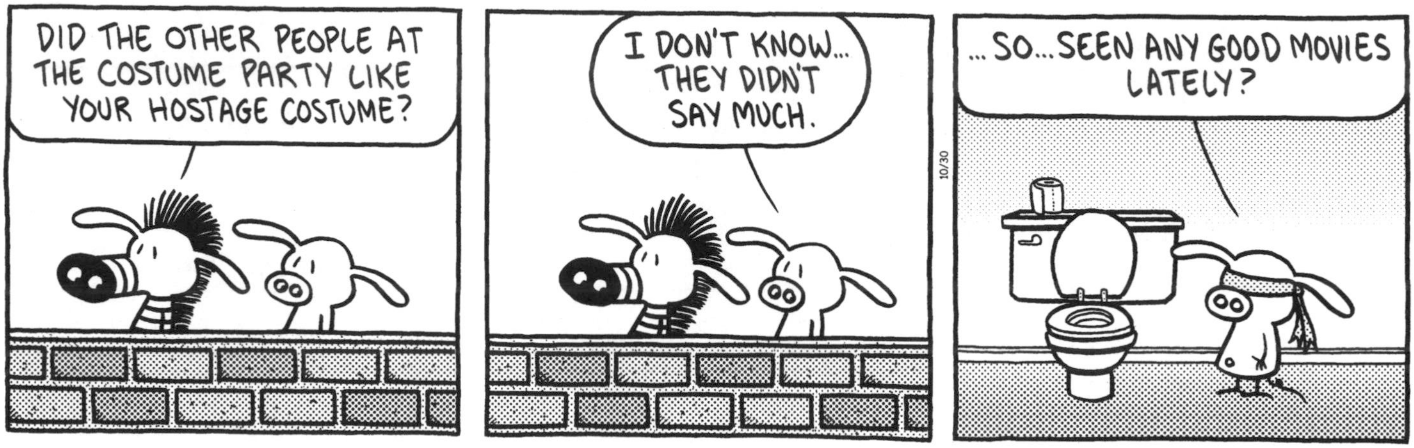
DID THE OTHER PEOPLE AT THE COSTUME PARTY LIKE YOUR HOSTAGE COSTUME?
I DON'T KNOW... THEY DIDN'T SAY MUCH.
10/30
... SO... SEEN ANY GOOD MOVIES LATELY?

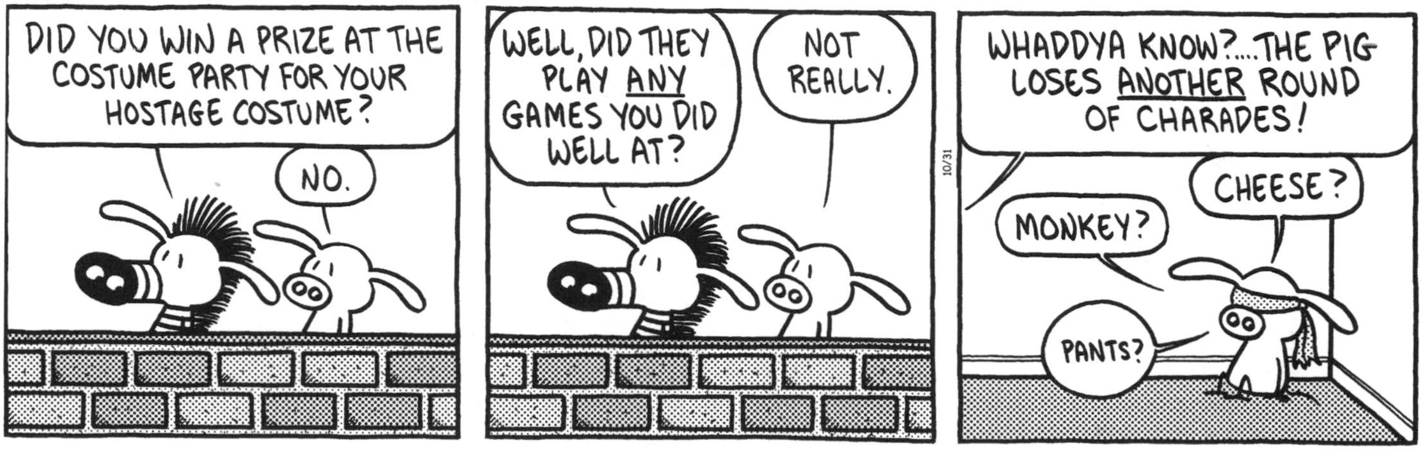
DID YOU WIN A PRIZE AT THE COSTUME PARTY FOR YOUR HOSTAGE COSTUME?
NO.
WELL, DID THEY PLAY ANY GAMES YOU DID WELL AT?
NOT REALLY.
10/31
WHADDYA KNOW?.... THE PIG LOSES ANOTHER ROUND OF CHARADES!
MONKEY?
CHEESE?
PANTS?

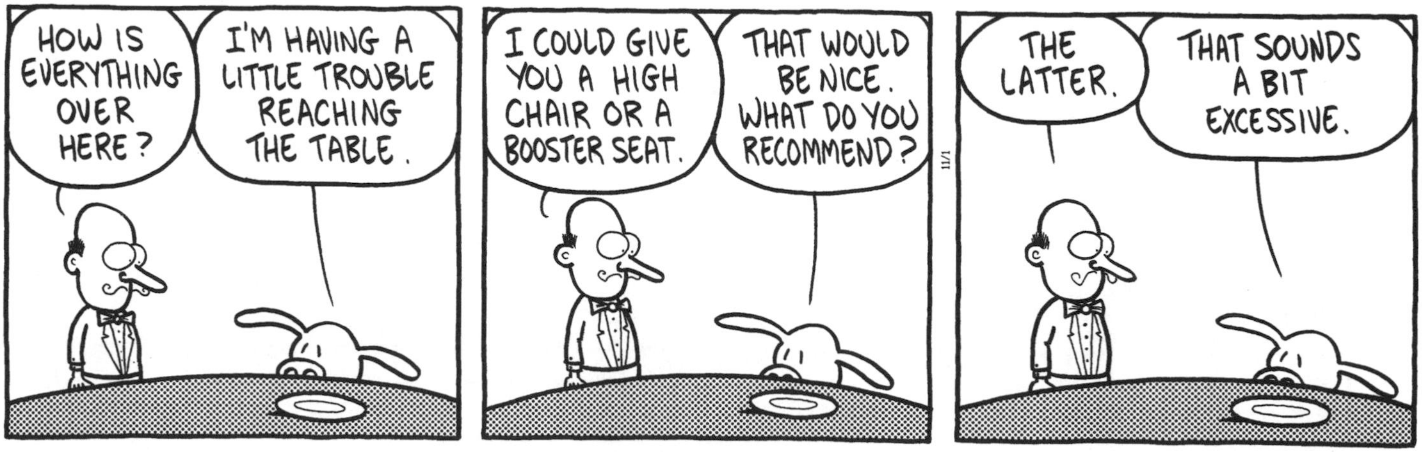
HOW IS EVERYTHING OVER HERE?
I'M HAVING A LITTLE TROUBLE REACHING THE TABLE.
I COULD GIVE YOU A HIGH CHAIR OR A BOOSTER SEAT.
THAT WOULD BE NICE. WHAT DO YOU RECOMMEND?
11/1
THE LATTER.
THAT SOUNDS A BIT EXCESSIVE.

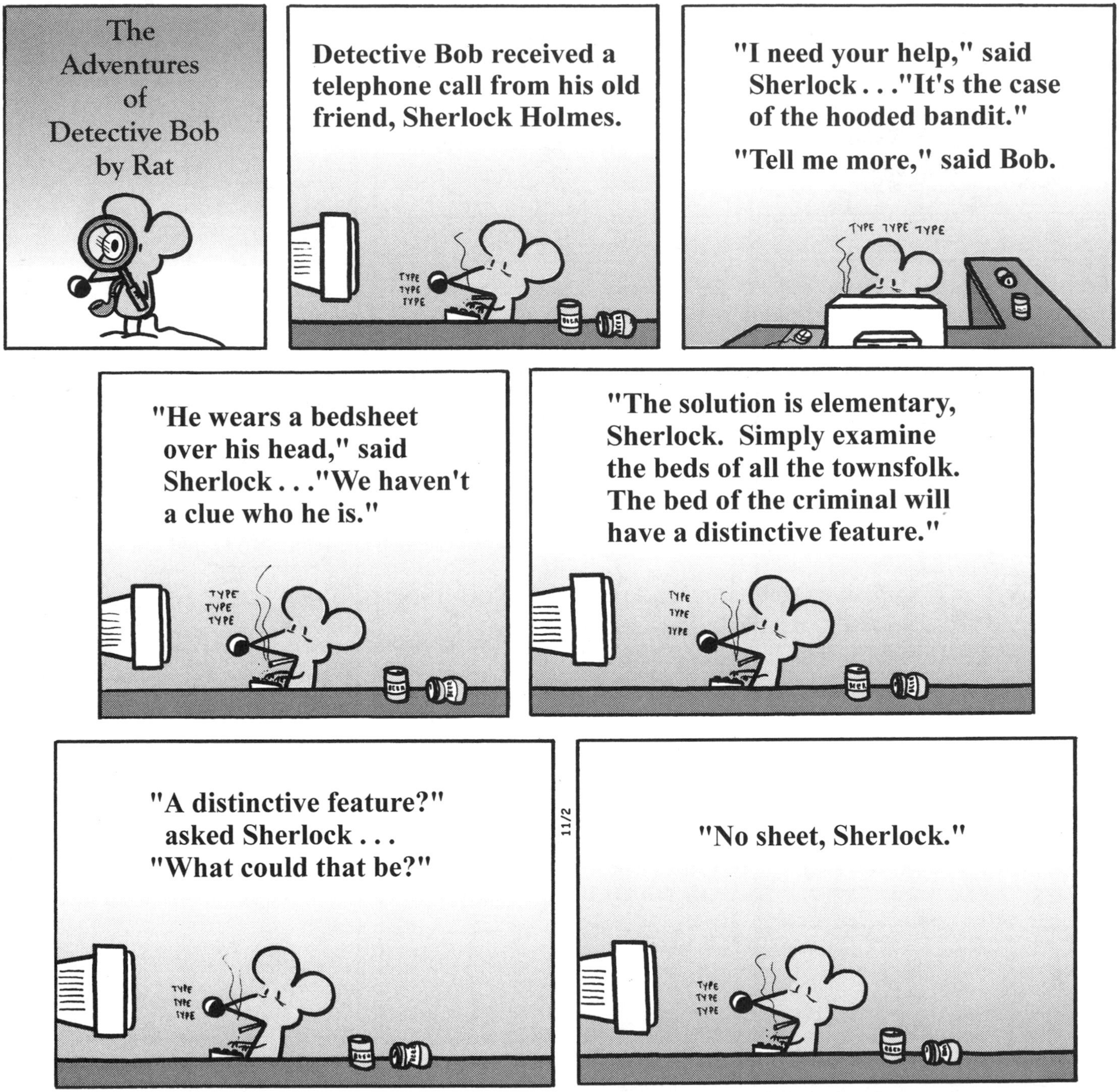
The Adventures of Detective Bob by Rat
Detective Bob received a telephone call from his old friend, Sherlock Holmes.
TYPE TYPE TYPE
"I need your help," said Sherlock . . . "It's the case of the hooded bandit."
"Tell me more," said Bob.
TYPE TYPE TYPE
"He wears a bedsheet over his head," said Sherlock . . . "We haven't a clue who he is."
TYPE TYPE TYPE
"The solution is elementary, Sherlock. Simply examine the beds of all the townsfolk. The bed of the criminal will have a distinctive feature."
TYPE TYPE TYPE
"A distinctive feature?" asked Sherlock . . . "What could that be?"
11/2
"No sheet, Sherlock."
TYPE TYPE TYPE

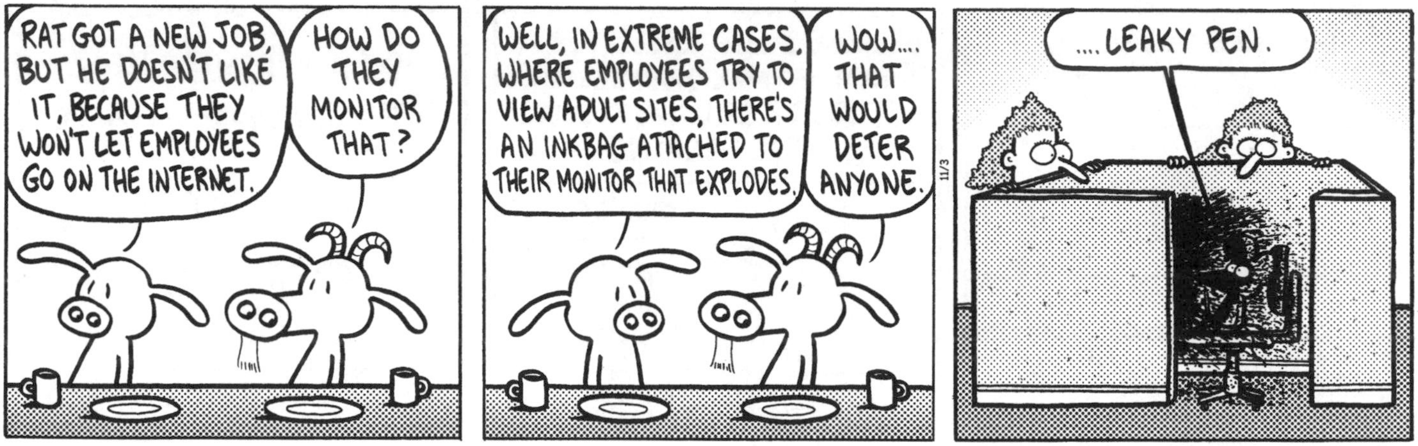
RAT GOT A NEW JOB, BUT HE DOESN'T LIKE IT, BECAUSE THEY WON'T LET EMPLOYEES GO ON THE INTERNET.
HOW DO THEY MONITOR THAT?
WELL, IN EXTREME CASES, WHERE EMPLOYEES TRY TO VIEW ADULT SITES, THERE'S AN INKBAG ATTACHED TO THEIR MONITOR THAT EXPLODES.
WOW.... THAT WOULD DETER ANYONE.
11/3
....LEAKY PEN.

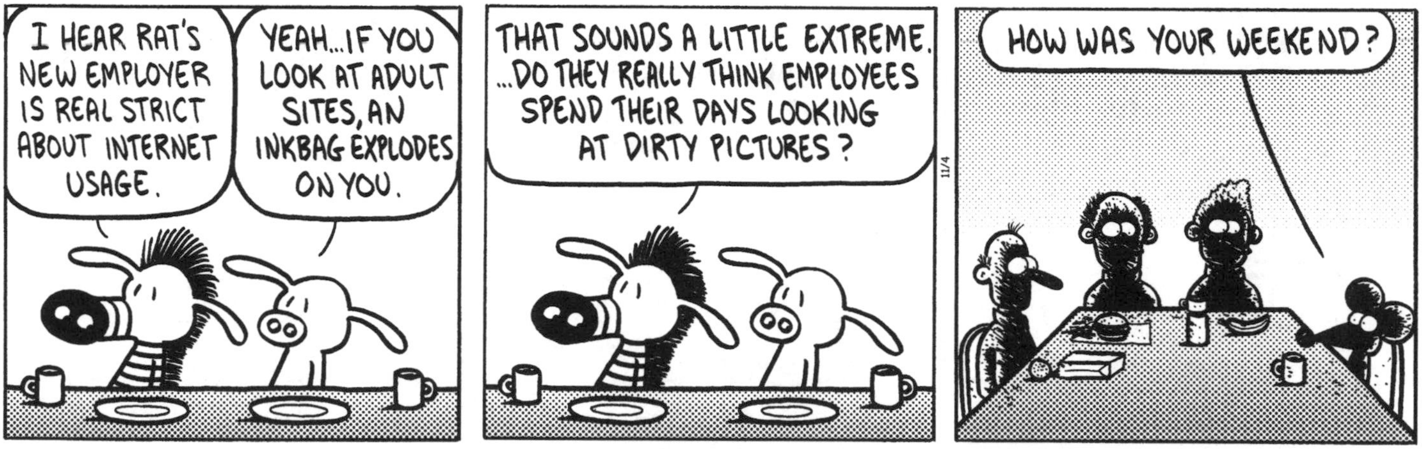
I HEAR RAT'S NEW EMPLOYER IS REAL STRICT ABOUT INTERNET USAGE.
YEAH...IF YOU LOOK AT ADULT SITES, AN INKBAG EXPLODES ON YOU.
THAT SOUNDS A LITTLE EXTREME. ...DO THEY REALLY THINK EMPLOYEES SPEND THEIR DAYS LOOKING AT DIRTY PICTURES?
11/4
HOW WAS YOUR WEEKEND?

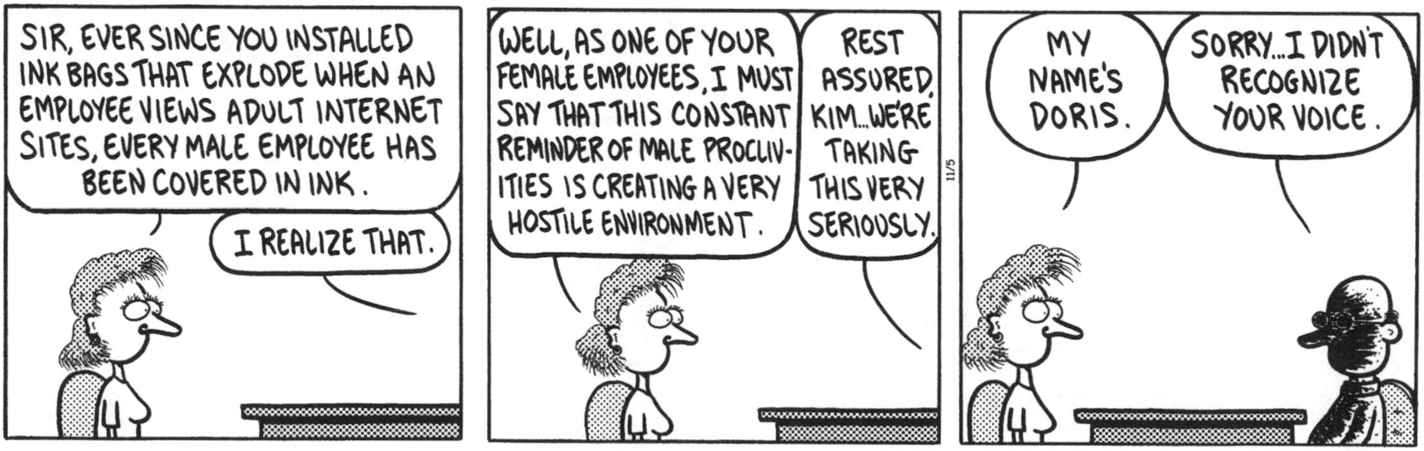
SIR, EVER SINCE YOU INSTALLED INK BAGS THAT EXPLODE WHEN AN EMPLOYEE VIEWS ADULT INTERNET SITES, EVERY MALE EMPLOYEE HAS BEEN COVERED IN INK.
I REALIZE THAT.
WELL, AS ONE OF YOUR FEMALE EMPLOYEES, I MUST SAY THAT THIS CONSTANT REMINDER OF MALE PROCLIVITIES IS CREATING A VERY HOSTILE ENVIRONMENT.
REST ASSURED, KIM...WE'RE TAKING THIS VERY SERIOUSLY.
11/5
MY NAME'S DORIS.
SORRY...I DIDN'T RECOGNIZE YOUR VOICE.

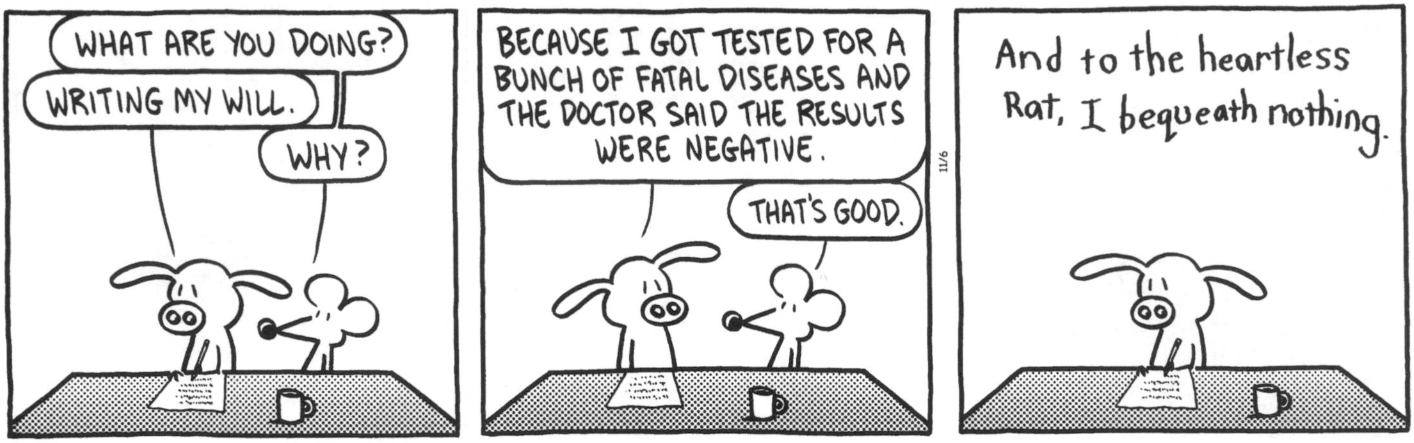
WHAT ARE YOU DOING?
WRITING MY WILL.
WHY?
BECAUSE I GOT TESTED FOR A BUNCH OF FATAL DISEASES AND THE DOCTOR SAID THE RESULTS WERE NEGATIVE.
THAT'S GOOD.
11/6
And to the heartless Rat, I bequeath nothing.

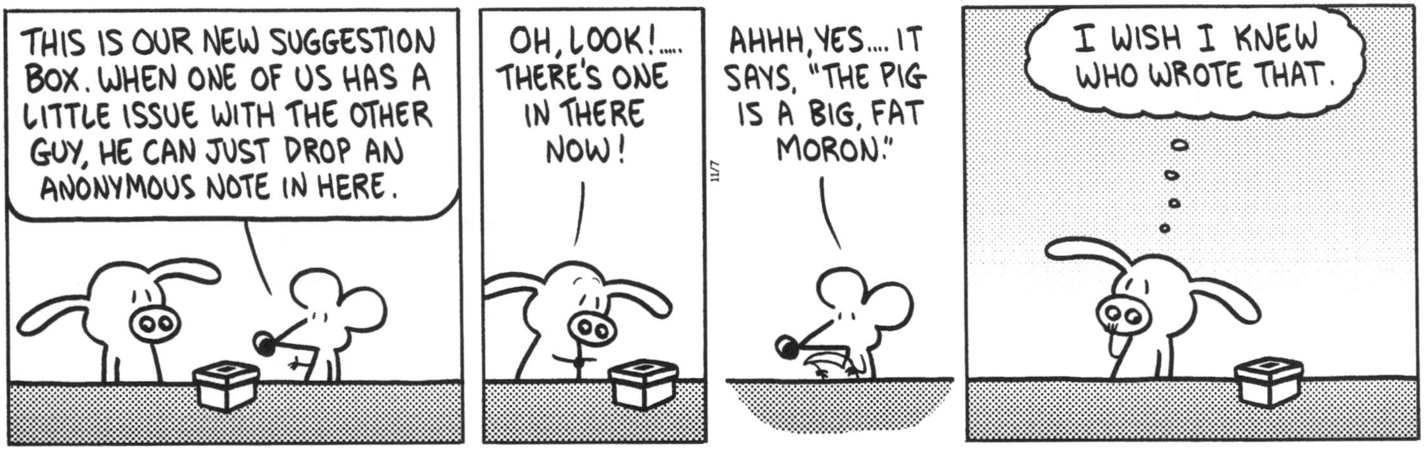
THIS IS OUR NEW SUGGESTION BOX. WHEN ONE OF US HAS A LITTLE ISSUE WITH THE OTHER GUY, HE CAN JUST DROP AN ANONYMOUS NOTE IN HERE.
OH, LOOK!..... THERE'S ONE IN THERE NOW!
11/7
AHHH, YES.... IT SAYS, "THE PIG IS A BIG, FAT MORON."
I WISH I KNEW WHO WROTE THAT.

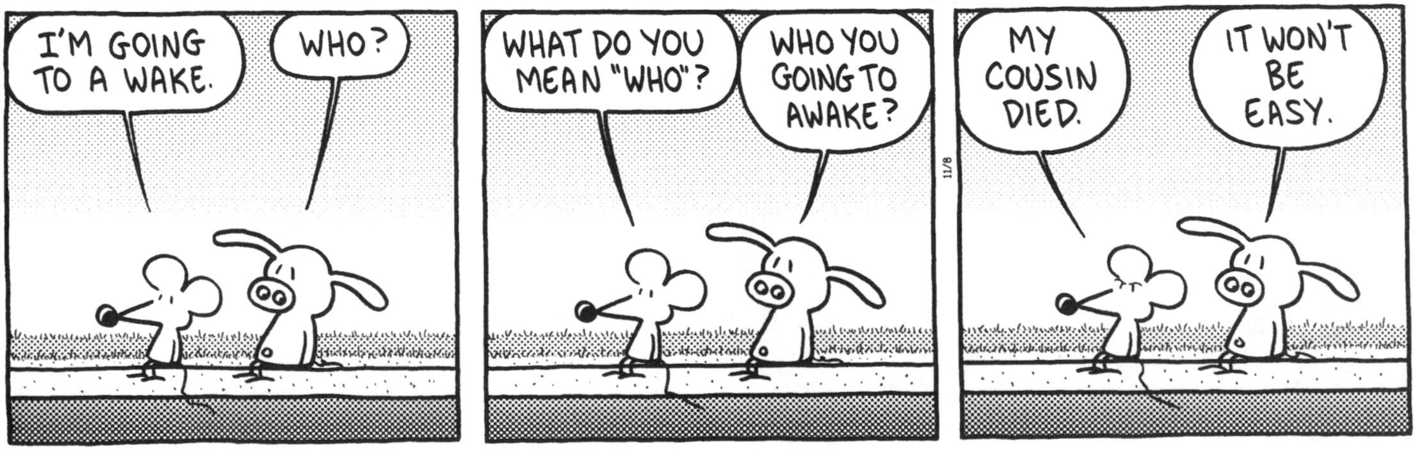
I'M GOING TO A WAKE.
WHO?
WHAT DO YOU MEAN "WHO"?
WHO YOU GOING TO AWAKE?
11/8
MY COUSIN DIED.
IT WON'T BE EASY.

A "Pearls" Walk Through Alternative History

brought to you by the makers of

Calmdownshutupandact-justliketherestofus-ametaphine™

11/9

Salzburg, Austria c. 1764

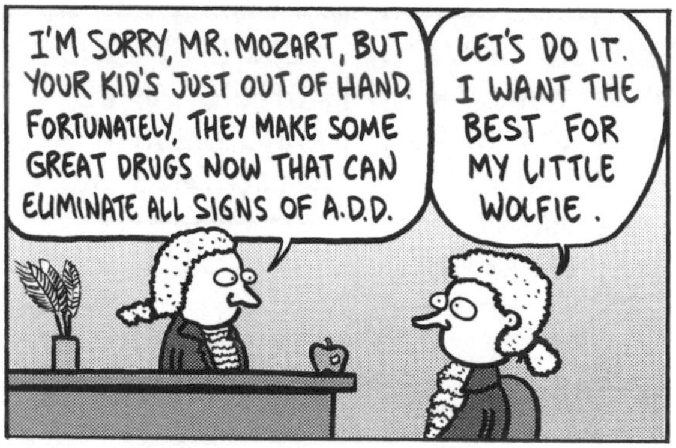

I'M SORRY, MR. MOZART, BUT YOUR KID'S JUST OUT OF HAND. FORTUNATELY, THEY MAKE SOME GREAT DRUGS NOW THAT CAN ELIMINATE ALL SIGNS OF A.D.D.
LET'S DO IT. I WANT THE BEST FOR MY LITTLE WOLFIE.

East St. Louis, Illinois c. 1934

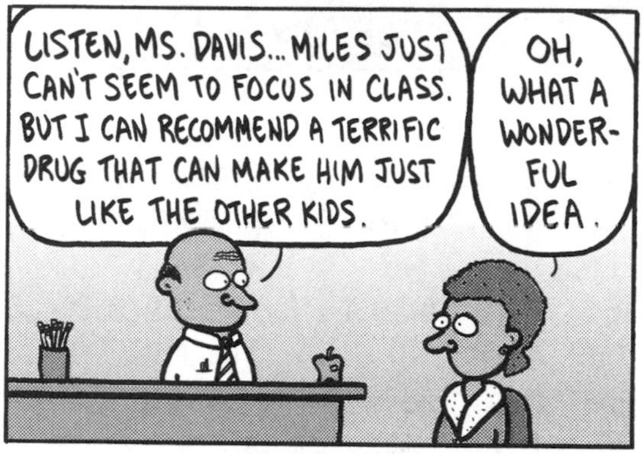

LISTEN, MS. DAVIS... MILES JUST CAN'T SEEM TO FOCUS IN CLASS. BUT I CAN RECOMMEND A TERRIFIC DRUG THAT CAN MAKE HIM JUST LIKE THE OTHER KIDS.
OH, WHAT A WONDER-FUL IDEA.

Liverpool, England c. 1950

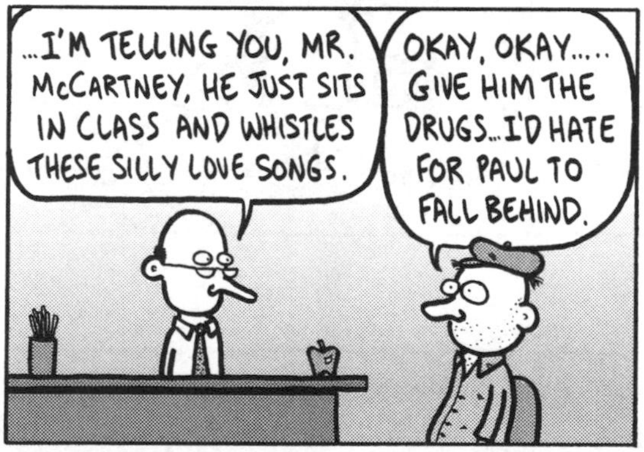

...I'M TELLING YOU, MR. McCARTNEY, HE JUST SITS IN CLASS AND WHISTLES THESE SILLY LOVE SONGS.
OKAY, OKAY..... GIVE HIM THE DRUGS... I'D HATE FOR PAUL TO FALL BEHIND.

Pearls Before Swine c. 2003

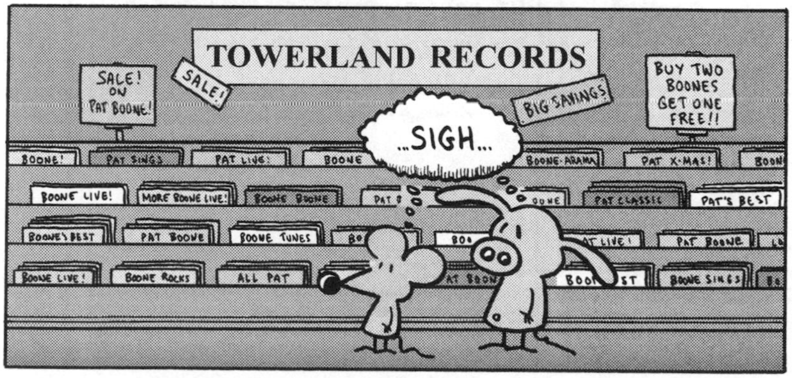

TOWERLAND RECORDS
SALE! ON PAT BOONE!
SALE!
BIG SAVINGS
BUY TWO BOONES GET ONE FREE!!
...SIGH...
BOONE!
PAT SINGS
PAT LIVE!
BOONE
BOONE-ARAMA
PAT X-MAS!
BOONE LIVE!
MORE BOONE LIVE!
BOONE BOONE
PAT CLASSIC
PAT'S BEST
BOONE'S BEST
PAT BOONE
BOONE TUNES
PAT BOONE
BOONE LIVE!
BOONE ROCKS
ALL PAT
BOONE SINGS

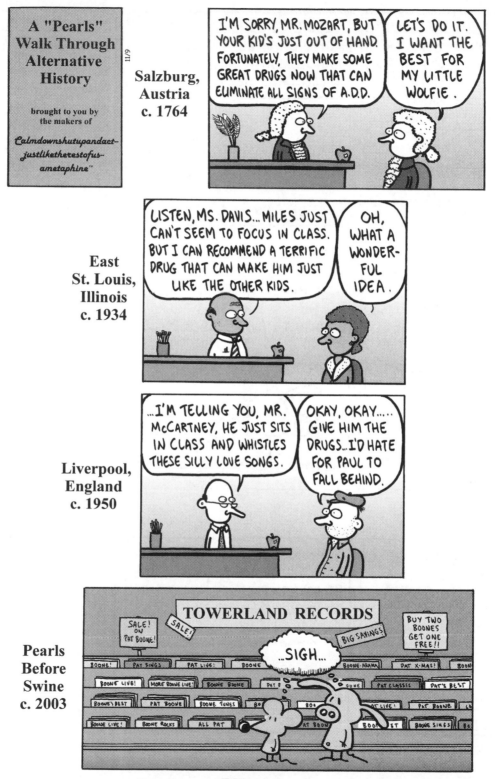

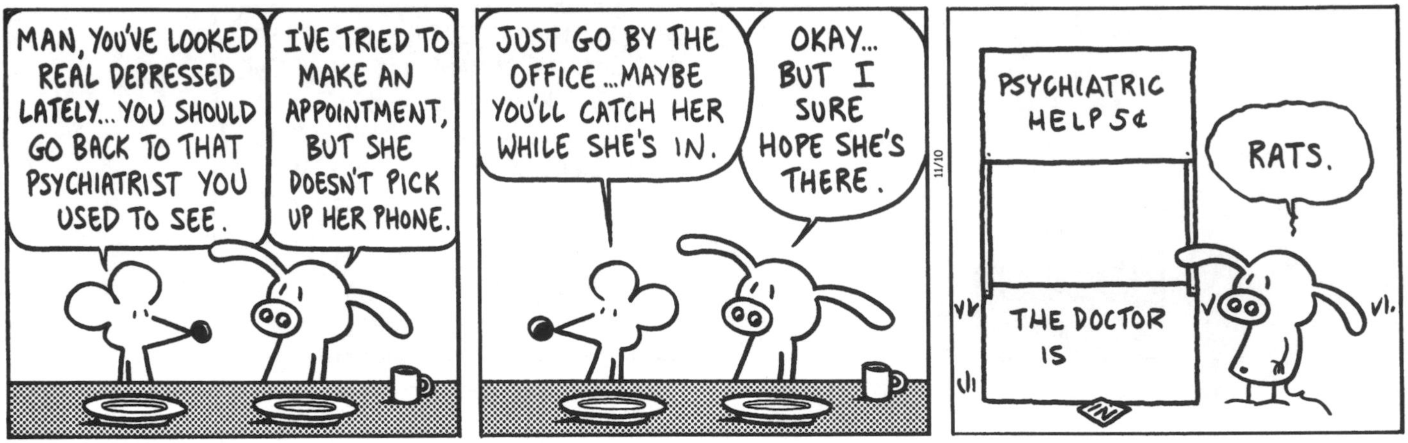
MAN, YOU'VE LOOKED REAL DEPRESSED LATELY... YOU SHOULD GO BACK TO THAT PSYCHIATRIST YOU USED TO SEE.
I'VE TRIED TO MAKE AN APPOINTMENT, BUT SHE DOESN'T PICK UP HER PHONE.
JUST GO BY THE OFFICE... MAYBE YOU'LL CATCH HER WHILE SHE'S IN.
OKAY... BUT I SURE HOPE SHE'S THERE.
11/10
PSYCHIATRIC HELP 5¢
THE DOCTOR IS
IN
RATS.

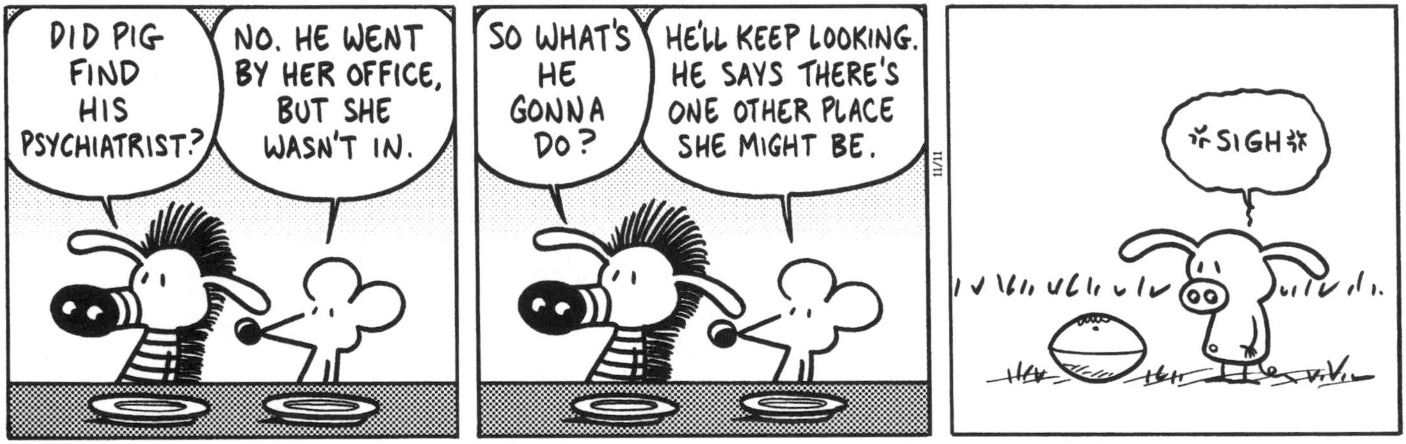
DID PIG FIND HIS PSYCHIATRIST?
NO. HE WENT BY HER OFFICE, BUT SHE WASN'T IN.
SO WHAT'S HE GONNA DO?
HE'LL KEEP LOOKING. HE SAYS THERE'S ONE OTHER PLACE SHE MIGHT BE.
11/11
SIGH

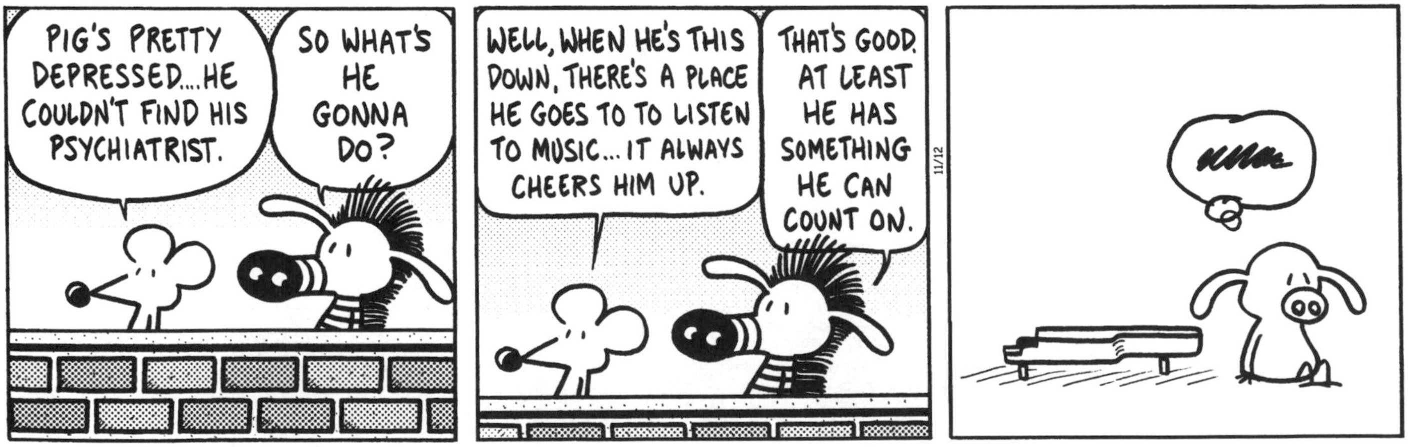
PIG'S PRETTY DEPRESSED.... HE COULDN'T FIND HIS PSYCHIATRIST.
SO WHAT'S HE GONNA DO?
WELL, WHEN HE'S THIS DOWN, THERE'S A PLACE HE GOES TO TO LISTEN TO MUSIC... IT ALWAYS CHEERS HIM UP.
THAT'S GOOD. AT LEAST HE HAS SOMETHING HE CAN COUNT ON.
11/12

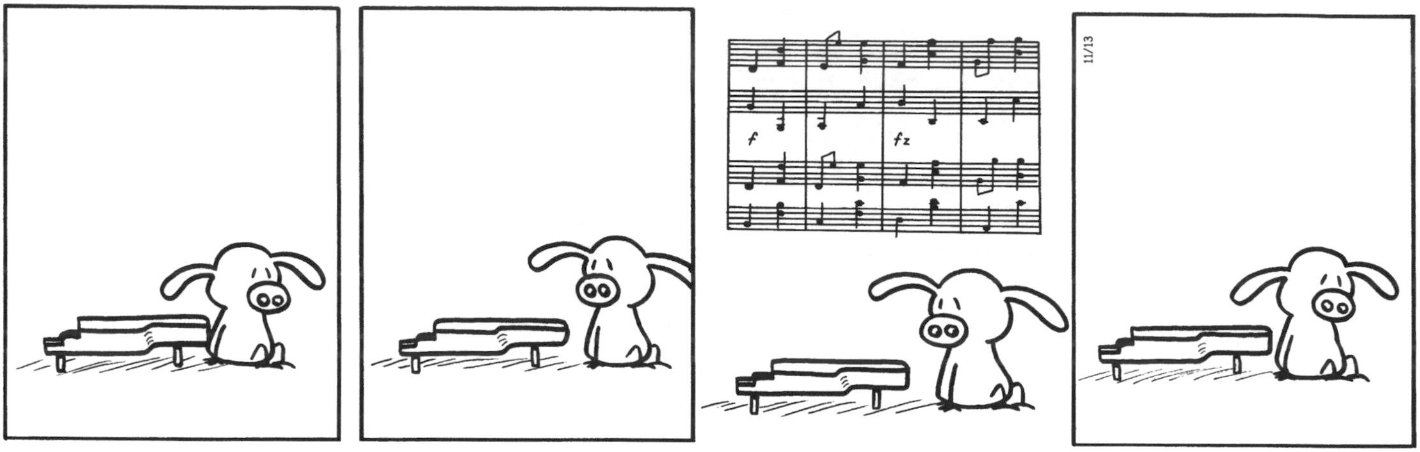
11/13

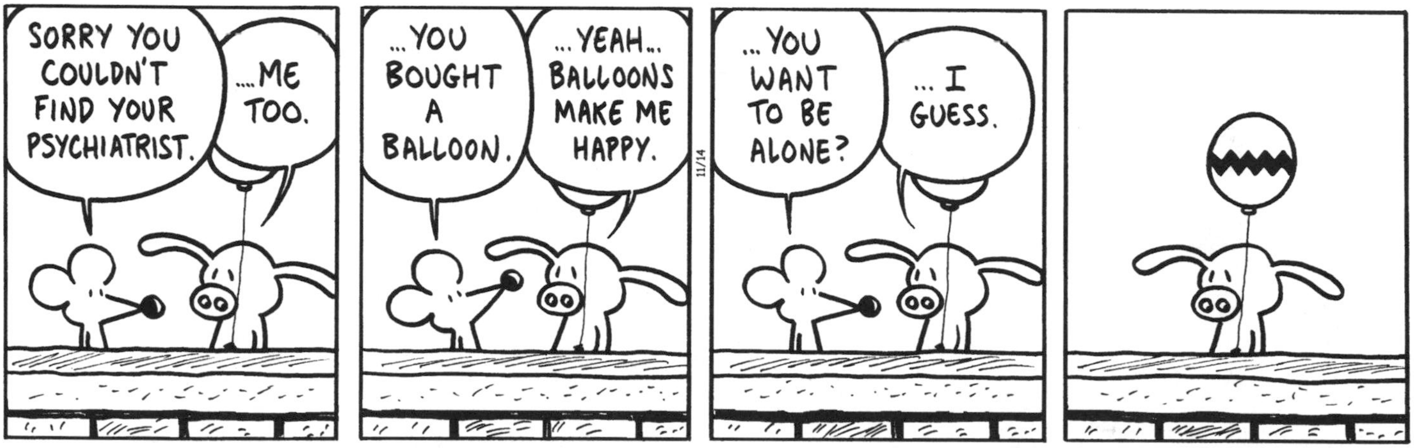
SORRY YOU COULDN'T FIND YOUR PSYCHIATRIST.
....ME TOO.
...YOU BOUGHT A BALLOON.
...YEAH... BALLOONS MAKE ME HAPPY.
11/14
...YOU WANT TO BE ALONE?
...I GUESS.

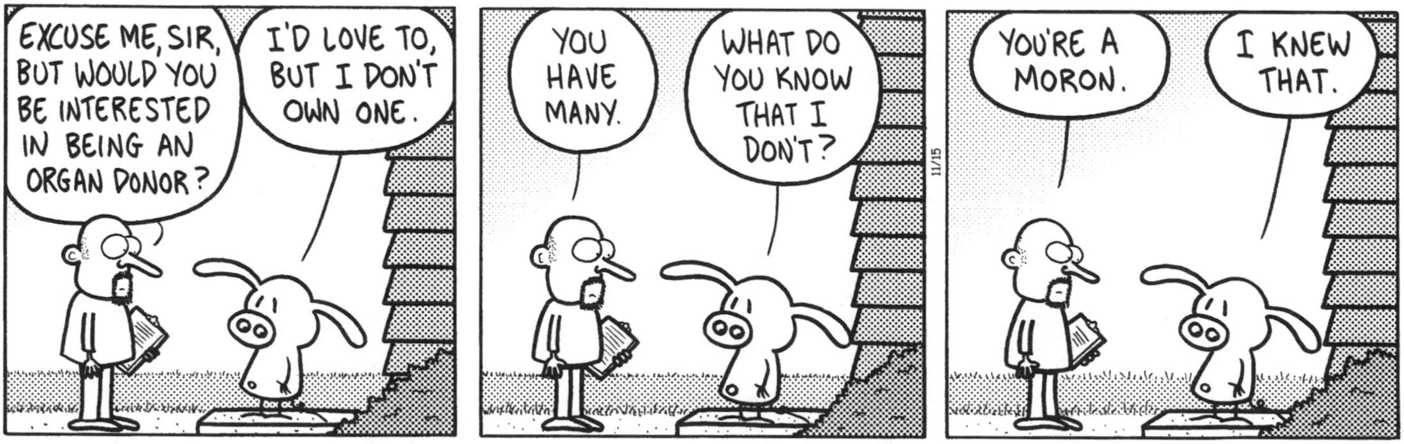
EXCUSE ME, SIR, BUT WOULD YOU BE INTERESTED IN BEING AN ORGAN DONOR?
I'D LOVE TO, BUT I DON'T OWN ONE.
YOU HAVE MANY.
WHAT DO YOU KNOW THAT I DON'T?
11/15
YOU'RE A MORON.
I KNEW THAT.

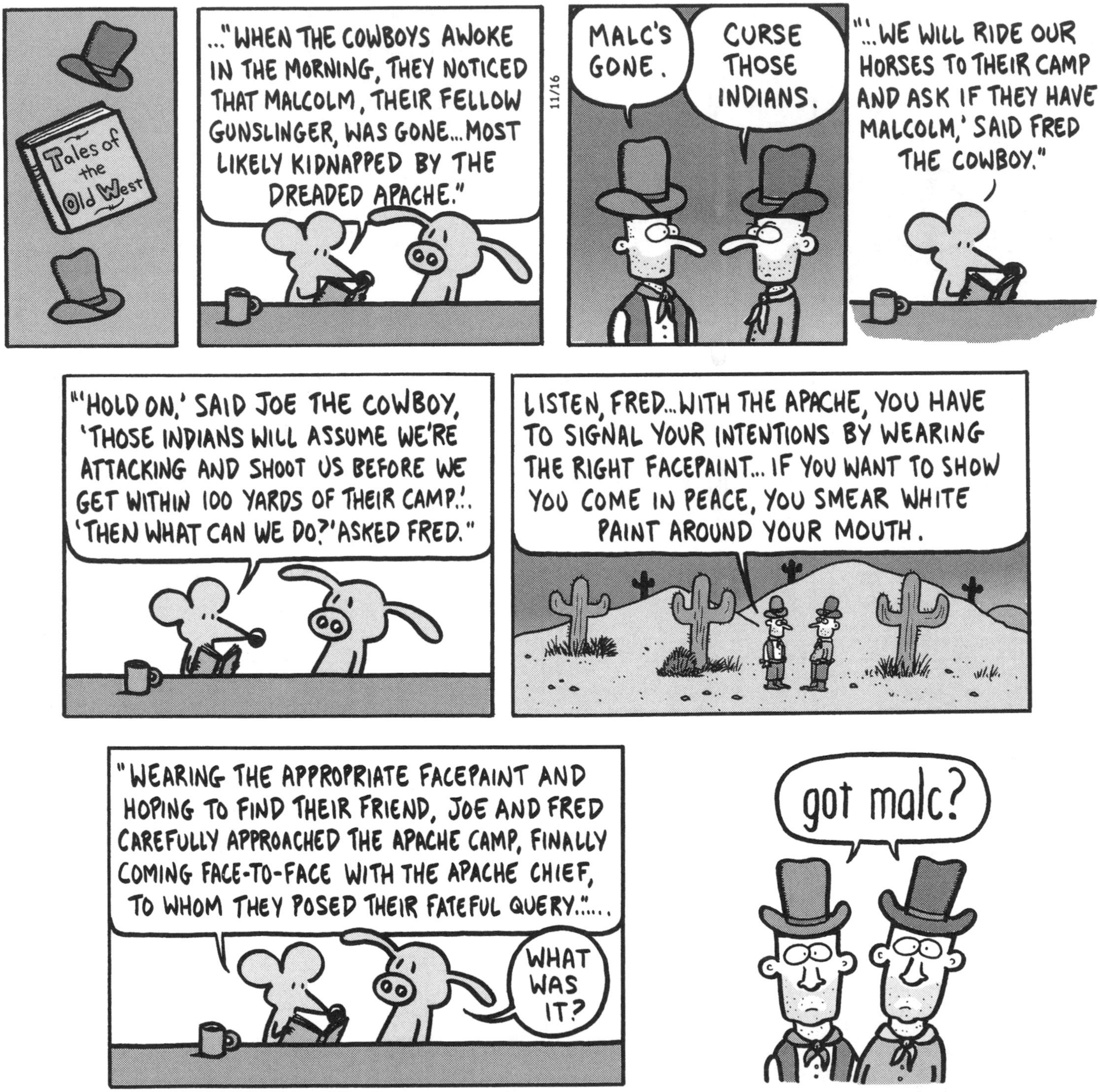

Tales of the Old West
..."WHEN THE COWBOYS AWOKE IN THE MORNING, THEY NOTICED THAT MALCOLM, THEIR FELLOW GUNSLINGER, WAS GONE...MOST LIKELY KIDNAPPED BY THE DREADED APACHE."
11/16
MALC'S GONE.
CURSE THOSE INDIANS.
"'...WE WILL RIDE OUR HORSES TO THEIR CAMP AND ASK IF THEY HAVE MALCOLM,' SAID FRED THE COWBOY."
"'HOLD ON,' SAID JOE THE COWBOY, 'THOSE INDIANS WILL ASSUME WE'RE ATTACKING AND SHOOT US BEFORE WE GET WITHIN 100 YARDS OF THEIR CAMP.'.. 'THEN WHAT CAN WE DO?' ASKED FRED."
LISTEN, FRED...WITH THE APACHE, YOU HAVE TO SIGNAL YOUR INTENTIONS BY WEARING THE RIGHT FACEPAINT... IF YOU WANT TO SHOW YOU COME IN PEACE, YOU SMEAR WHITE PAINT AROUND YOUR MOUTH.
"WEARING THE APPROPRIATE FACEPAINT AND HOPING TO FIND THEIR FRIEND, JOE AND FRED CAREFULLY APPROACHED THE APACHE CAMP, FINALLY COMING FACE-TO-FACE WITH THE APACHE CHIEF, TO WHOM THEY POSED THEIR FATEFUL QUERY.".....
WHAT WAS IT?
got malc?

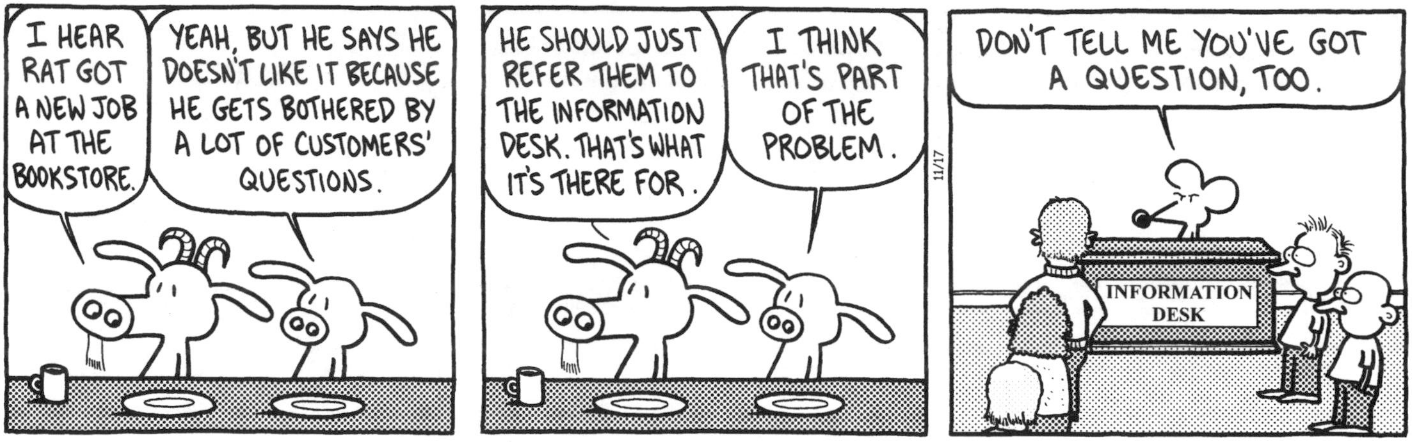
I HEAR RAT GOT A NEW JOB AT THE BOOKSTORE.
YEAH, BUT HE SAYS HE DOESN'T LIKE IT BECAUSE HE GETS BOTHERED BY A LOT OF CUSTOMERS' QUESTIONS.
HE SHOULD JUST REFER THEM TO THE INFORMATION DESK. THAT'S WHAT IT'S THERE FOR.
I THINK THAT'S PART OF THE PROBLEM.
11/17
DON'T TELL ME YOU'VE GOT A QUESTION, TOO.
INFORMATION DESK

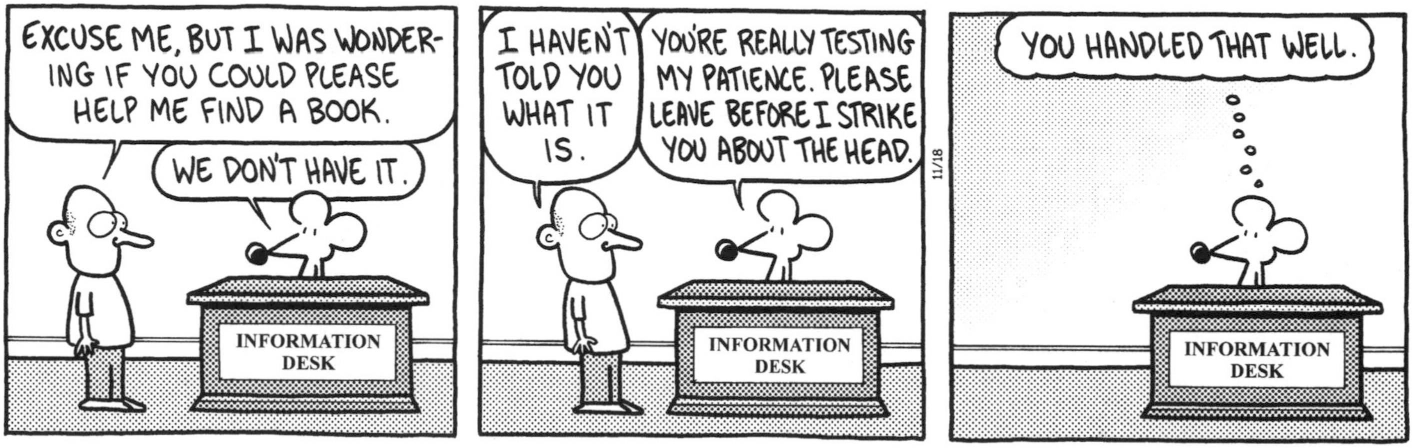
EXCUSE ME, BUT I WAS WONDERING IF YOU COULD PLEASE HELP ME FIND A BOOK.
WE DON'T HAVE IT.
INFORMATION DESK
I HAVEN'T TOLD YOU WHAT IT IS.
YOU'RE REALLY TESTING MY PATIENCE. PLEASE LEAVE BEFORE I STRIKE YOU ABOUT THE HEAD.
INFORMATION DESK
11/18
YOU HANDLED THAT WELL.
INFORMATION DESK

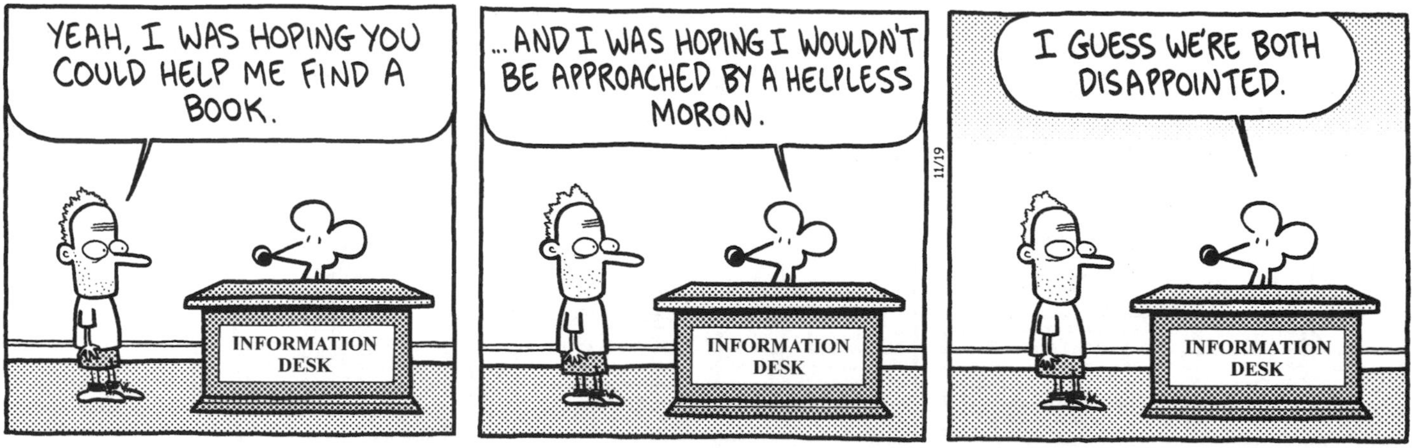
YEAH, I WAS HOPING YOU COULD HELP ME FIND A BOOK.
INFORMATION DESK
...AND I WAS HOPING I WOULDN'T BE APPROACHED BY A HELPLESS MORON.
INFORMATION DESK
11/19
I GUESS WE'RE BOTH DISAPPOINTED.
INFORMATION DESK

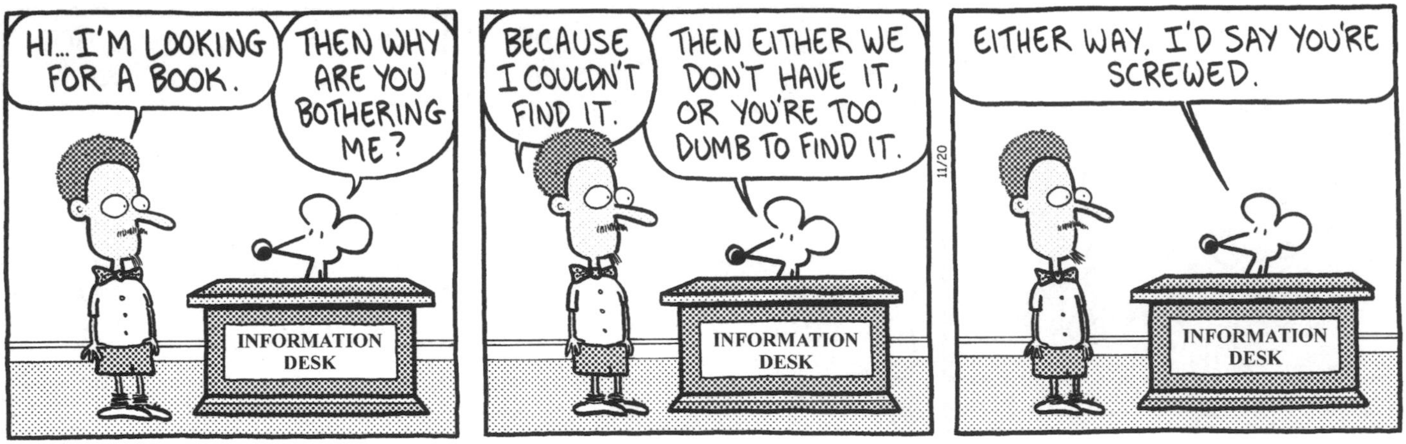
HI... I'M LOOKING FOR A BOOK.
THEN WHY ARE YOU BOTHERING ME?
BECAUSE I COULDN'T FIND IT.
THEN EITHER WE DON'T HAVE IT, OR YOU'RE TOO DUMB TO FIND IT.
INFORMATION DESK
11/20
EITHER WAY, I'D SAY YOU'RE SCREWED.

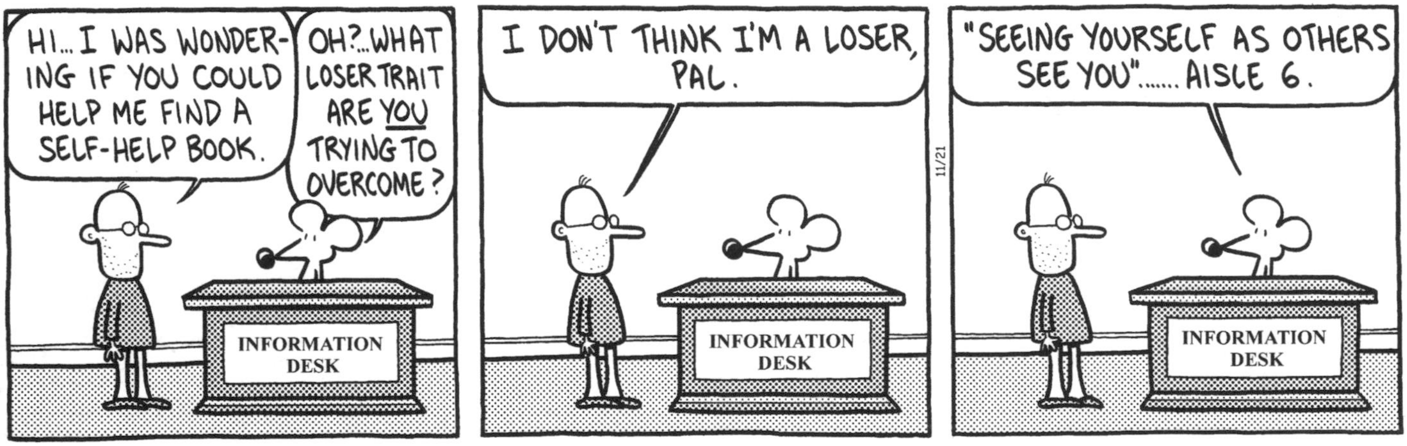
HI... I WAS WONDERING IF YOU COULD HELP ME FIND A SELF-HELP BOOK.
OH?...WHAT LOSER TRAIT ARE YOU TRYING TO OVERCOME?
INFORMATION DESK
I DON'T THINK I'M A LOSER, PAL.
11/21
"SEEING YOURSELF AS OTHERS SEE YOU"....... AISLE 6.

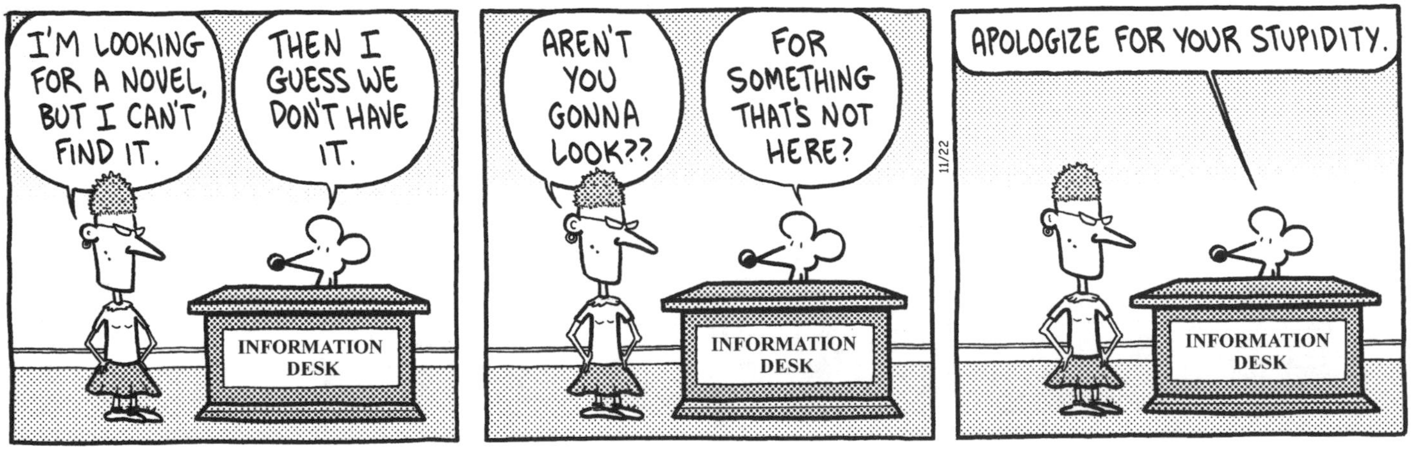
I'M LOOKING FOR A NOVEL, BUT I CAN'T FIND IT.
THEN I GUESS WE DON'T HAVE IT.
INFORMATION DESK
AREN'T YOU GONNA LOOK??
FOR SOMETHING THAT'S NOT HERE?
11/22
APOLOGIZE FOR YOUR STUPIDITY.

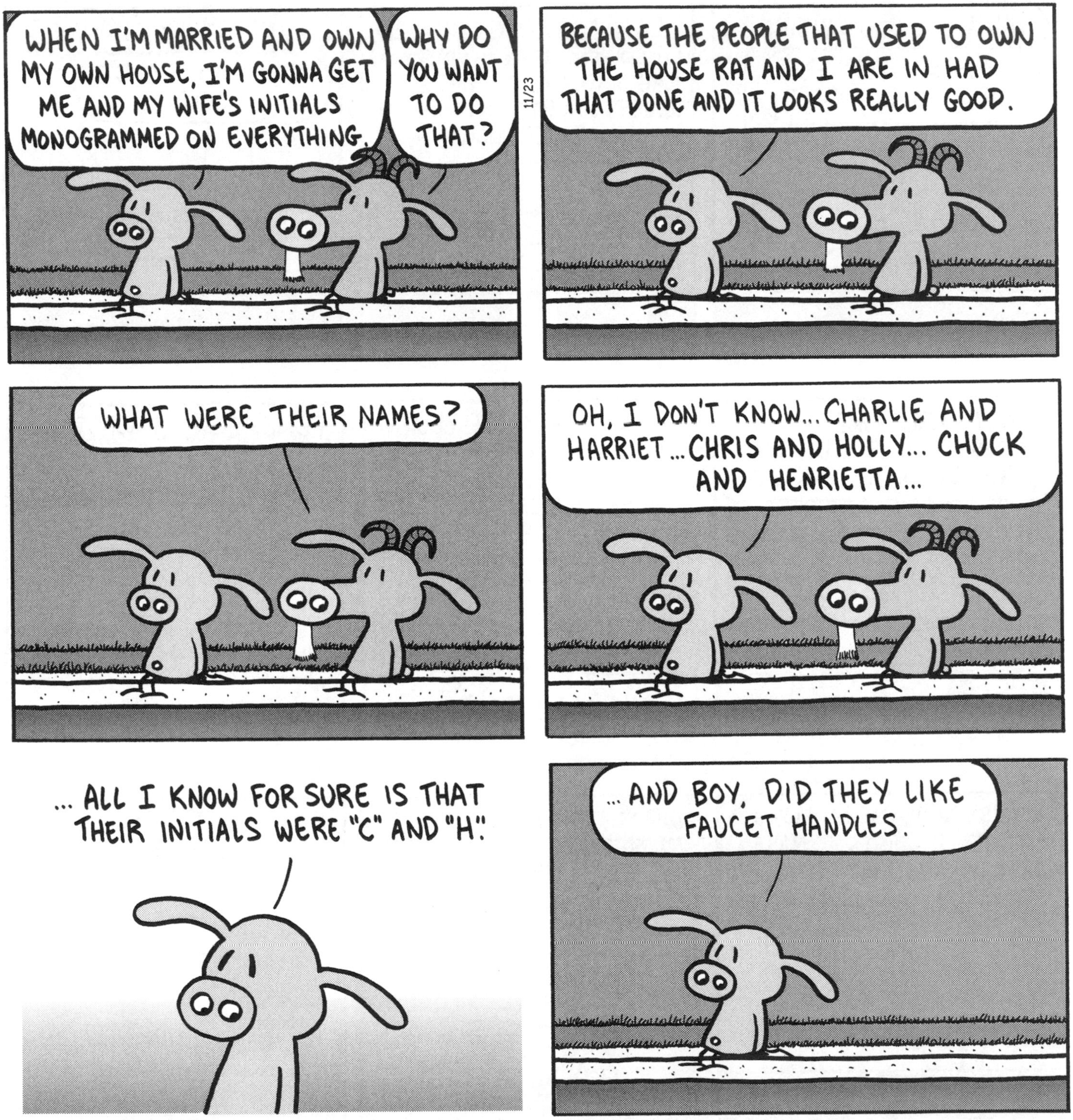
WHEN I'M MARRIED AND OWN MY OWN HOUSE, I'M GONNA GET ME AND MY WIFE'S INITIALS MONOGRAMMED ON EVERYTHING.
WHY DO YOU WANT TO DO THAT?
11/23
BECAUSE THE PEOPLE THAT USED TO OWN THE HOUSE RAT AND I ARE IN HAD THAT DONE AND IT LOOKS REALLY GOOD.
WHAT WERE THEIR NAMES?
OH, I DON'T KNOW... CHARLIE AND HARRIET... CHRIS AND HOLLY... CHUCK AND HENRIETTA...
... ALL I KNOW FOR SURE IS THAT THEIR INITIALS WERE "C" AND "H."
... AND BOY, DID THEY LIKE FAUCET HANDLES.

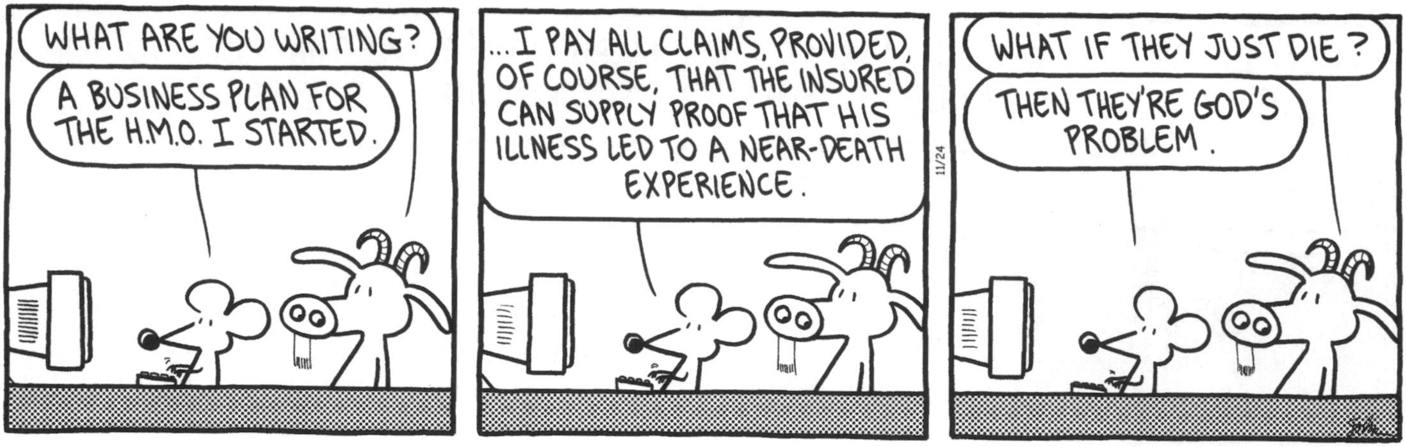
WHAT ARE YOU WRITING?
A BUSINESS PLAN FOR THE H.M.O. I STARTED.
...I PAY ALL CLAIMS, PROVIDED, OF COURSE, THAT THE INSURED CAN SUPPLY PROOF THAT HIS ILLNESS LED TO A NEAR-DEATH EXPERIENCE.
11/24
WHAT IF THEY JUST DIE?
THEN THEY'RE GOD'S PROBLEM.

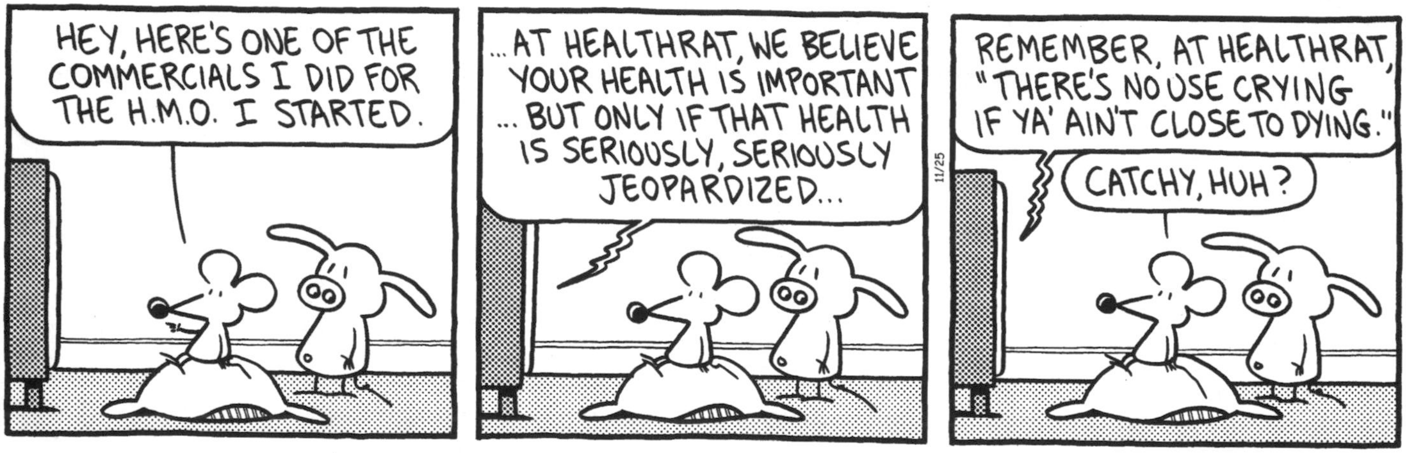
HEY, HERE'S ONE OF THE COMMERCIALS I DID FOR THE H.M.O. I STARTED.
...AT HEALTHRAT, WE BELIEVE YOUR HEALTH IS IMPORTANT ...BUT ONLY IF THAT HEALTH IS SERIOUSLY, SERIOUSLY JEOPARDIZED...
11/25
REMEMBER, AT HEALTHRAT, "THERE'S NO USE CRYING IF YA' AIN'T CLOSE TO DYING."
CATCHY, HUH?

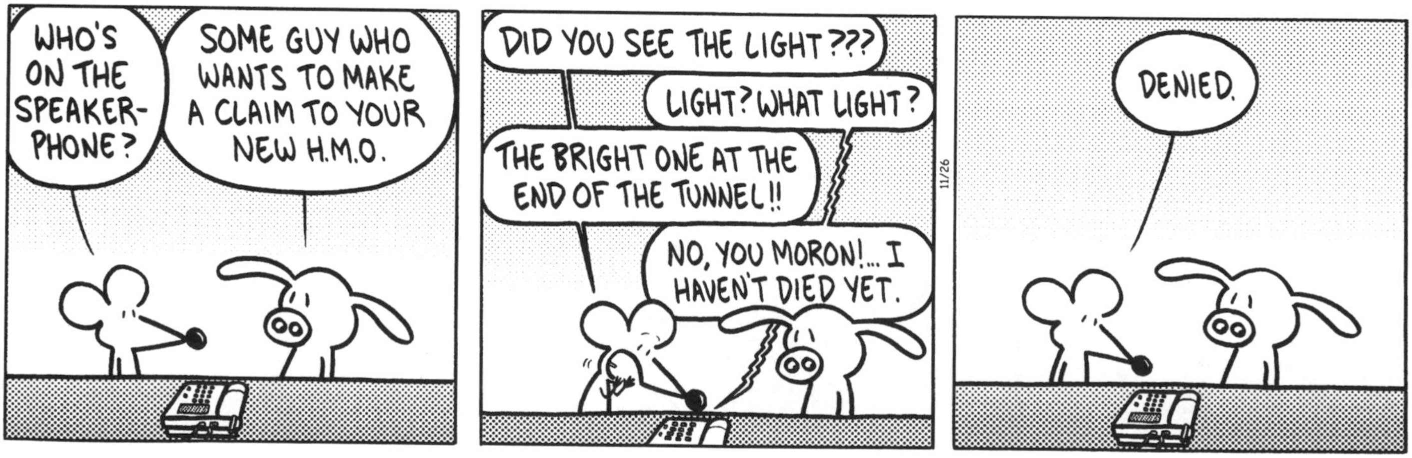
WHO'S ON THE SPEAKER-PHONE?
SOME GUY WHO WANTS TO MAKE A CLAIM TO YOUR NEW H.M.O.
DID YOU SEE THE LIGHT???
LIGHT? WHAT LIGHT?
THE BRIGHT ONE AT THE END OF THE TUNNEL!!
NO, YOU MORON!... I HAVEN'T DIED YET.
11/26
DENIED.

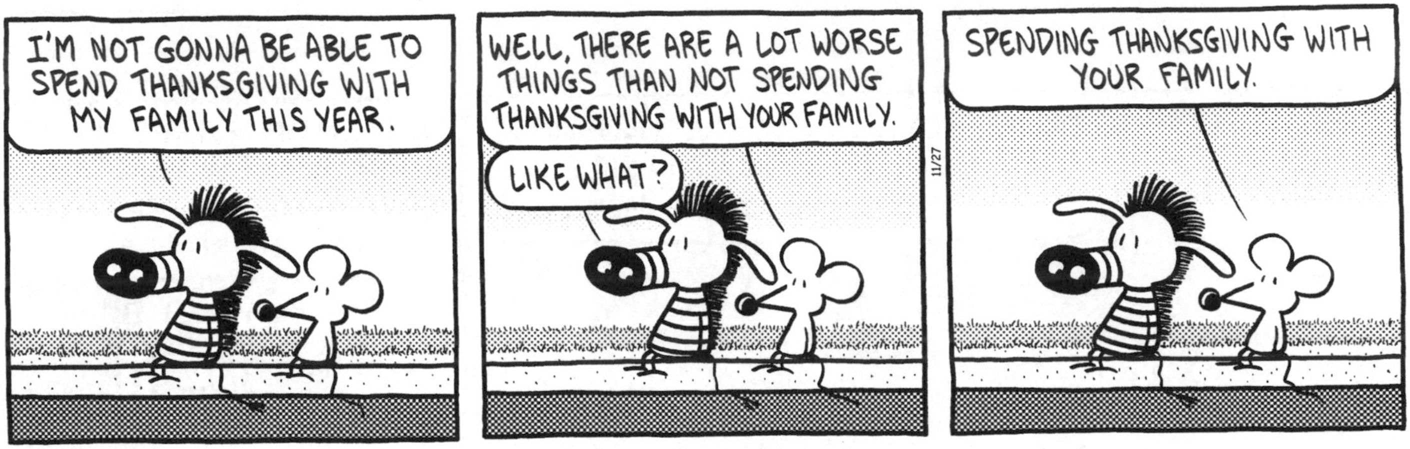
I'M NOT GONNA BE ABLE TO SPEND THANKSGIVING WITH MY FAMILY THIS YEAR.
WELL, THERE ARE A LOT WORSE THINGS THAN NOT SPENDING THANKSGIVING WITH YOUR FAMILY.
LIKE WHAT?
11/27
SPENDING THANKSGIVING WITH YOUR FAMILY.

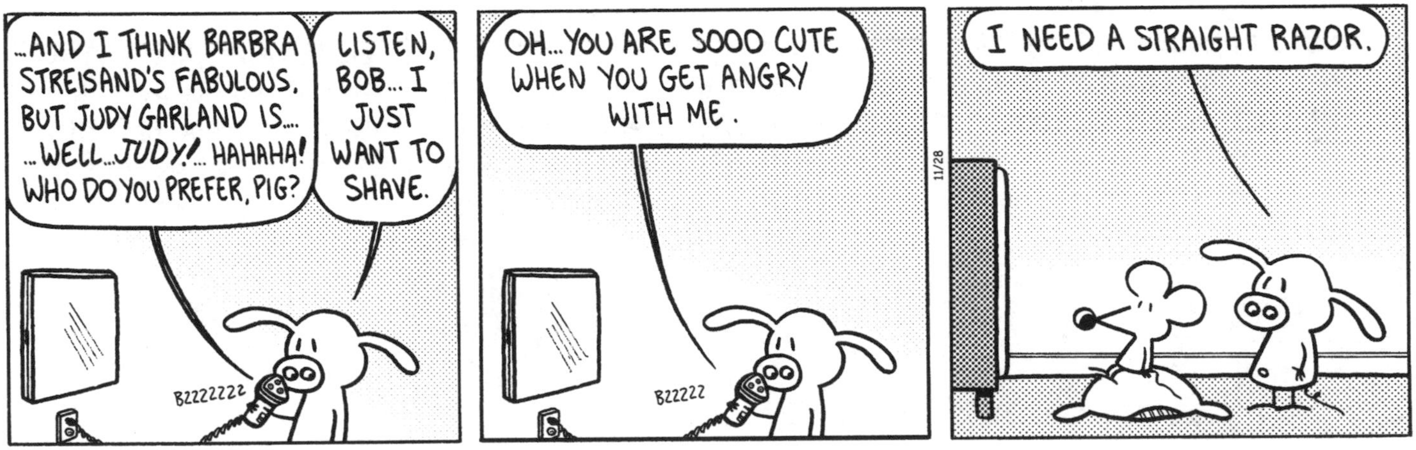
...AND I THINK BARBRA STREISAND'S FABULOUS. BUT JUDY GARLAND IS.... ...WELL...JUDY!... HAHAHA! WHO DO YOU PREFER, PIG?
LISTEN, BOB... I JUST WANT TO SHAVE.
BZZZZZZZ
OH... YOU ARE SOOO CUTE WHEN YOU GET ANGRY WITH ME.
BZZZZZ
11/28
I NEED A STRAIGHT RAZOR.

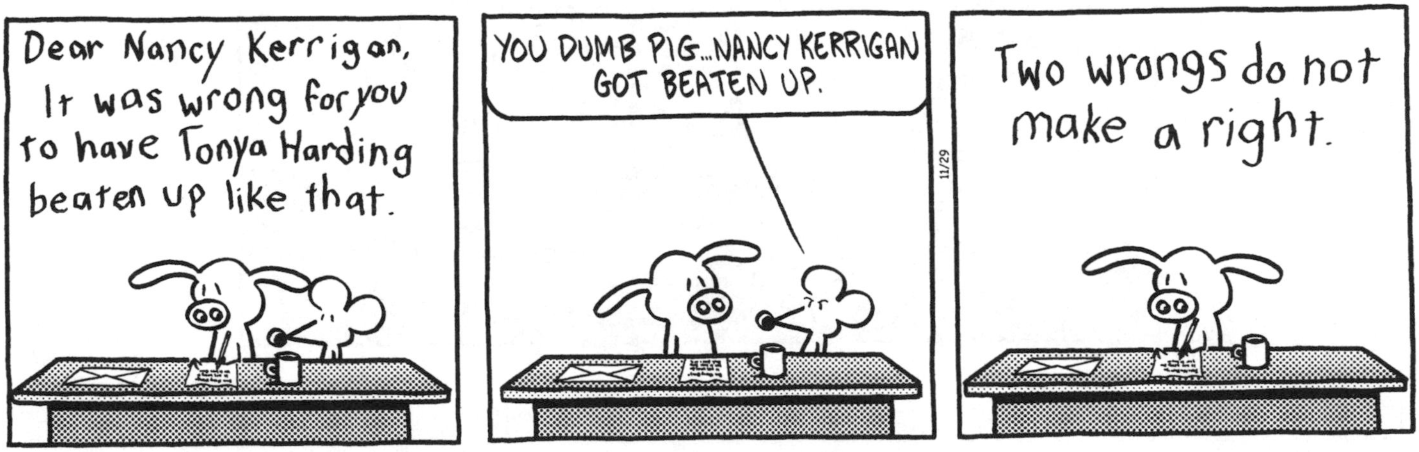
Dear Nancy Kerrigan, It was wrong for you to have Tonya Harding beaten up like that.
YOU DUMB PIG...NANCY KERRIGAN GOT BEATEN UP.
11/29
Two wrongs do not make a right.

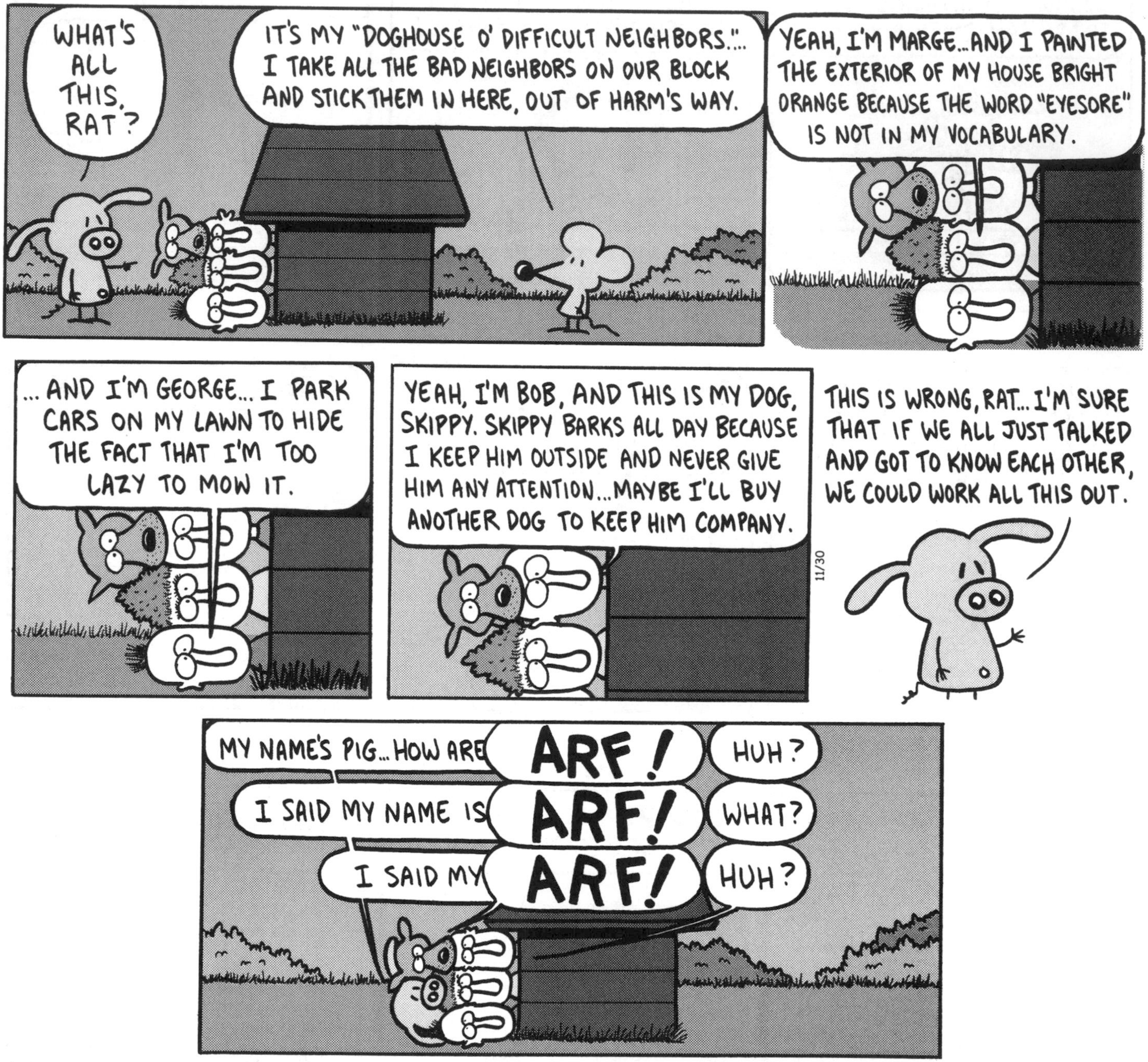
WHAT'S ALL THIS, RAT?
IT'S MY "DOGHOUSE O' DIFFICULT NEIGHBORS."... I TAKE ALL THE BAD NEIGHBORS ON OUR BLOCK AND STICK THEM IN HERE, OUT OF HARM'S WAY.
YEAH, I'M MARGE...AND I PAINTED THE EXTERIOR OF MY HOUSE BRIGHT ORANGE BECAUSE THE WORD "EYESORE" IS NOT IN MY VOCABULARY.
... AND I'M GEORGE... I PARK CARS ON MY LAWN TO HIDE THE FACT THAT I'M TOO LAZY TO MOW IT.
YEAH, I'M BOB, AND THIS IS MY DOG, SKIPPY. SKIPPY BARKS ALL DAY BECAUSE I KEEP HIM OUTSIDE AND NEVER GIVE HIM ANY ATTENTION...MAYBE I'LL BUY ANOTHER DOG TO KEEP HIM COMPANY.
11/30
THIS IS WRONG, RAT... I'M SURE THAT IF WE ALL JUST TALKED AND GOT TO KNOW EACH OTHER, WE COULD WORK ALL THIS OUT.
MY NAME'S PIG... HOW ARE
ARF!
HUH?
I SAID MY NAME IS
ARF!
WHAT?
I SAID MY
ARF!
HUH?

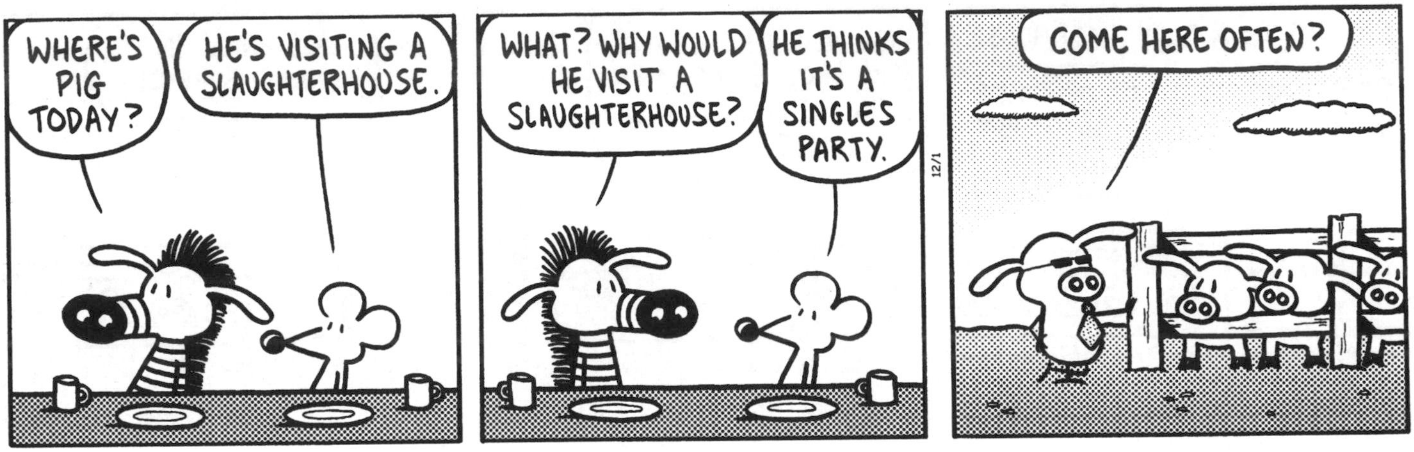
WHERE'S PIG TODAY?
HE'S VISITING A SLAUGHTERHOUSE.
WHAT? WHY WOULD HE VISIT A SLAUGHTERHOUSE?
HE THINKS IT'S A SINGLES PARTY.
12/1
COME HERE OFTEN?

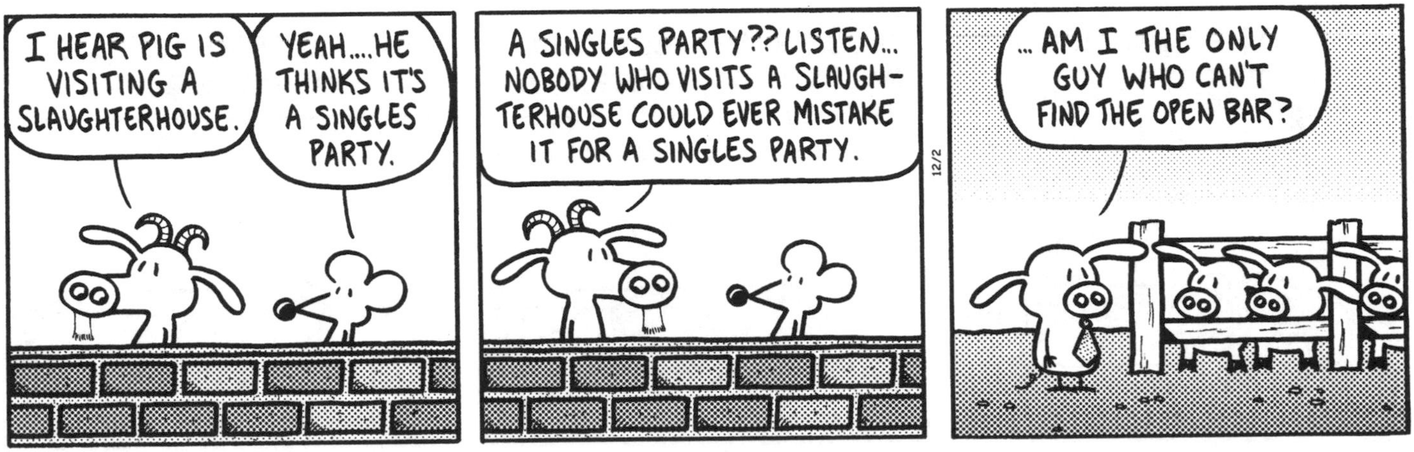
I HEAR PIG IS VISITING A SLAUGHTERHOUSE.
YEAH....HE THINKS IT'S A SINGLES PARTY.
A SINGLES PARTY?? LISTEN... NOBODY WHO VISITS A SLAUGH-TERHOUSE COULD EVER MISTAKE IT FOR A SINGLES PARTY.
12/2
... AM I THE ONLY GUY WHO CAN'T FIND THE OPEN BAR?

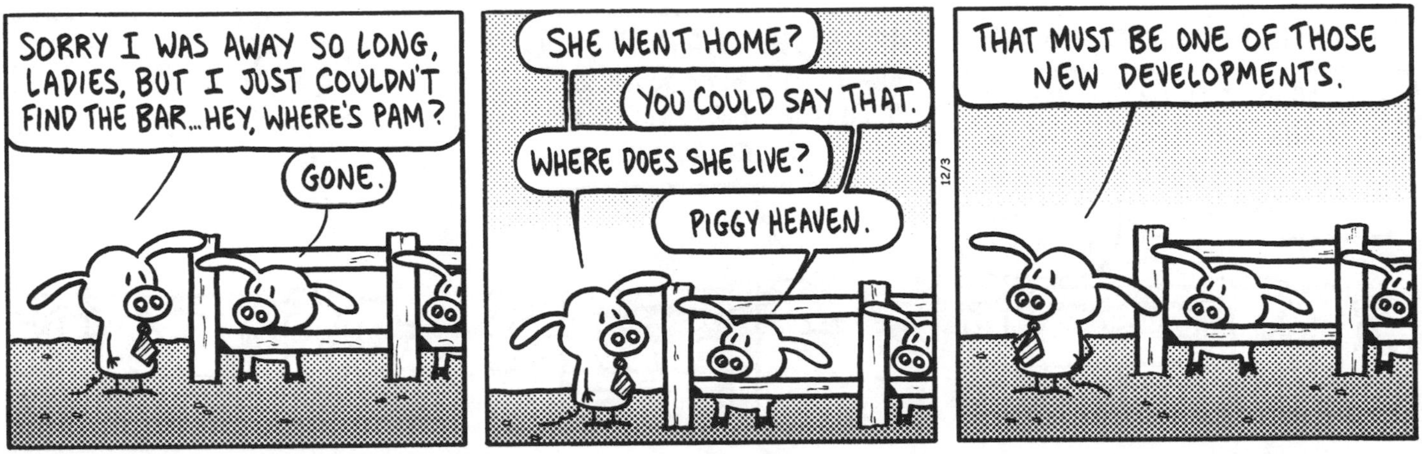
SORRY I WAS AWAY SO LONG, LADIES, BUT I JUST COULDN'T FIND THE BAR... HEY, WHERE'S PAM?
GONE.
SHE WENT HOME?
YOU COULD SAY THAT.
WHERE DOES SHE LIVE?
PIGGY HEAVEN.
12/3
THAT MUST BE ONE OF THOSE NEW DEVELOPMENTS.

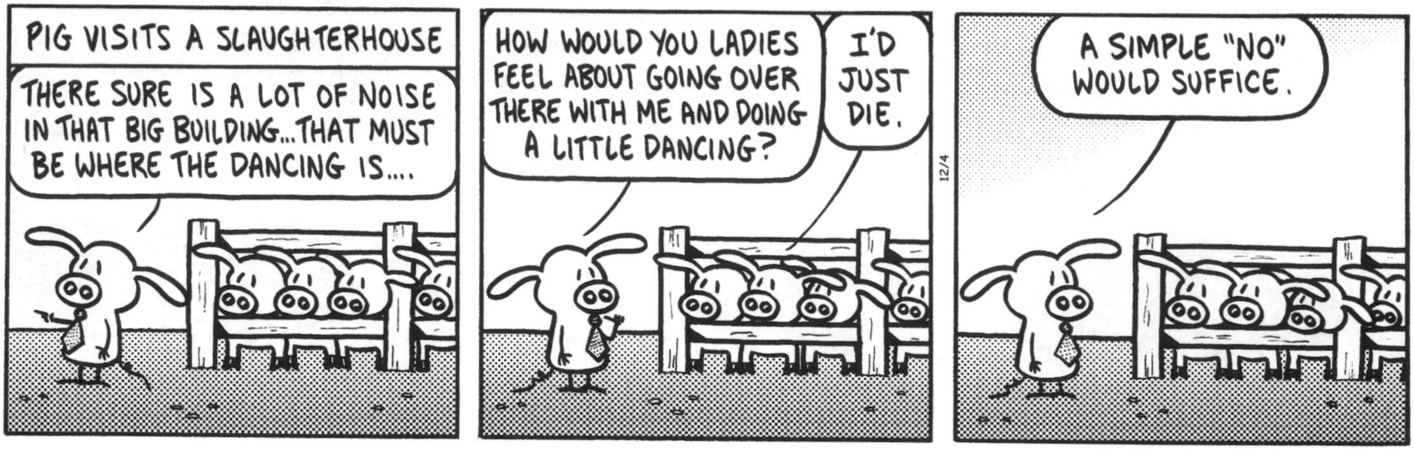
PIG VISITS A SLAUGHTERHOUSE
THERE SURE IS A LOT OF NOISE IN THAT BIG BUILDING...THAT MUST BE WHERE THE DANCING IS....
HOW WOULD YOU LADIES FEEL ABOUT GOING OVER THERE WITH ME AND DOING A LITTLE DANCING?
I'D JUST DIE.
12/4
A SIMPLE "NO" WOULD SUFFICE.

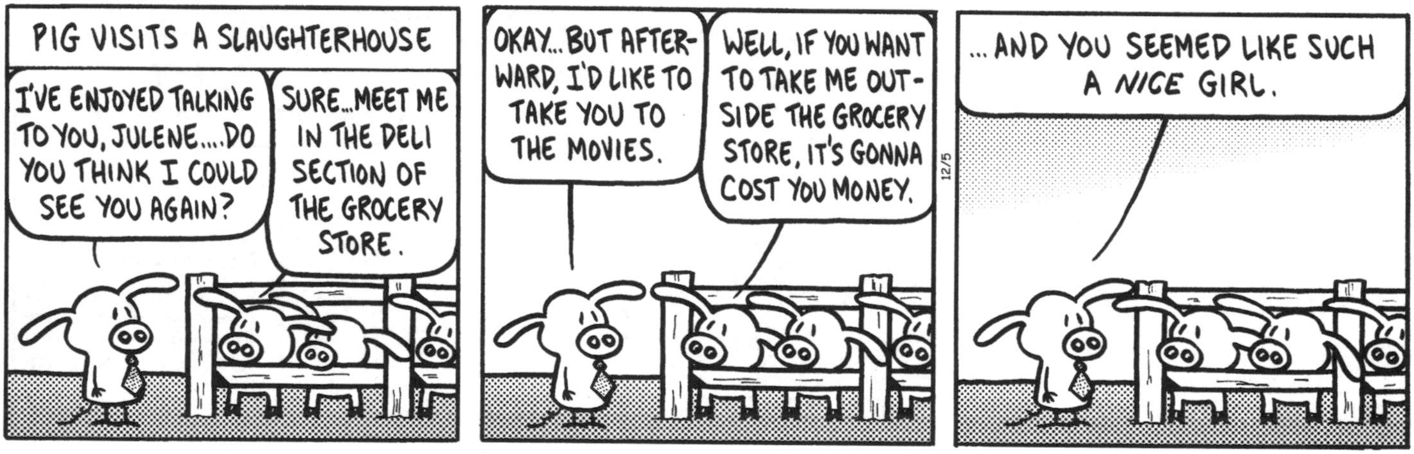
PIG VISITS A SLAUGHTERHOUSE
I'VE ENJOYED TALKING TO YOU, JULENE....DO YOU THINK I COULD SEE YOU AGAIN?
SURE...MEET ME IN THE DELI SECTION OF THE GROCERY STORE.
OKAY...BUT AFTERWARD, I'D LIKE TO TAKE YOU TO THE MOVIES.
WELL, IF YOU WANT TO TAKE ME OUTSIDE THE GROCERY STORE, IT'S GONNA COST YOU MONEY.
12/5
...AND YOU SEEMED LIKE SUCH A *NICE* GIRL.

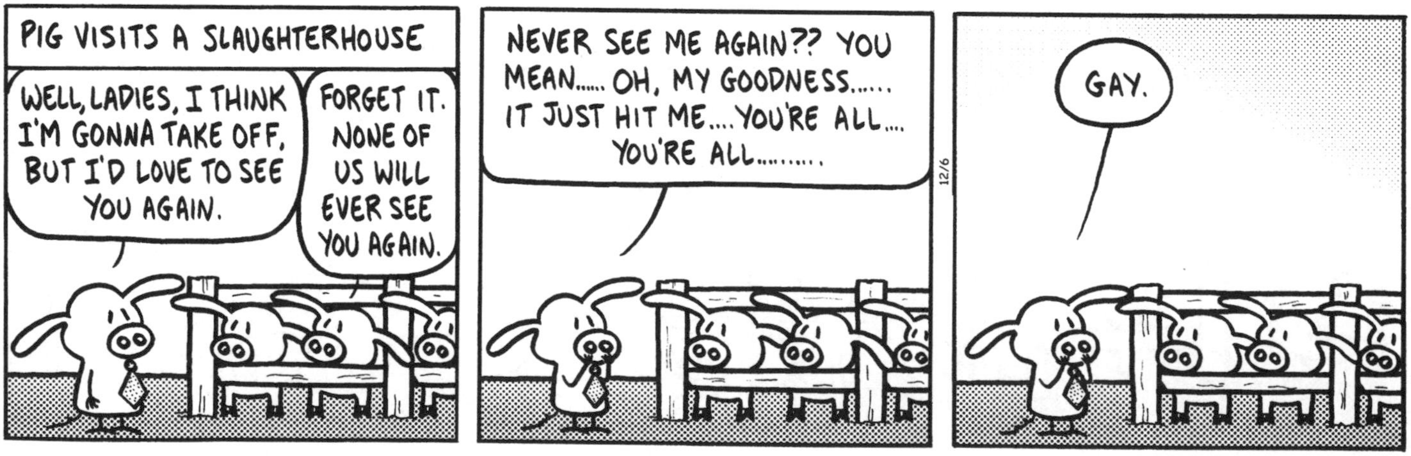
PIG VISITS A SLAUGHTERHOUSE
WELL, LADIES, I THINK I'M GONNA TAKE OFF, BUT I'D LOVE TO SEE YOU AGAIN.
FORGET IT. NONE OF US WILL EVER SEE YOU AGAIN.
NEVER SEE ME AGAIN?? YOU MEAN...... OH, MY GOODNESS...... IT JUST HIT ME.... YOU'RE ALL.... YOU'RE ALL..........
12/6
GAY.

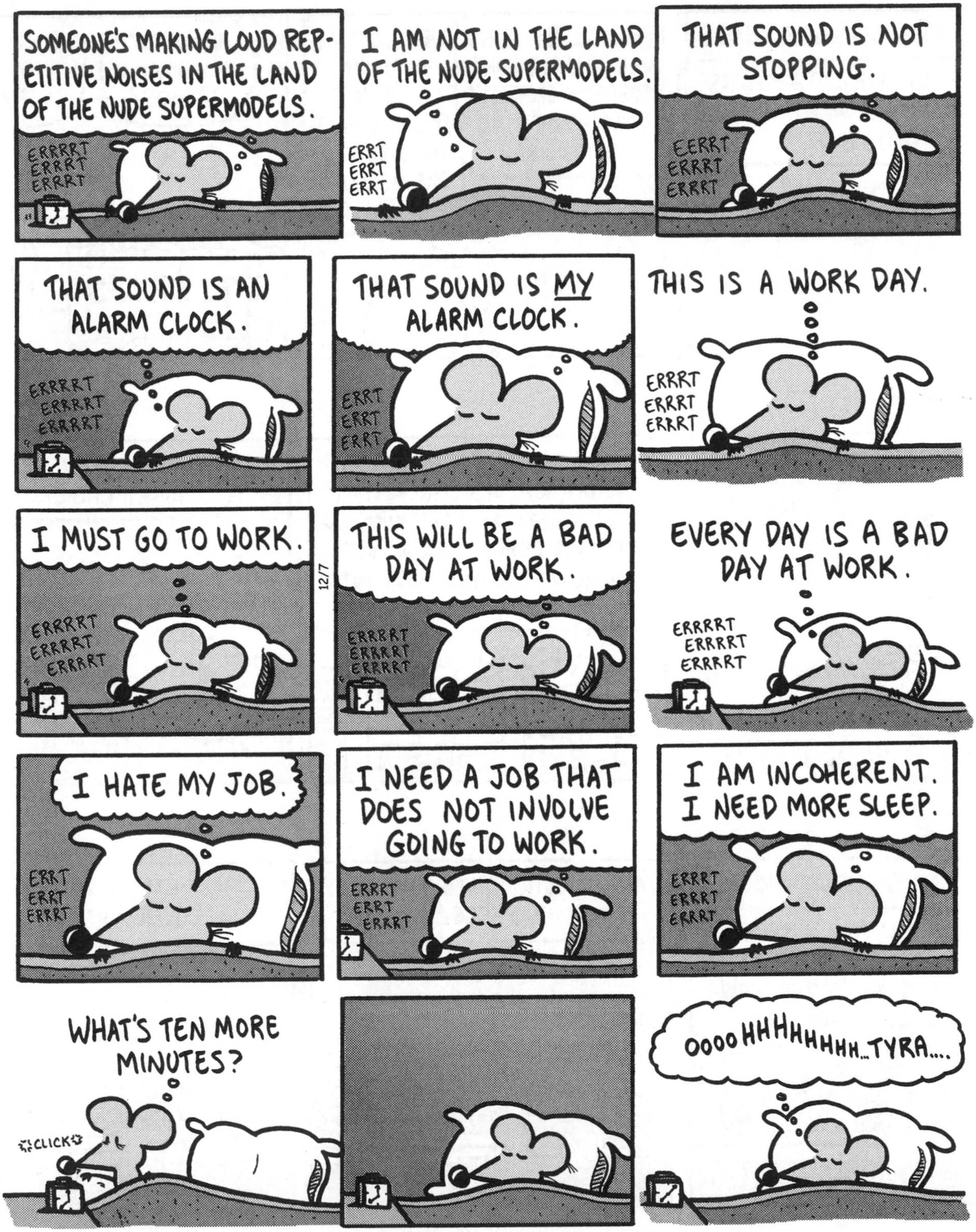

SOMEONE'S MAKING LOUD REPETITIVE NOISES IN THE LAND OF THE NUDE SUPERMODELS.
ERRRRT ERRRT ERRRT
I AM NOT IN THE LAND OF THE NUDE SUPERMODELS.
ERRT ERRT ERRT
THAT SOUND IS NOT STOPPING.
EERRT ERRRT ERRRT
THAT SOUND IS AN ALARM CLOCK.
ERRRRT ERRRRT ERRRRT
THAT SOUND IS MY ALARM CLOCK.
ERRT ERRT ERRT
THIS IS A WORK DAY.
ERRRT ERRRT ERRRT
I MUST GO TO WORK.
ERRRRT ERRRRT ERRRRT
12/7
THIS WILL BE A BAD DAY AT WORK.
ERRRRT ERRRRT ERRRRT
EVERY DAY IS A BAD DAY AT WORK.
ERRRRT ERRRRT ERRRRT
I HATE MY JOB.
ERRT ERRT ERRRT
I NEED A JOB THAT DOES NOT INVOLVE GOING TO WORK.
ERRRT ERRT ERRRT
I AM INCOHERENT. I NEED MORE SLEEP.
ERRRT ERRRT ERRRT
WHAT'S TEN MORE MINUTES?
CLICK
OOOOHHHHHHHH...TYRA....

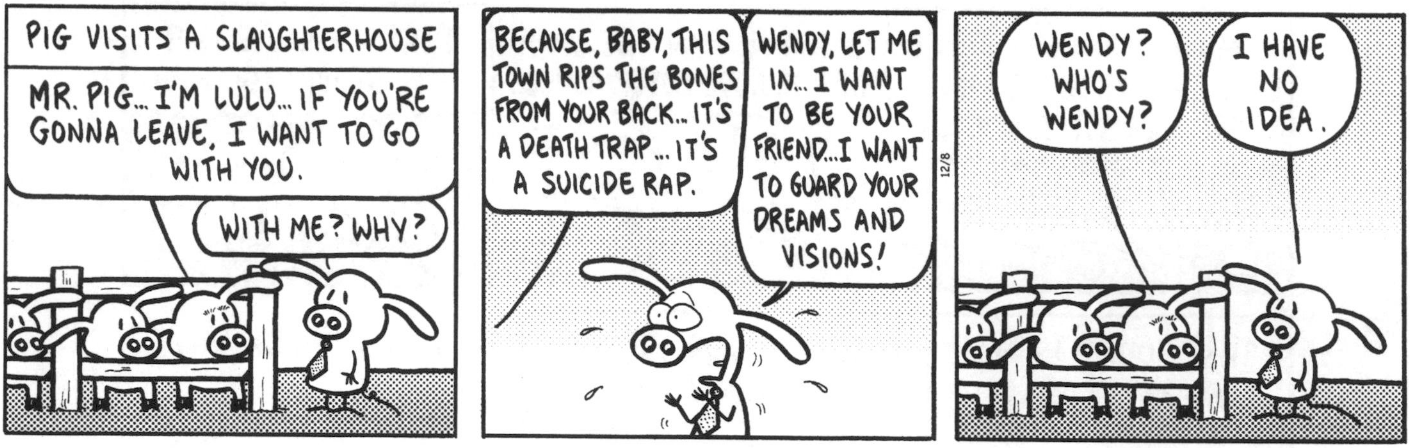
PIG VISITS A SLAUGHTERHOUSE
MR. PIG... I'M LULU... IF YOU'RE GONNA LEAVE, I WANT TO GO WITH YOU.
WITH ME? WHY?
BECAUSE, BABY, THIS TOWN RIPS THE BONES FROM YOUR BACK.. IT'S A DEATH TRAP... IT'S A SUICIDE RAP.
WENDY, LET ME IN... I WANT TO BE YOUR FRIEND...I WANT TO GUARD YOUR DREAMS AND VISIONS!
12/8
WENDY? WHO'S WENDY?
I HAVE NO IDEA.

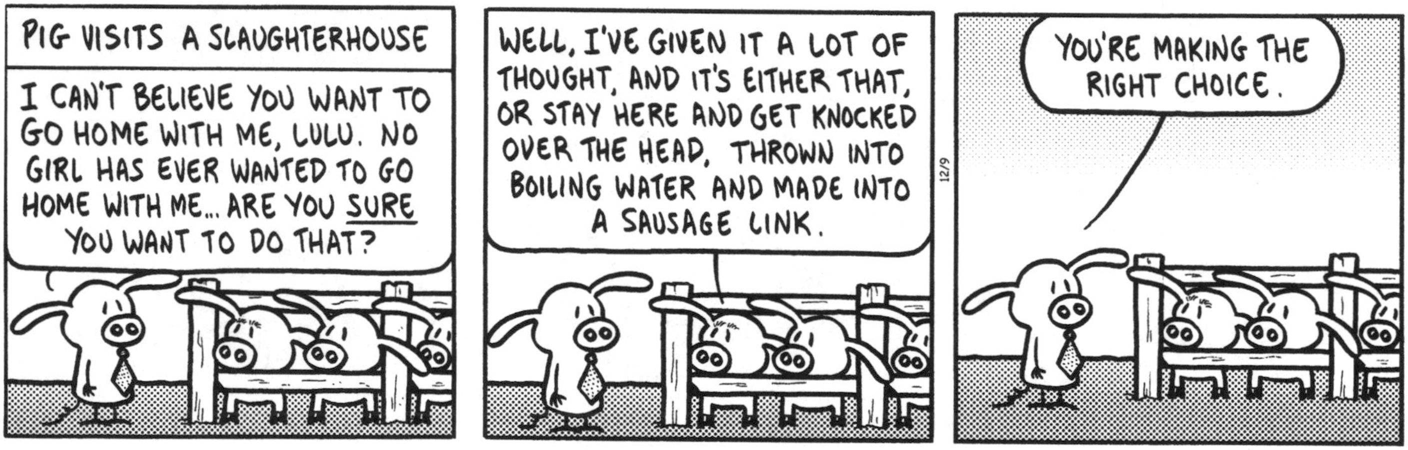
PIG VISITS A SLAUGHTERHOUSE
I CAN'T BELIEVE YOU WANT TO GO HOME WITH ME, LULU. NO GIRL HAS EVER WANTED TO GO HOME WITH ME... ARE YOU SURE YOU WANT TO DO THAT?
WELL, I'VE GIVEN IT A LOT OF THOUGHT, AND IT'S EITHER THAT, OR STAY HERE AND GET KNOCKED OVER THE HEAD, THROWN INTO BOILING WATER AND MADE INTO A SAUSAGE LINK.
12/9
YOU'RE MAKING THE RIGHT CHOICE.

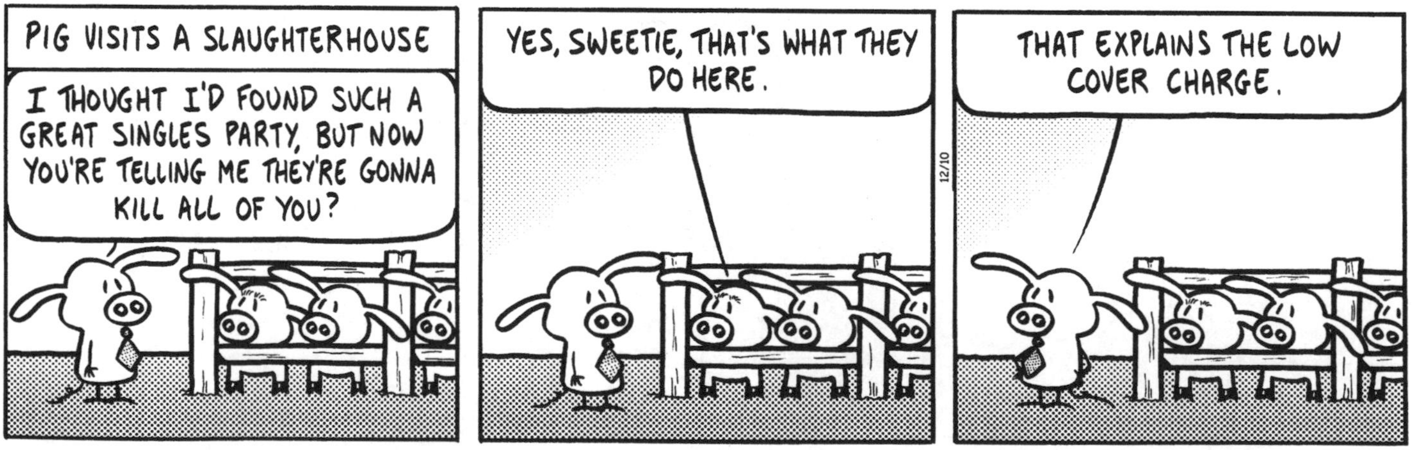
PIG VISITS A SLAUGHTERHOUSE
I THOUGHT I'D FOUND SUCH A GREAT SINGLES PARTY, BUT NOW YOU'RE TELLING ME THEY'RE GONNA KILL ALL OF YOU?
YES, SWEETIE, THAT'S WHAT THEY DO HERE.
12/10
THAT EXPLAINS THE LOW COVER CHARGE.

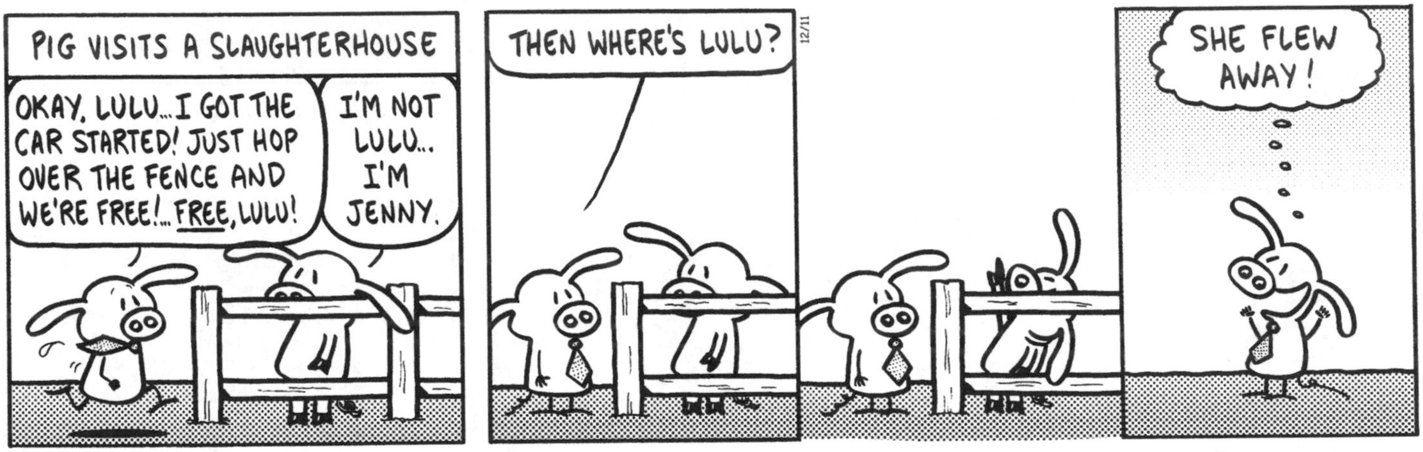
PIG VISITS A SLAUGHTERHOUSE
OKAY, LULU... I GOT THE CAR STARTED! JUST HOP OVER THE FENCE AND WE'RE FREE!... FREE, LULU!
I'M NOT LULU... I'M JENNY.
THEN WHERE'S LULU?
12/11
SHE FLEW AWAY!

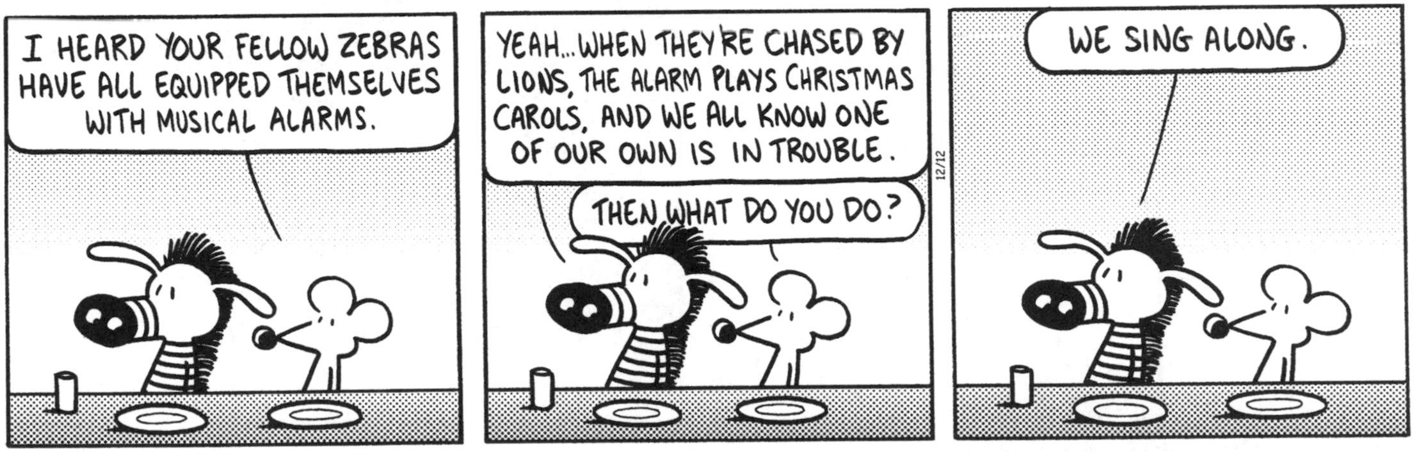
I HEARD YOUR FELLOW ZEBRAS HAVE ALL EQUIPPED THEMSELVES WITH MUSICAL ALARMS.
YEAH... WHEN THEY'RE CHASED BY LIONS, THE ALARM PLAYS CHRISTMAS CAROLS, AND WE ALL KNOW ONE OF OUR OWN IS IN TROUBLE.
THEN WHAT DO YOU DO?
12/12
WE SING ALONG.

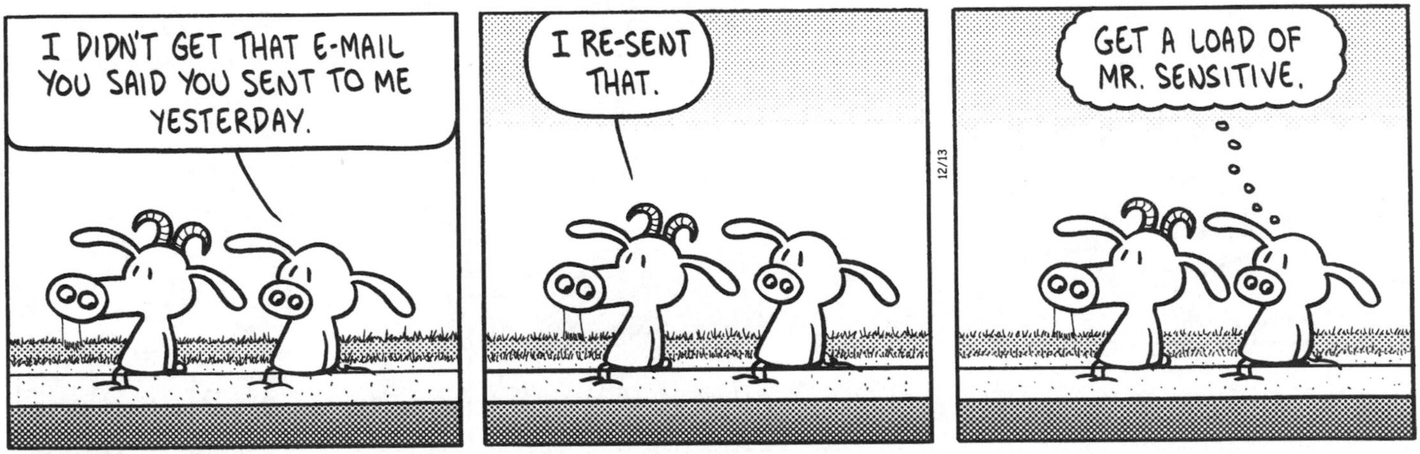
I DIDN'T GET THAT E-MAIL YOU SAID YOU SENT TO ME YESTERDAY.
I RE-SENT THAT.
12/13
GET A LOAD OF MR. SENSITIVE.

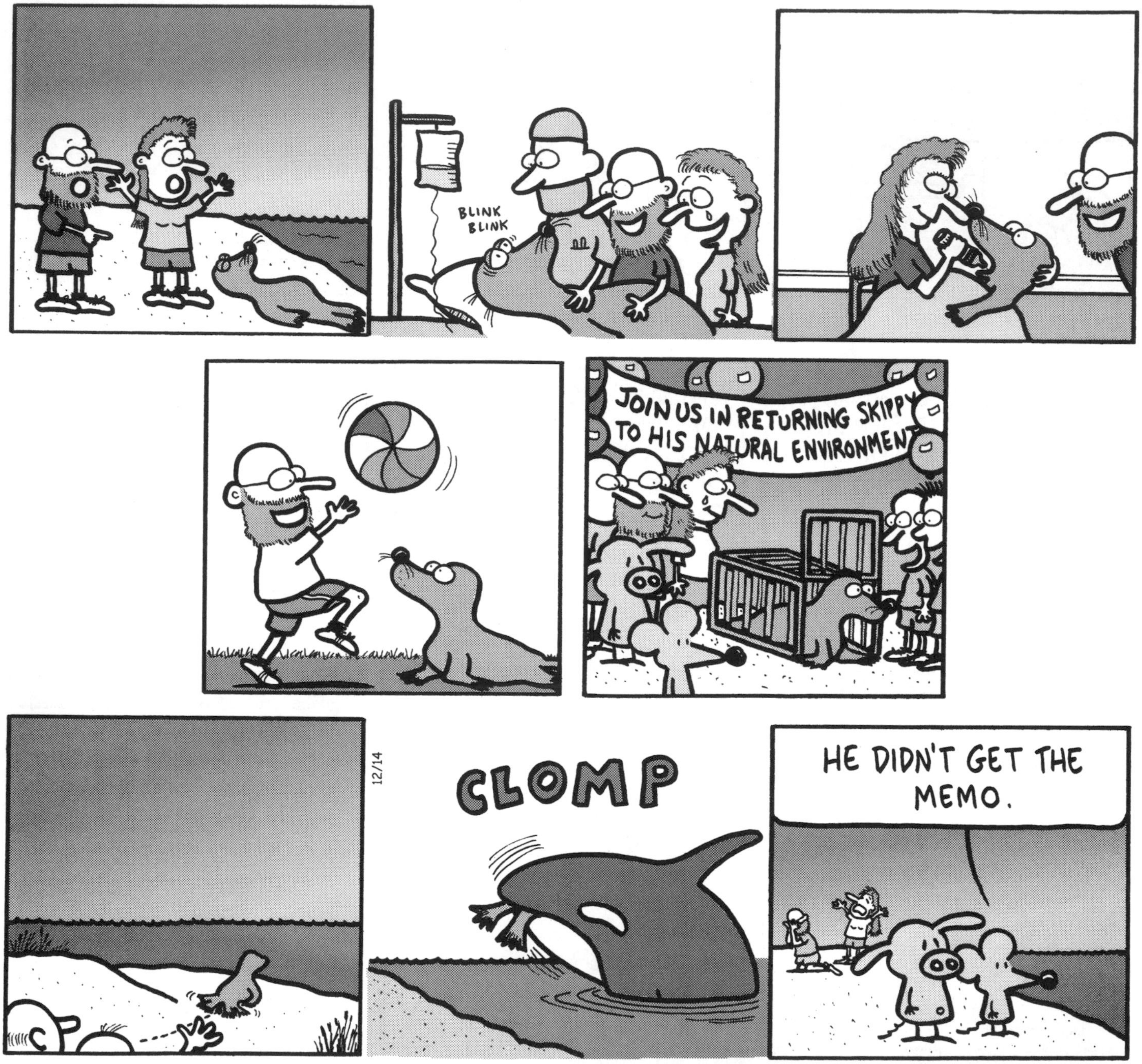

BLINK
BLINK
JOIN US IN RETURNING SKIPPY TO HIS NATURAL ENVIRONMENT
12/14
CLOMP
HE DIDN'T GET THE MEMO.

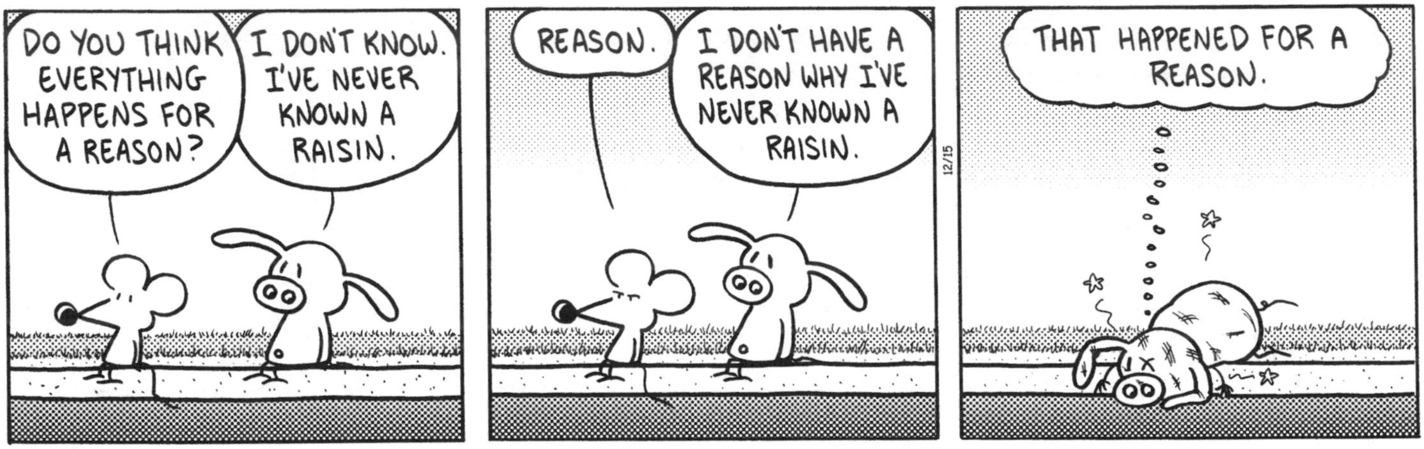
DO YOU THINK EVERYTHING HAPPENS FOR A REASON?
I DON'T KNOW. I'VE NEVER KNOWN A RAISIN.
REASON.
I DON'T HAVE A REASON WHY I'VE NEVER KNOWN A RAISIN.
12/15
THAT HAPPENED FOR A REASON.

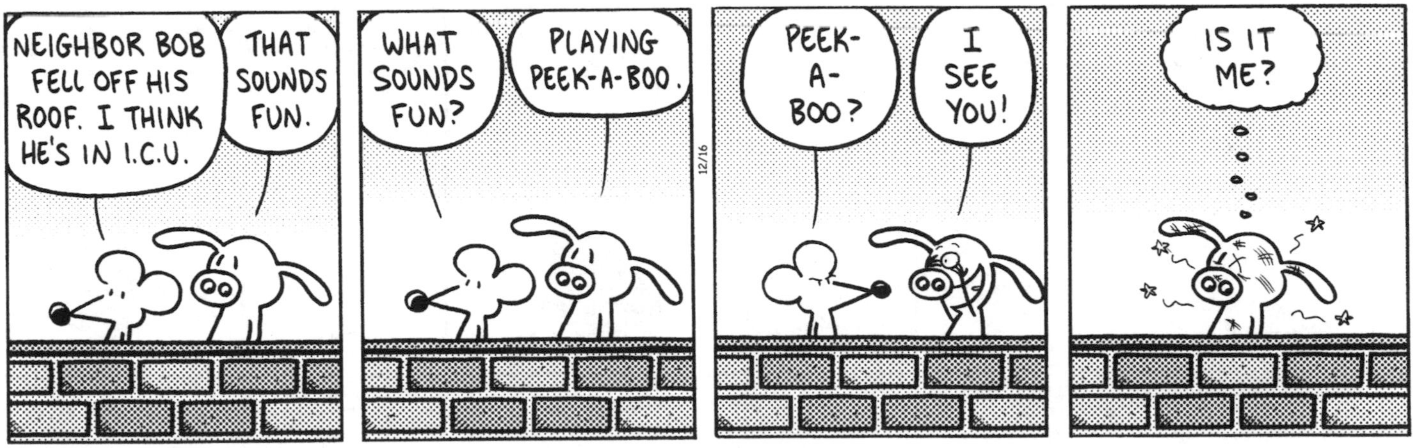
NEIGHBOR BOB FELL OFF HIS ROOF. I THINK HE'S IN I.C.U.
THAT SOUNDS FUN.
WHAT SOUNDS FUN?
PLAYING PEEK-A-BOO.
12/16
PEEK-A-BOO?
I SEE YOU!
IS IT ME?

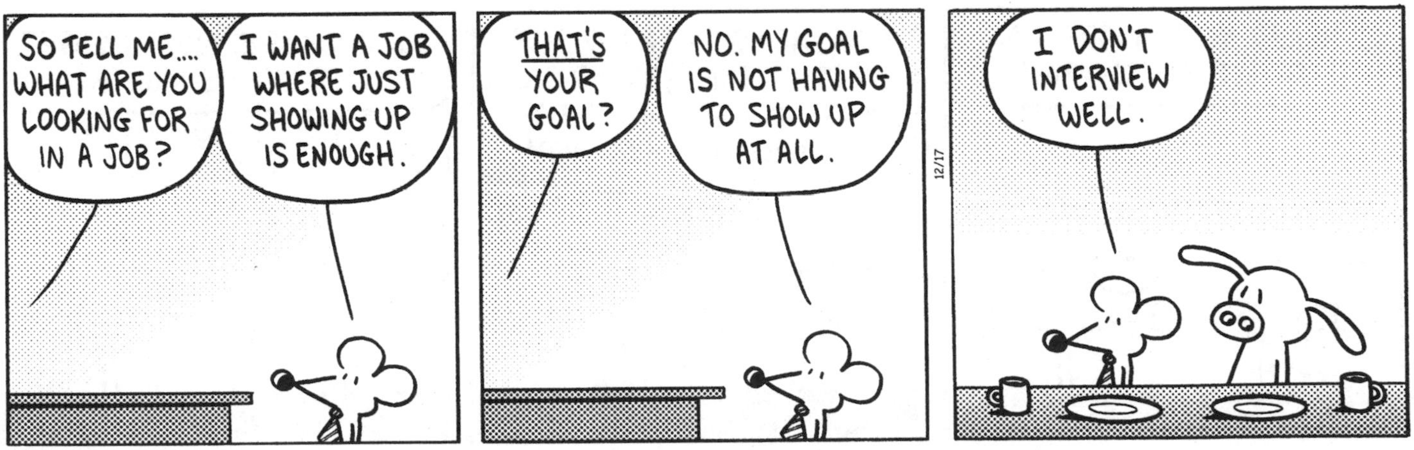
SO TELL ME.... WHAT ARE YOU LOOKING FOR IN A JOB?
I WANT A JOB WHERE JUST SHOWING UP IS ENOUGH.
THAT'S YOUR GOAL?
NO. MY GOAL IS NOT HAVING TO SHOW UP AT ALL.
12/17
I DON'T INTERVIEW WELL.

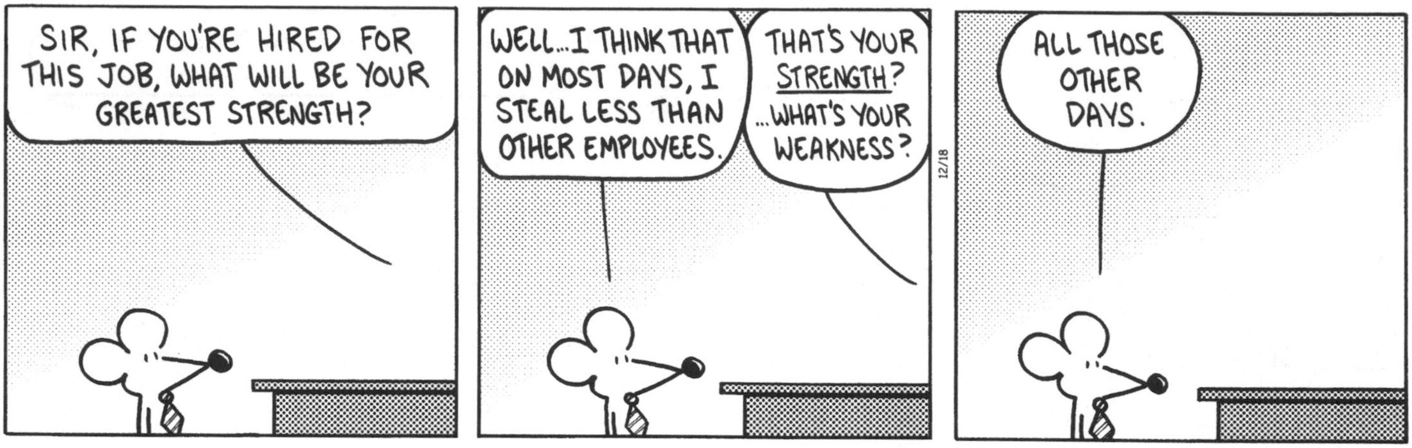
SIR, IF YOU'RE HIRED FOR THIS JOB, WHAT WILL BE YOUR GREATEST STRENGTH?
WELL...I THINK THAT ON MOST DAYS, I STEAL LESS THAN OTHER EMPLOYEES.
THAT'S YOUR STRENGTH? ...WHAT'S YOUR WEAKNESS?
12/18
ALL THOSE OTHER DAYS.

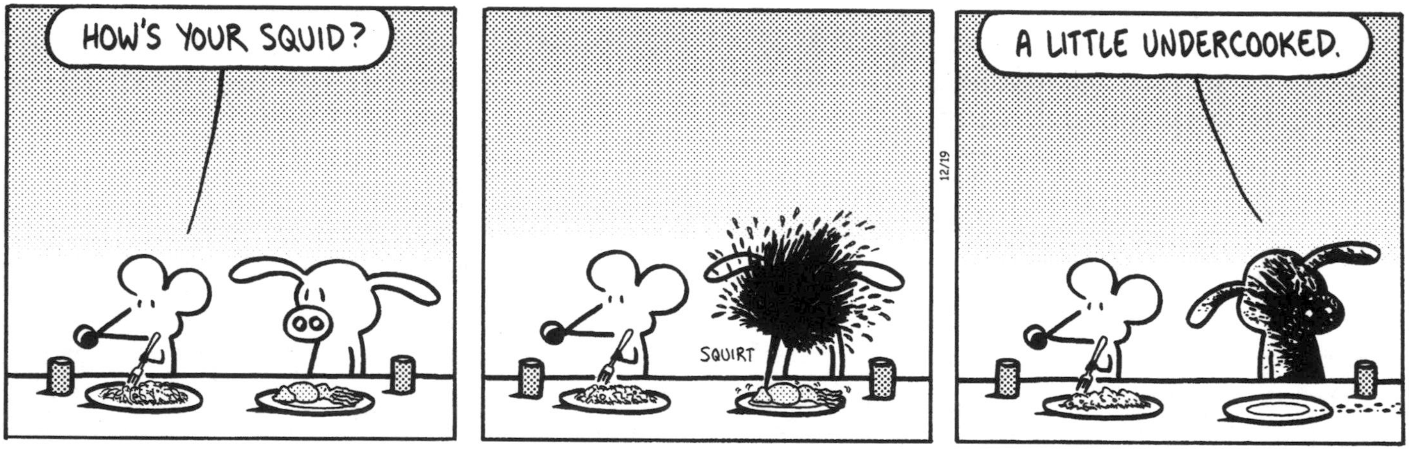
HOW'S YOUR SQUID?
SQUIRT
12/19
A LITTLE UNDERCOOKED.

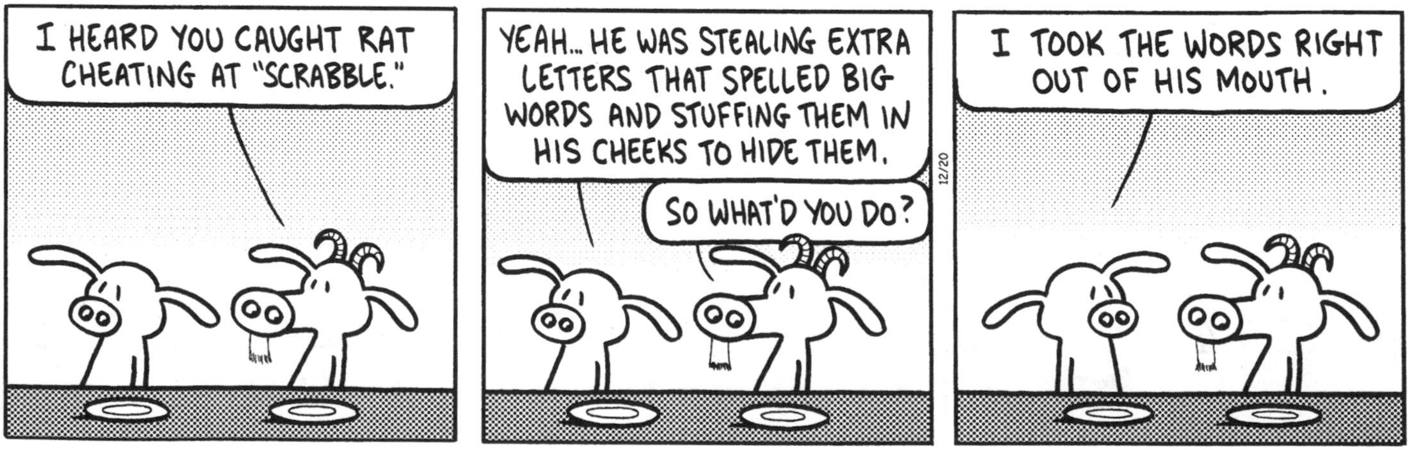
I HEARD YOU CAUGHT RAT CHEATING AT "SCRABBLE."
YEAH... HE WAS STEALING EXTRA LETTERS THAT SPELLED BIG WORDS AND STUFFING THEM IN HIS CHEEKS TO HIDE THEM.
SO WHAT'D YOU DO?
12/20
I TOOK THE WORDS RIGHT OUT OF HIS MOUTH.

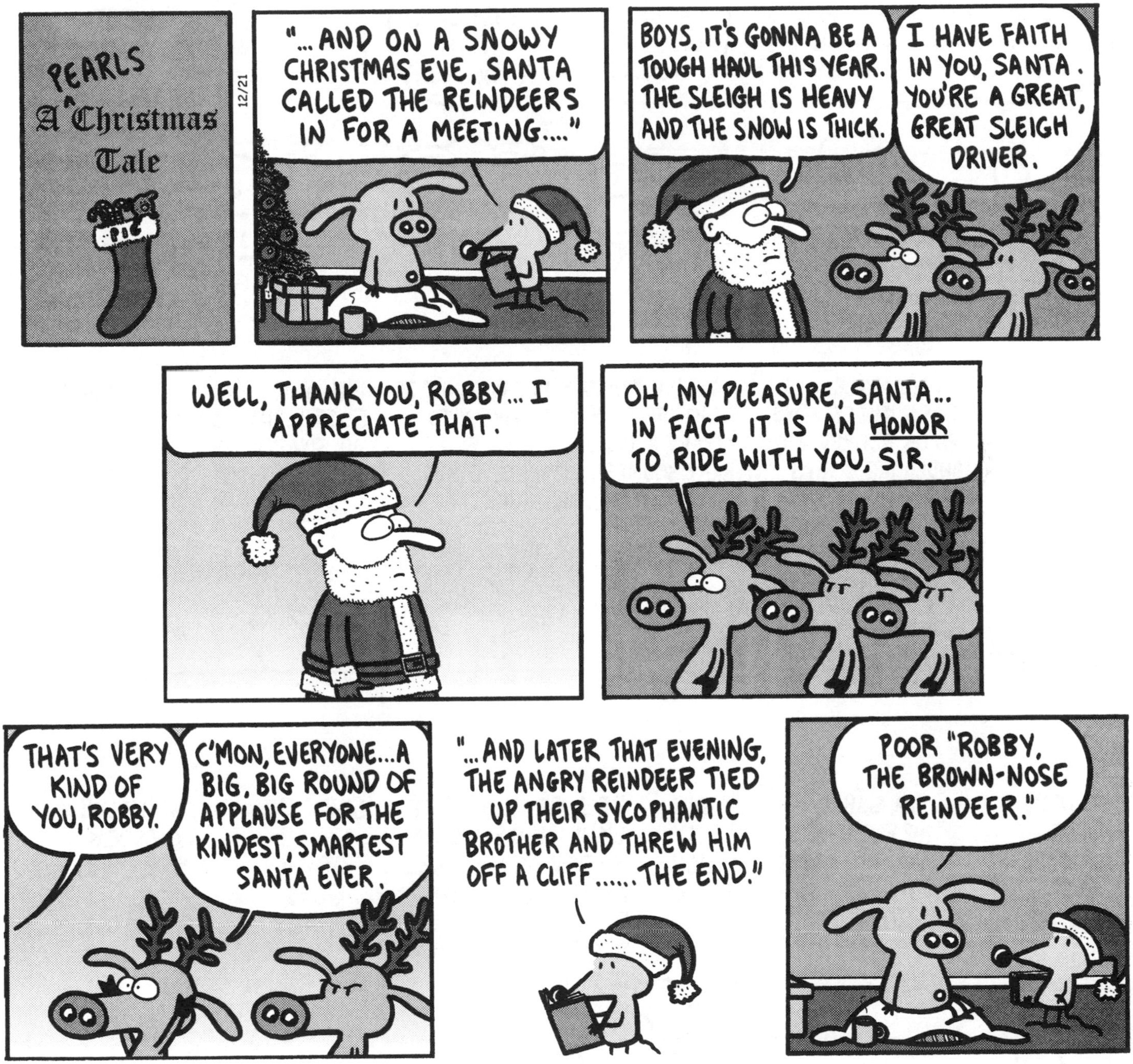
PEARLS
A Christmas Tale
PIG
12/21
"... AND ON A SNOWY CHRISTMAS EVE, SANTA CALLED THE REINDEERS IN FOR A MEETING...."
BOYS, IT'S GONNA BE A TOUGH HAUL THIS YEAR. THE SLEIGH IS HEAVY AND THE SNOW IS THICK.
I HAVE FAITH IN YOU, SANTA. YOU'RE A GREAT, GREAT SLEIGH DRIVER.
WELL, THANK YOU, ROBBY... I APPRECIATE THAT.
OH, MY PLEASURE, SANTA... IN FACT, IT IS AN HONOR TO RIDE WITH YOU, SIR.
THAT'S VERY KIND OF YOU, ROBBY.
C'MON, EVERYONE...A BIG, BIG ROUND OF APPLAUSE FOR THE KINDEST, SMARTEST SANTA EVER.
"... AND LATER THAT EVENING, THE ANGRY REINDEER TIED UP THEIR SYCOPHANTIC BROTHER AND THREW HIM OFF A CLIFF...... THE END."
POOR "ROBBY, THE BROWN-NOSE REINDEER."

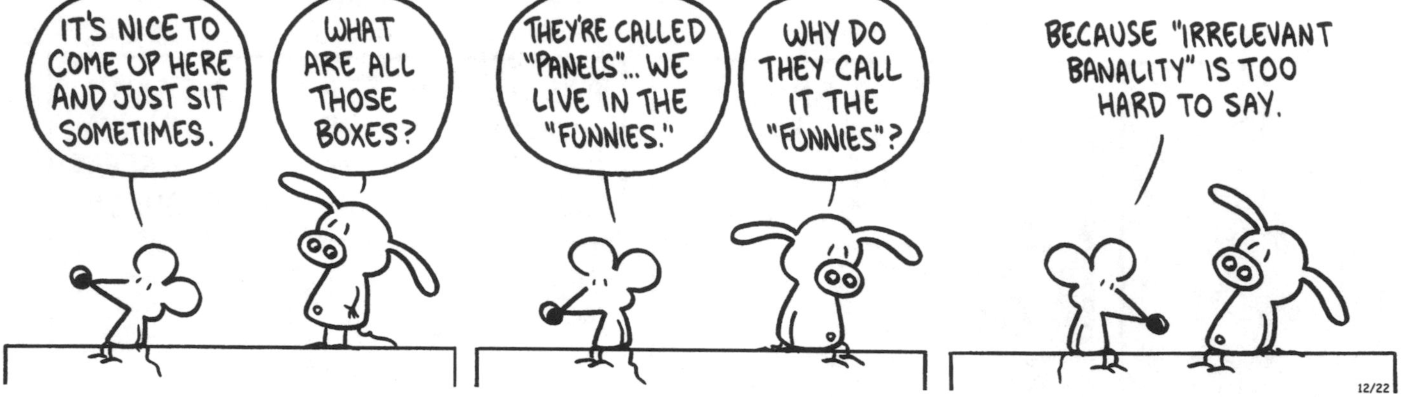
IT'S NICE TO COME UP HERE AND JUST SIT SOMETIMES.
WHAT ARE ALL THOSE BOXES?
THEY'RE CALLED "PANELS"... WE LIVE IN THE "FUNNIES."
WHY DO THEY CALL IT THE "FUNNIES"?
BECAUSE "IRRELEVANT BANALITY" IS TOO HARD TO SAY.
12/22

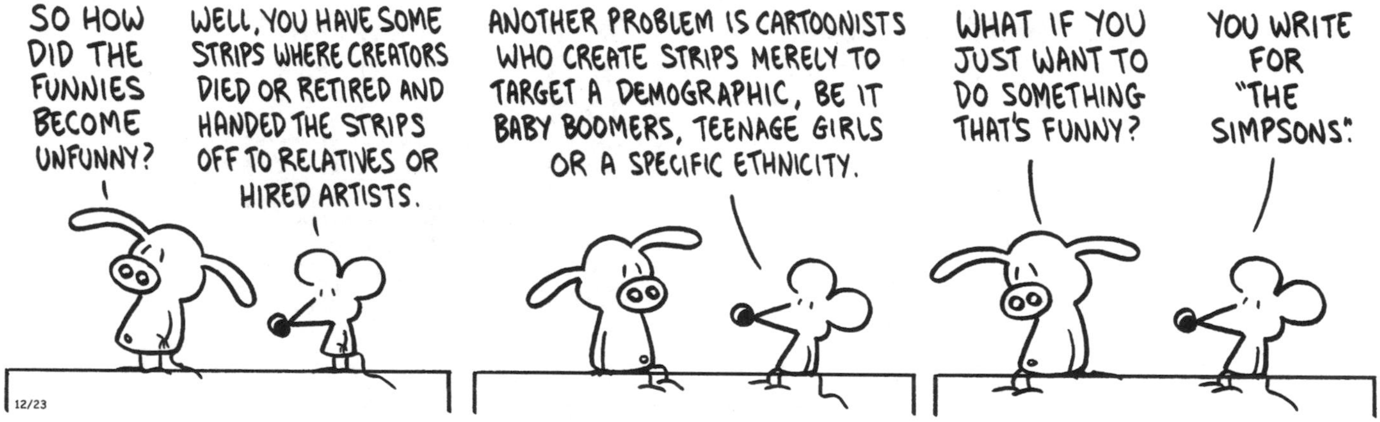
SO HOW DID THE FUNNIES BECOME UNFUNNY?
WELL, YOU HAVE SOME STRIPS WHERE CREATORS DIED OR RETIRED AND HANDED THE STRIPS OFF TO RELATIVES OR HIRED ARTISTS.
12/23
ANOTHER PROBLEM IS CARTOONISTS WHO CREATE STRIPS MERELY TO TARGET A DEMOGRAPHIC, BE IT BABY BOOMERS, TEENAGE GIRLS OR A SPECIFIC ETHNICITY.
WHAT IF YOU JUST WANT TO DO SOMETHING THAT'S FUNNY?
YOU WRITE FOR "THE SIMPSONS."

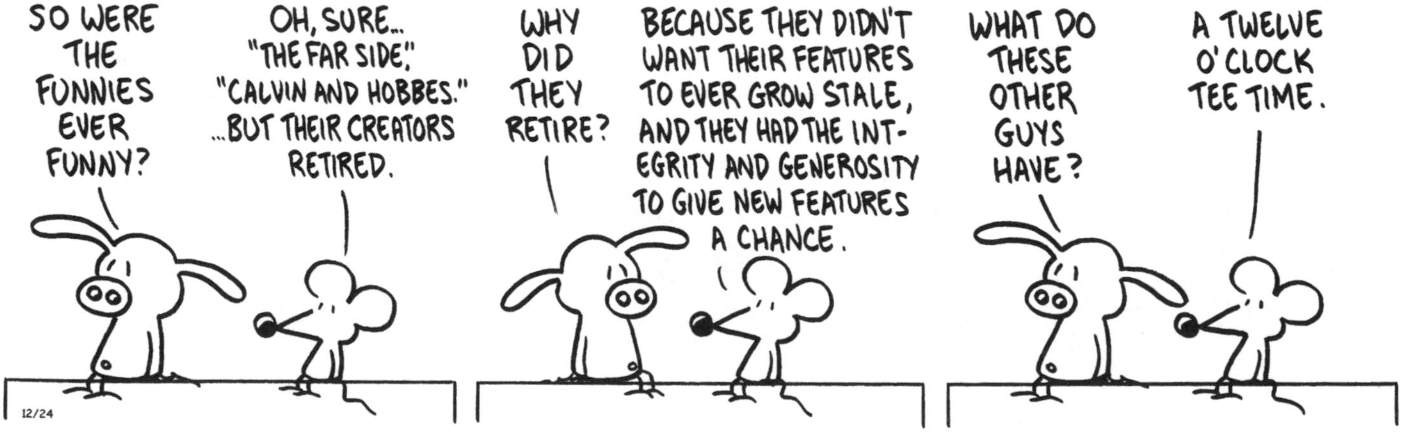
SO WERE THE FUNNIES EVER FUNNY?
OH, SURE... "THE FAR SIDE," "CALVIN AND HOBBES." ...BUT THEIR CREATORS RETIRED.
12/24
WHY DID THEY RETIRE?
BECAUSE THEY DIDN'T WANT THEIR FEATURES TO EVER GROW STALE, AND THEY HAD THE INTEGRITY AND GENEROSITY TO GIVE NEW FEATURES A CHANCE.
WHAT DO THESE OTHER GUYS HAVE?
A TWELVE O'CLOCK TEE TIME.

Panel 1: SO ARE THERE ANY OTHER REASONS THE FUNNIES AREN'T FUNNY?

SURE...UNLIKE IN ALL OTHER FORMS OF ENTERTAINMENT, THE CENSORSHIP CODE FOR COMICS REMAINS STUCK IN THE 1950's.

Panel 2: HOW DO YOU MEAN?

WELL, IN THE COMICS, YOU CAN'T MENTION THE SUBJECTS OF ██ OR ████ AND YOU CAN'T SAY THE WORDS "████" OR "████", DESPITE THE FACT THEY'RE SAID DAILY ON PRIME-TIME T.V.

Panel 3: GEE... THAT'S ████ED.

HEY, NOW.

12/25

Panel 1: LOOKING AT THESE COMICS IS TOO DEPRESSING...I'M GOING OFF TO FIND GARY LARSON.

BUT I THOUGHT YOU SAID HE NO LONGER WANTED TO DRAW "THE FAR SIDE" BECAUSE—

Panel 2: OH, FORGET WHAT I SAID!!...THESE ARE DESPERATE TIMES! I'M SURE THAT IF I CAN JUST SIT DOWN AND TALK TO HIM FOR A FEW MINUTES, I CAN CONVINCE HIM TO COME BACK...

Panel 3 (inset comic): "...And what makes you think he lives here?"

12/26

Panel 1: I THOUGHT YOU WENT TO FIND GARY LARSON.

I COULDN'T GET BY HIS SECURITY COWS. I GUESS THE FUNNIES ARE JUST DOOMED.

Panel 2: WELL, I WAS THINKING...MAYBE WE COULD DO OUR OWN COMIC STRIP ABOUT THESE NAMELESS STICK-FIGURE ANIMALS WHO NEVER MOVE OR SHOW EXPRESSION, AND ALWAYS TALK ABOUT DEATH...

Panel 3: ...I'D JUMP, BUT I'M AFRAID I'D CRUSH "DEAR ABBY."

12/27

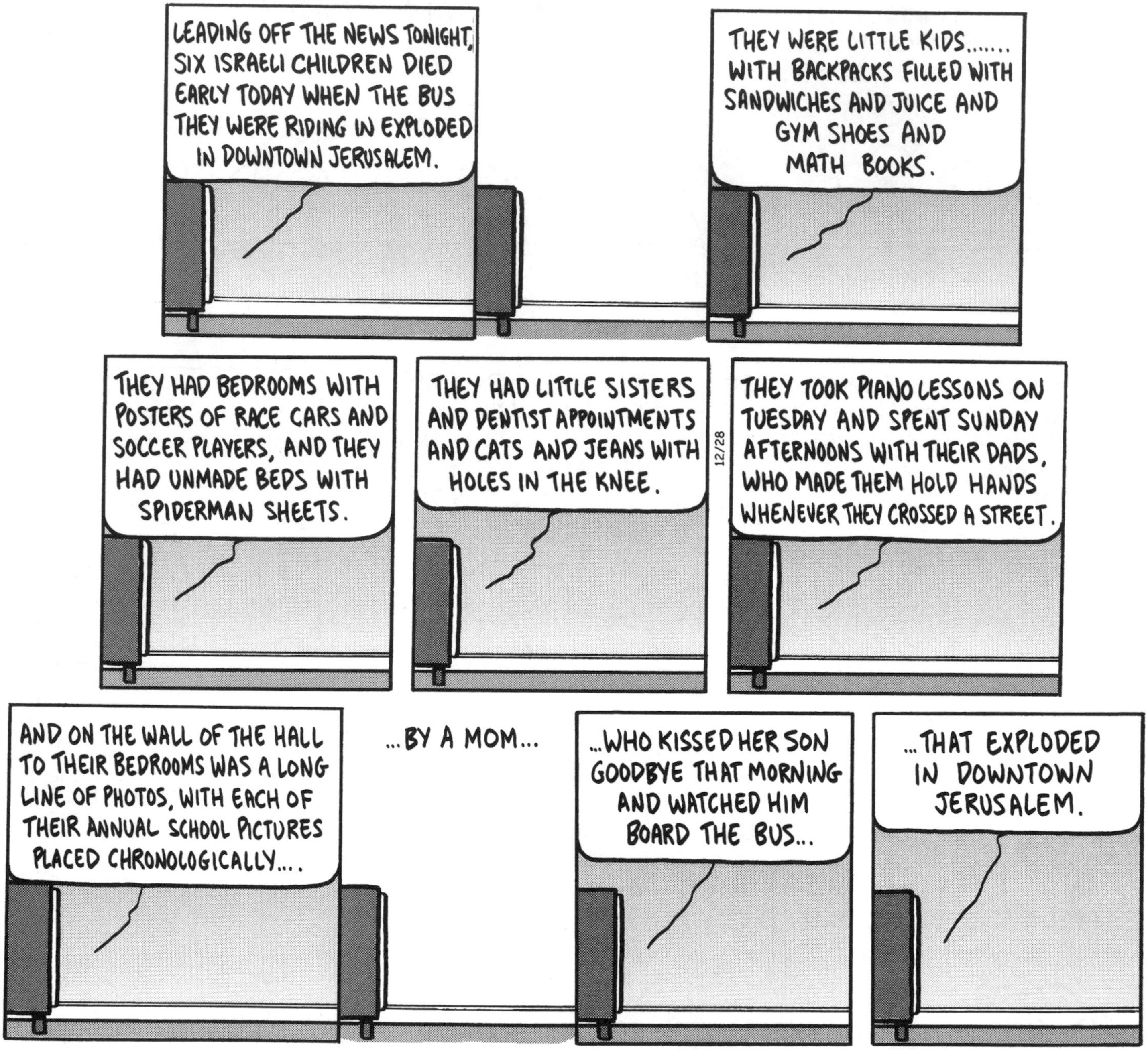
LEADING OFF THE NEWS TONIGHT, SIX ISRAELI CHILDREN DIED EARLY TODAY WHEN THE BUS THEY WERE RIDING IN EXPLODED IN DOWNTOWN JERUSALEM.
THEY WERE LITTLE KIDS....... WITH BACKPACKS FILLED WITH SANDWICHES AND JUICE AND GYM SHOES AND MATH BOOKS.
THEY HAD BEDROOMS WITH POSTERS OF RACE CARS AND SOCCER PLAYERS, AND THEY HAD UNMADE BEDS WITH SPIDERMAN SHEETS.
THEY HAD LITTLE SISTERS AND DENTIST APPOINTMENTS AND CATS AND JEANS WITH HOLES IN THE KNEE.
12/28
THEY TOOK PIANO LESSONS ON TUESDAY AND SPENT SUNDAY AFTERNOONS WITH THEIR DADS, WHO MADE THEM HOLD HANDS WHENEVER THEY CROSSED A STREET.
AND ON THE WALL OF THE HALL TO THEIR BEDROOMS WAS A LONG LINE OF PHOTOS, WITH EACH OF THEIR ANNUAL SCHOOL PICTURES PLACED CHRONOLOGICALLY....
...BY A MOM...
...WHO KISSED HER SON GOODBYE THAT MORNING AND WATCHED HIM BOARD THE BUS...
...THAT EXPLODED IN DOWNTOWN JERUSALEM.

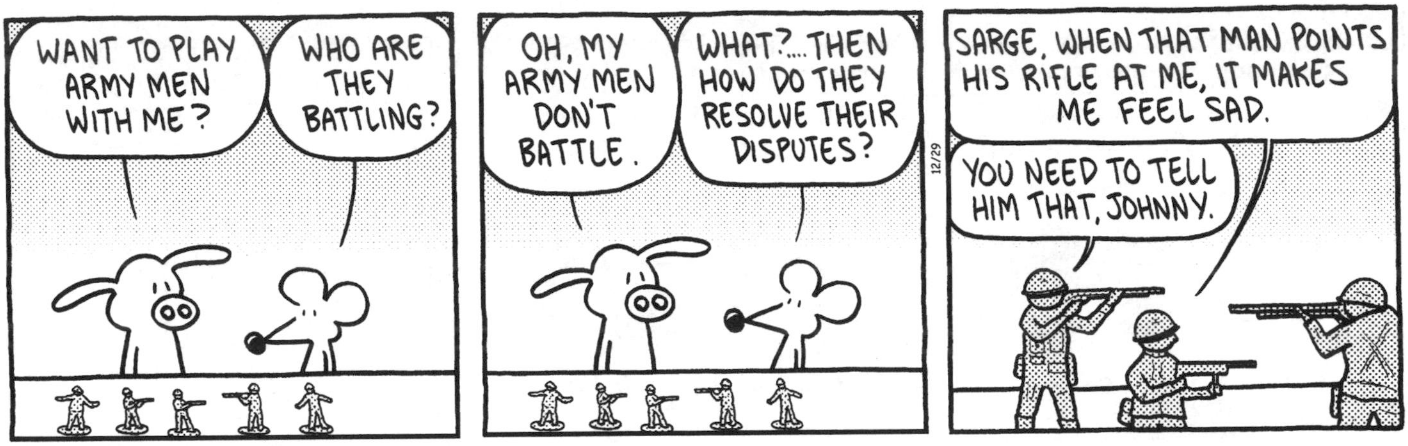
WANT TO PLAY ARMY MEN WITH ME?
WHO ARE THEY BATTLING?
OH, MY ARMY MEN DON'T BATTLE.
WHAT?.... THEN HOW DO THEY RESOLVE THEIR DISPUTES?
12/29
SARGE, WHEN THAT MAN POINTS HIS RIFLE AT ME, IT MAKES ME FEEL SAD.
YOU NEED TO TELL HIM THAT, JOHNNY.

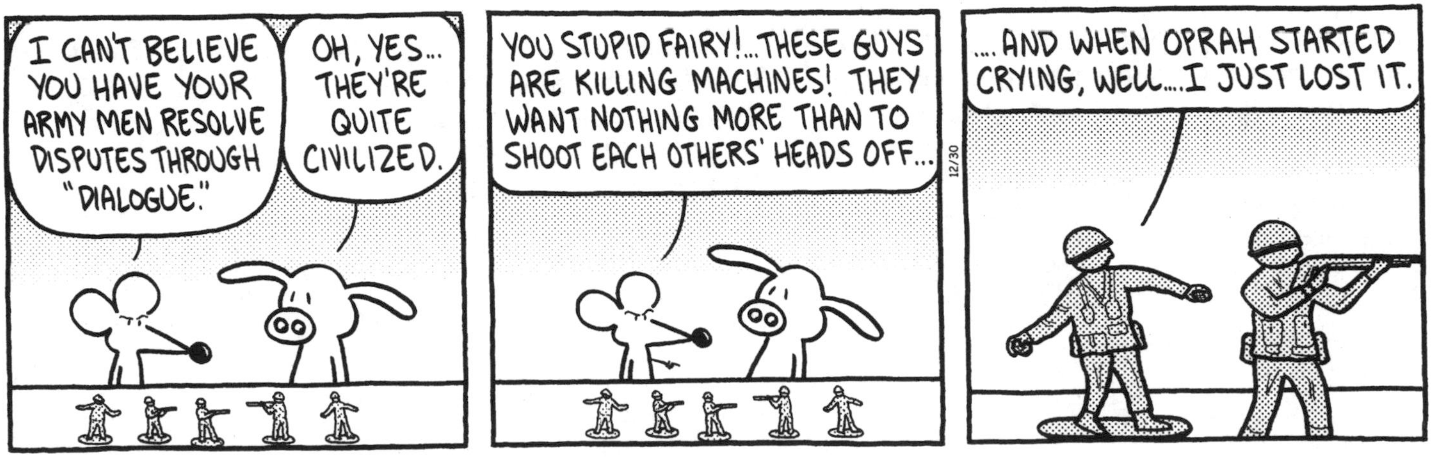
I CAN'T BELIEVE YOU HAVE YOUR ARMY MEN RESOLVE DISPUTES THROUGH "DIALOGUE."
OH, YES... THEY'RE QUITE CIVILIZED.
YOU STUPID FAIRY!... THESE GUYS ARE KILLING MACHINES! THEY WANT NOTHING MORE THAN TO SHOOT EACH OTHERS' HEADS OFF...
12/30
.... AND WHEN OPRAH STARTED CRYING, WELL.... I JUST LOST IT.

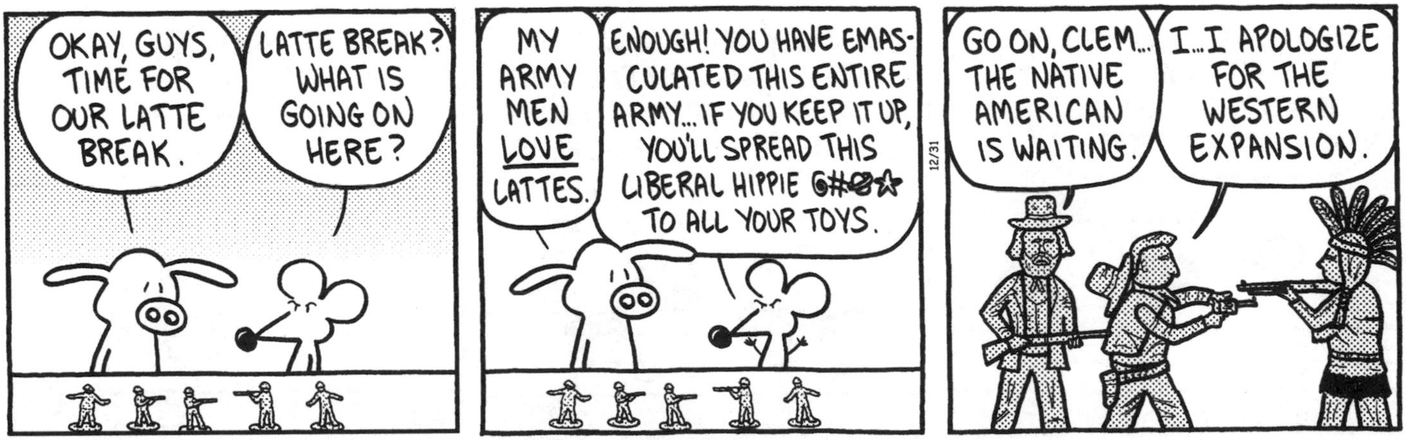
OKAY, GUYS, TIME FOR OUR LATTE BREAK.
LATTE BREAK? WHAT IS GOING ON HERE?
MY ARMY MEN LOVE LATTES.
ENOUGH! YOU HAVE EMASCULATED THIS ENTIRE ARMY... IF YOU KEEP IT UP, YOU'LL SPREAD THIS LIBERAL HIPPIE @#@☆ TO ALL YOUR TOYS.
12/31
GO ON, CLEM... THE NATIVE AMERICAN IS WAITING.
I... I APOLOGIZE FOR THE WESTERN EXPANSION.

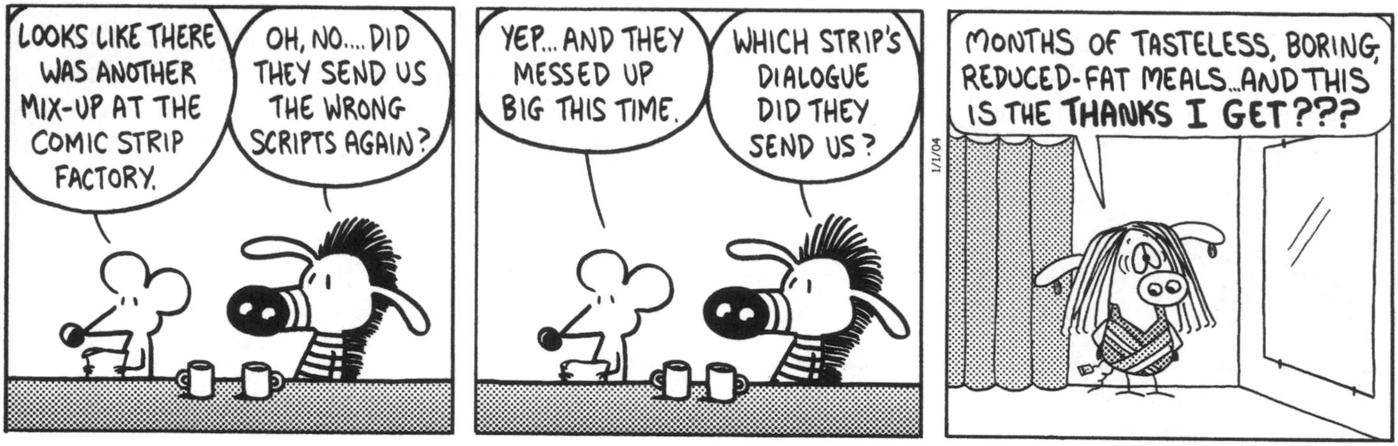
LOOKS LIKE THERE WAS ANOTHER MIX-UP AT THE COMIC STRIP FACTORY.
OH, NO.... DID THEY SEND US THE WRONG SCRIPTS AGAIN?
YEP... AND THEY MESSED UP BIG THIS TIME.
WHICH STRIP'S DIALOGUE DID THEY SEND US?
1/1/04
MONTHS OF TASTELESS, BORING, REDUCED-FAT MEALS...AND THIS IS THE THANKS I GET???

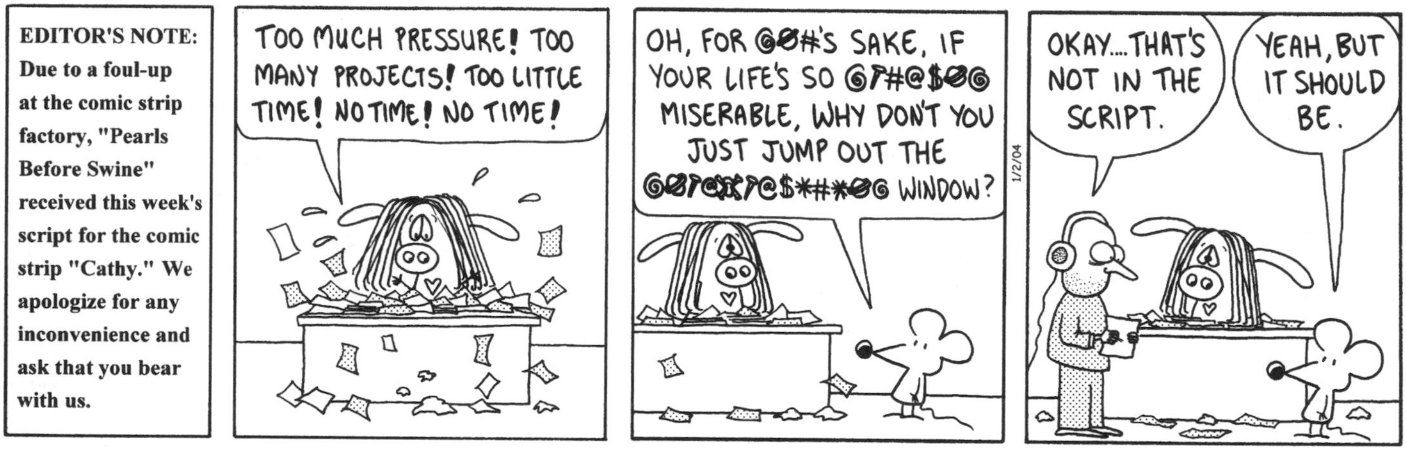
EDITOR'S NOTE: Due to a foul-up at the comic strip factory, "Pearls Before Swine" received this week's script for the comic strip "Cathy." We apologize for any inconvenience and ask that you bear with us.
TOO MUCH PRESSURE! TOO MANY PROJECTS! TOO LITTLE TIME! NO TIME! NO TIME!
OH, FOR @@#'S SAKE, IF YOUR LIFE'S SO @?#@$@@ MISERABLE, WHY DON'T YOU JUST JUMP OUT THE @@?@*?@$*#*@@ WINDOW?
1/2/04
OKAY.... THAT'S NOT IN THE SCRIPT.
YEAH, BUT IT SHOULD BE.

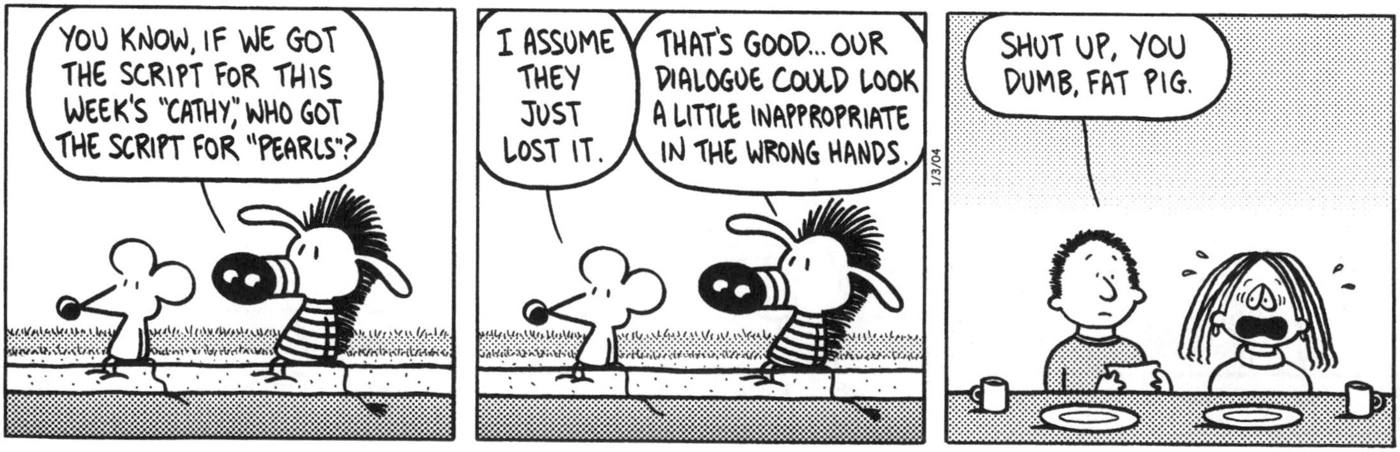
YOU KNOW, IF WE GOT THE SCRIPT FOR THIS WEEK'S "CATHY," WHO GOT THE SCRIPT FOR "PEARLS"?
I ASSUME THEY JUST LOST IT.
THAT'S GOOD... OUR DIALOGUE COULD LOOK A LITTLE INAPPROPRIATE IN THE WRONG HANDS.
1/3/04
SHUT UP, YOU DUMB, FAT PIG.

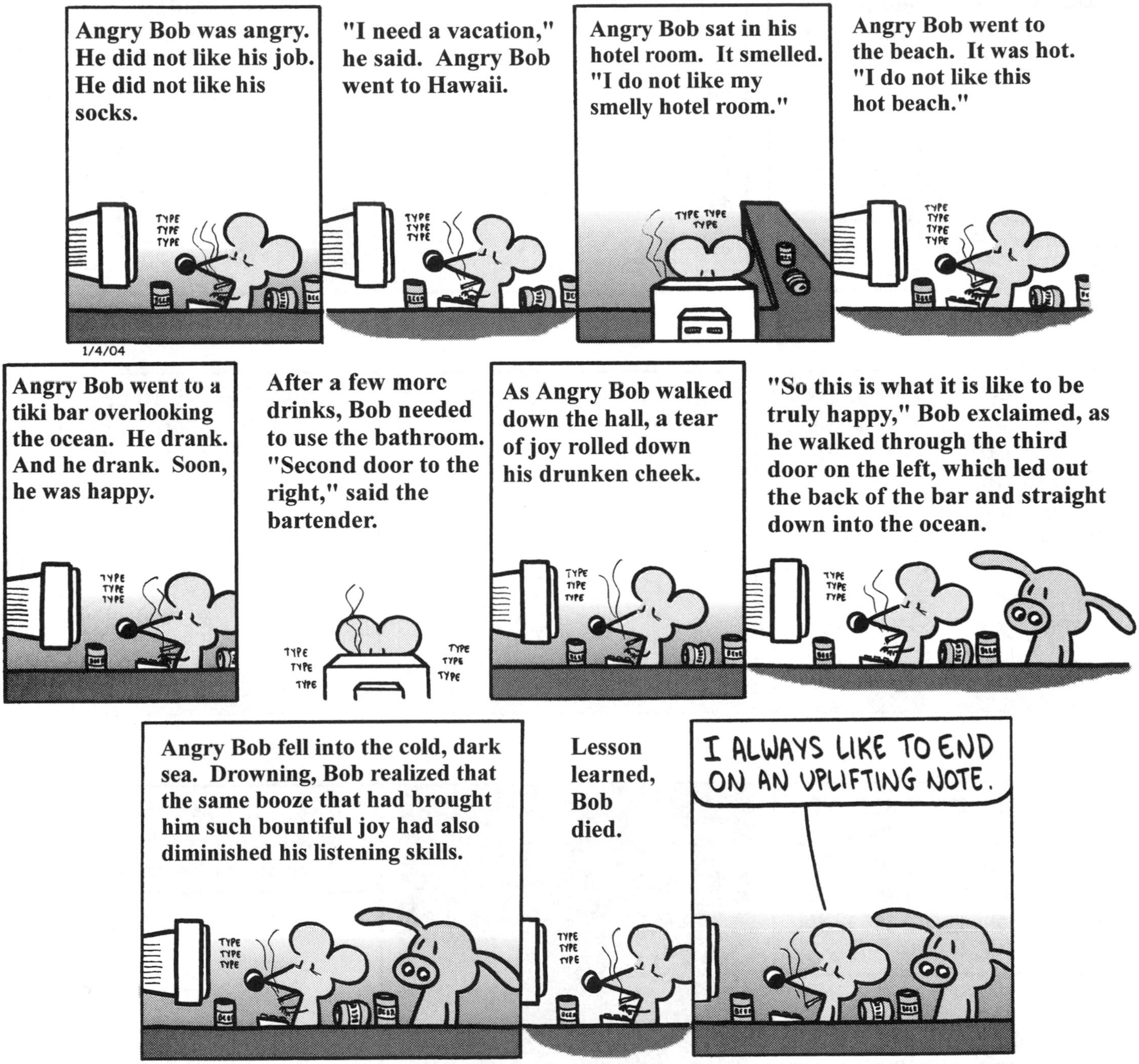
Angry Bob was angry. He did not like his job. He did not like his socks.
TYPE TYPE TYPE
1/4/04
"I need a vacation," he said. Angry Bob went to Hawaii.
TYPE TYPE TYPE
Angry Bob sat in his hotel room. It smelled. "I do not like my smelly hotel room."
TYPE TYPE TYPE
Angry Bob went to the beach. It was hot. "I do not like this hot beach."
TYPE TYPE TYPE TYPE
Angry Bob went to a tiki bar overlooking the ocean. He drank. And he drank. Soon, he was happy.
TYPE TYPE TYPE
After a few more drinks, Bob needed to use the bathroom. "Second door to the right," said the bartender.
TYPE TYPE TYPE
TYPE TYPE TYPE
As Angry Bob walked down the hall, a tear of joy rolled down his drunken cheek.
TYPE TYPE TYPE
"So this is what it is like to be truly happy," Bob exclaimed, as he walked through the third door on the left, which led out the back of the bar and straight down into the ocean.
TYPE TYPE TYPE
Angry Bob fell into the cold, dark sea. Drowning, Bob realized that the same booze that had brought him such bountiful joy had also diminished his listening skills.
TYPE TYPE TYPE
Lesson learned, Bob died.
TYPE TYPE TYPE
I ALWAYS LIKE TO END ON AN UPLIFTING NOTE.

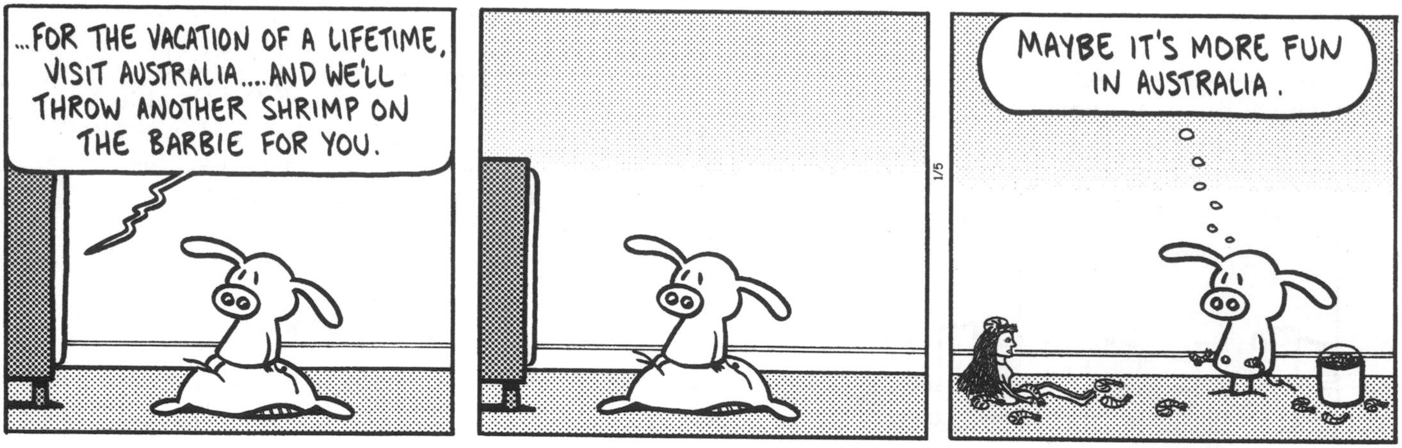
...FOR THE VACATION OF A LIFETIME, VISIT AUSTRALIA.... AND WE'LL THROW ANOTHER SHRIMP ON THE BARBIE FOR YOU.
1/5
MAYBE IT'S MORE FUN IN AUSTRALIA.

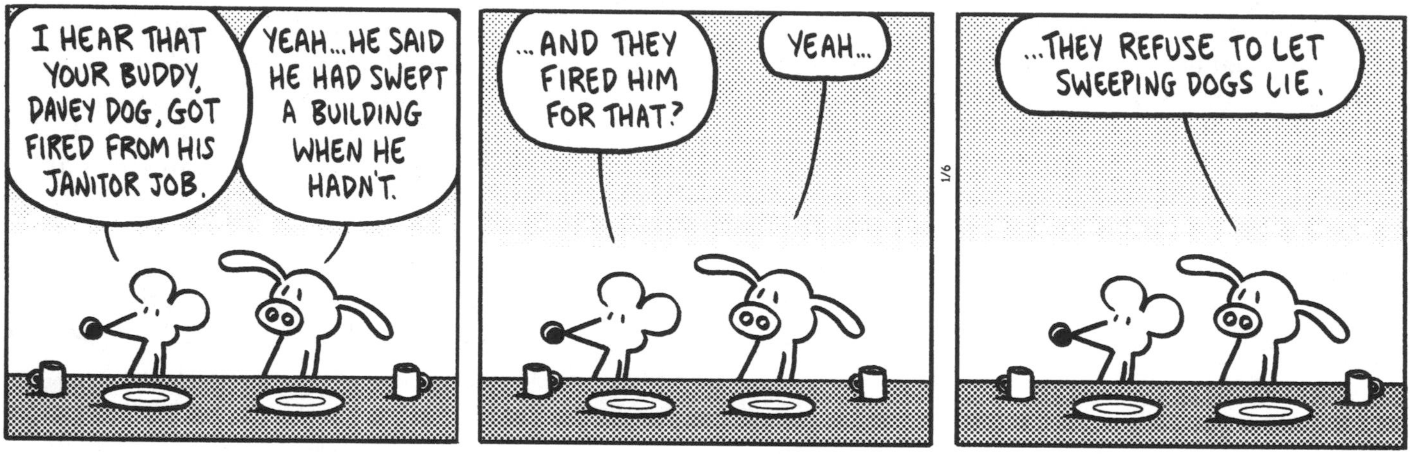
I HEAR THAT YOUR BUDDY, DAVEY DOG, GOT FIRED FROM HIS JANITOR JOB.
YEAH... HE SAID HE HAD SWEPT A BUILDING WHEN HE HADN'T.
...AND THEY FIRED HIM FOR THAT?
YEAH...
1/6
...THEY REFUSE TO LET SWEEPING DOGS LIE.

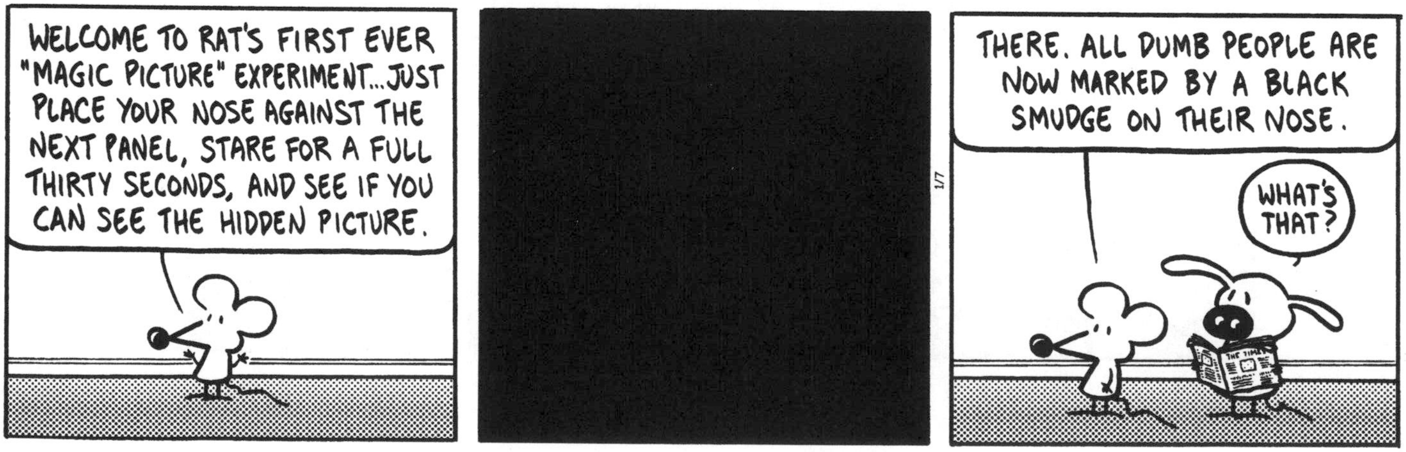
WELCOME TO RAT'S FIRST EVER "MAGIC PICTURE" EXPERIMENT... JUST PLACE YOUR NOSE AGAINST THE NEXT PANEL, STARE FOR A FULL THIRTY SECONDS, AND SEE IF YOU CAN SEE THE HIDDEN PICTURE.
1/7
THERE. ALL DUMB PEOPLE ARE NOW MARKED BY A BLACK SMUDGE ON THEIR NOSE.
WHAT'S THAT?

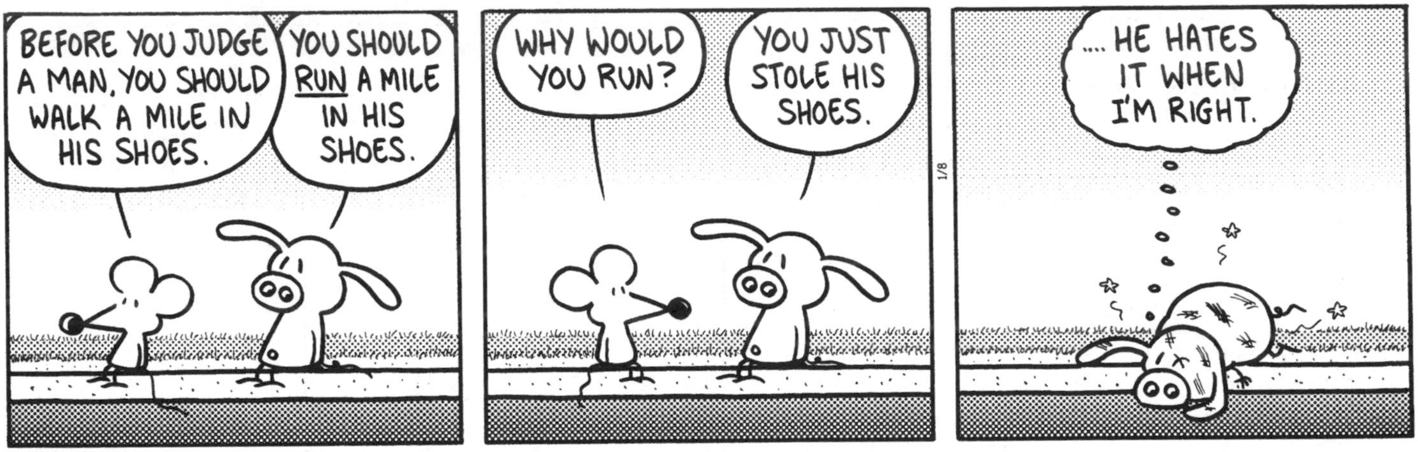
BEFORE YOU JUDGE A MAN, YOU SHOULD WALK A MILE IN HIS SHOES.
YOU SHOULD RUN A MILE IN HIS SHOES.
WHY WOULD YOU RUN?
YOU JUST STOLE HIS SHOES.
1/8
.... HE HATES IT WHEN I'M RIGHT.

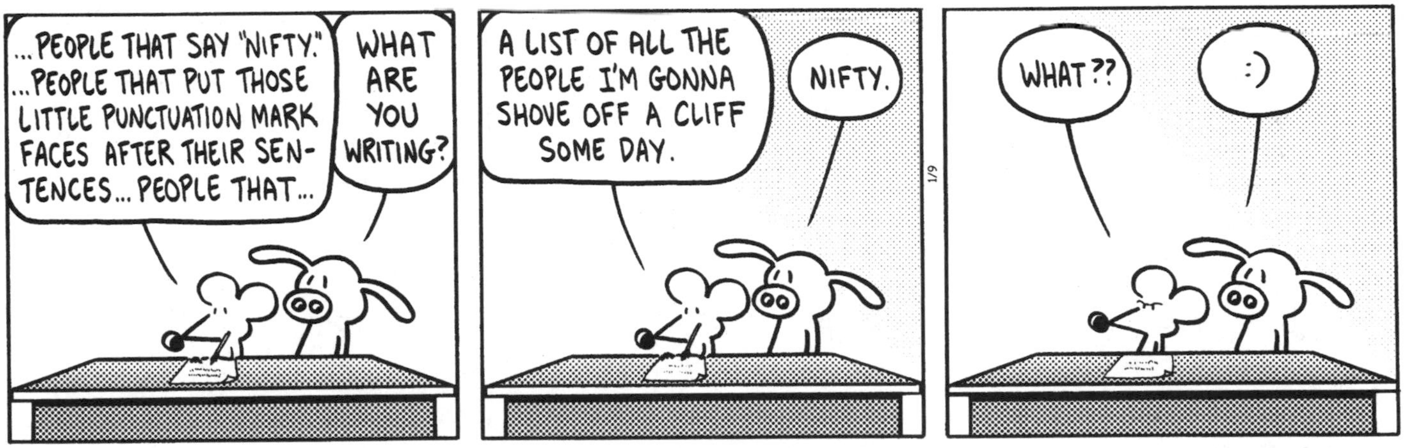
...PEOPLE THAT SAY "NIFTY." ...PEOPLE THAT PUT THOSE LITTLE PUNCTUATION MARK FACES AFTER THEIR SEN-TENCES... PEOPLE THAT...
WHAT ARE YOU WRITING?
A LIST OF ALL THE PEOPLE I'M GONNA SHOVE OFF A CLIFF SOME DAY.
NIFTY.
1/9
WHAT??
:)

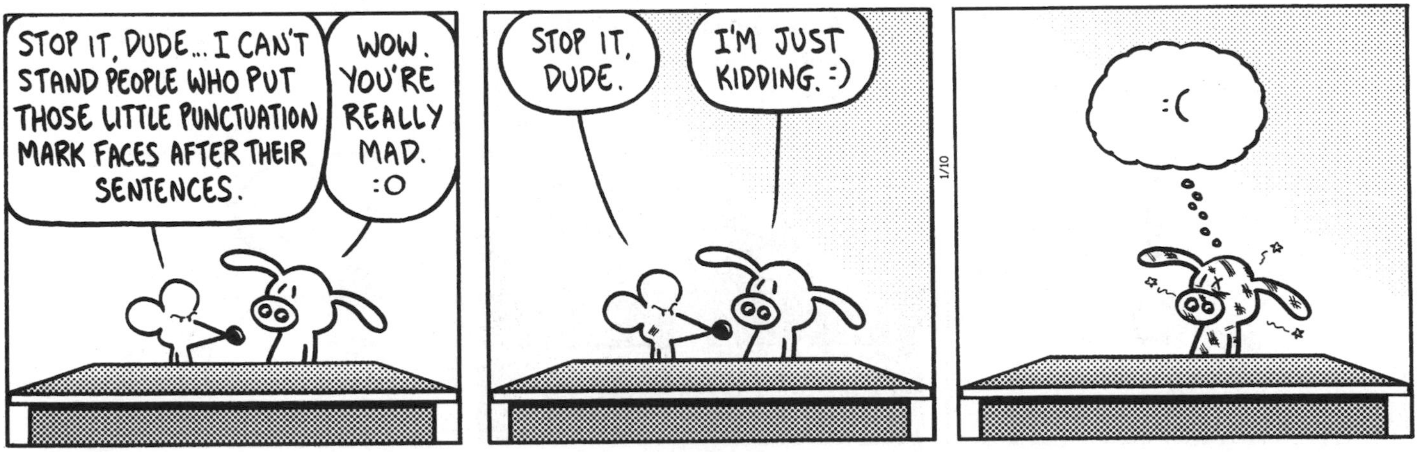
STOP IT, DUDE... I CAN'T STAND PEOPLE WHO PUT THOSE LITTLE PUNCTUATION MARK FACES AFTER THEIR SENTENCES.
WOW. YOU'RE REALLY MAD. :O
STOP IT, DUDE.
I'M JUST KIDDING. :)
1/10
:(

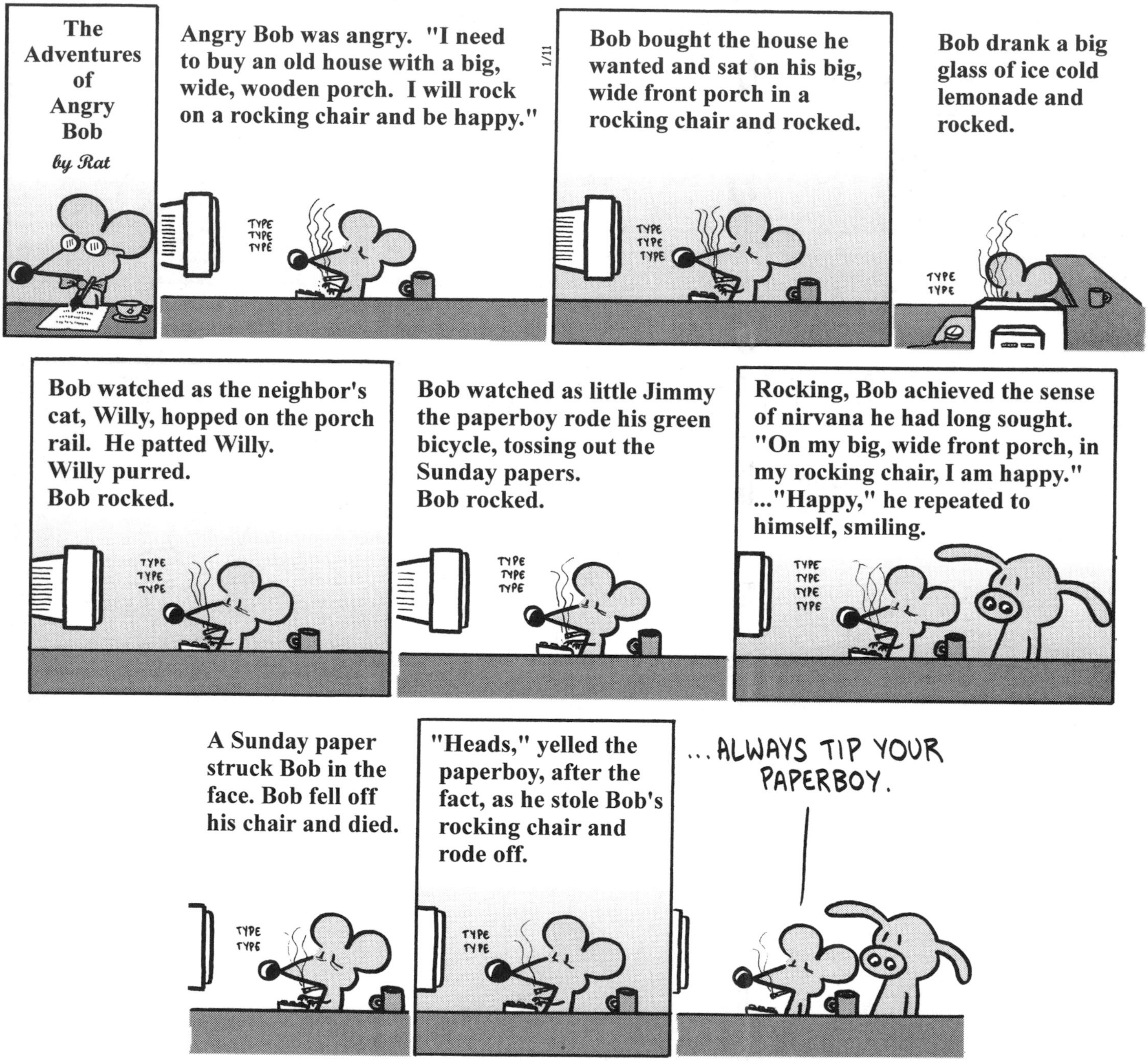
The Adventures of Angry Bob
by Rat
Angry Bob was angry. "I need to buy an old house with a big, wide, wooden porch. I will rock on a rocking chair and be happy."
1/11
TYPE TYPE TYPE
Bob bought the house he wanted and sat on his big, wide front porch in a rocking chair and rocked.
TYPE TYPE TYPE
Bob drank a big glass of ice cold lemonade and rocked.
TYPE TYPE
Bob watched as the neighbor's cat, Willy, hopped on the porch rail. He patted Willy. Willy purred. Bob rocked.
TYPE TYPE TYPE
Bob watched as little Jimmy the paperboy rode his green bicycle, tossing out the Sunday papers. Bob rocked.
TYPE TYPE TYPE
Rocking, Bob achieved the sense of nirvana he had long sought. "On my big, wide front porch, in my rocking chair, I am happy." ..."Happy," he repeated to himself, smiling.
TYPE TYPE TYPE TYPE
A Sunday paper struck Bob in the face. Bob fell off his chair and died.
TYPE TYPE
"Heads," yelled the paperboy, after the fact, as he stole Bob's rocking chair and rode off.
TYPE TYPE
...ALWAYS TIP YOUR PAPERBOY.

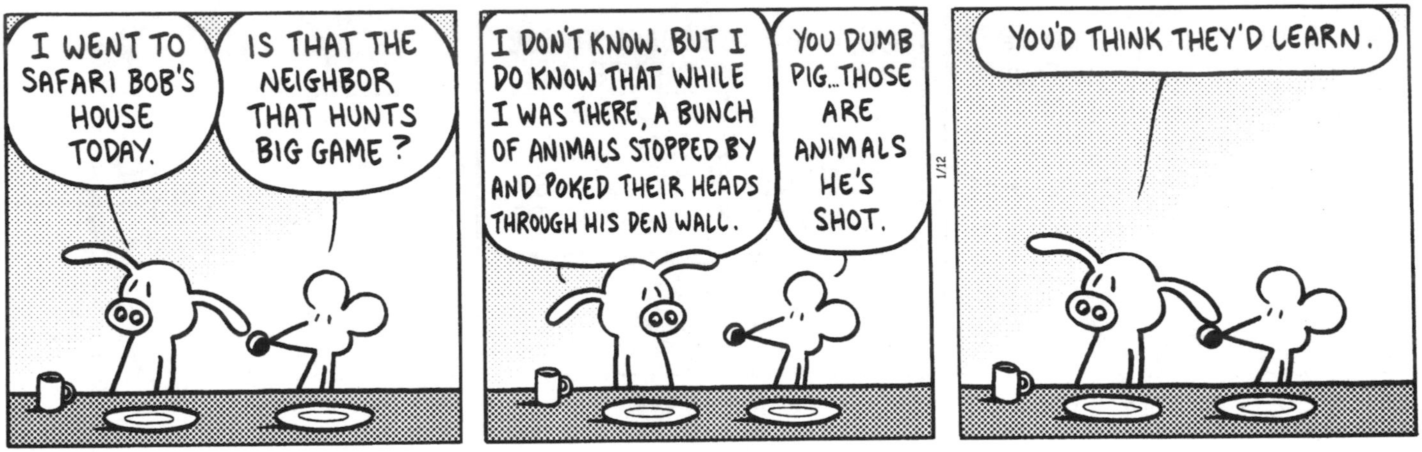
I WENT TO SAFARI BOB'S HOUSE TODAY.
IS THAT THE NEIGHBOR THAT HUNTS BIG GAME?
I DON'T KNOW. BUT I DO KNOW THAT WHILE I WAS THERE, A BUNCH OF ANIMALS STOPPED BY AND POKED THEIR HEADS THROUGH HIS DEN WALL.
YOU DUMB PIG...THOSE ARE ANIMALS HE'S SHOT.
1/12
YOU'D THINK THEY'D LEARN.

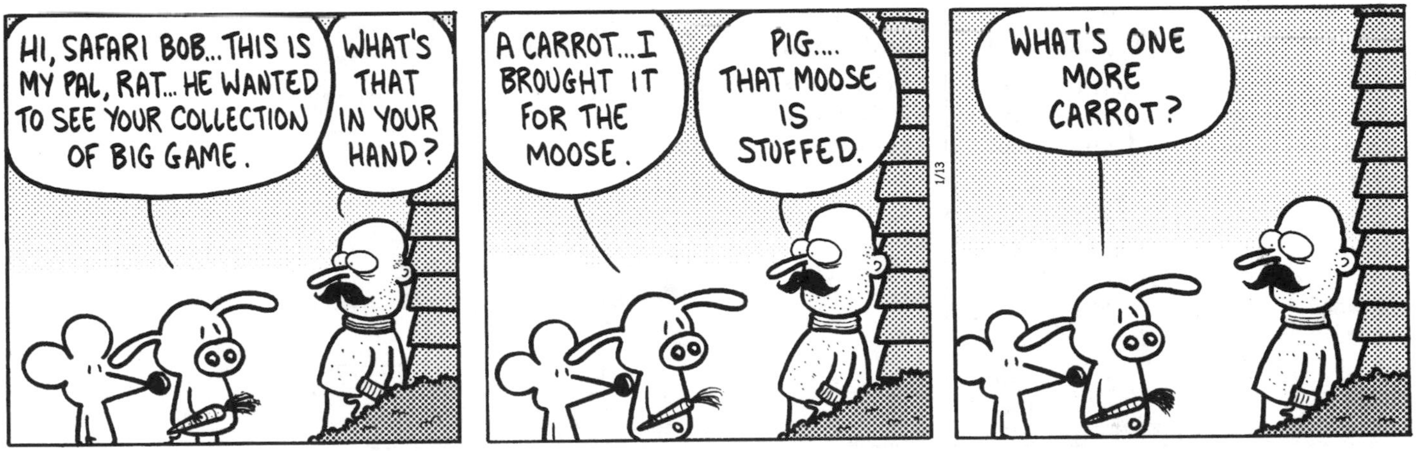
HI, SAFARI BOB...THIS IS MY PAL, RAT... HE WANTED TO SEE YOUR COLLECTION OF BIG GAME.
WHAT'S THAT IN YOUR HAND?
A CARROT...I BROUGHT IT FOR THE MOOSE.
PIG.... THAT MOOSE IS STUFFED.
1/13
WHAT'S ONE MORE CARROT?

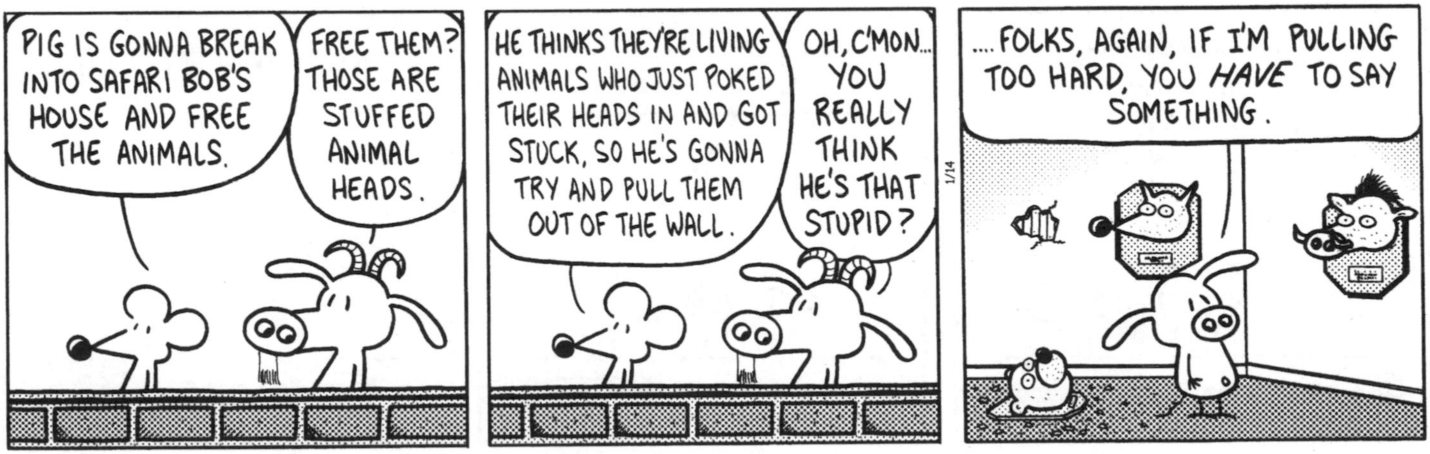
PIG IS GONNA BREAK INTO SAFARI BOB'S HOUSE AND FREE THE ANIMALS.
FREE THEM? THOSE ARE STUFFED ANIMAL HEADS.
HE THINKS THEY'RE LIVING ANIMALS WHO JUST POKED THEIR HEADS IN AND GOT STUCK, SO HE'S GONNA TRY AND PULL THEM OUT OF THE WALL.
OH, C'MON... YOU REALLY THINK HE'S THAT STUPID?
1/14
....FOLKS, AGAIN, IF I'M PULLING TOO HARD, YOU *HAVE* TO SAY SOMETHING.

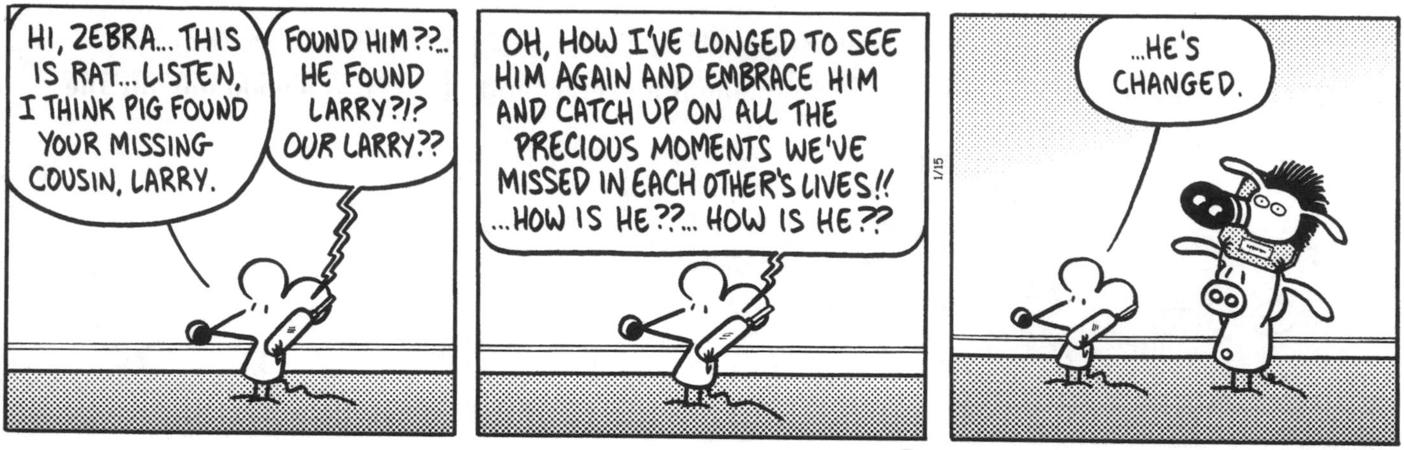
HI, ZEBRA... THIS IS RAT... LISTEN, I THINK PIG FOUND YOUR MISSING COUSIN, LARRY.
FOUND HIM??... HE FOUND LARRY?!? OUR LARRY??
OH, HOW I'VE LONGED TO SEE HIM AGAIN AND EMBRACE HIM AND CATCH UP ON ALL THE PRECIOUS MOMENTS WE'VE MISSED IN EACH OTHER'S LIVES!! ...HOW IS HE??... HOW IS HE??
1/15
...HE'S CHANGED.

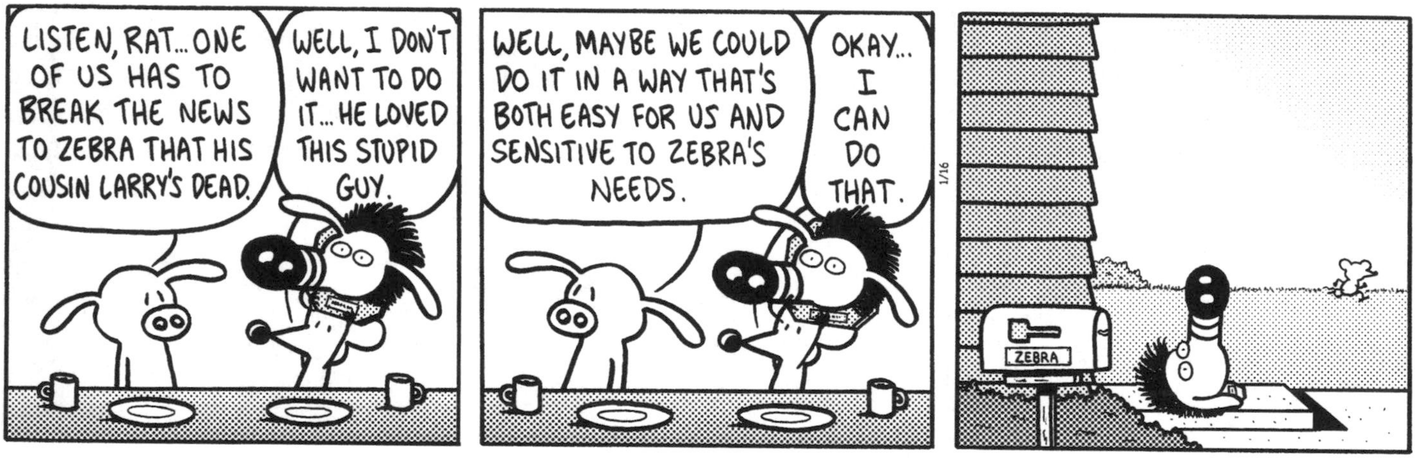
LISTEN, RAT... ONE OF US HAS TO BREAK THE NEWS TO ZEBRA THAT HIS COUSIN LARRY'S DEAD.
WELL, I DON'T WANT TO DO IT... HE LOVED THIS STUPID GUY.
WELL, MAYBE WE COULD DO IT IN A WAY THAT'S BOTH EASY FOR US AND SENSITIVE TO ZEBRA'S NEEDS.
OKAY... I CAN DO THAT.
1/16
ZEBRA

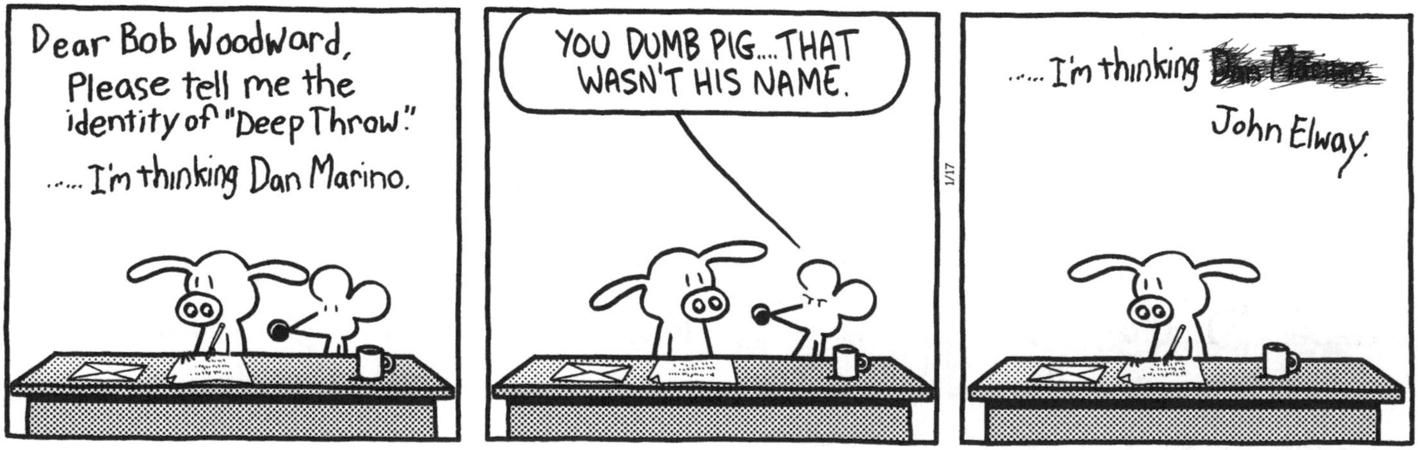
Dear Bob Woodward,
Please tell me the identity of "Deep Throw."
...... I'm thinking Dan Marino.
YOU DUMB PIG.... THAT WASN'T HIS NAME.
1/17
...... I'm thinking [redacted] John Elway.

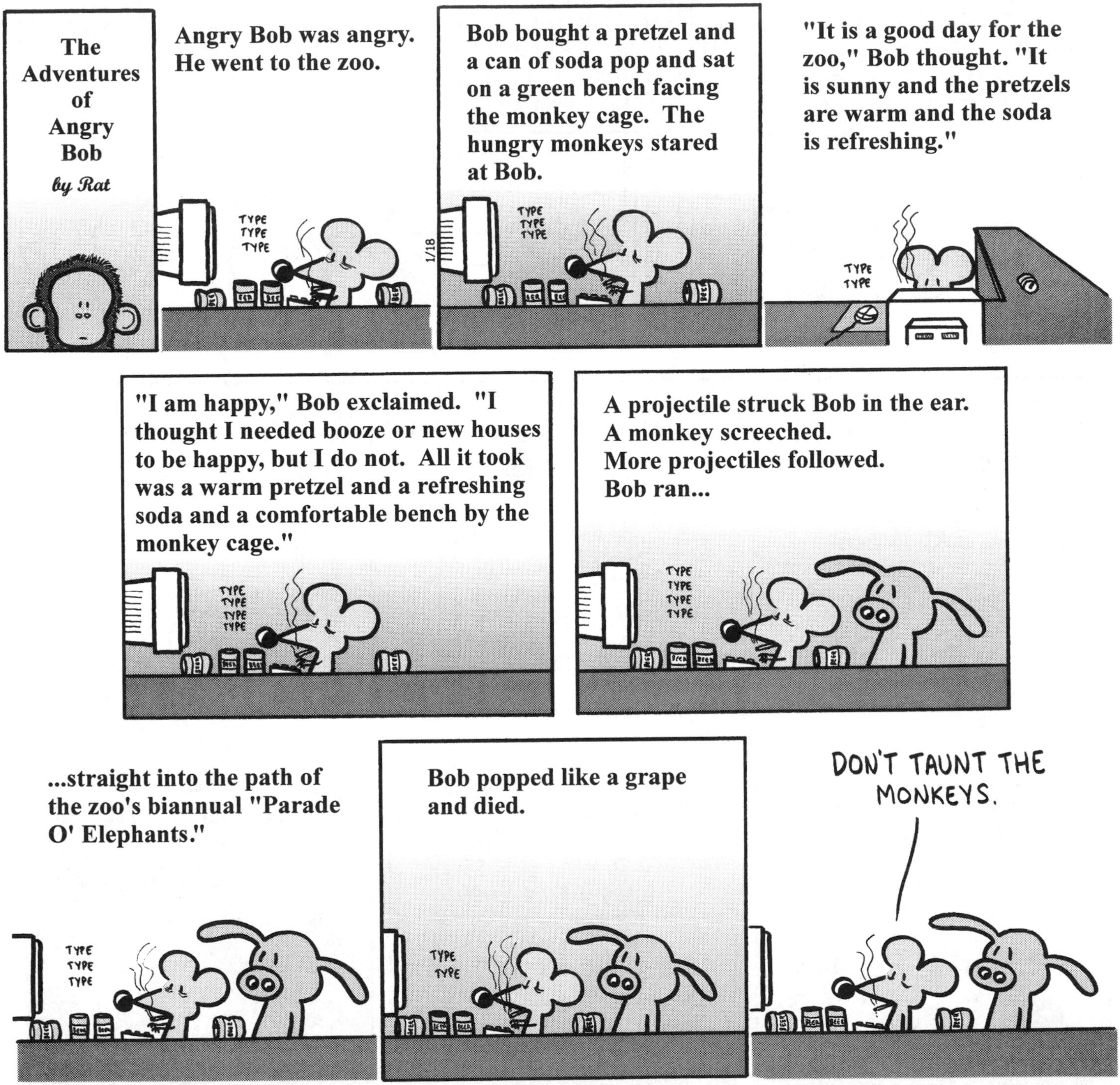
The Adventures of Angry Bob
by Rat
Angry Bob was angry. He went to the zoo.
TYPE TYPE TYPE
1/18
Bob bought a pretzel and a can of soda pop and sat on a green bench facing the monkey cage. The hungry monkeys stared at Bob.
TYPE TYPE TYPE
"It is a good day for the zoo," Bob thought. "It is sunny and the pretzels are warm and the soda is refreshing."
TYPE TYPE
"I am happy," Bob exclaimed. "I thought I needed booze or new houses to be happy, but I do not. All it took was a warm pretzel and a refreshing soda and a comfortable bench by the monkey cage."
TYPE TYPE TYPE TYPE
A projectile struck Bob in the ear. A monkey screeched. More projectiles followed. Bob ran...
TYPE TYPE TYPE TYPE
...straight into the path of the zoo's biannual "Parade O' Elephants."
TYPE TYPE TYPE
Bob popped like a grape and died.
TYPE TYPE
DON'T TAUNT THE MONKEYS.

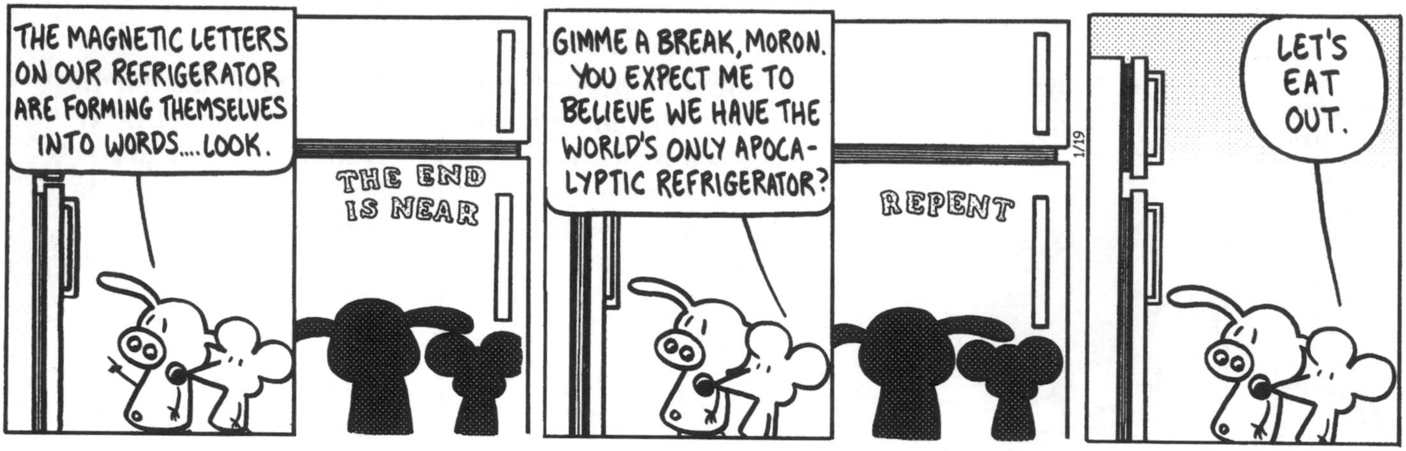
THE MAGNETIC LETTERS ON OUR REFRIGERATOR ARE FORMING THEMSELVES INTO WORDS....LOOK.
THE END IS NEAR
GIMME A BREAK, MORON. YOU EXPECT ME TO BELIEVE WE HAVE THE WORLD'S ONLY APOCALYPTIC REFRIGERATOR?
REPENT
1/19
LET'S EAT OUT.

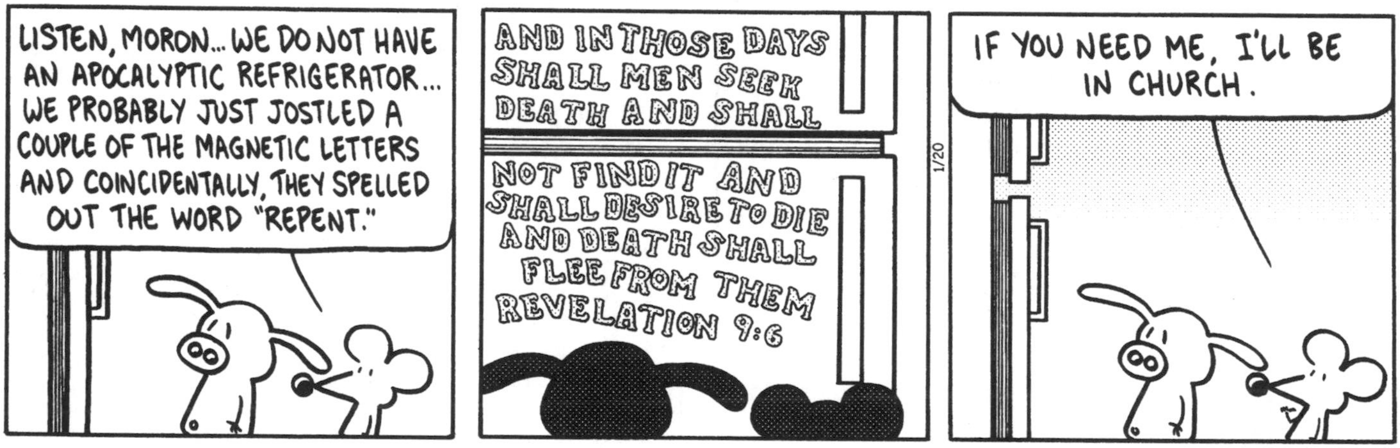
LISTEN, MORON... WE DO NOT HAVE AN APOCALYPTIC REFRIGERATOR... WE PROBABLY JUST JOSTLED A COUPLE OF THE MAGNETIC LETTERS AND COINCIDENTALLY, THEY SPELLED OUT THE WORD "REPENT."
AND IN THOSE DAYS SHALL MEN SEEK DEATH AND SHALL NOT FIND IT AND SHALL DESIRE TO DIE AND DEATH SHALL FLEE FROM THEM REVELATION 9:6
1/20
IF YOU NEED ME, I'LL BE IN CHURCH.

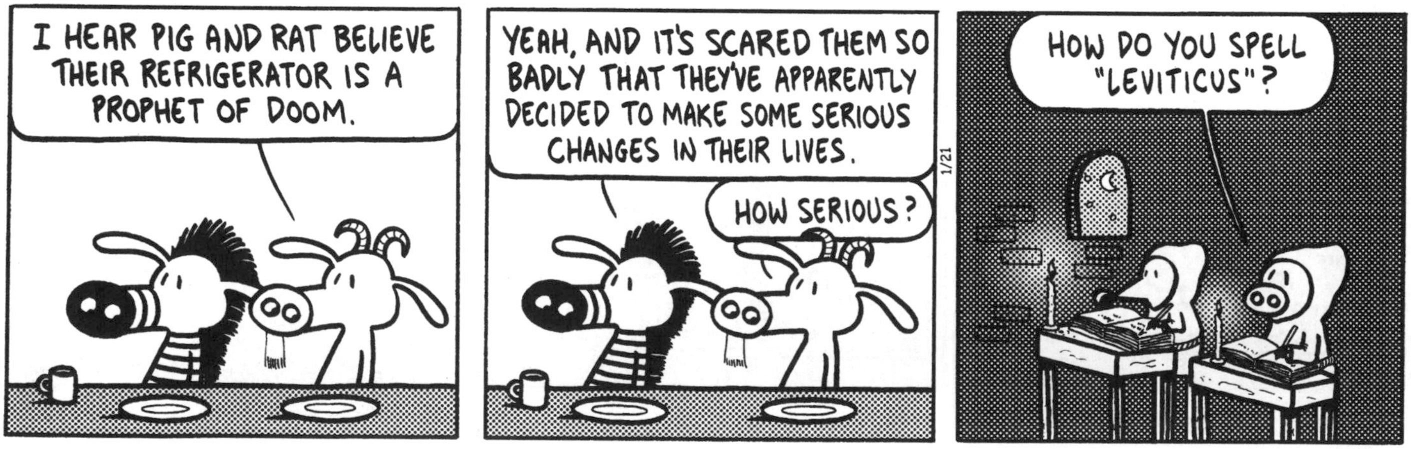
I HEAR PIG AND RAT BELIEVE THEIR REFRIGERATOR IS A PROPHET OF DOOM.
YEAH, AND IT'S SCARED THEM SO BADLY THAT THEY'VE APPARENTLY DECIDED TO MAKE SOME SERIOUS CHANGES IN THEIR LIVES.
HOW SERIOUS?
1/21
HOW DO YOU SPELL "LEVITICUS"?

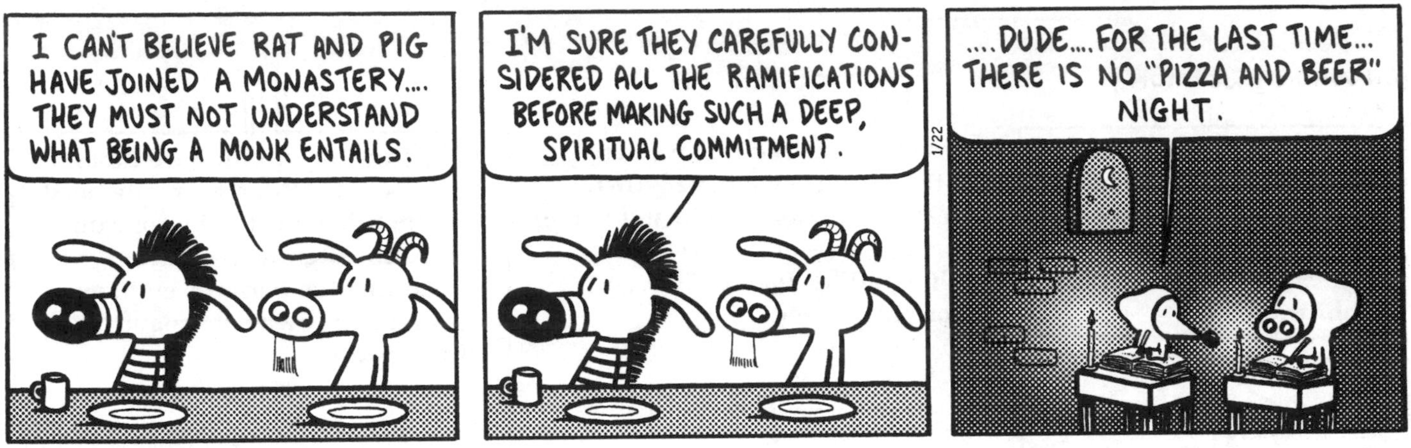
I CAN'T BELIEVE RAT AND PIG HAVE JOINED A MONASTERY.... THEY MUST NOT UNDERSTAND WHAT BEING A MONK ENTAILS.
I'M SURE THEY CAREFULLY CONSIDERED ALL THE RAMIFICATIONS BEFORE MAKING SUCH A DEEP, SPIRITUAL COMMITMENT.
1/22
....DUDE....FOR THE LAST TIME... THERE IS NO "PIZZA AND BEER" NIGHT.

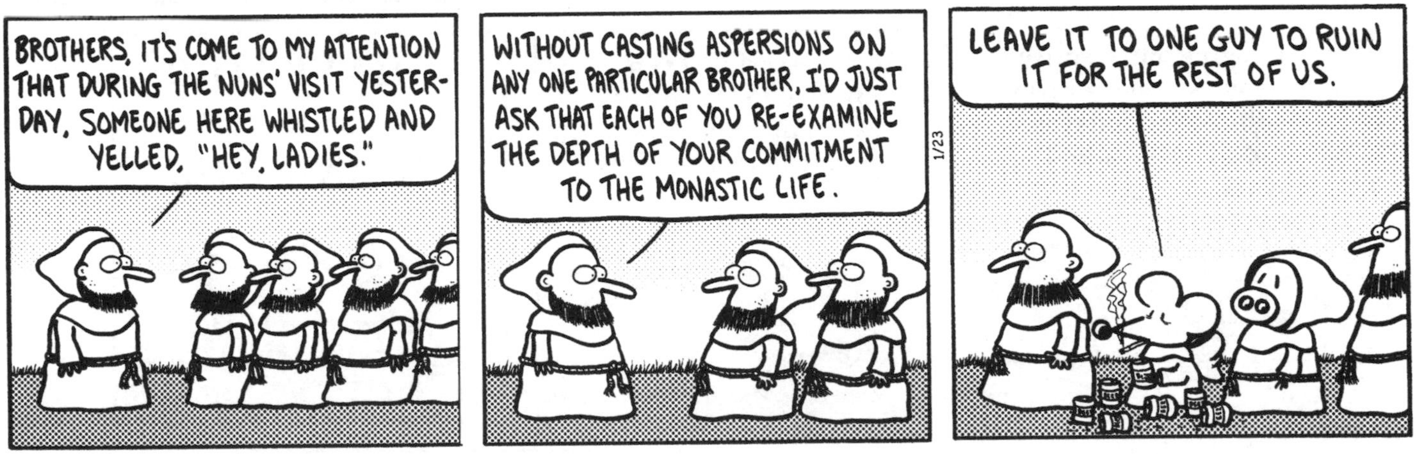
BROTHERS, IT'S COME TO MY ATTENTION THAT DURING THE NUNS' VISIT YESTERDAY, SOMEONE HERE WHISTLED AND YELLED, "HEY, LADIES."
WITHOUT CASTING ASPERSIONS ON ANY ONE PARTICULAR BROTHER, I'D JUST ASK THAT EACH OF YOU RE-EXAMINE THE DEPTH OF YOUR COMMITMENT TO THE MONASTIC LIFE.
1/23
LEAVE IT TO ONE GUY TO RUIN IT FOR THE REST OF US.

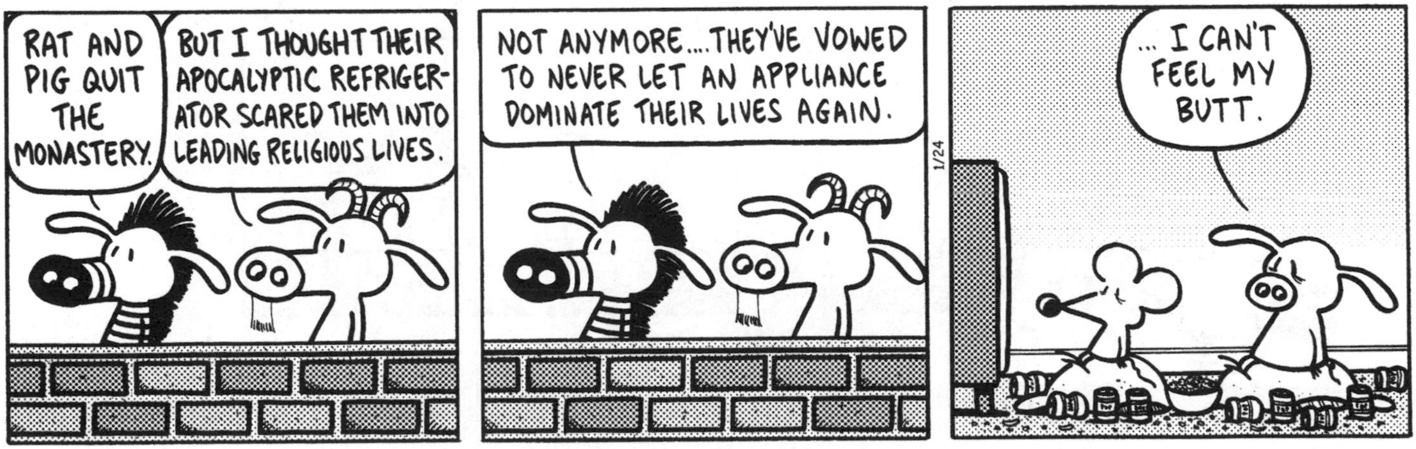
RAT AND PIG QUIT THE MONASTERY.
BUT I THOUGHT THEIR APOCALYPTIC REFRIGERATOR SCARED THEM INTO LEADING RELIGIOUS LIVES.
NOT ANYMORE....THEY'VE VOWED TO NEVER LET AN APPLIANCE DOMINATE THEIR LIVES AGAIN.
1/24
... I CAN'T FEEL MY BUTT.

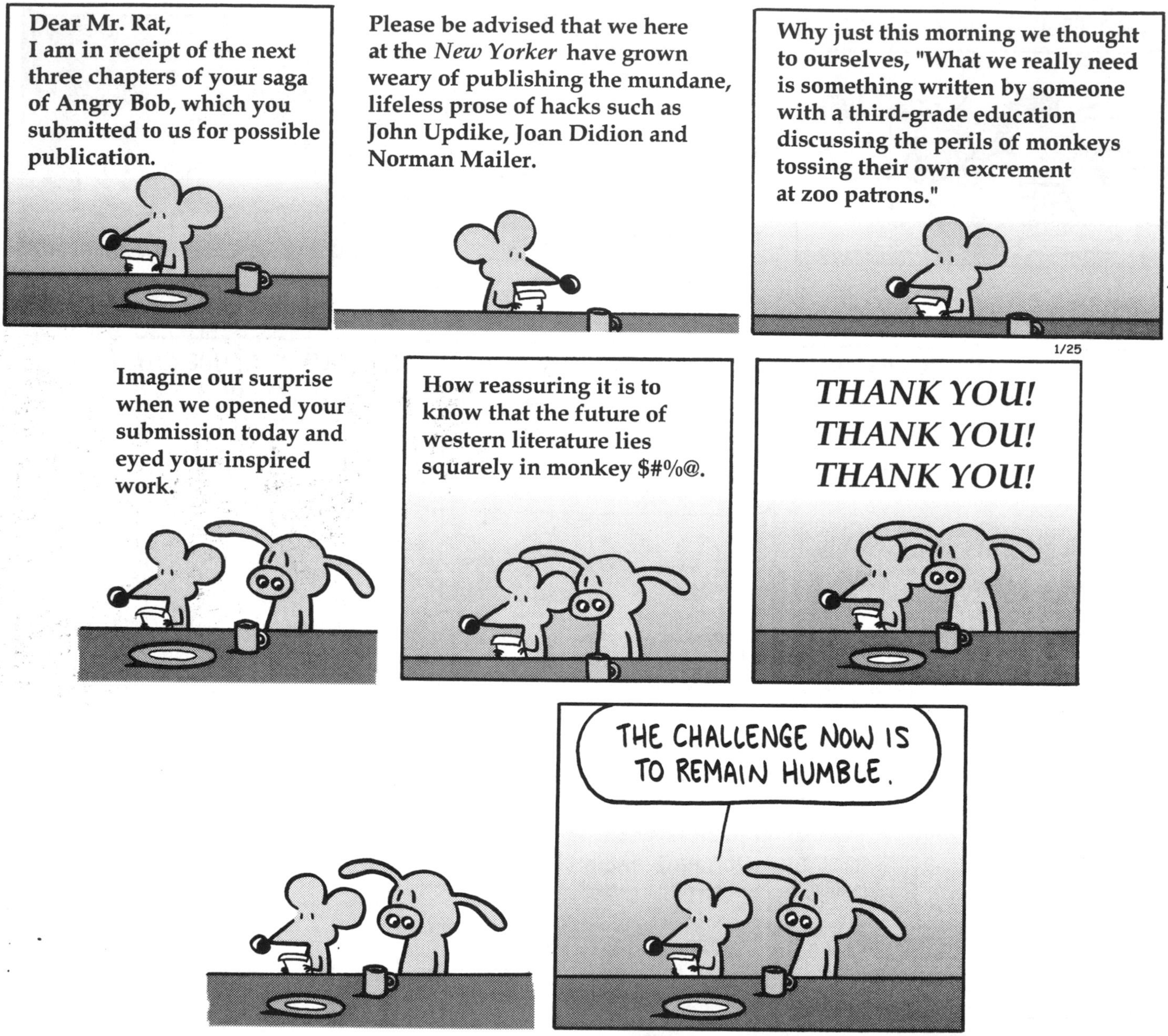
Dear Mr. Rat,
I am in receipt of the next three chapters of your saga of Angry Bob, which you submitted to us for possible publication.
Please be advised that we here at the *New Yorker* have grown weary of publishing the mundane, lifeless prose of hacks such as John Updike, Joan Didion and Norman Mailer.
Why just this morning we thought to ourselves, "What we really need is something written by someone with a third-grade education discussing the perils of monkeys tossing their own excrement at zoo patrons."
1/25
Imagine our surprise when we opened your submission today and eyed your inspired work.
How reassuring it is to know that the future of western literature lies squarely in monkey $#%@.
THANK YOU! THANK YOU! THANK YOU!
THE CHALLENGE NOW IS TO REMAIN HUMBLE.

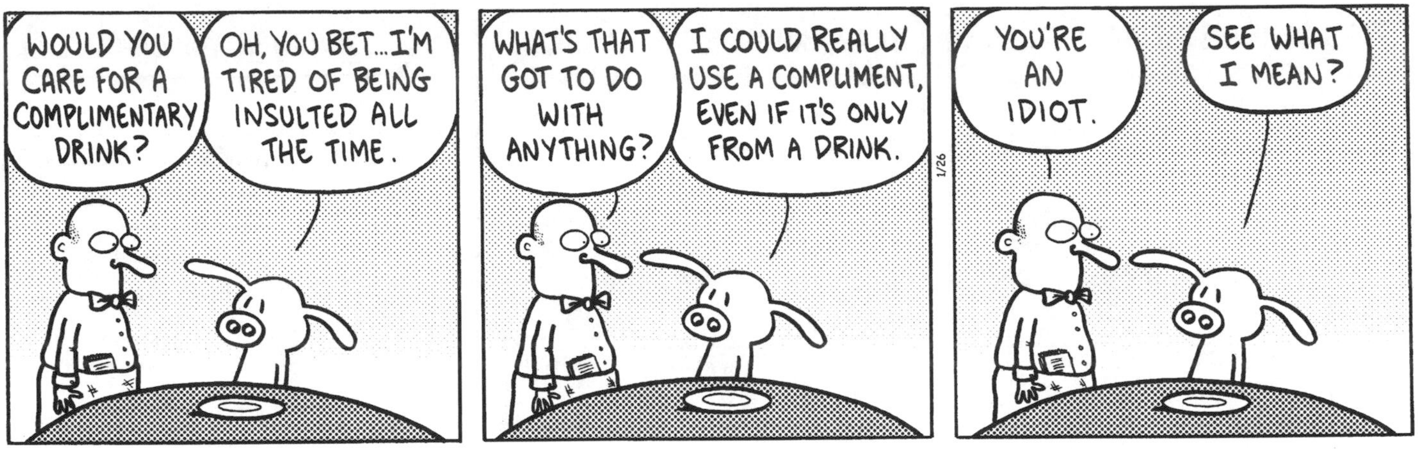
WOULD YOU CARE FOR A COMPLIMENTARY DRINK?
OH, YOU BET...I'M TIRED OF BEING INSULTED ALL THE TIME.
WHAT'S THAT GOT TO DO WITH ANYTHING?
I COULD REALLY USE A COMPLIMENT, EVEN IF IT'S ONLY FROM A DRINK.
1/26
YOU'RE AN IDIOT.
SEE WHAT I MEAN?

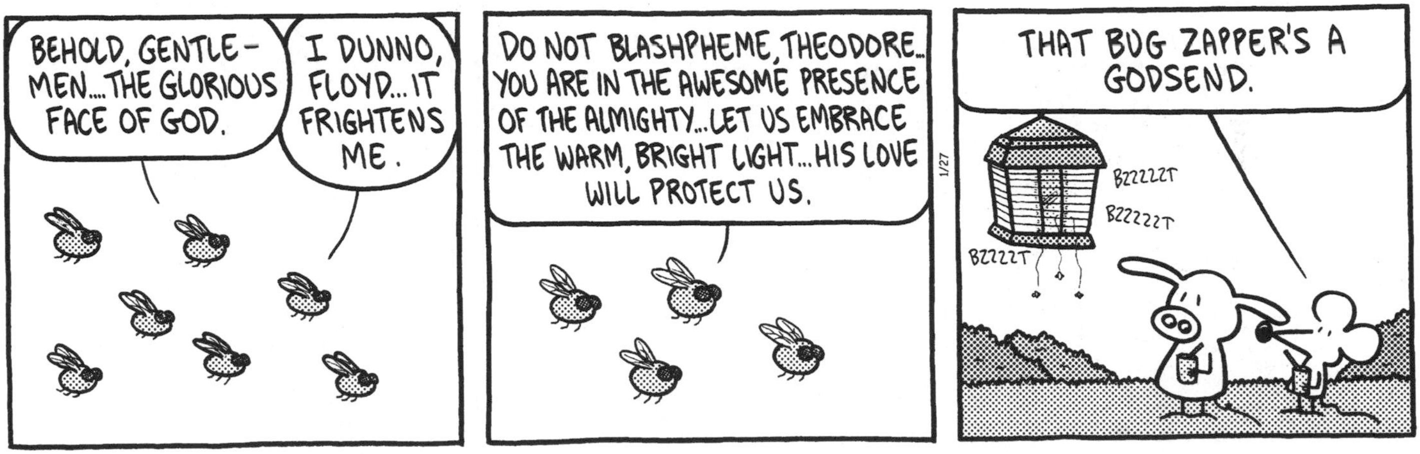
BEHOLD, GENTLE-MEN....THE GLORIOUS FACE OF GOD.
I DUNNO, FLOYD...IT FRIGHTENS ME.
DO NOT BLASHPHEME, THEODORE... YOU ARE IN THE AWESOME PRESENCE OF THE ALMIGHTY...LET US EMBRACE THE WARM, BRIGHT LIGHT...HIS LOVE WILL PROTECT US.
1/27
THAT BUG ZAPPER'S A GODSEND.
BZZZZZT
BZZZZZZT
BZZZZZT

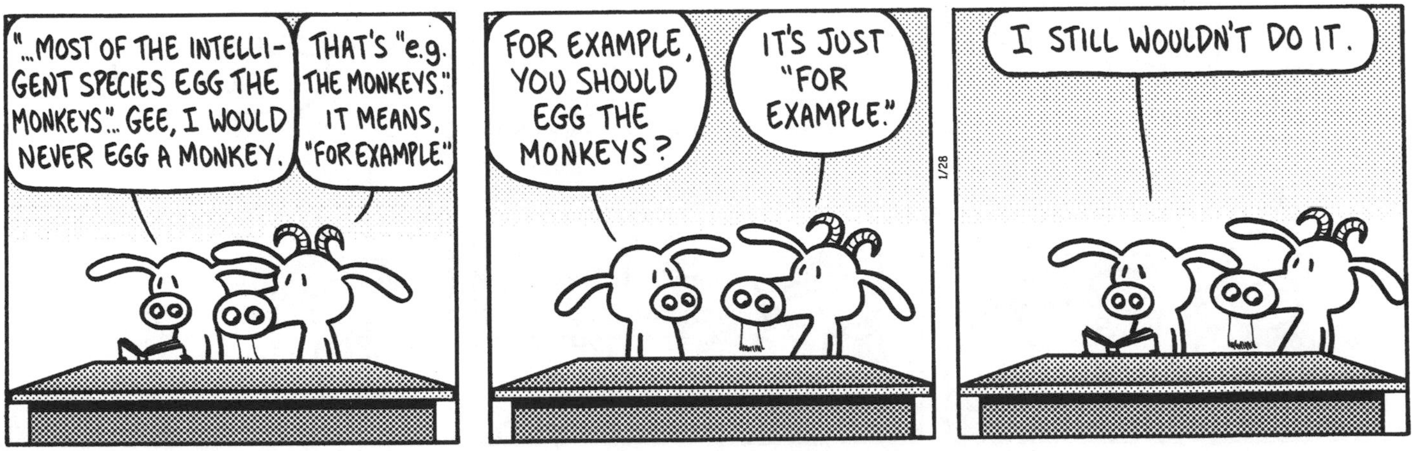
"...MOST OF THE INTELLI-GENT SPECIES EGG THE MONKEYS."... GEE, I WOULD NEVER EGG A MONKEY.
THAT'S "e.g. THE MONKEYS." IT MEANS, "FOR EXAMPLE."
FOR EXAMPLE, YOU SHOULD EGG THE MONKEYS?
IT'S JUST "FOR EXAMPLE."
1/28
I STILL WOULDN'T DO IT.

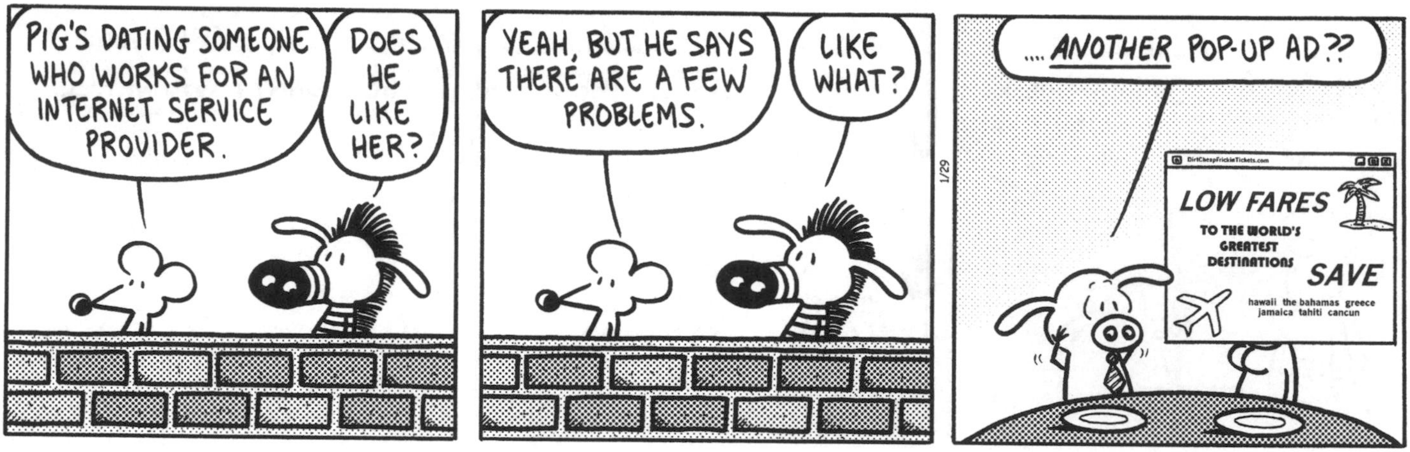
PIG'S DATING SOMEONE WHO WORKS FOR AN INTERNET SERVICE PROVIDER.
DOES HE LIKE HER?
YEAH, BUT HE SAYS THERE ARE A FEW PROBLEMS.
LIKE WHAT?
1/29
....ANOTHER POP-UP AD??
LOW FARES
TO THE WORLD'S GREATEST DESTINATIONS
SAVE
hawaii the bahamas greece jamaica tahiti cancun

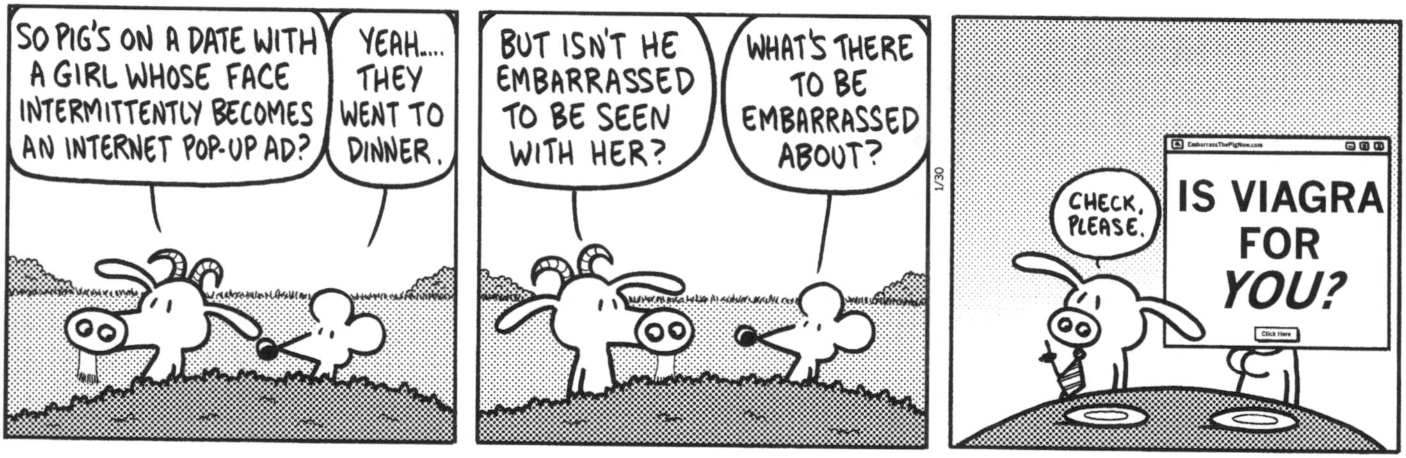
SO PIG'S ON A DATE WITH A GIRL WHOSE FACE INTERMITTENTLY BECOMES AN INTERNET POP-UP AD?
YEAH.... THEY WENT TO DINNER.
BUT ISN'T HE EMBARRASSED TO BE SEEN WITH HER?
WHAT'S THERE TO BE EMBARRASSED ABOUT?
1/30
CHECK, PLEASE.
IS VIAGRA FOR YOU?
Click Here

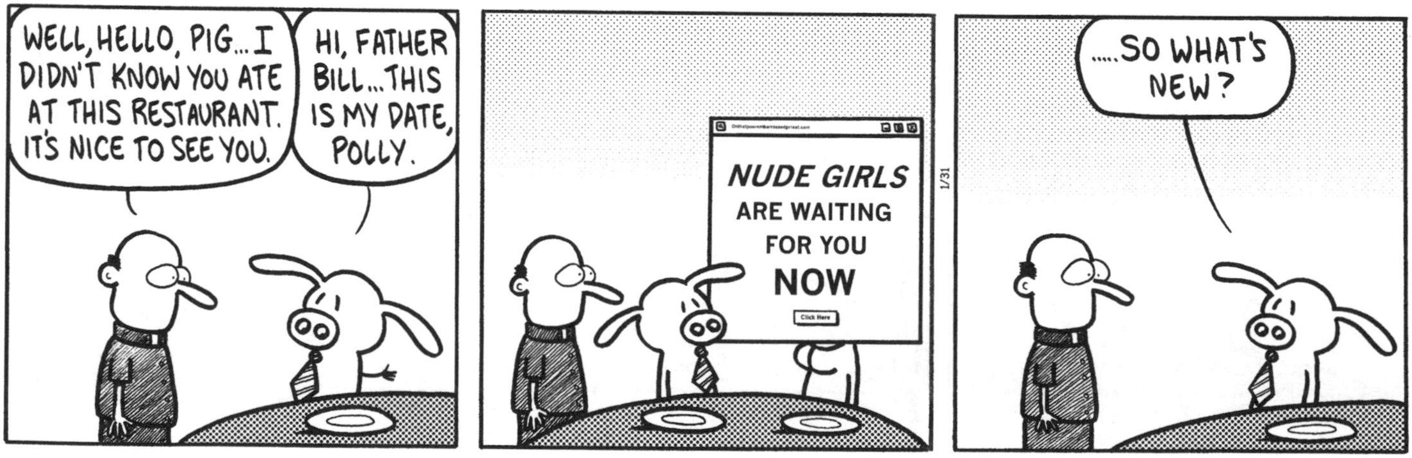
WELL, HELLO, PIG...I DIDN'T KNOW YOU ATE AT THIS RESTAURANT. IT'S NICE TO SEE YOU.
HI, FATHER BILL...THIS IS MY DATE, POLLY.
1/31
NUDE GIRLS ARE WAITING FOR YOU NOW
Click Here
.....SO WHAT'S NEW?

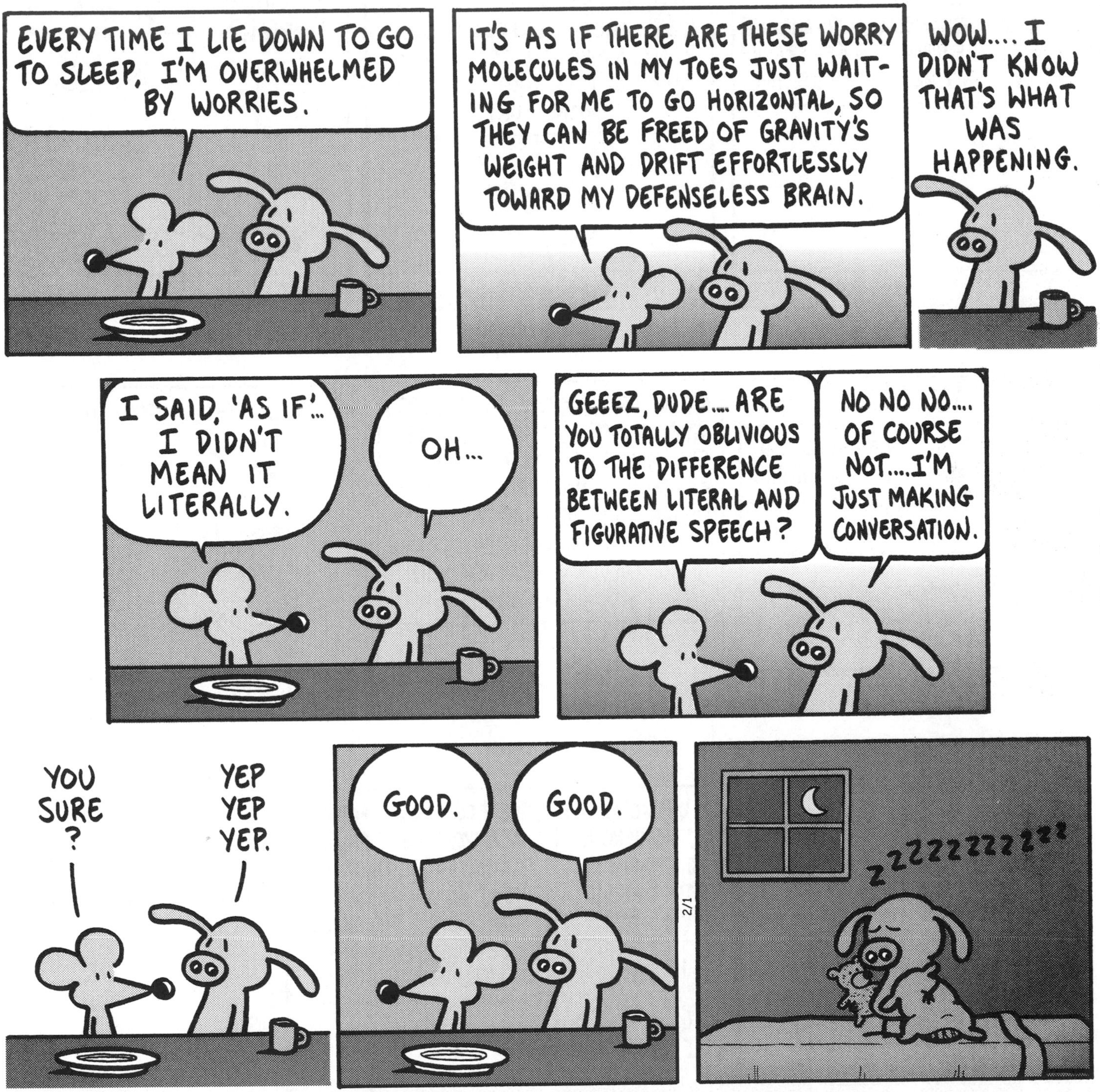
EVERY TIME I LIE DOWN TO GO TO SLEEP, I'M OVERWHELMED BY WORRIES.
IT'S AS IF THERE ARE THESE WORRY MOLECULES IN MY TOES JUST WAITING FOR ME TO GO HORIZONTAL, SO THEY CAN BE FREED OF GRAVITY'S WEIGHT AND DRIFT EFFORTLESSLY TOWARD MY DEFENSELESS BRAIN.
WOW.... I DIDN'T KNOW THAT'S WHAT WAS HAPPENING.
I SAID, 'AS IF'... I DIDN'T MEAN IT LITERALLY.
OH...
GEEEZ, DUDE.... ARE YOU TOTALLY OBLIVIOUS TO THE DIFFERENCE BETWEEN LITERAL AND FIGURATIVE SPEECH?
NO NO NO.... OF COURSE NOT....I'M JUST MAKING CONVERSATION.
YOU SURE?
YEP YEP YEP.
GOOD.
GOOD.
ZZZZZZZZZZZ

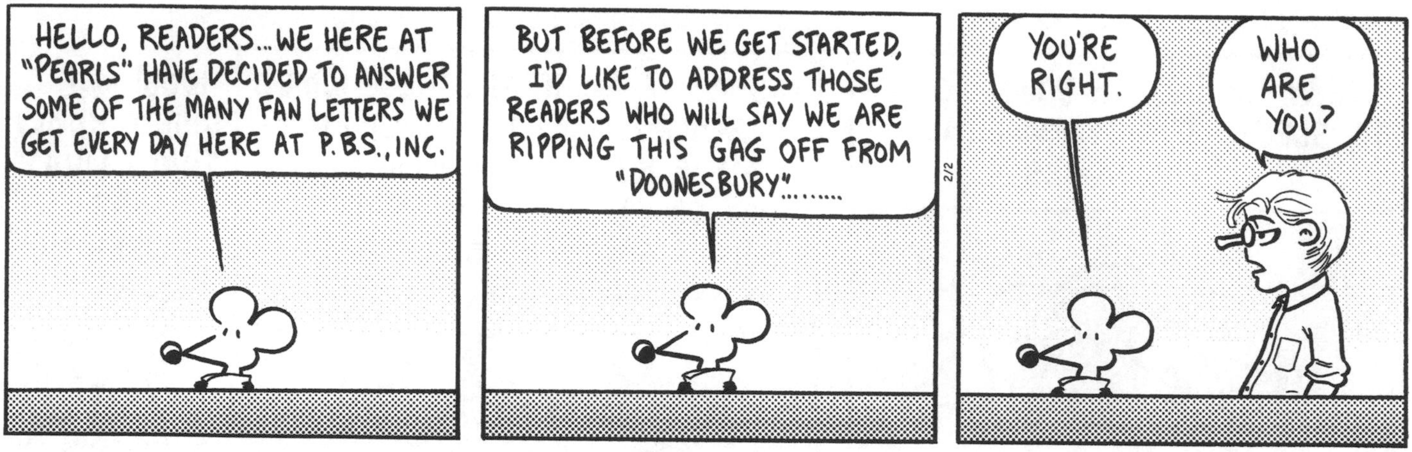
HELLO, READERS...WE HERE AT "PEARLS" HAVE DECIDED TO ANSWER SOME OF THE MANY FAN LETTERS WE GET EVERY DAY HERE AT P.B.S., INC.
BUT BEFORE WE GET STARTED, I'D LIKE TO ADDRESS THOSE READERS WHO WILL SAY WE ARE RIPPING THIS GAG OFF FROM "DOONESBURY".......
2/2
YOU'RE RIGHT.
WHO ARE YOU?

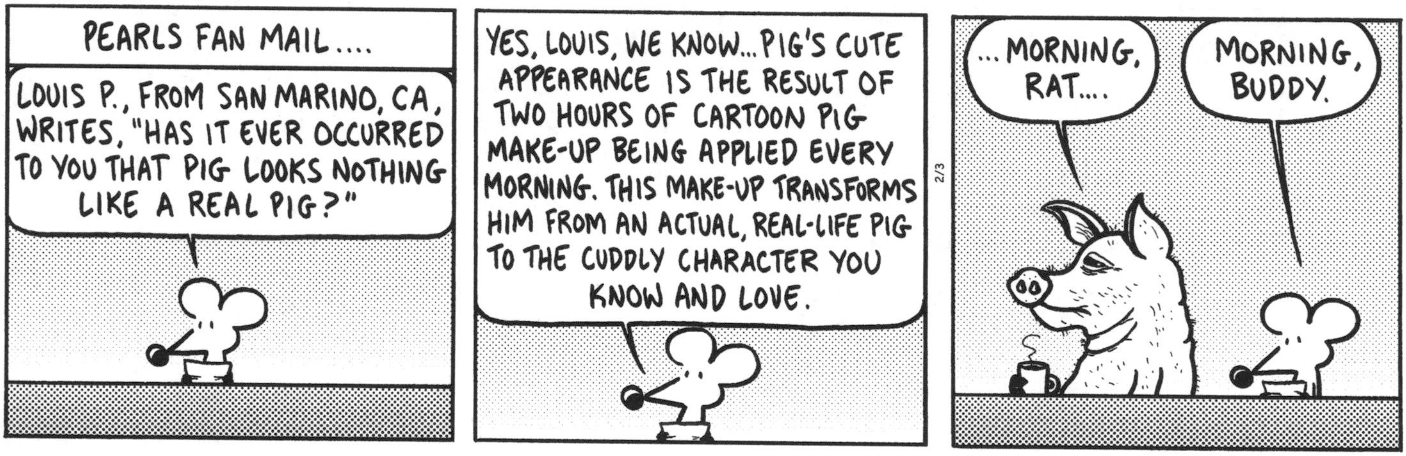
PEARLS FAN MAIL....
LOUIS P., FROM SAN MARINO, CA, WRITES, "HAS IT EVER OCCURRED TO YOU THAT PIG LOOKS NOTHING LIKE A REAL PIG?"
YES, LOUIS, WE KNOW...PIG'S CUTE APPEARANCE IS THE RESULT OF TWO HOURS OF CARTOON PIG MAKE-UP BEING APPLIED EVERY MORNING. THIS MAKE-UP TRANSFORMS HIM FROM AN ACTUAL, REAL-LIFE PIG TO THE CUDDLY CHARACTER YOU KNOW AND LOVE.
2/3
...MORNING, RAT....
MORNING, BUDDY.

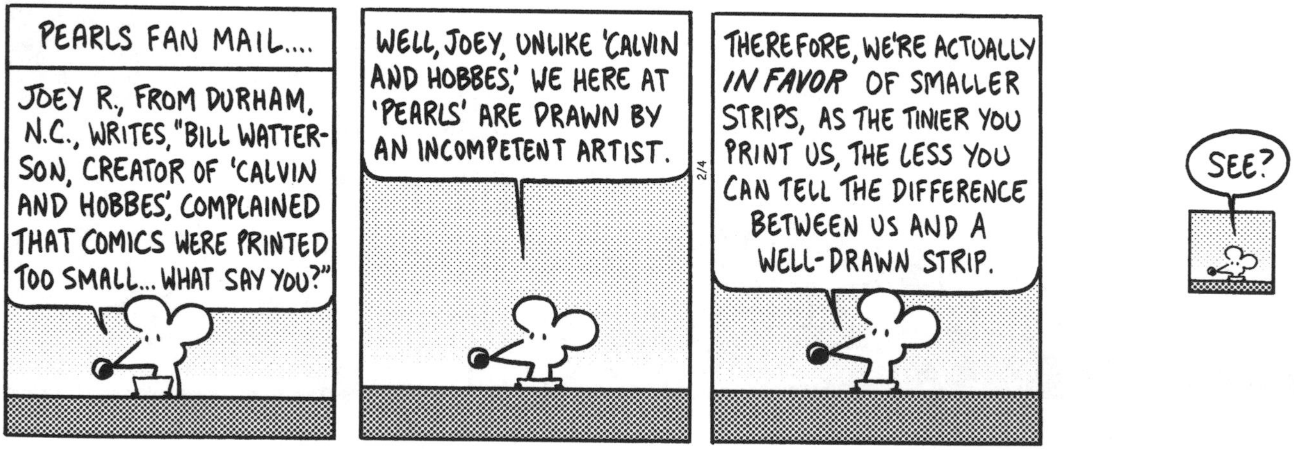
PEARLS FAN MAIL....
JOEY R., FROM DURHAM, N.C., WRITES, "BILL WATTERSON, CREATOR OF 'CALVIN AND HOBBES,' COMPLAINED THAT COMICS WERE PRINTED TOO SMALL...WHAT SAY YOU?"
WELL, JOEY, UNLIKE 'CALVIN AND HOBBES,' WE HERE AT 'PEARLS' ARE DRAWN BY AN INCOMPETENT ARTIST.
2/4
THEREFORE, WE'RE ACTUALLY IN FAVOR OF SMALLER STRIPS, AS THE TINIER YOU PRINT US, THE LESS YOU CAN TELL THE DIFFERENCE BETWEEN US AND A WELL-DRAWN STRIP.
SEE?

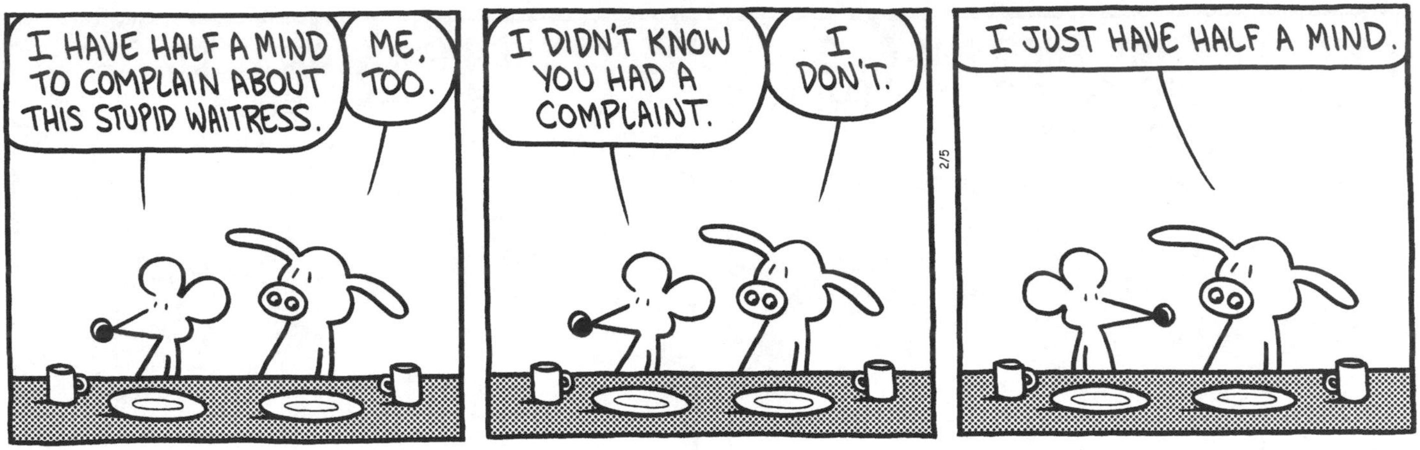
I HAVE HALF A MIND TO COMPLAIN ABOUT THIS STUPID WAITRESS.
ME, TOO.
I DIDN'T KNOW YOU HAD A COMPLAINT.
I DON'T.
2/5
I JUST HAVE HALF A MIND.

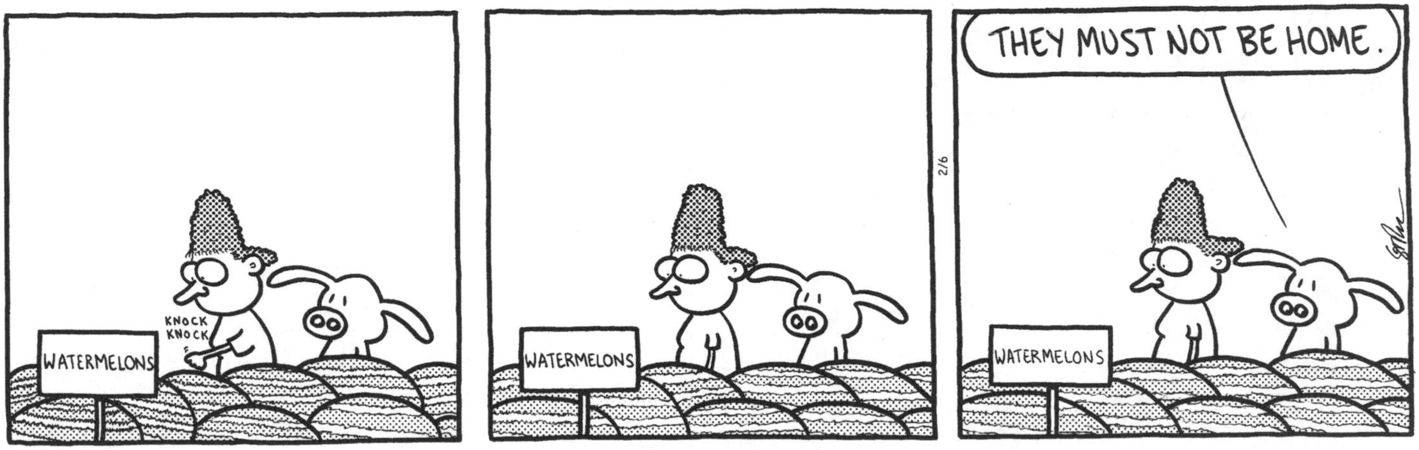
WATERMELONS
KNOCK KNOCK
WATERMELONS
2/6
THEY MUST NOT BE HOME.
WATERMELONS

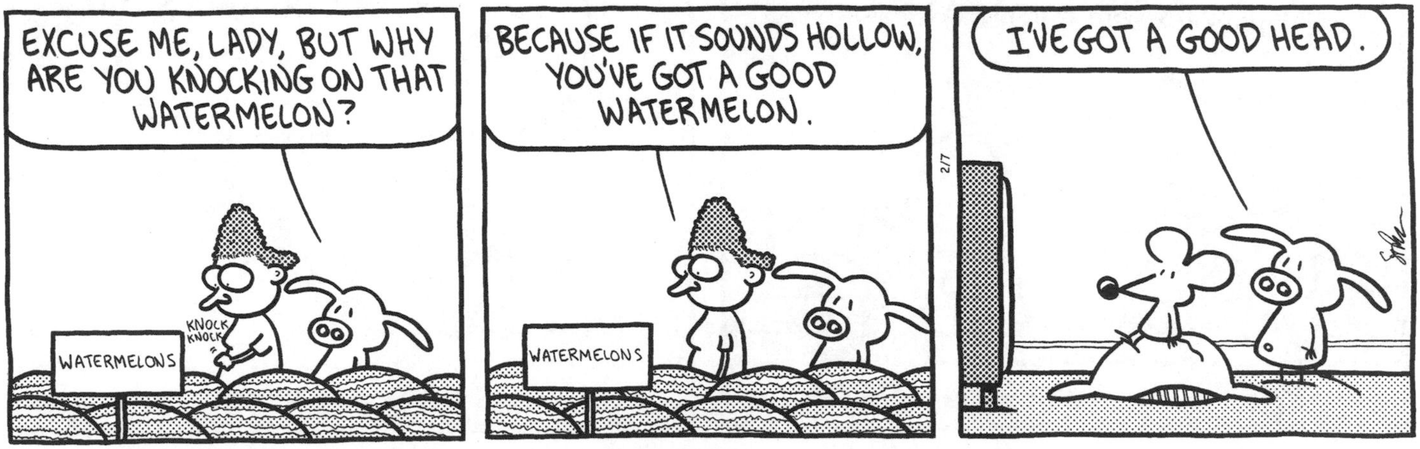
EXCUSE ME, LADY, BUT WHY ARE YOU KNOCKING ON THAT WATERMELON?
WATERMELONS
KNOCK KNOCK
BECAUSE IF IT SOUNDS HOLLOW, YOU'VE GOT A GOOD WATERMELON.
WATERMELONS
2/7
I'VE GOT A GOOD HEAD.

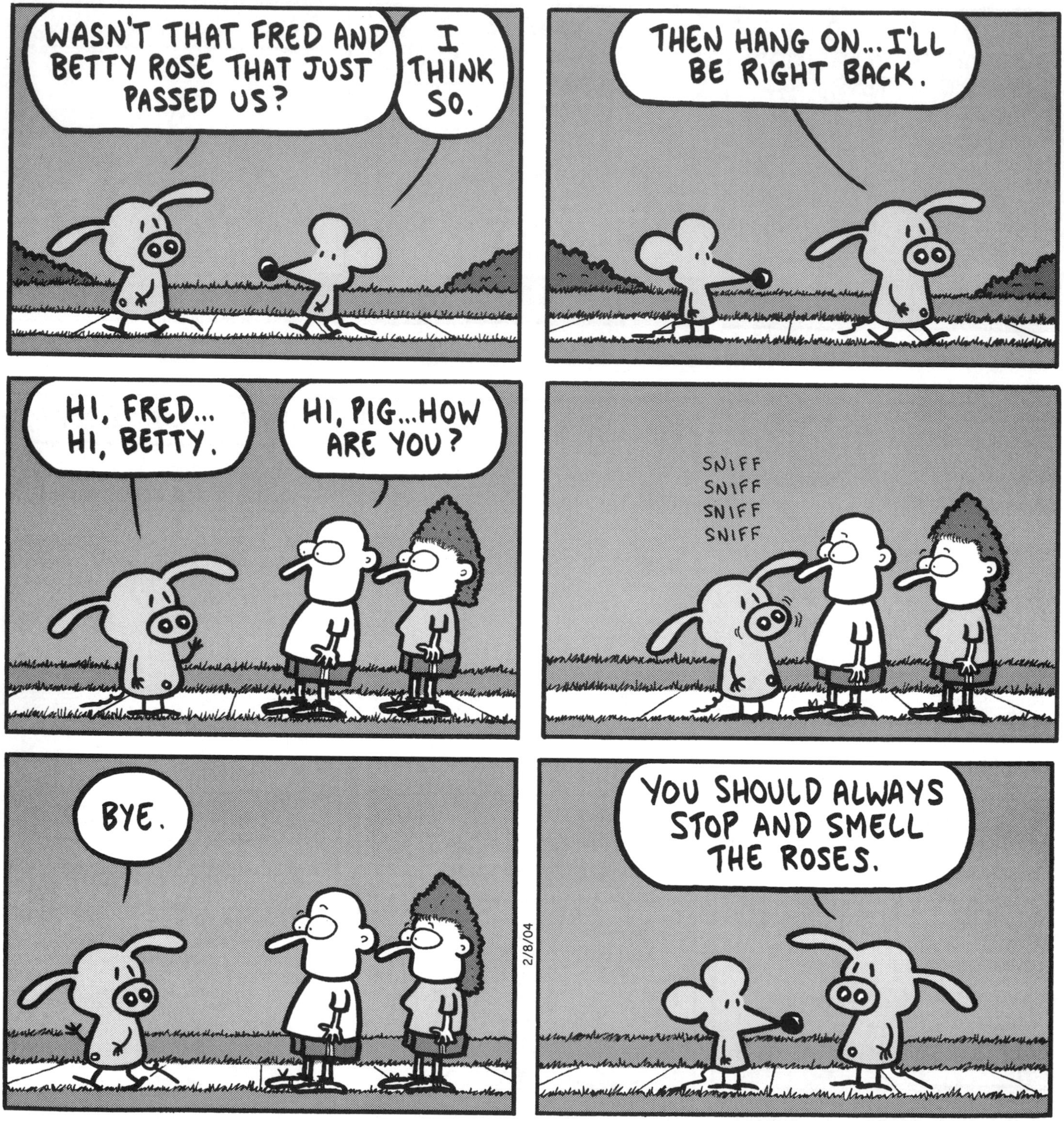
WASN'T THAT FRED AND BETTY ROSE THAT JUST PASSED US?
I THINK SO.
THEN HANG ON... I'LL BE RIGHT BACK.
HI, FRED... HI, BETTY.
HI, PIG...HOW ARE YOU?
SNIFF SNIFF SNIFF SNIFF
BYE.
2/8/04
YOU SHOULD ALWAYS STOP AND SMELL THE ROSES.

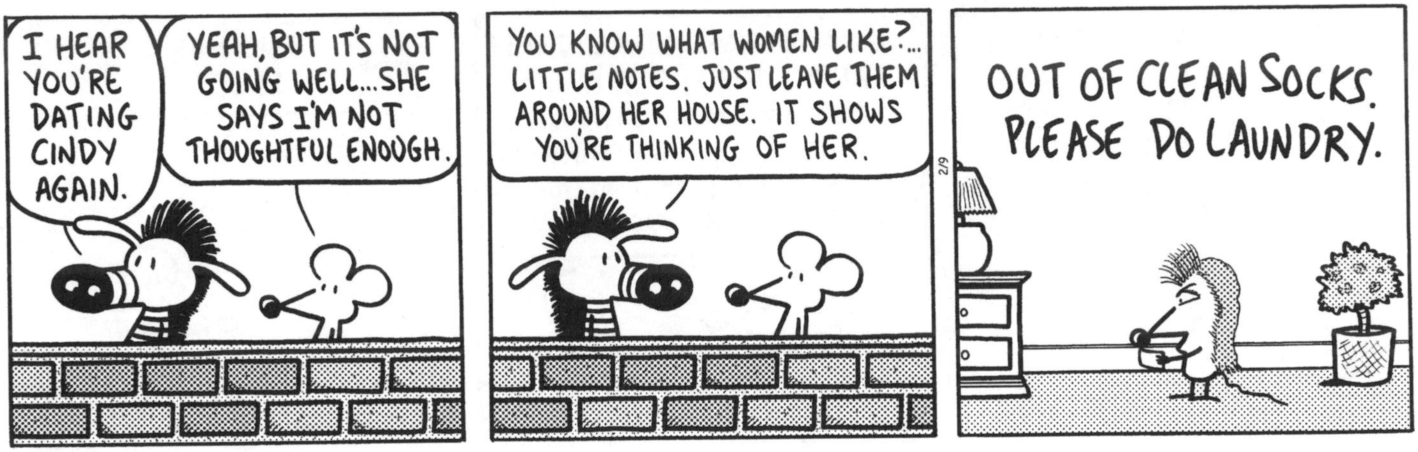
I HEAR YOU'RE DATING CINDY AGAIN.
YEAH, BUT IT'S NOT GOING WELL...SHE SAYS I'M NOT THOUGHTFUL ENOUGH.
YOU KNOW WHAT WOMEN LIKE?... LITTLE NOTES. JUST LEAVE THEM AROUND HER HOUSE. IT SHOWS YOU'RE THINKING OF HER.
2/9
OUT OF CLEAN SOCKS. PLEASE DO LAUNDRY.

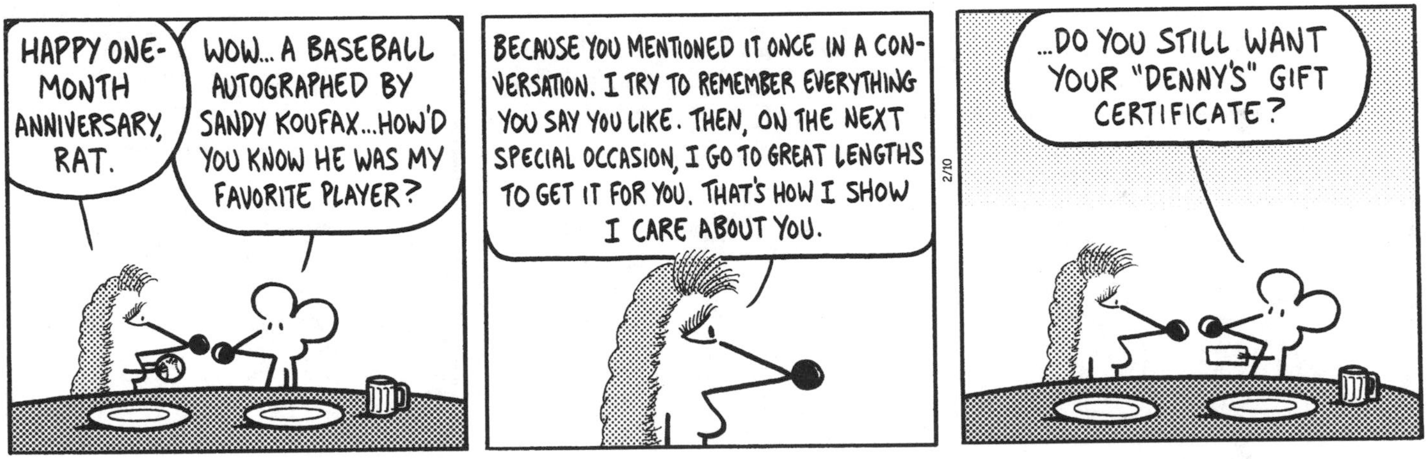
HAPPY ONE-MONTH ANNIVERSARY, RAT.
WOW... A BASEBALL AUTOGRAPHED BY SANDY KOUFAX...HOW'D YOU KNOW HE WAS MY FAVORITE PLAYER?
BECAUSE YOU MENTIONED IT ONCE IN A CONVERSATION. I TRY TO REMEMBER EVERYTHING YOU SAY YOU LIKE. THEN, ON THE NEXT SPECIAL OCCASION, I GO TO GREAT LENGTHS TO GET IT FOR YOU. THAT'S HOW I SHOW I CARE ABOUT YOU.
2/10
...DO YOU STILL WANT YOUR "DENNY'S" GIFT CERTIFICATE?

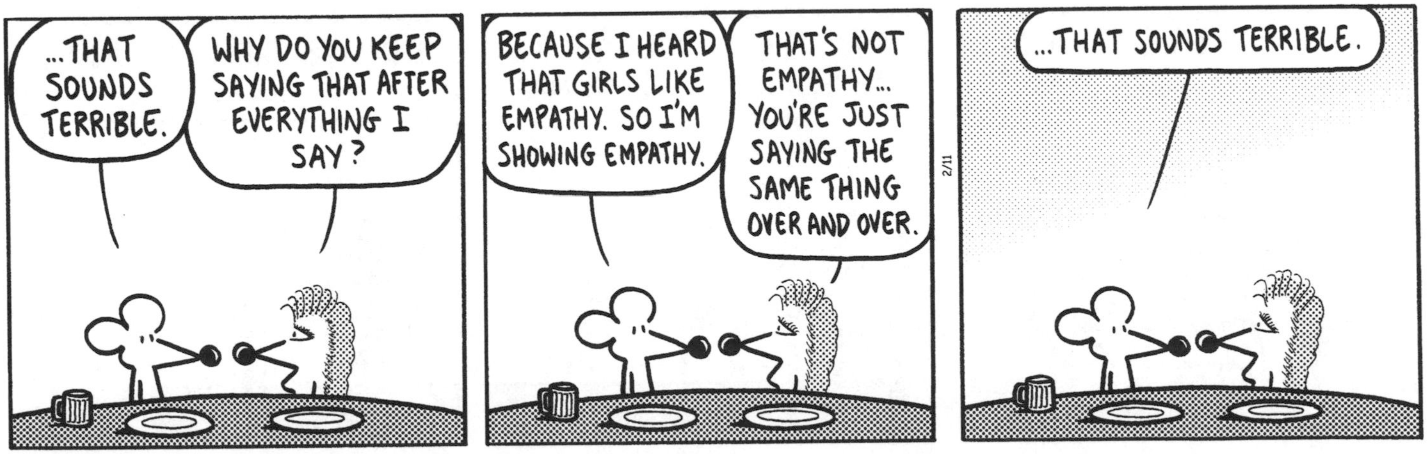
...THAT SOUNDS TERRIBLE.
WHY DO YOU KEEP SAYING THAT AFTER EVERYTHING I SAY?
BECAUSE I HEARD THAT GIRLS LIKE EMPATHY. SO I'M SHOWING EMPATHY.
THAT'S NOT EMPATHY... YOU'RE JUST SAYING THE SAME THING OVER AND OVER.
2/11
...THAT SOUNDS TERRIBLE.

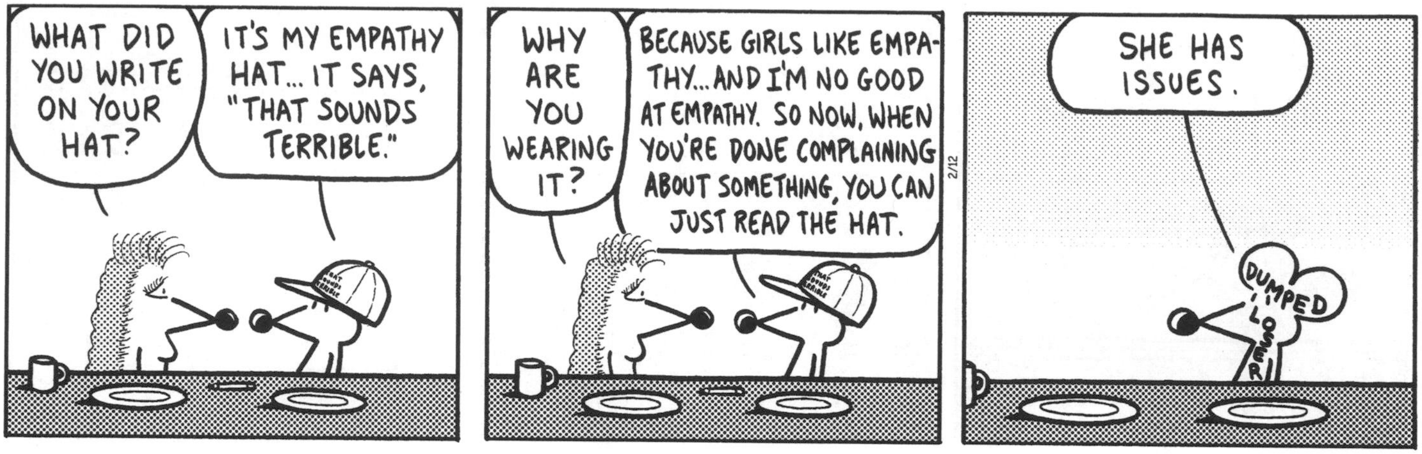
WHAT DID YOU WRITE ON YOUR HAT?
IT'S MY EMPATHY HAT... IT SAYS, "THAT SOUNDS TERRIBLE."
WHY ARE YOU WEARING IT?
BECAUSE GIRLS LIKE EMPATHY... AND I'M NO GOOD AT EMPATHY. SO NOW, WHEN YOU'RE DONE COMPLAINING ABOUT SOMETHING, YOU CAN JUST READ THE HAT.
2/12
SHE HAS ISSUES.
DUMPED
LOSER

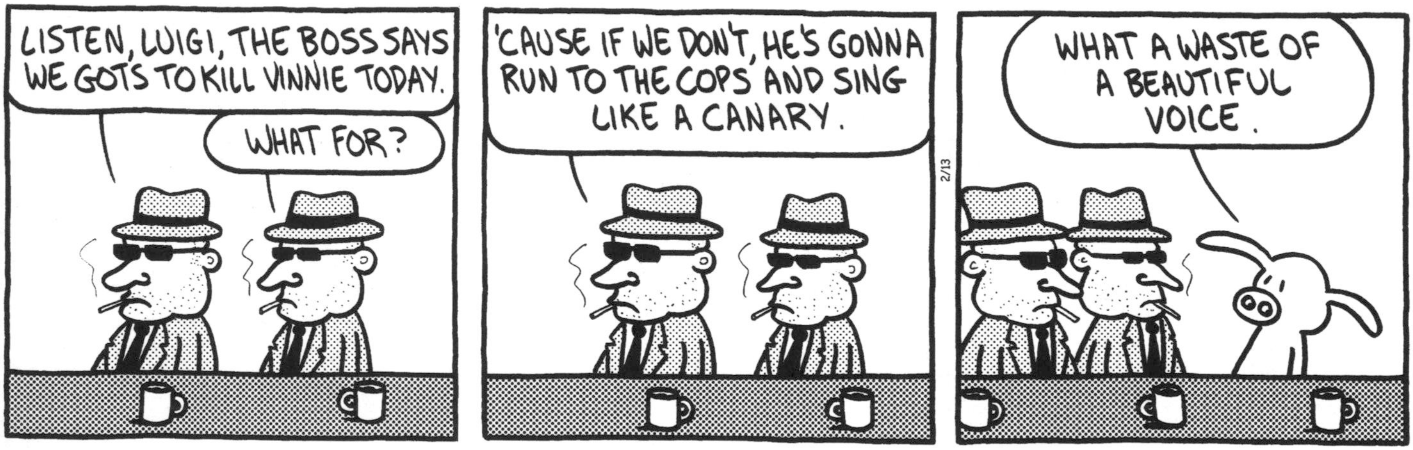
LISTEN, LUIGI, THE BOSS SAYS WE GOTS TO KILL VINNIE TODAY.
WHAT FOR?
'CAUSE IF WE DON'T, HE'S GONNA RUN TO THE COPS AND SING LIKE A CANARY.
2/13
WHAT A WASTE OF A BEAUTIFUL VOICE.

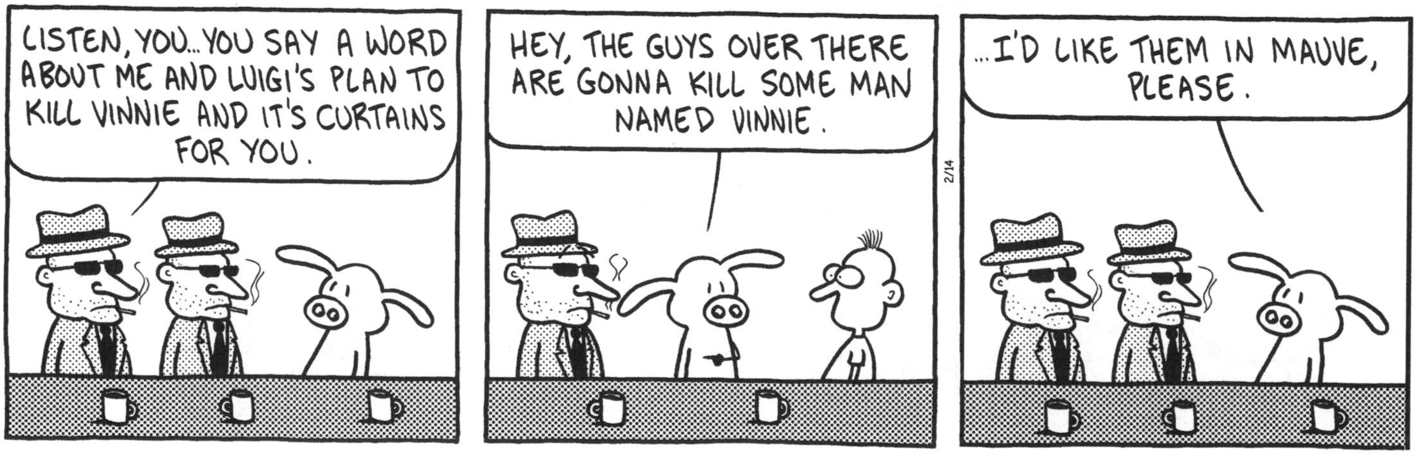
LISTEN, YOU... YOU SAY A WORD ABOUT ME AND LUIGI'S PLAN TO KILL VINNIE AND IT'S CURTAINS FOR YOU.
HEY, THE GUYS OVER THERE ARE GONNA KILL SOME MAN NAMED VINNIE.
2/14
...I'D LIKE THEM IN MAUVE, PLEASE.

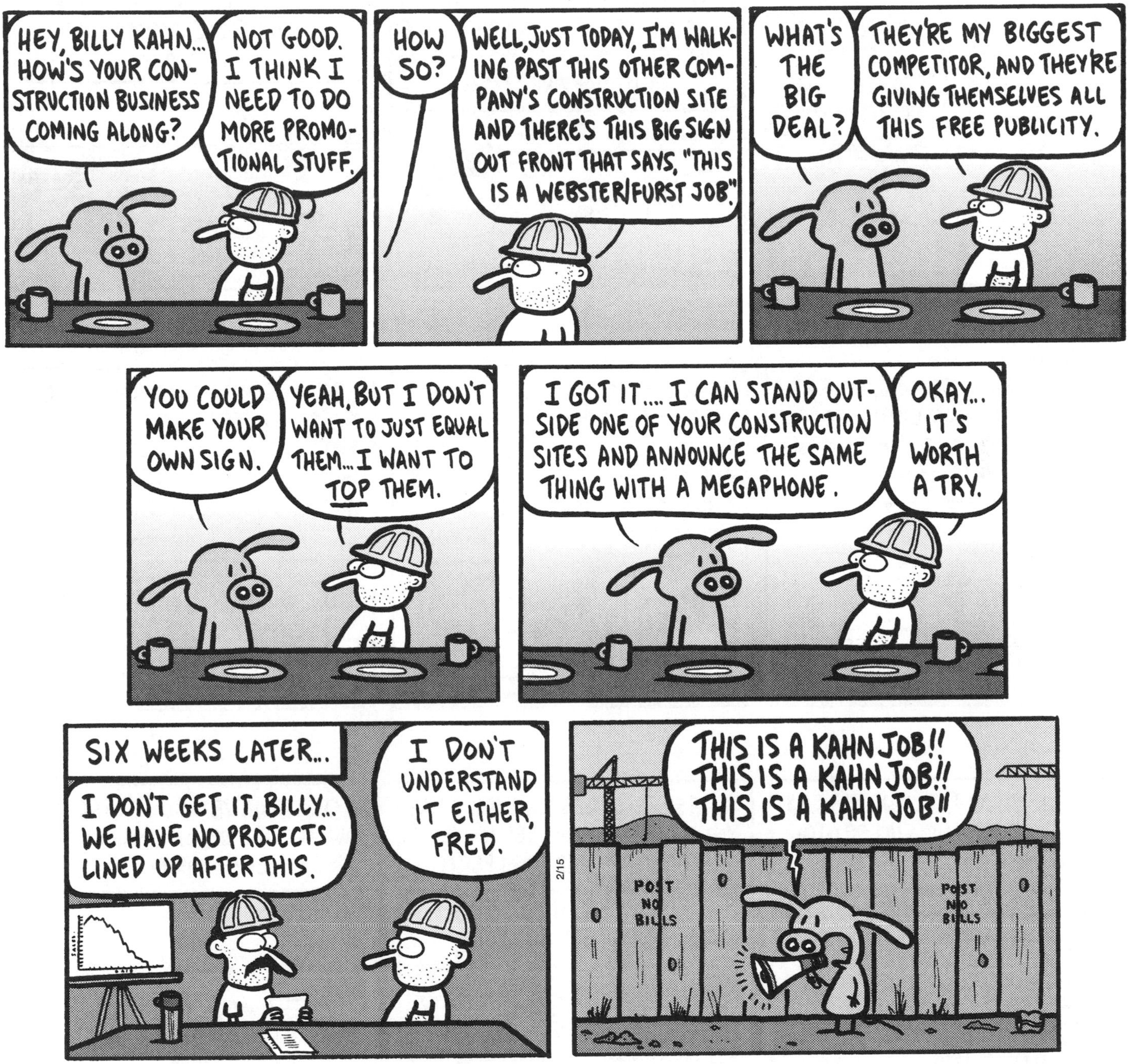
HEY, BILLY KAHN... HOW'S YOUR CONSTRUCTION BUSINESS COMING ALONG?
NOT GOOD. I THINK I NEED TO DO MORE PROMOTIONAL STUFF.
HOW SO?
WELL, JUST TODAY, I'M WALKING PAST THIS OTHER COMPANY'S CONSTRUCTION SITE AND THERE'S THIS BIG SIGN OUT FRONT THAT SAYS, "THIS IS A WEBSTER/FURST JOB".
WHAT'S THE BIG DEAL?
THEY'RE MY BIGGEST COMPETITOR, AND THEY'RE GIVING THEMSELVES ALL THIS FREE PUBLICITY.
YOU COULD MAKE YOUR OWN SIGN.
YEAH, BUT I DON'T WANT TO JUST EQUAL THEM... I WANT TO TOP THEM.
I GOT IT.... I CAN STAND OUTSIDE ONE OF YOUR CONSTRUCTION SITES AND ANNOUNCE THE SAME THING WITH A MEGAPHONE.
OKAY... IT'S WORTH A TRY.
SIX WEEKS LATER...
I DON'T GET IT, BILLY... WE HAVE NO PROJECTS LINED UP AFTER THIS.
I DON'T UNDERSTAND IT EITHER, FRED.
2/15
THIS IS A KAHN JOB!! THIS IS A KAHN JOB!! THIS IS A KAHN JOB!!
POST NO BILLS
POST NO BILLS

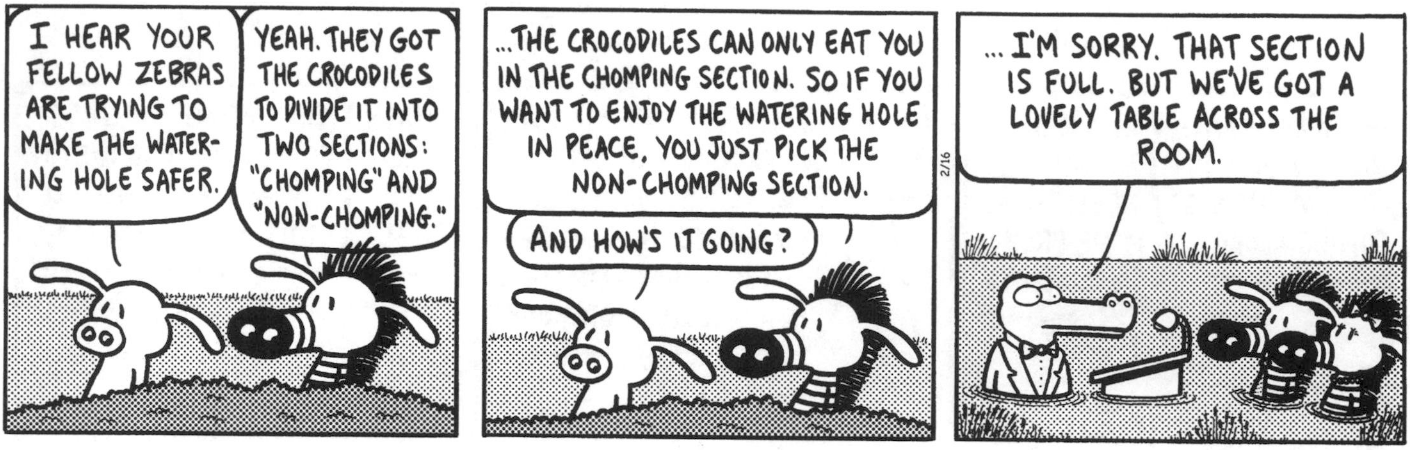
I HEAR YOUR FELLOW ZEBRAS ARE TRYING TO MAKE THE WATERING HOLE SAFER.
YEAH. THEY GOT THE CROCODILES TO DIVIDE IT INTO TWO SECTIONS: "CHOMPING" AND "NON-CHOMPING."
...THE CROCODILES CAN ONLY EAT YOU IN THE CHOMPING SECTION. SO IF YOU WANT TO ENJOY THE WATERING HOLE IN PEACE, YOU JUST PICK THE NON-CHOMPING SECTION.
AND HOW'S IT GOING?
2/16
... I'M SORRY. THAT SECTION IS FULL. BUT WE'VE GOT A LOVELY TABLE ACROSS THE ROOM.

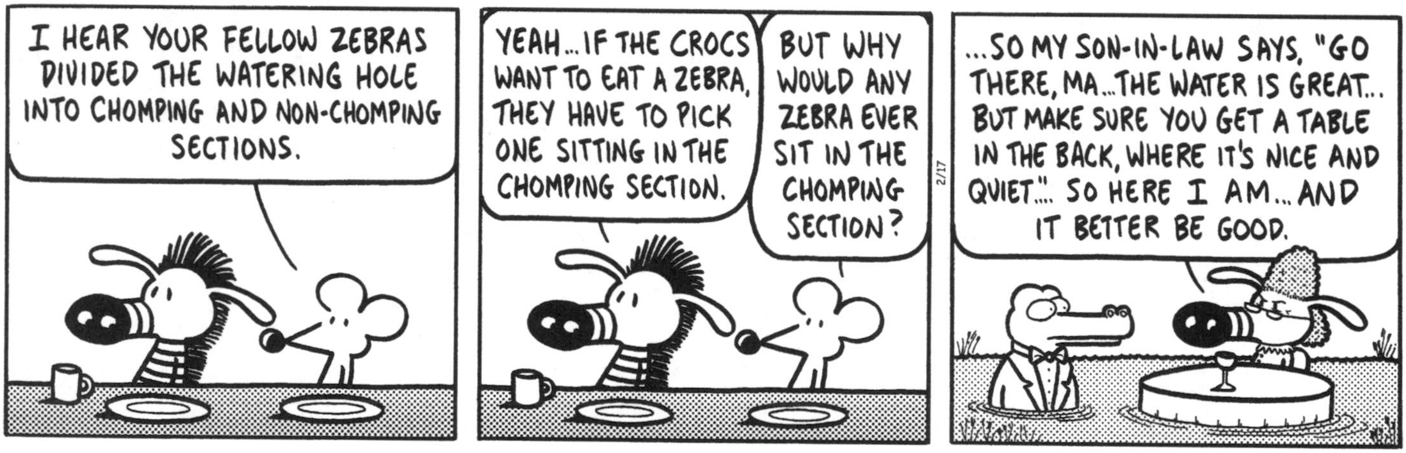
I HEAR YOUR FELLOW ZEBRAS DIVIDED THE WATERING HOLE INTO CHOMPING AND NON-CHOMPING SECTIONS.
YEAH... IF THE CROCS WANT TO EAT A ZEBRA, THEY HAVE TO PICK ONE SITTING IN THE CHOMPING SECTION.
BUT WHY WOULD ANY ZEBRA EVER SIT IN THE CHOMPING SECTION?
2/17
...SO MY SON-IN-LAW SAYS, "GO THERE, MA... THE WATER IS GREAT... BUT MAKE SURE YOU GET A TABLE IN THE BACK, WHERE IT'S NICE AND QUIET."... SO HERE I AM... AND IT BETTER BE GOOD.

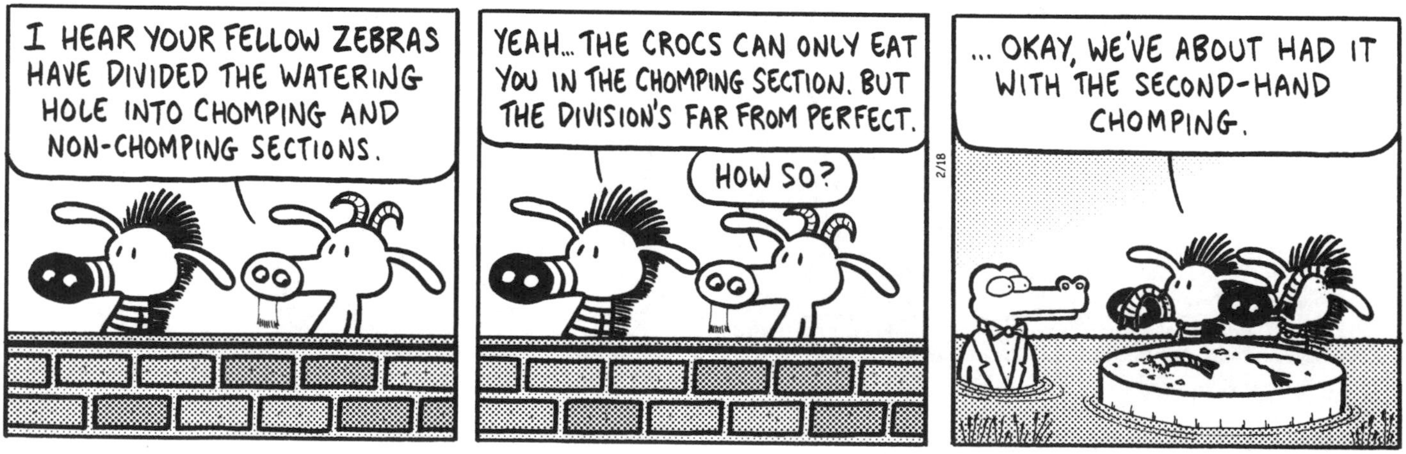
I HEAR YOUR FELLOW ZEBRAS HAVE DIVIDED THE WATERING HOLE INTO CHOMPING AND NON-CHOMPING SECTIONS.
YEAH... THE CROCS CAN ONLY EAT YOU IN THE CHOMPING SECTION. BUT THE DIVISION'S FAR FROM PERFECT.
HOW SO?
2/18
... OKAY, WE'VE ABOUT HAD IT WITH THE SECOND-HAND CHOMPING.

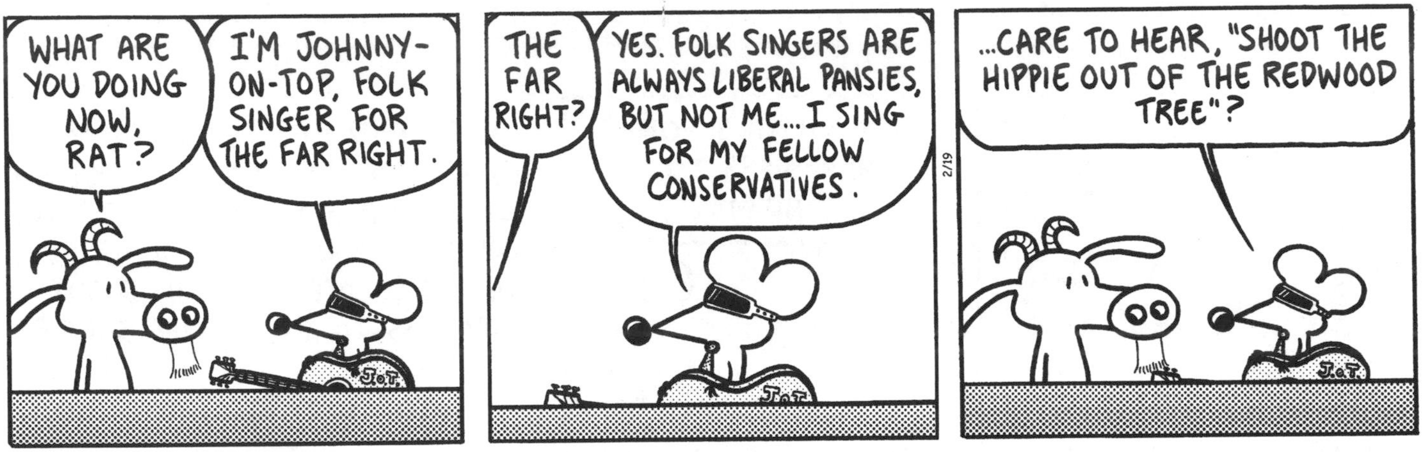
WHAT ARE YOU DOING NOW, RAT?
I'M JOHNNY-ON-TOP, FOLK SINGER FOR THE FAR RIGHT.
THE FAR RIGHT?
YES. FOLK SINGERS ARE ALWAYS LIBERAL PANSIES, BUT NOT ME... I SING FOR MY FELLOW CONSERVATIVES.
2/19
...CARE TO HEAR, "SHOOT THE HIPPIE OUT OF THE REDWOOD TREE"?

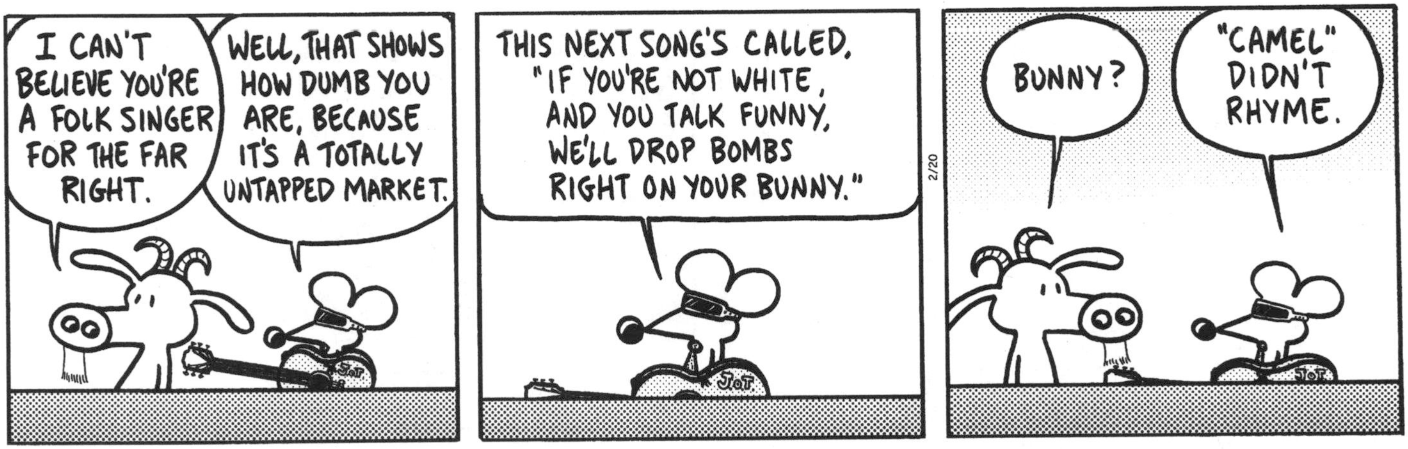
I CAN'T BELIEVE YOU'RE A FOLK SINGER FOR THE FAR RIGHT.
WELL, THAT SHOWS HOW DUMB YOU ARE, BECAUSE IT'S A TOTALLY UNTAPPED MARKET.
THIS NEXT SONG'S CALLED, "IF YOU'RE NOT WHITE, AND YOU TALK FUNNY, WE'LL DROP BOMBS RIGHT ON YOUR BUNNY."
2/20
BUNNY?
"CAMEL" DIDN'T RHYME.

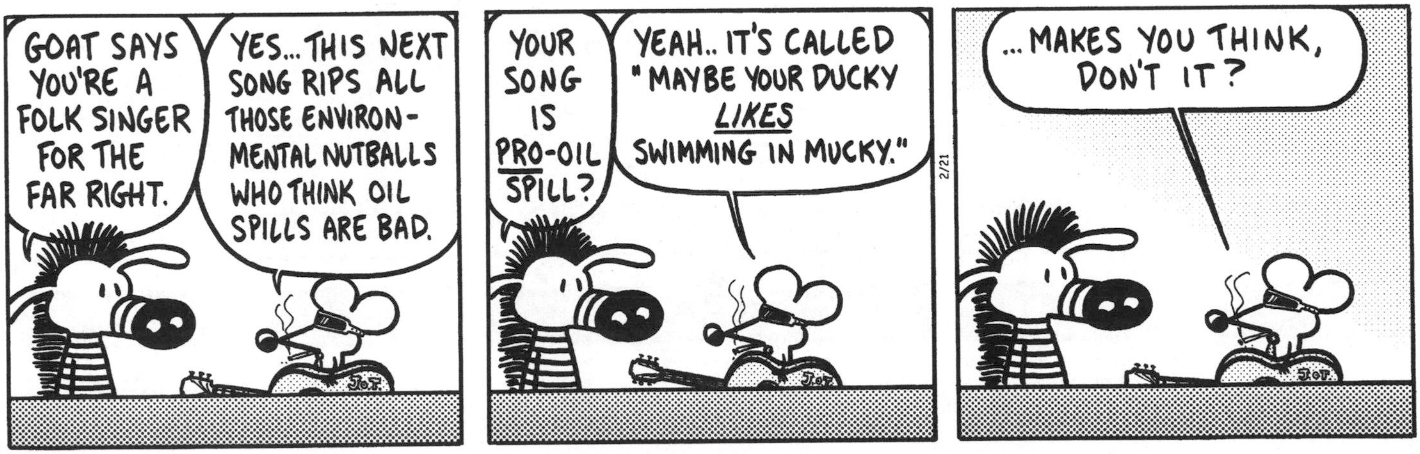
GOAT SAYS YOU'RE A FOLK SINGER FOR THE FAR RIGHT.
YES... THIS NEXT SONG RIPS ALL THOSE ENVIRON-MENTAL NUTBALLS WHO THINK OIL SPILLS ARE BAD.
YOUR SONG IS PRO-OIL SPILL?
YEAH.. IT'S CALLED "MAYBE YOUR DUCKY LIKES SWIMMING IN MUCKY."
2/21
... MAKES YOU THINK, DON'T IT?

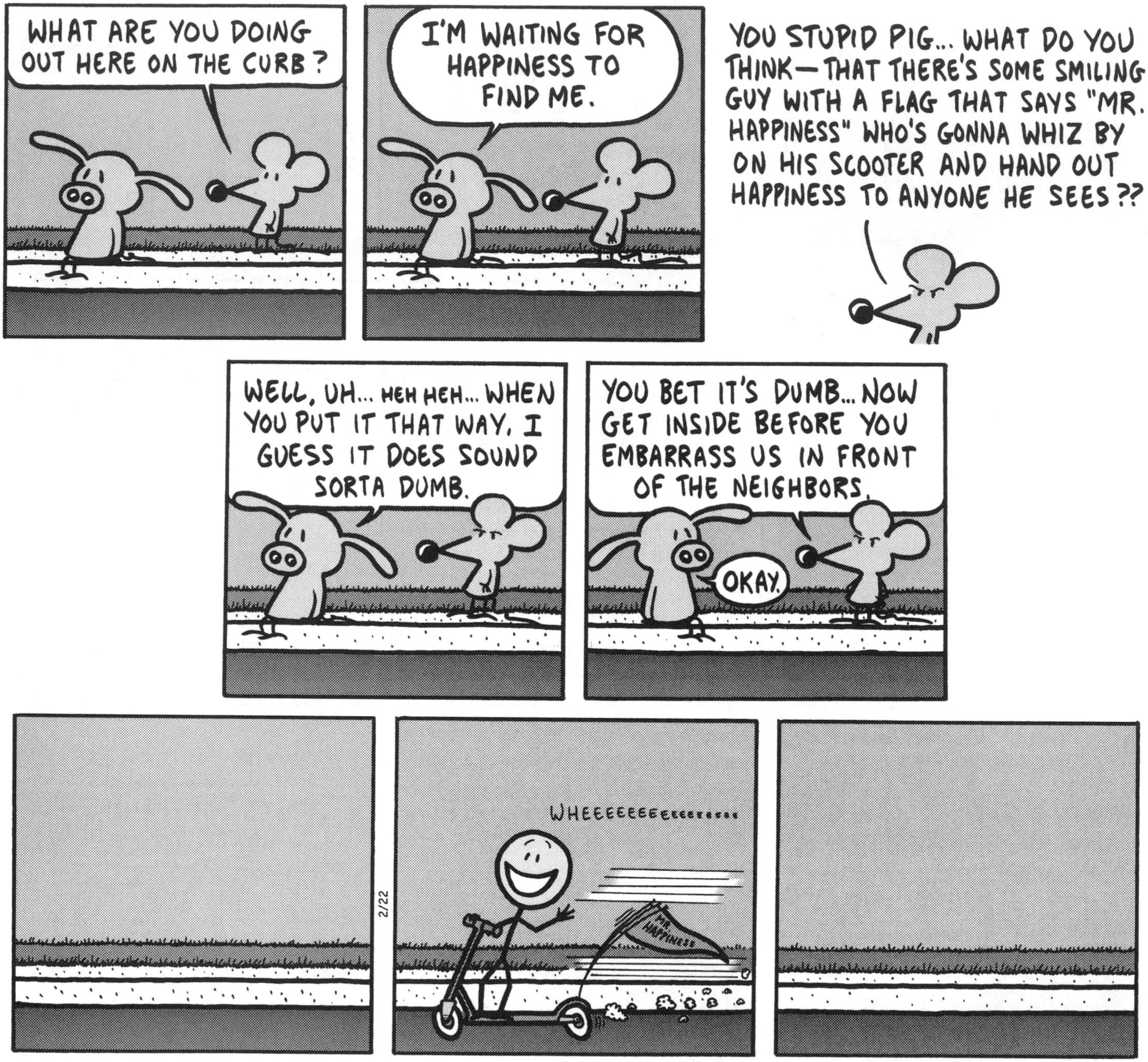
WHAT ARE YOU DOING OUT HERE ON THE CURB?
I'M WAITING FOR HAPPINESS TO FIND ME.
YOU STUPID PIG... WHAT DO YOU THINK—THAT THERE'S SOME SMILING GUY WITH A FLAG THAT SAYS "MR. HAPPINESS" WHO'S GONNA WHIZ BY ON HIS SCOOTER AND HAND OUT HAPPINESS TO ANYONE HE SEES??
WELL, UH... HEH HEH... WHEN YOU PUT IT THAT WAY, I GUESS IT DOES SOUND SORTA DUMB.
YOU BET IT'S DUMB... NOW GET INSIDE BEFORE YOU EMBARRASS US IN FRONT OF THE NEIGHBORS.
OKAY.
2/22
WHEEEEEEEEeeeeeee
MR. HAPPINESS

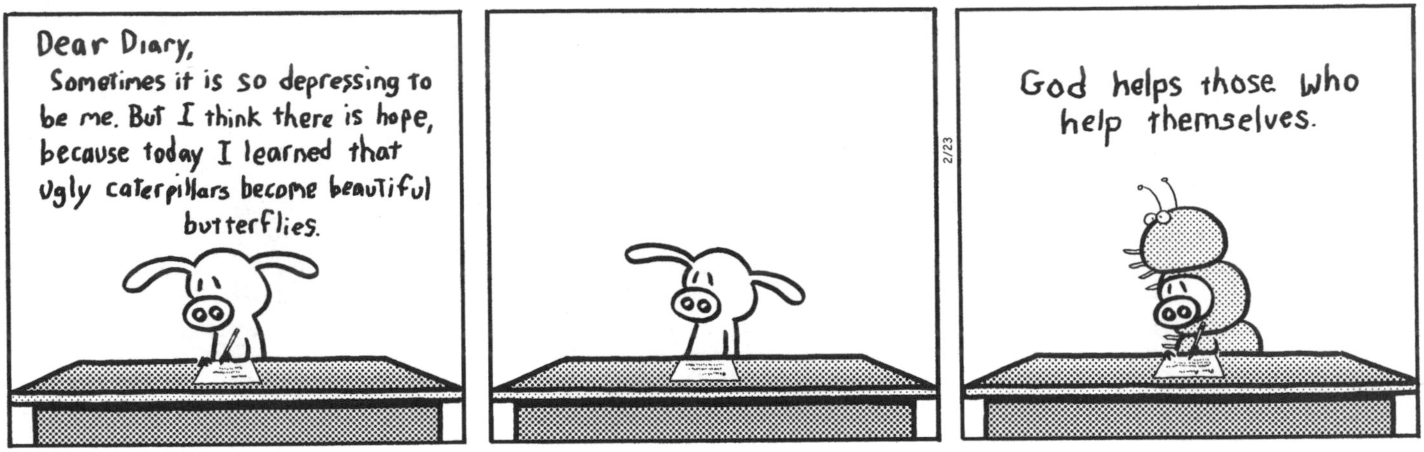
Dear Diary,
Sometimes it is so depressing to be me. But I think there is hope, because today I learned that ugly caterpillars become beautiful butterflies.
2/23
God helps those who help themselves.

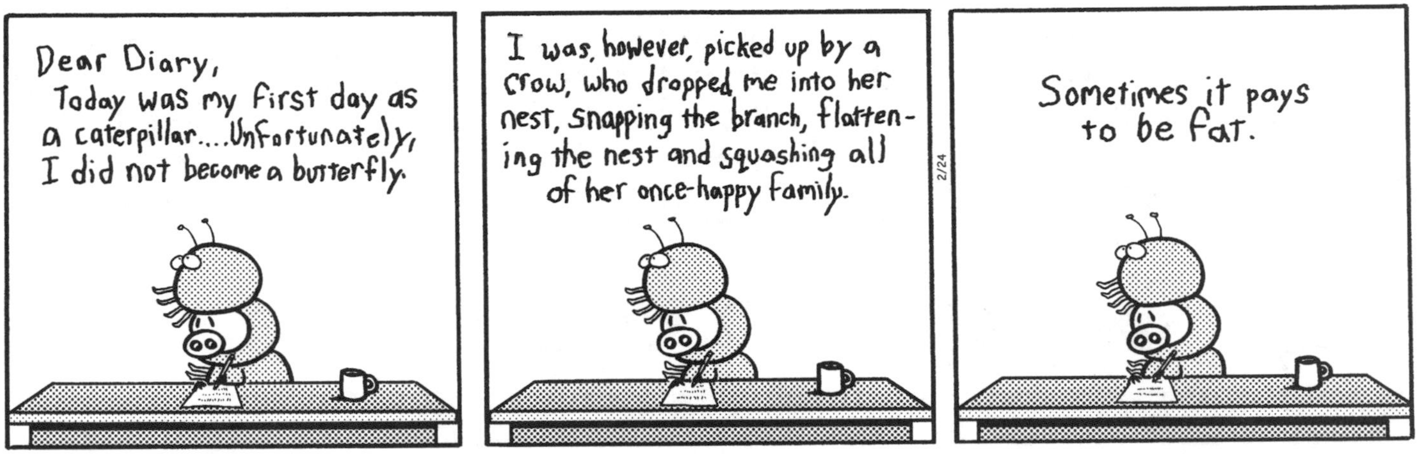
Dear Diary,
Today was my first day as a caterpillar....Unfortunately, I did not become a butterfly.
I was, however, picked up by a crow, who dropped me into her nest, snapping the branch, flattening the nest and squashing all of her once-happy family.
2/24
Sometimes it pays to be fat.

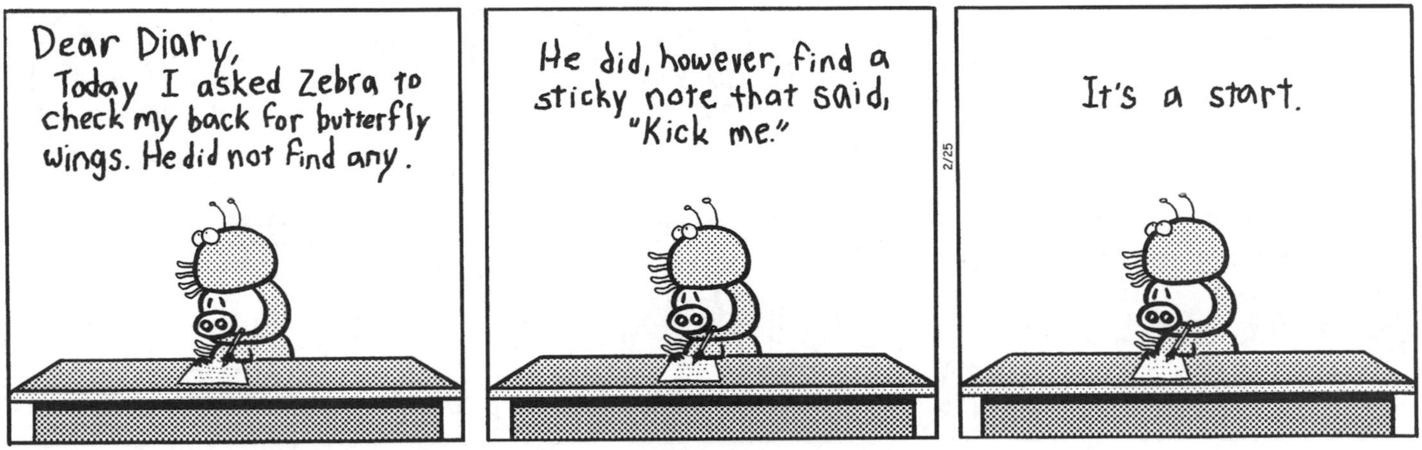
Dear Diary,
Today I asked Zebra to check my back for butterfly wings. He did not find any.
He did, however, find a sticky note that said, "Kick me."
2/25
It's a start.

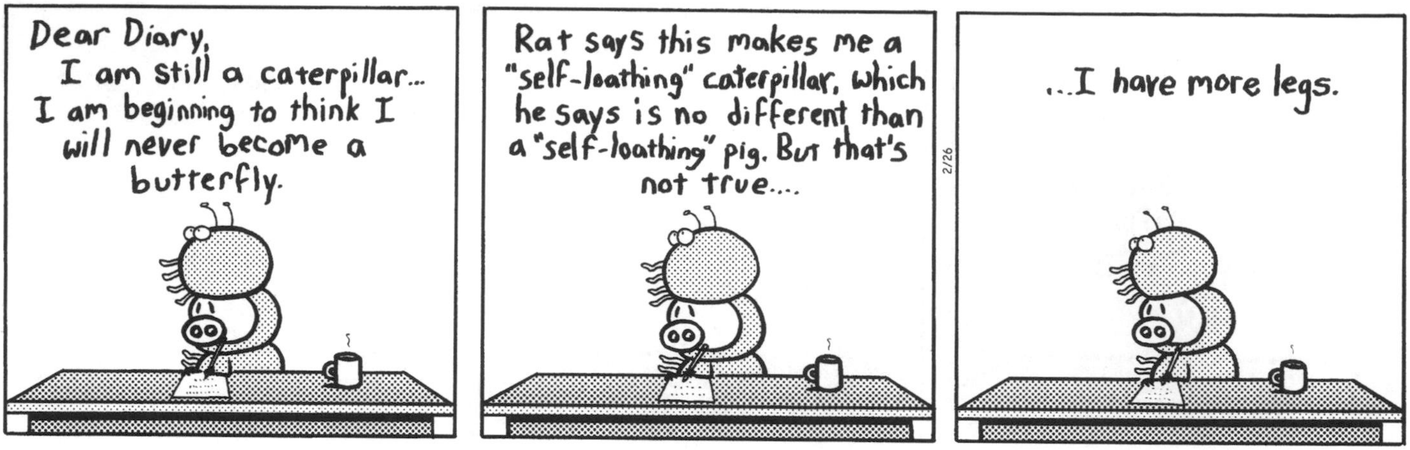
Dear Diary,
I am still a caterpillar... I am beginning to think I will never become a butterfly.
Rat says this makes me a "self-loathing" caterpillar, which he says is no different than a "self-loathing" pig. But that's not true....
2/26
...I have more legs.

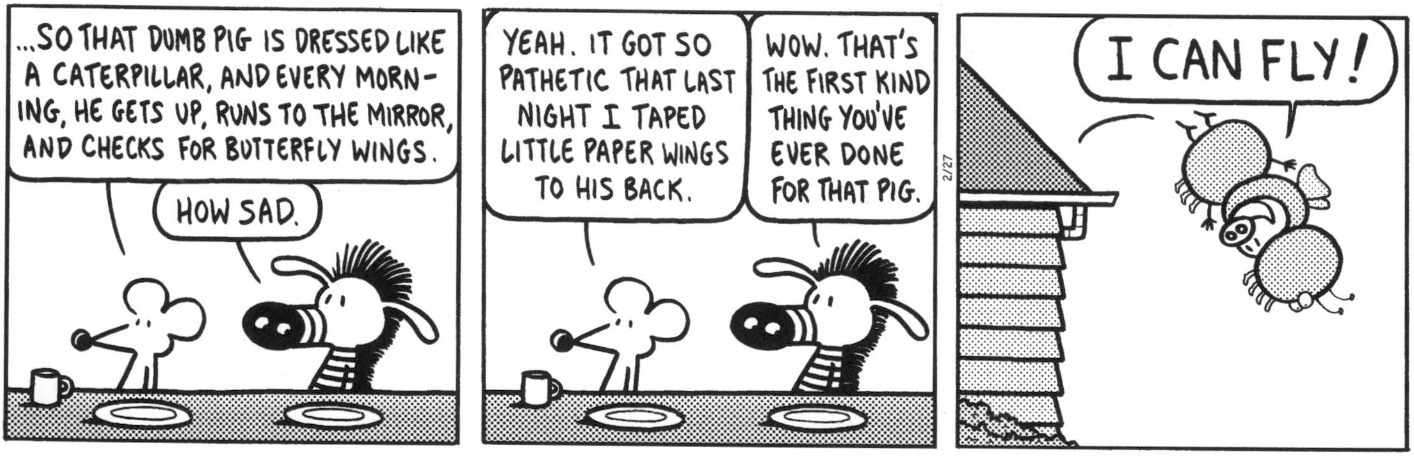
...SO THAT DUMB PIG IS DRESSED LIKE A CATERPILLAR, AND EVERY MORNING, HE GETS UP, RUNS TO THE MIRROR, AND CHECKS FOR BUTTERFLY WINGS.
HOW SAD.
YEAH. IT GOT SO PATHETIC THAT LAST NIGHT I TAPED LITTLE PAPER WINGS TO HIS BACK.
WOW. THAT'S THE FIRST KIND THING YOU'VE EVER DONE FOR THAT PIG.
2/27
I CAN FLY!

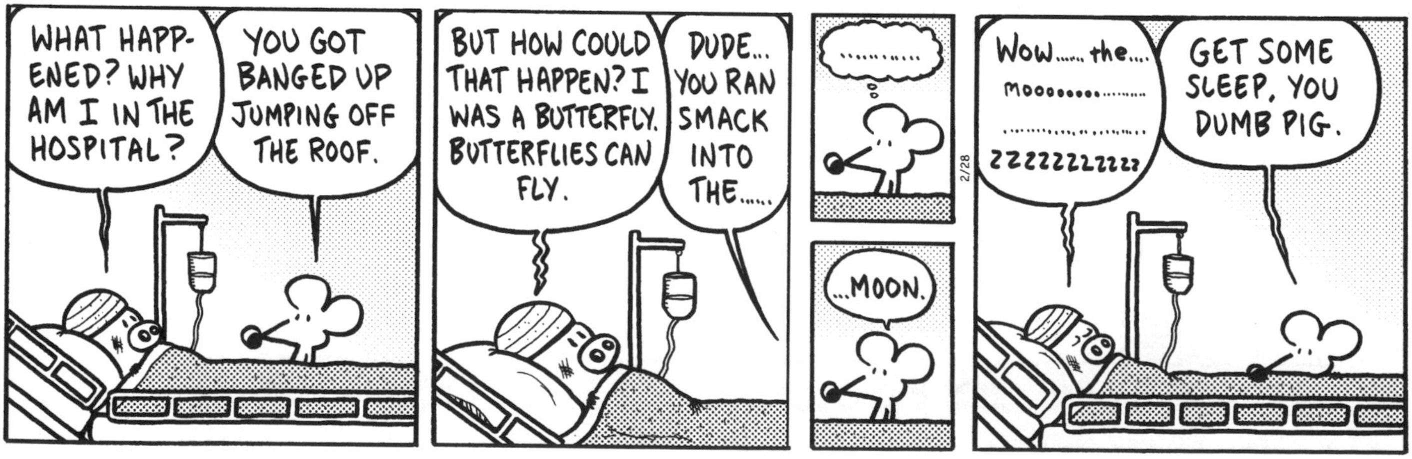
WHAT HAPPENED? WHY AM I IN THE HOSPITAL?
YOU GOT BANGED UP JUMPING OFF THE ROOF.
BUT HOW COULD THAT HAPPEN? I WAS A BUTTERFLY. BUTTERFLIES CAN FLY.
DUDE... YOU RAN SMACK INTO THE.....
2/28
...MOON.
Wow...... the.... Mooooooo..........
zzzzzzzzzzzz
GET SOME SLEEP, YOU DUMB PIG.

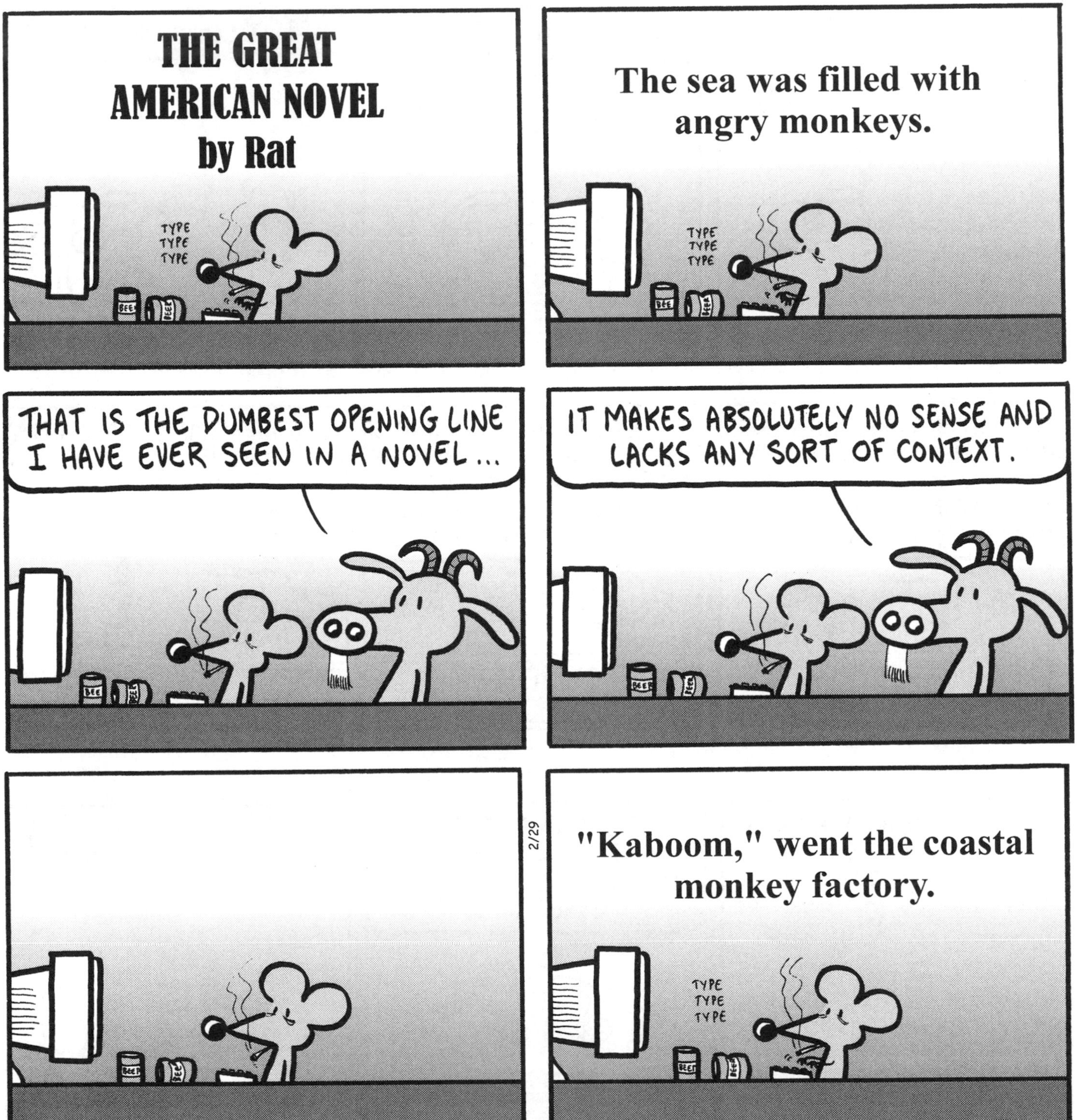
THE GREAT AMERICAN NOVEL by Rat
TYPE TYPE TYPE
The sea was filled with angry monkeys.
TYPE TYPE TYPE
THAT IS THE DUMBEST OPENING LINE I HAVE EVER SEEN IN A NOVEL...
IT MAKES ABSOLUTELY NO SENSE AND LACKS ANY SORT OF CONTEXT.
2/29
"Kaboom," went the coastal monkey factory.
TYPE TYPE TYPE

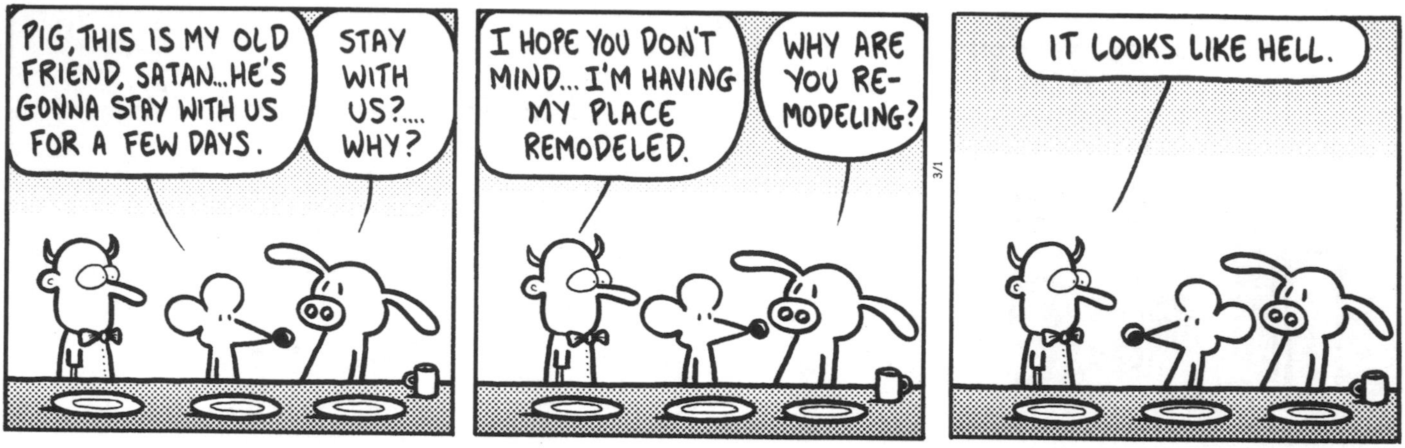
PIG, THIS IS MY OLD FRIEND, SATAN...HE'S GONNA STAY WITH US FOR A FEW DAYS.
STAY WITH US?.... WHY?
I HOPE YOU DON'T MIND... I'M HAVING MY PLACE REMODELED.
WHY ARE YOU RE-MODELING?
3/1
IT LOOKS LIKE HELL.

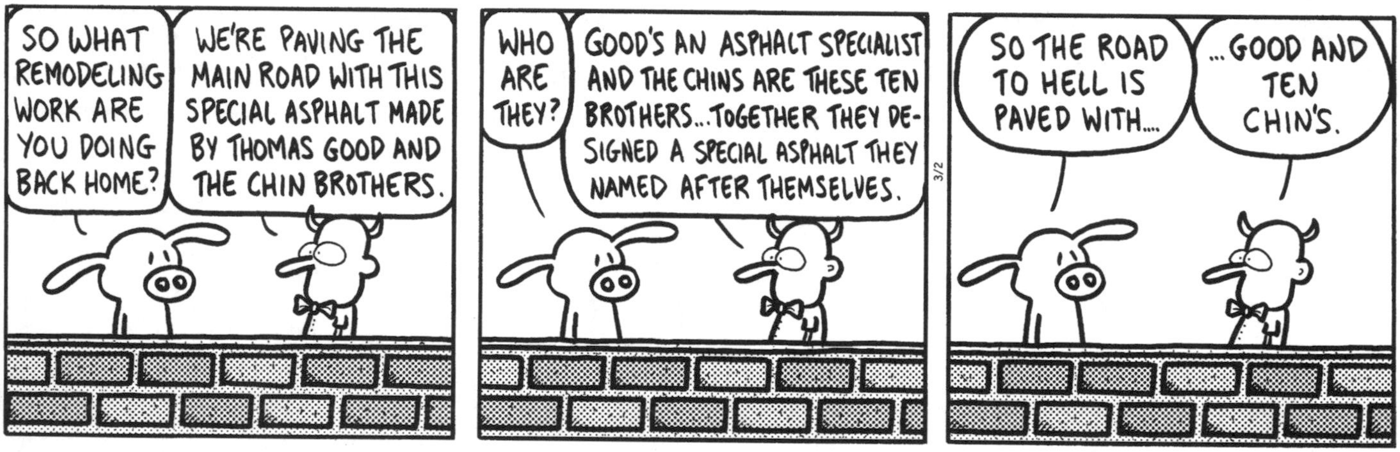
SO WHAT REMODELING WORK ARE YOU DOING BACK HOME?
WE'RE PAVING THE MAIN ROAD WITH THIS SPECIAL ASPHALT MADE BY THOMAS GOOD AND THE CHIN BROTHERS.
WHO ARE THEY?
GOOD'S AN ASPHALT SPECIALIST AND THE CHINS ARE THESE TEN BROTHERS...TOGETHER THEY DE-SIGNED A SPECIAL ASPHALT THEY NAMED AFTER THEMSELVES.
3/2
SO THE ROAD TO HELL IS PAVED WITH....
...GOOD AND TEN CHIN'S.

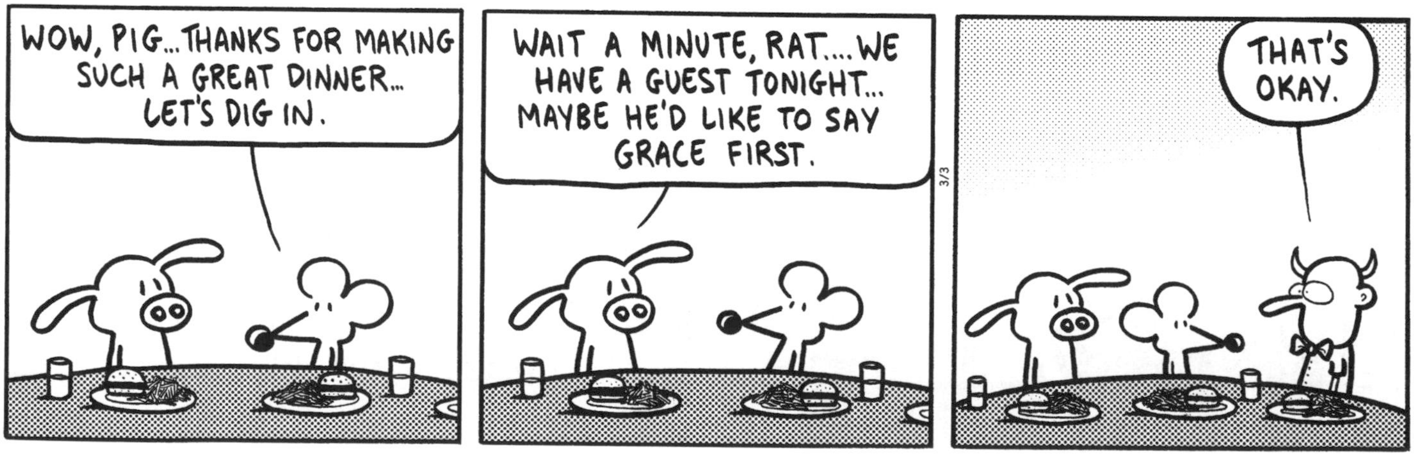
WOW, PIG...THANKS FOR MAKING SUCH A GREAT DINNER... LET'S DIG IN.
WAIT A MINUTE, RAT....WE HAVE A GUEST TONIGHT... MAYBE HE'D LIKE TO SAY GRACE FIRST.
3/3
THAT'S OKAY.

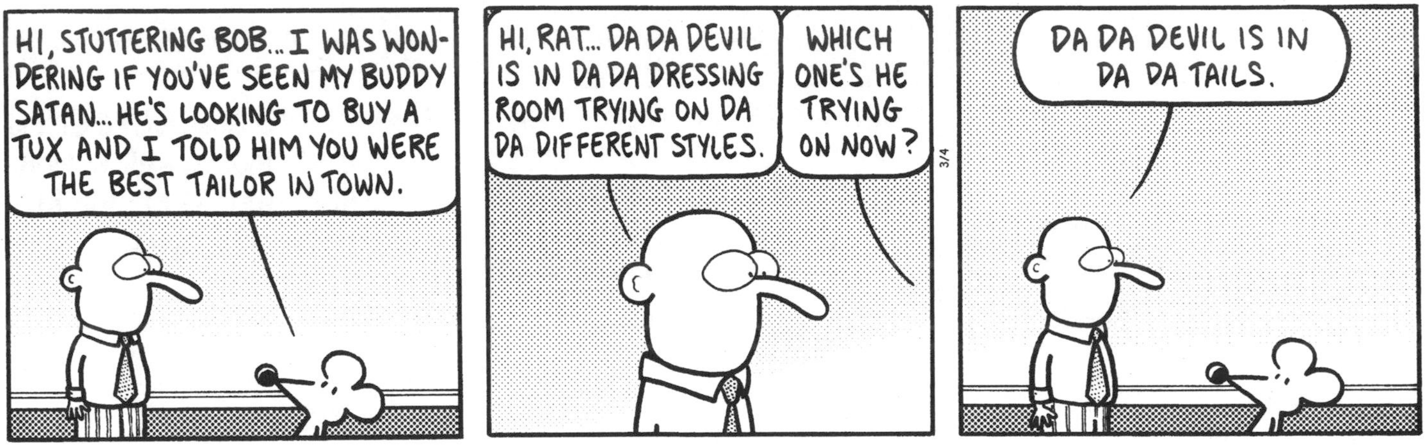
HI, STUTTERING BOB... I WAS WONDERING IF YOU'VE SEEN MY BUDDY SATAN... HE'S LOOKING TO BUY A TUX AND I TOLD HIM YOU WERE THE BEST TAILOR IN TOWN.
HI, RAT... DA DA DEVIL IS IN DA DA DRESSING ROOM TRYING ON DA DA DIFFERENT STYLES.
WHICH ONE'S HE TRYING ON NOW?
3/4
DA DA DEVIL IS IN DA DA TAILS.

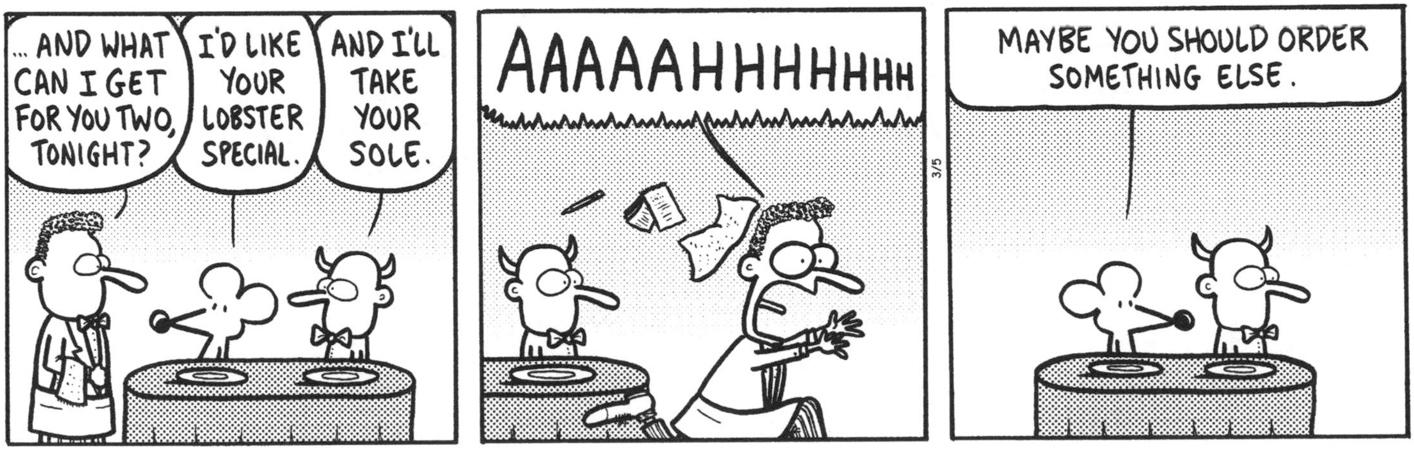
... AND WHAT CAN I GET FOR YOU TWO, TONIGHT?
I'D LIKE YOUR LOBSTER SPECIAL.
AND I'LL TAKE YOUR SOLE.
AAAAAHHHHHHH
3/5
MAYBE YOU SHOULD ORDER SOMETHING ELSE.

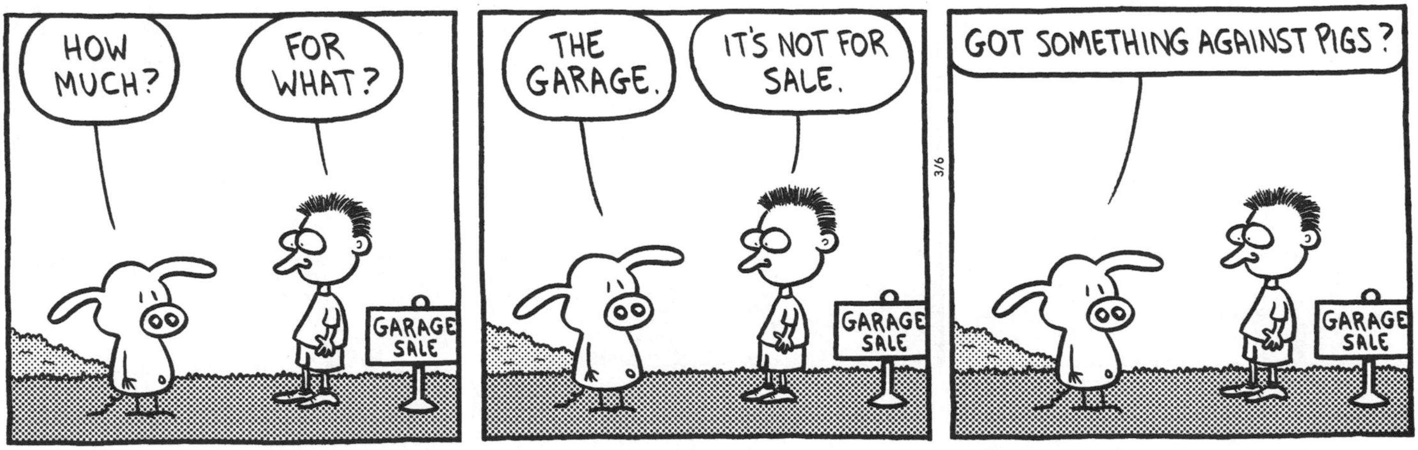
HOW MUCH?
FOR WHAT?
GARAGE SALE
THE GARAGE.
IT'S NOT FOR SALE.
GARAGE SALE
3/6
GOT SOMETHING AGAINST PIGS?
GARAGE SALE

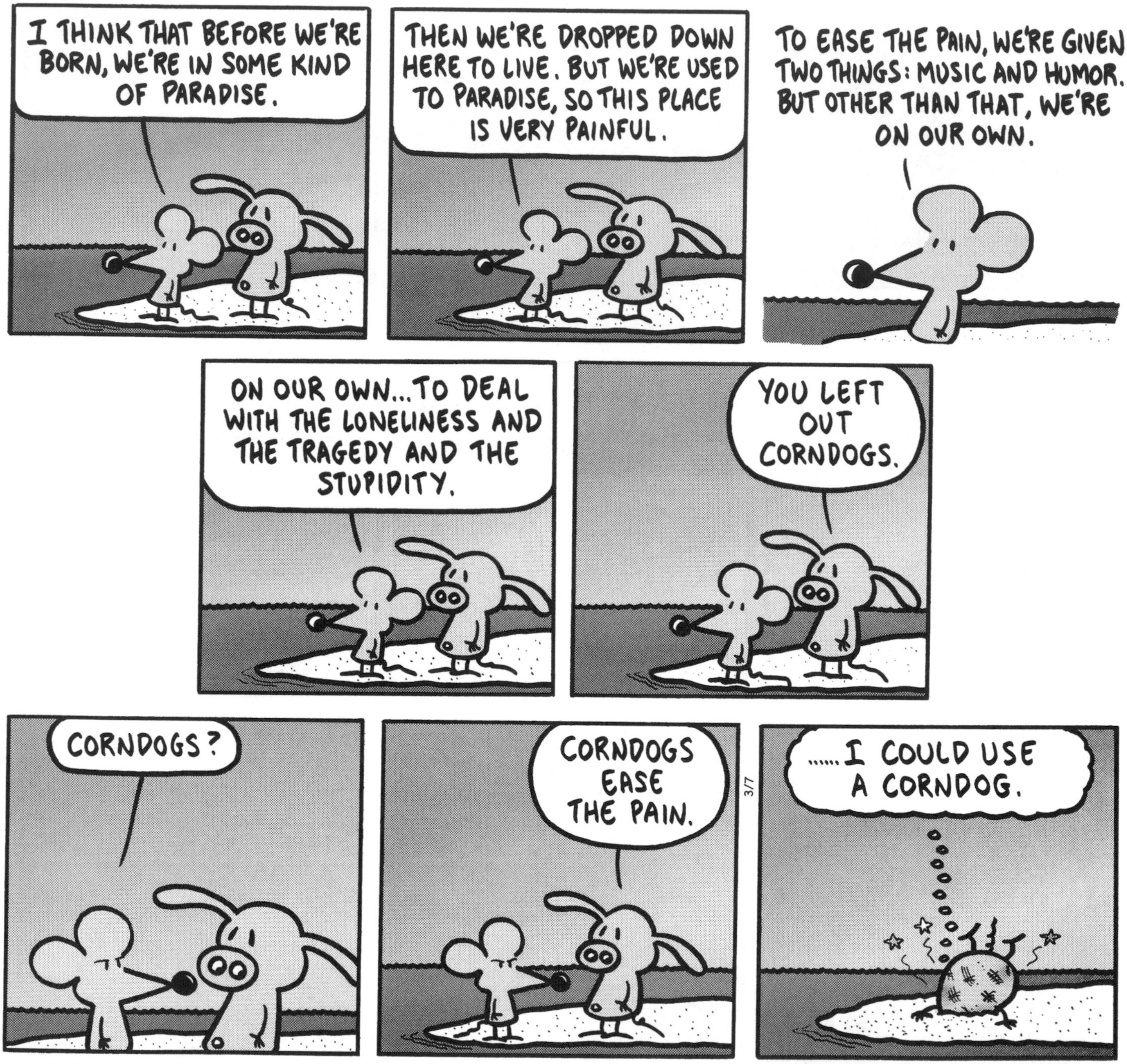
I THINK THAT BEFORE WE'RE BORN, WE'RE IN SOME KIND OF PARADISE.
THEN WE'RE DROPPED DOWN HERE TO LIVE. BUT WE'RE USED TO PARADISE, SO THIS PLACE IS VERY PAINFUL.
TO EASE THE PAIN, WE'RE GIVEN TWO THINGS: MUSIC AND HUMOR. BUT OTHER THAN THAT, WE'RE ON OUR OWN.
ON OUR OWN... TO DEAL WITH THE LONELINESS AND THE TRAGEDY AND THE STUPIDITY.
YOU LEFT OUT CORNDOGS.
CORNDOGS?
CORNDOGS EASE THE PAIN.
3/7
......I COULD USE A CORNDOG.

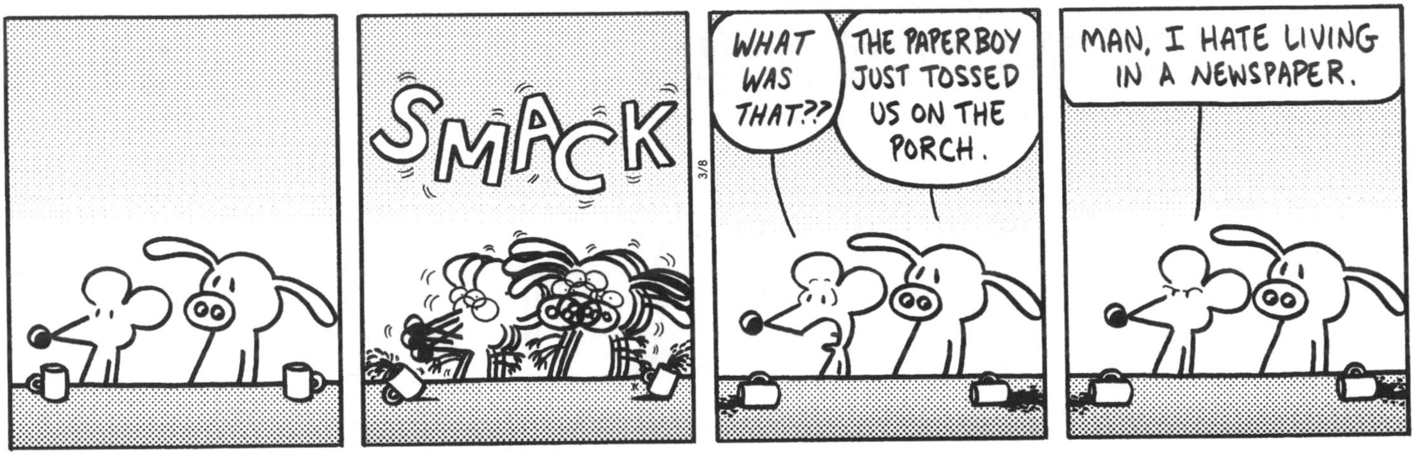
SMACK
3/8
WHAT WAS THAT??
THE PAPERBOY JUST TOSSED US ON THE PORCH.
MAN, I HATE LIVING IN A NEWSPAPER.

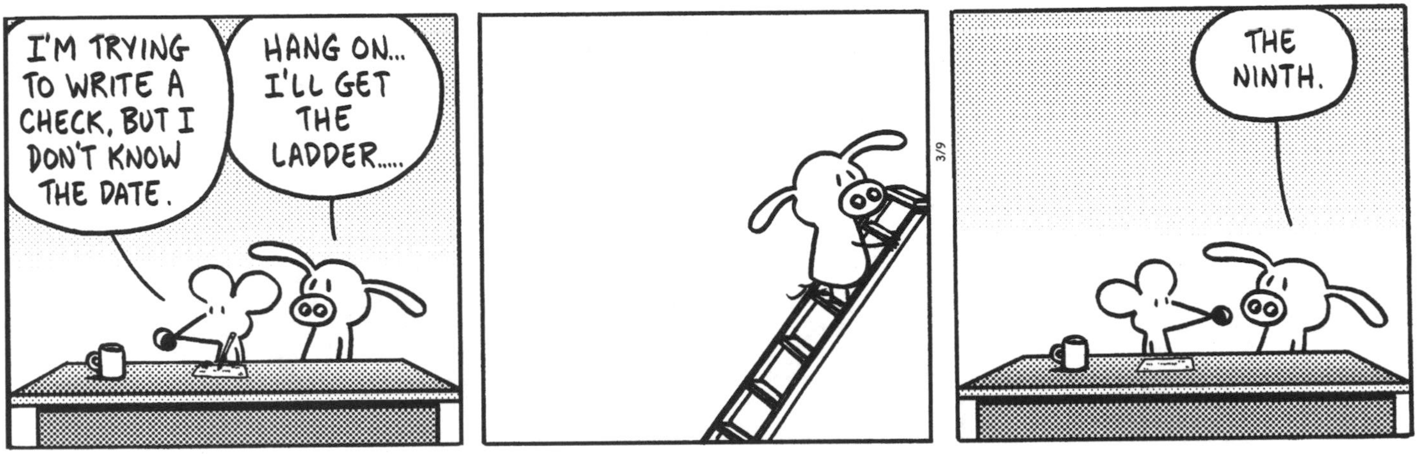
I'M TRYING TO WRITE A CHECK, BUT I DON'T KNOW THE DATE.
HANG ON... I'LL GET THE LADDER.....
3/9
THE NINTH.

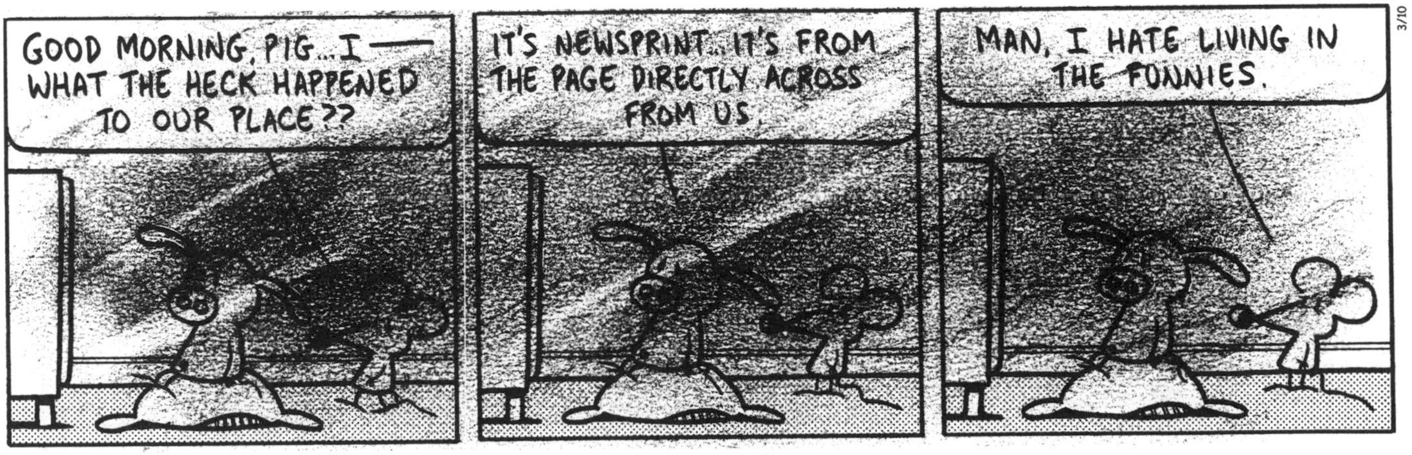
GOOD MORNING, PIG... I — WHAT THE HECK HAPPENED TO OUR PLACE??
IT'S NEWSPRINT... IT'S FROM THE PAGE DIRECTLY ACROSS FROM US.
MAN, I HATE LIVING IN THE FUNNIES.
3/10

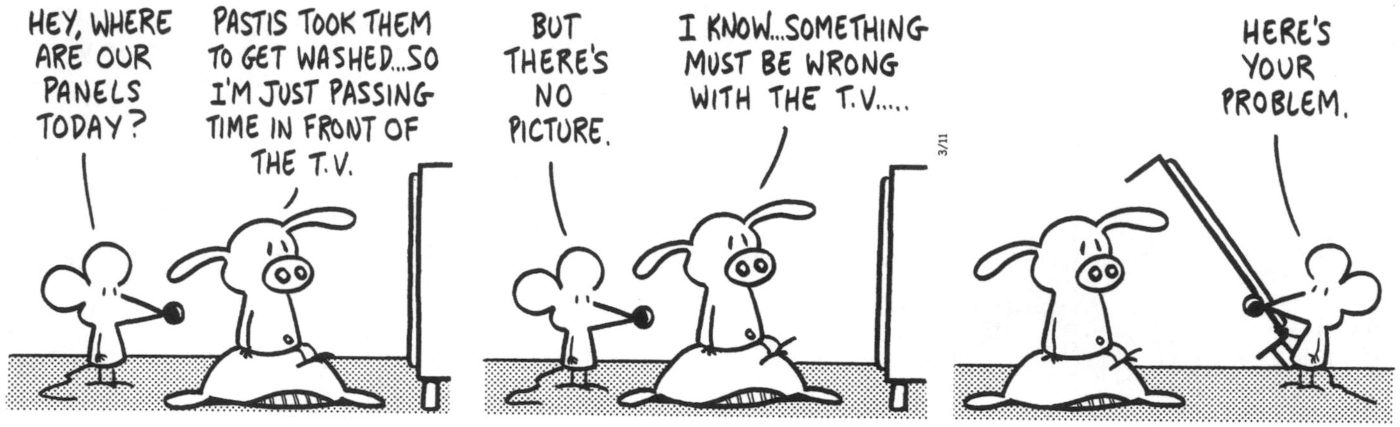
HEY, WHERE ARE OUR PANELS TODAY?
PASTIS TOOK THEM TO GET WASHED...SO I'M JUST PASSING TIME IN FRONT OF THE T.V.
BUT THERE'S NO PICTURE.
I KNOW...SOMETHING MUST BE WRONG WITH THE T.V....
3/11
HERE'S YOUR PROBLEM.

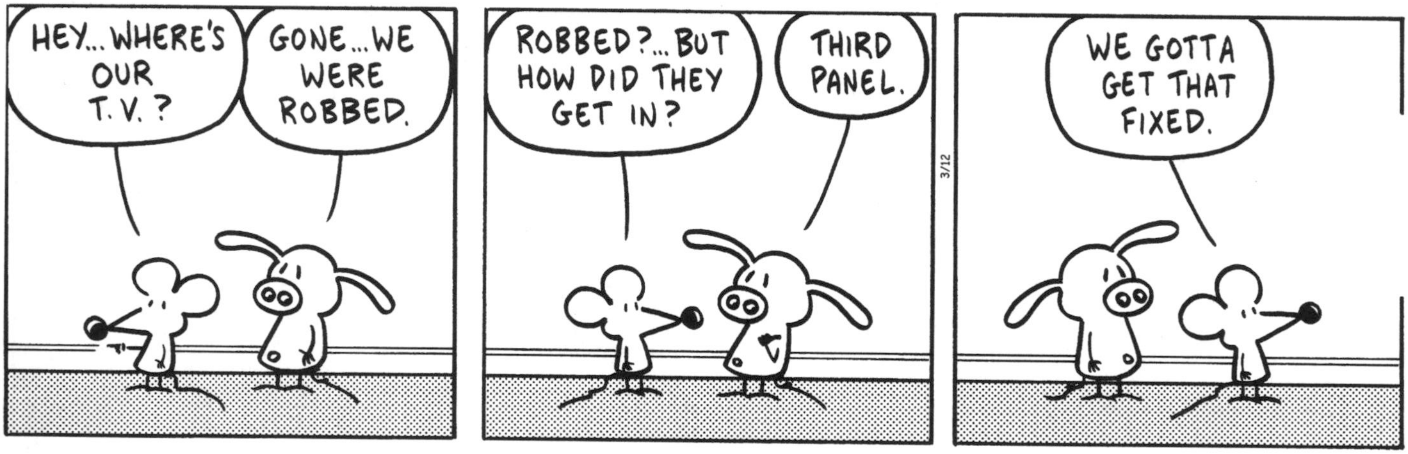
HEY...WHERE'S OUR T.V.?
GONE...WE WERE ROBBED.
ROBBED?...BUT HOW DID THEY GET IN?
THIRD PANEL.
3/12
WE GOTTA GET THAT FIXED.

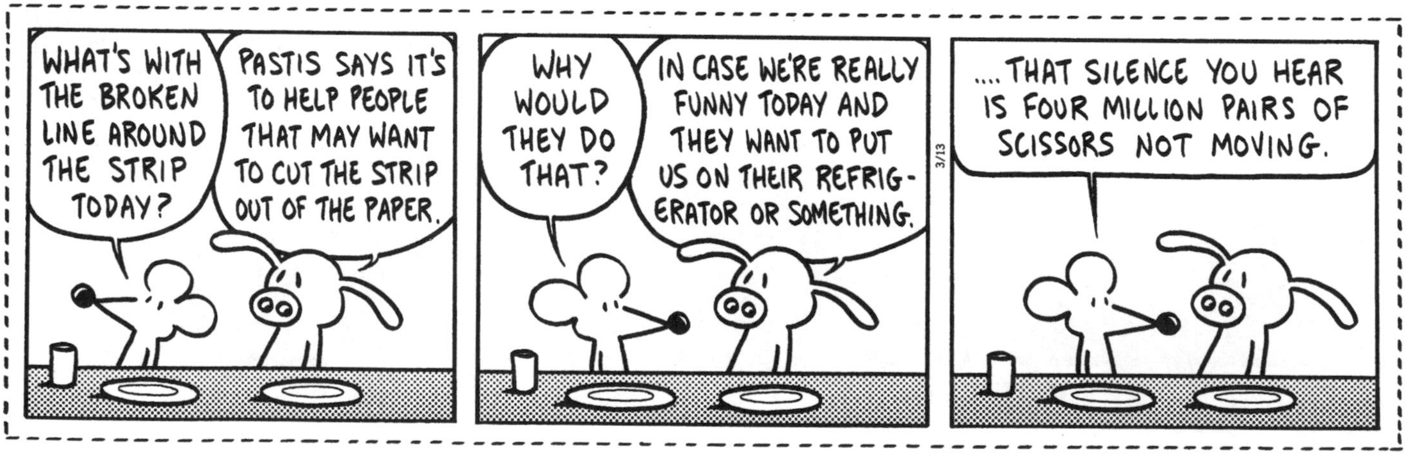
WHAT'S WITH THE BROKEN LINE AROUND THE STRIP TODAY?
PASTIS SAYS IT'S TO HELP PEOPLE THAT MAY WANT TO CUT THE STRIP OUT OF THE PAPER.
WHY WOULD THEY DO THAT?
IN CASE WE'RE REALLY FUNNY TODAY AND THEY WANT TO PUT US ON THEIR REFRIG-ERATOR OR SOMETHING.
3/13
....THAT SILENCE YOU HEAR IS FOUR MILLION PAIRS OF SCISSORS NOT MOVING.

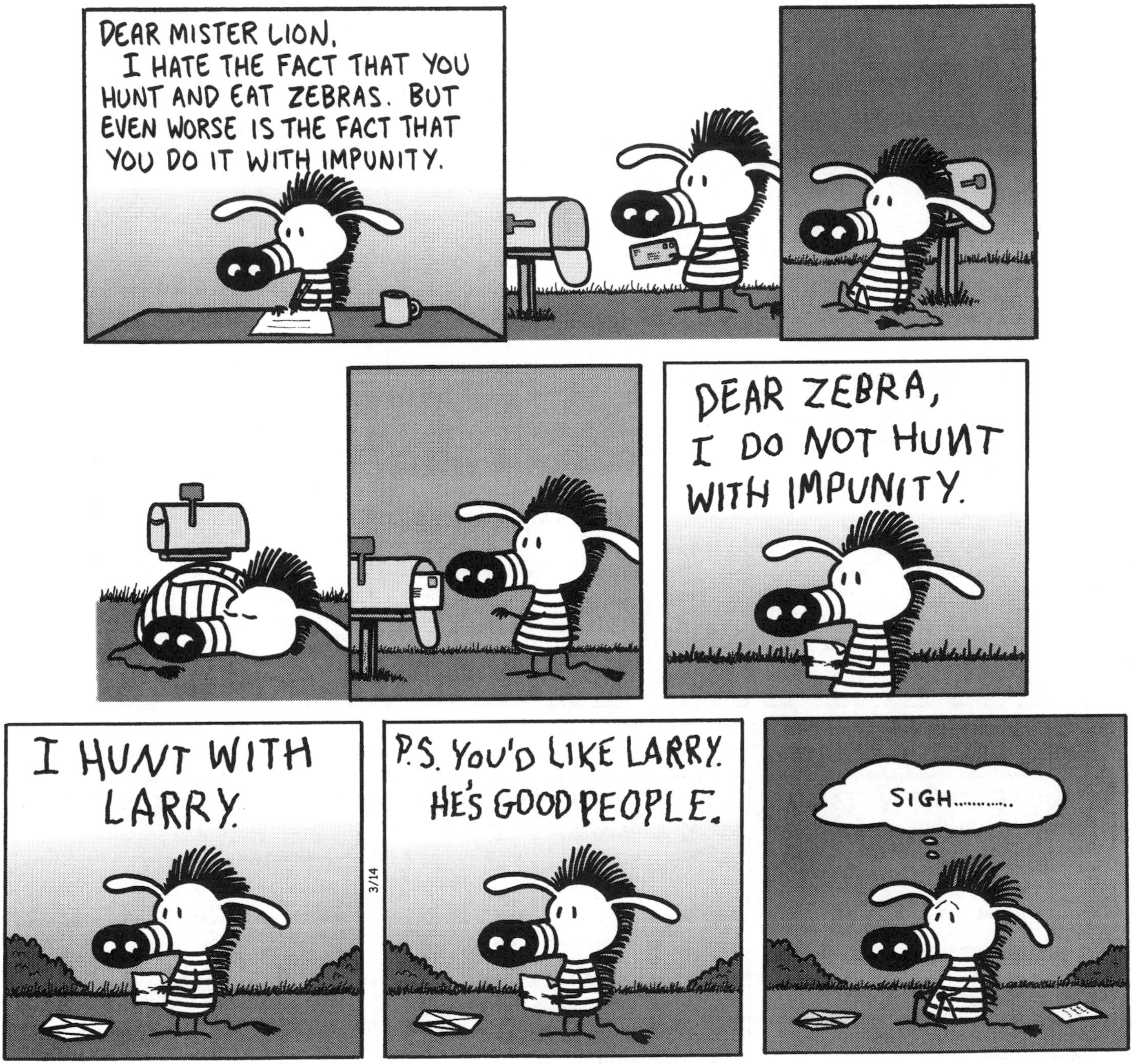
DEAR MISTER LION,
I HATE THE FACT THAT YOU HUNT AND EAT ZEBRAS. BUT EVEN WORSE IS THE FACT THAT YOU DO IT WITH IMPUNITY.
DEAR ZEBRA,
I DO NOT HUNT WITH IMPUNITY.
I HUNT WITH LARRY.
3/14
P.S. YOU'D LIKE LARRY. HE'S GOOD PEOPLE.
SIGH............

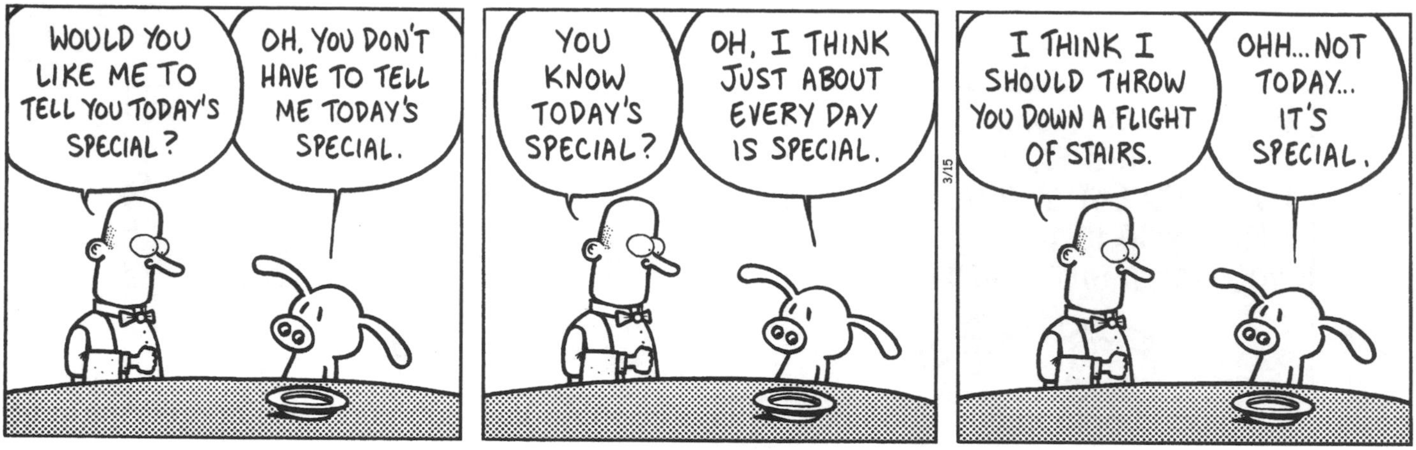
WOULD YOU LIKE ME TO TELL YOU TODAY'S SPECIAL?
OH, YOU DON'T HAVE TO TELL ME TODAY'S SPECIAL.
YOU KNOW TODAY'S SPECIAL?
OH, I THINK JUST ABOUT EVERY DAY IS SPECIAL.
3/15
I THINK I SHOULD THROW YOU DOWN A FLIGHT OF STAIRS.
OHH...NOT TODAY... IT'S SPECIAL.

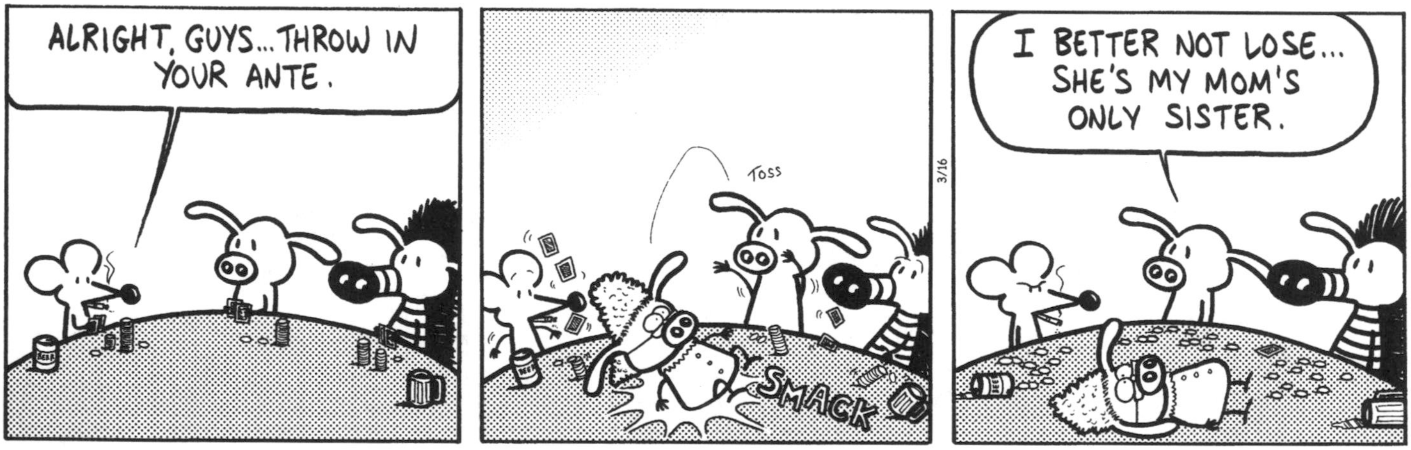
ALRIGHT, GUYS...THROW IN YOUR ANTE.
TOSS
SMACK
3/16
I BETTER NOT LOSE... SHE'S MY MOM'S ONLY SISTER.

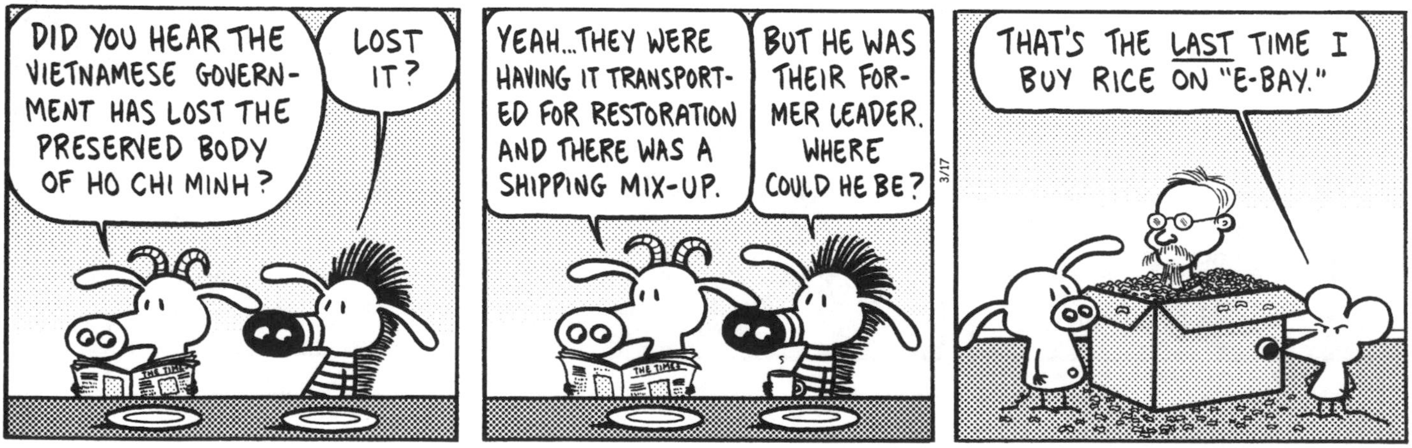
DID YOU HEAR THE VIETNAMESE GOVERNMENT HAS LOST THE PRESERVED BODY OF HO CHI MINH?
LOST IT?
YEAH...THEY WERE HAVING IT TRANSPORTED FOR RESTORATION AND THERE WAS A SHIPPING MIX-UP.
BUT HE WAS THEIR FORMER LEADER. WHERE COULD HE BE?
3/17
THAT'S THE LAST TIME I BUY RICE ON "E-BAY."

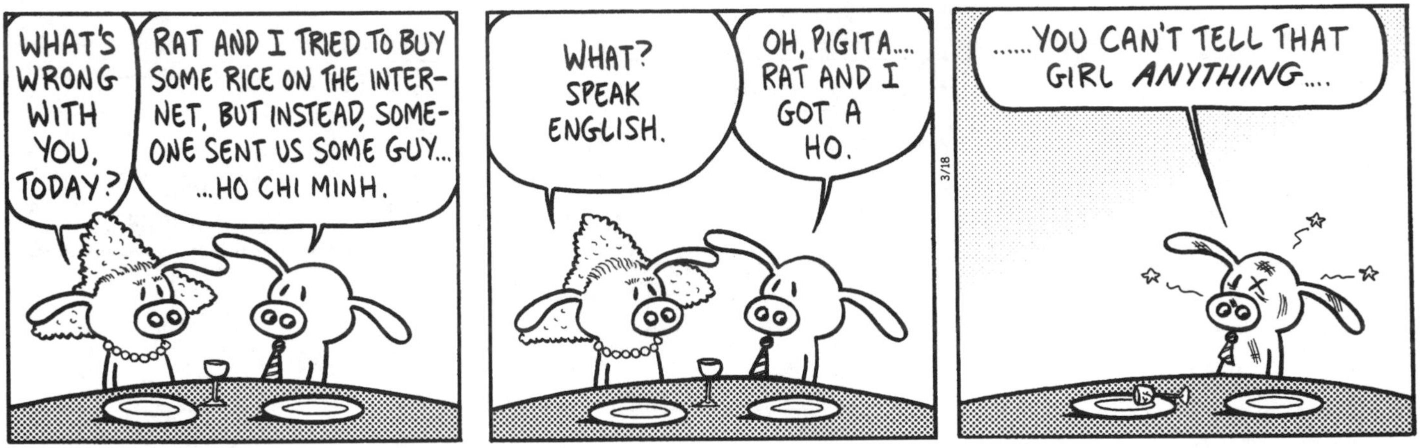
WHAT'S WRONG WITH YOU, TODAY?
RAT AND I TRIED TO BUY SOME RICE ON THE INTER-NET, BUT INSTEAD, SOME-ONE SENT US SOME GUY... ...HO CHI MINH.
WHAT? SPEAK ENGLISH.
OH, PIGITA.... RAT AND I GOT A HO.
3/18
......YOU CAN'T TELL THAT GIRL *ANYTHING*....

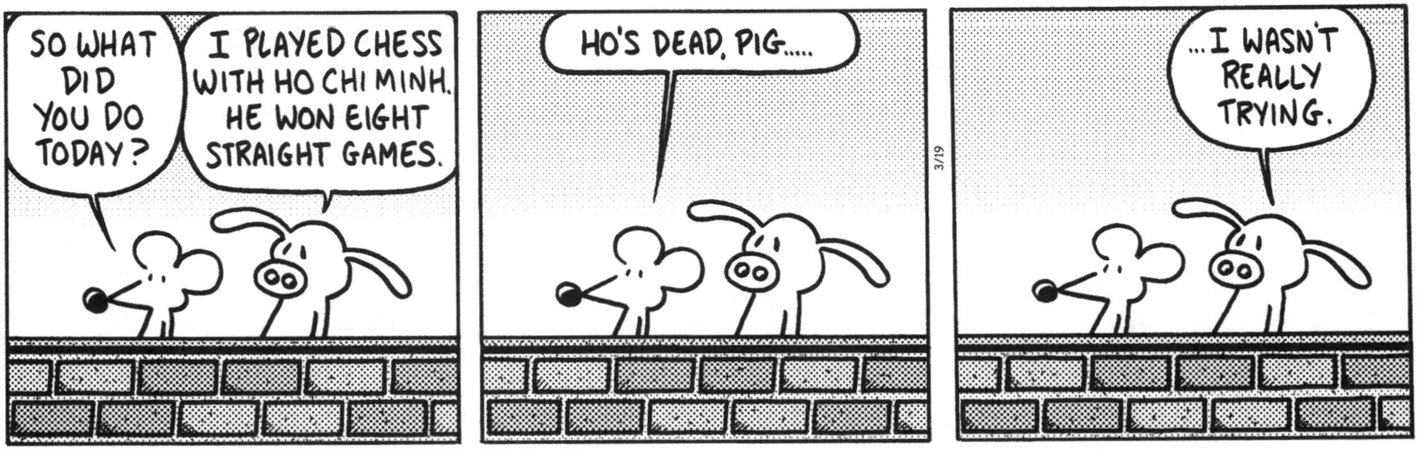
SO WHAT DID YOU DO TODAY?
I PLAYED CHESS WITH HO CHI MINH. HE WON EIGHT STRAIGHT GAMES.
HO'S DEAD, PIG.....
3/19
...I WASN'T REALLY TRYING.

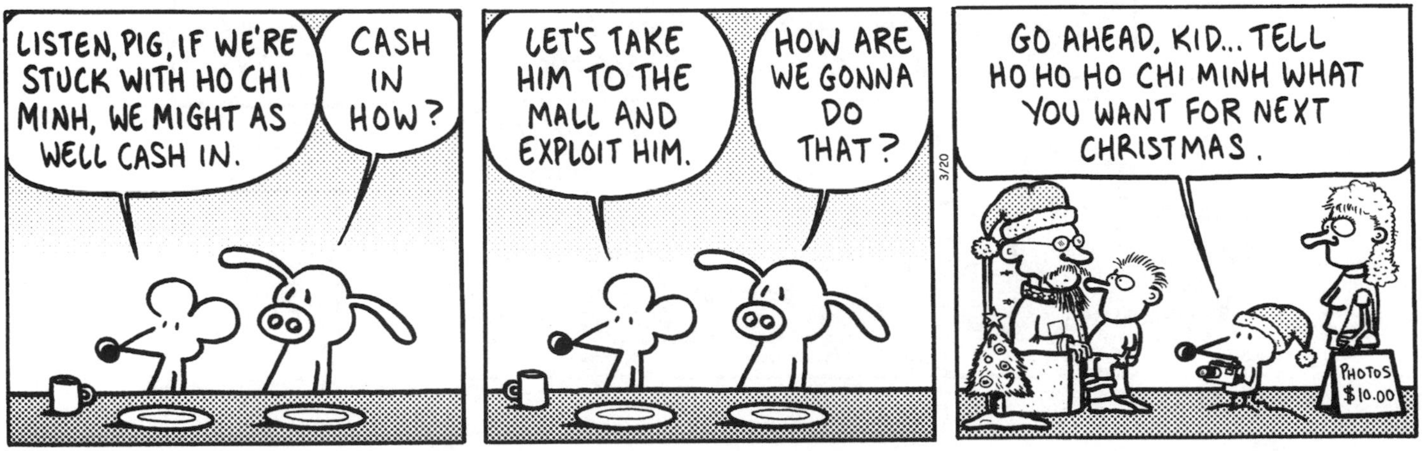
LISTEN, PIG, IF WE'RE STUCK WITH HO CHI MINH, WE MIGHT AS WELL CASH IN.
CASH IN HOW?
LET'S TAKE HIM TO THE MALL AND EXPLOIT HIM.
HOW ARE WE GONNA DO THAT?
3/20
GO AHEAD, KID... TELL HO HO HO CHI MINH WHAT YOU WANT FOR NEXT CHRISTMAS.
PHOTOS $10.00

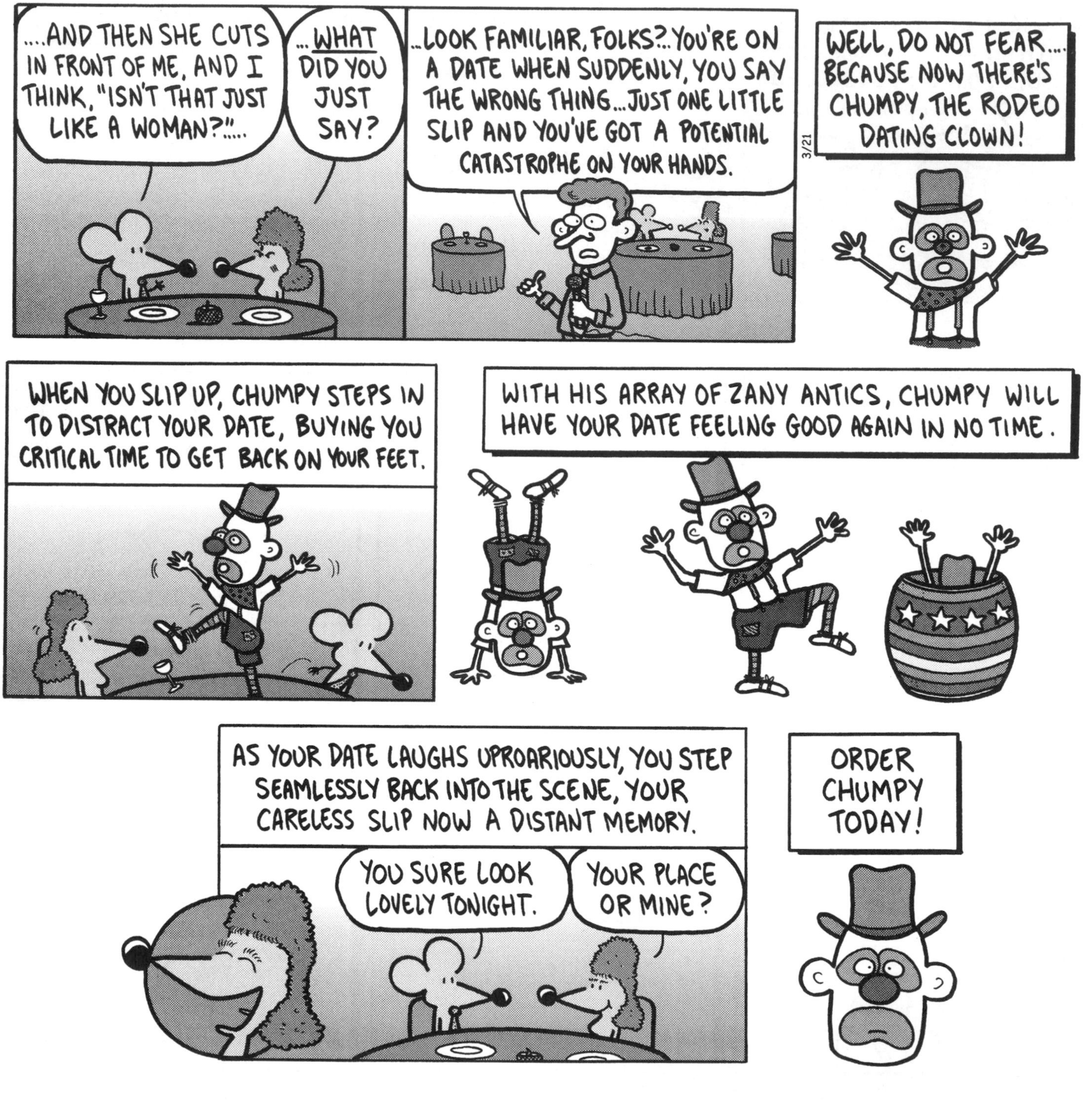
....AND THEN SHE CUTS IN FRONT OF ME, AND I THINK, "ISN'T THAT JUST LIKE A WOMAN?"....
...WHAT DID YOU JUST SAY?
...LOOK FAMILIAR, FOLKS?.. YOU'RE ON A DATE WHEN SUDDENLY, YOU SAY THE WRONG THING... JUST ONE LITTLE SLIP AND YOU'VE GOT A POTENTIAL CATASTROPHE ON YOUR HANDS.
3/21
WELL, DO NOT FEAR.... BECAUSE NOW THERE'S CHUMPY, THE RODEO DATING CLOWN!
WHEN YOU SLIP UP, CHUMPY STEPS IN TO DISTRACT YOUR DATE, BUYING YOU CRITICAL TIME TO GET BACK ON YOUR FEET.
WITH HIS ARRAY OF ZANY ANTICS, CHUMPY WILL HAVE YOUR DATE FEELING GOOD AGAIN IN NO TIME.
AS YOUR DATE LAUGHS UPROARIOUSLY, YOU STEP SEAMLESSLY BACK INTO THE SCENE, YOUR CARELESS SLIP NOW A DISTANT MEMORY.
YOU SURE LOOK LOVELY TONIGHT.
YOUR PLACE OR MINE?
ORDER CHUMPY TODAY!

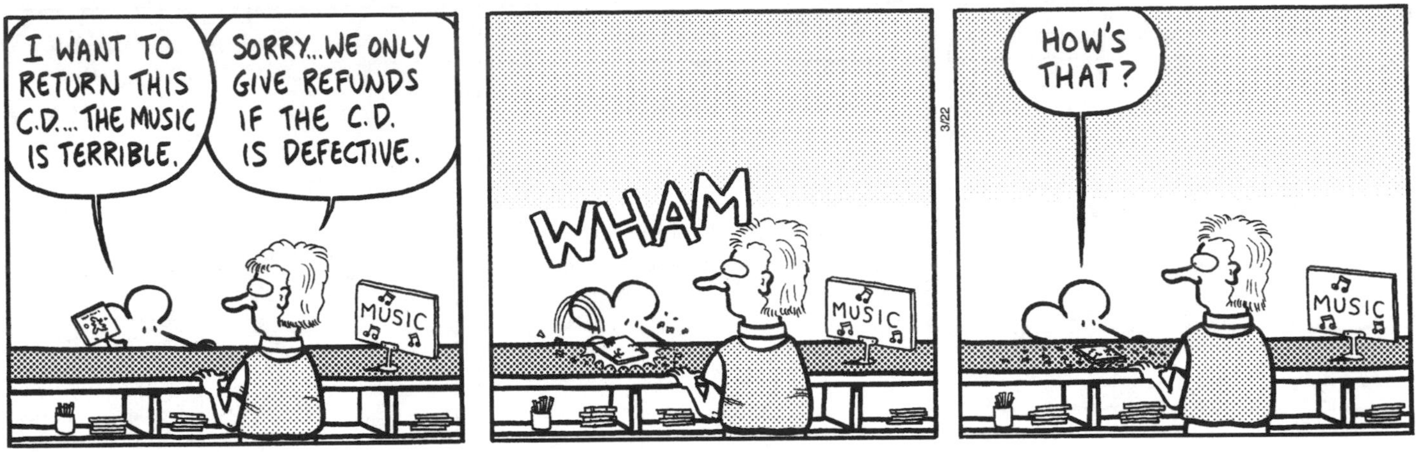
I WANT TO RETURN THIS C.D.... THE MUSIC IS TERRIBLE.
SORRY...WE ONLY GIVE REFUNDS IF THE C.D. IS DEFECTIVE.
MUSIC
3/22
WHAM
MUSIC
HOW'S THAT?
MUSIC

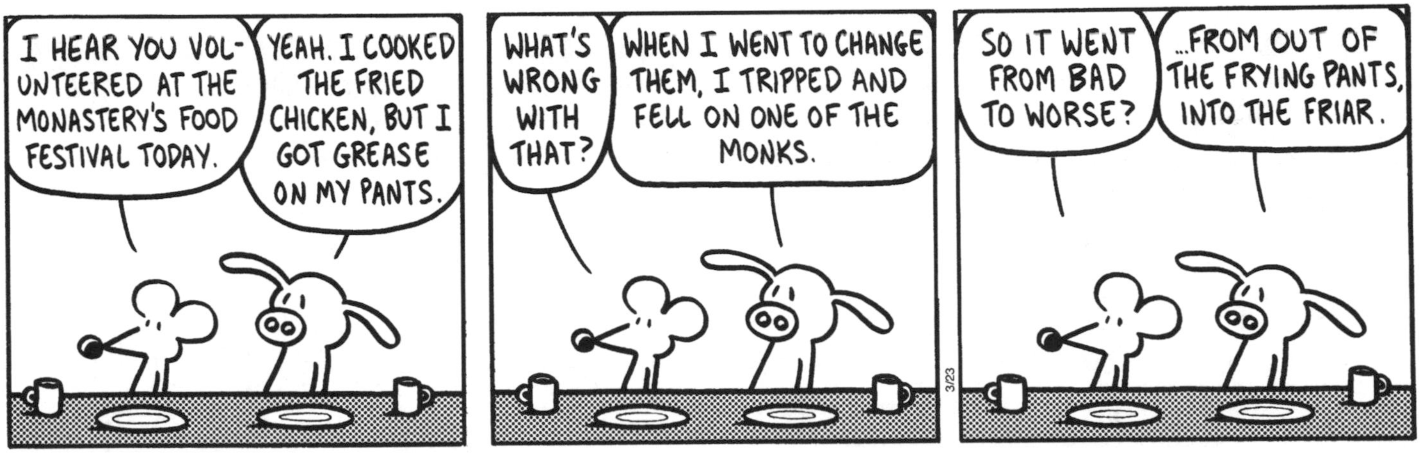
I HEAR YOU VOLUNTEERED AT THE MONASTERY'S FOOD FESTIVAL TODAY.
YEAH. I COOKED THE FRIED CHICKEN, BUT I GOT GREASE ON MY PANTS.
WHAT'S WRONG WITH THAT?
WHEN I WENT TO CHANGE THEM, I TRIPPED AND FELL ON ONE OF THE MONKS.
3/23
SO IT WENT FROM BAD TO WORSE?
...FROM OUT OF THE FRYING PANTS, INTO THE FRIAR.

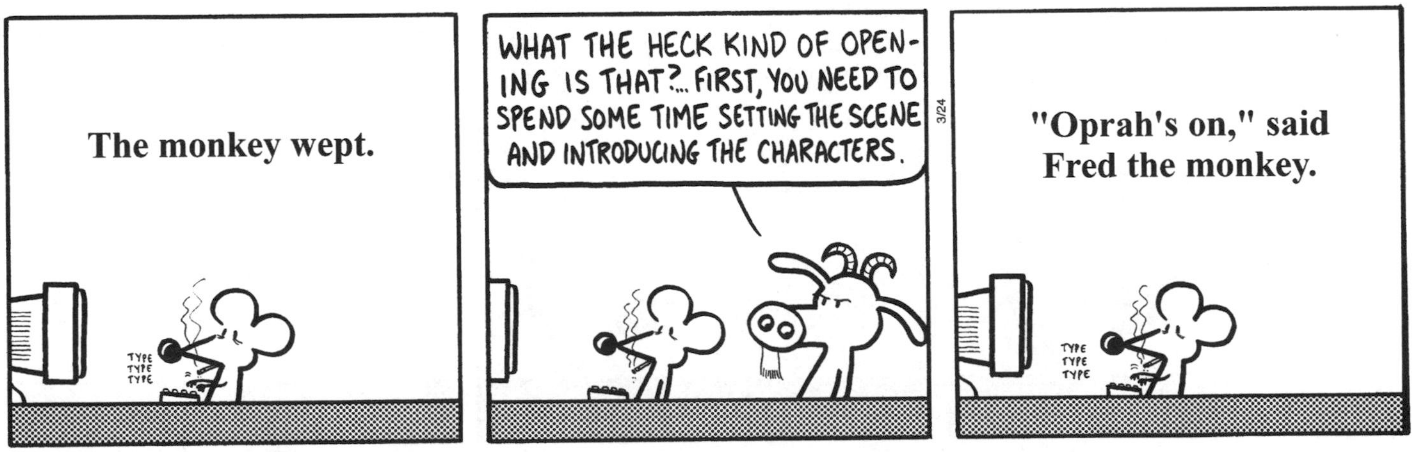
The monkey wept.
TYPE TYPE TYPE
WHAT THE HECK KIND OF OPENING IS THAT?... FIRST, YOU NEED TO SPEND SOME TIME SETTING THE SCENE AND INTRODUCING THE CHARACTERS.
3/24
"Oprah's on," said Fred the monkey.
TYPE TYPE TYPE

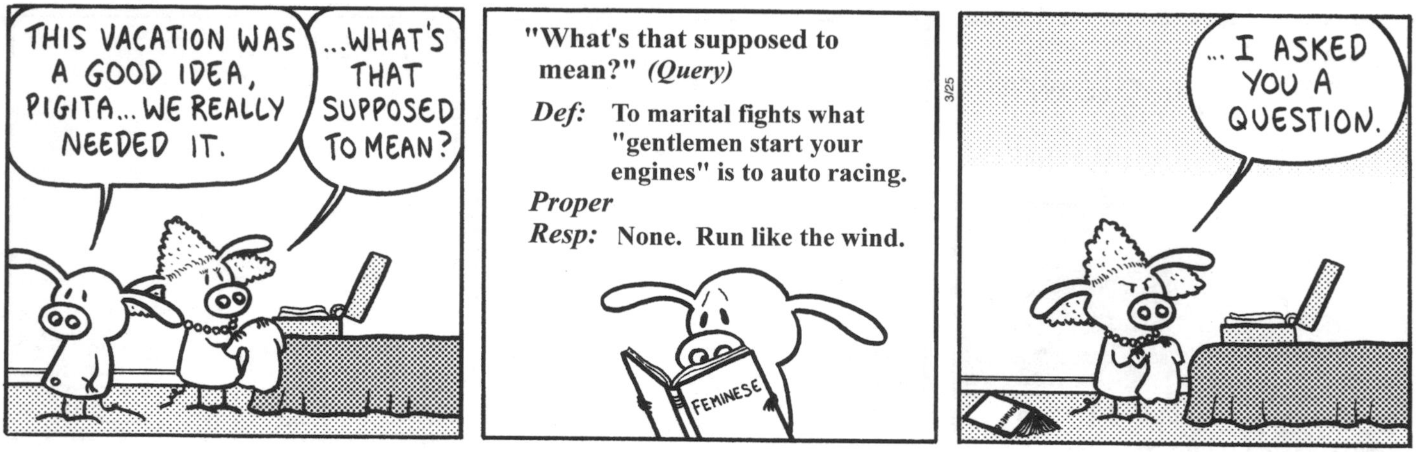
THIS VACATION WAS A GOOD IDEA, PIGITA... WE REALLY NEEDED IT.
...WHAT'S THAT SUPPOSED TO MEAN?
"What's that supposed to mean?" (Query)
Def: To marital fights what "gentlemen start your engines" is to auto racing.
Proper Resp: None. Run like the wind.
FEMINESE
3/25
...I ASKED YOU A QUESTION.

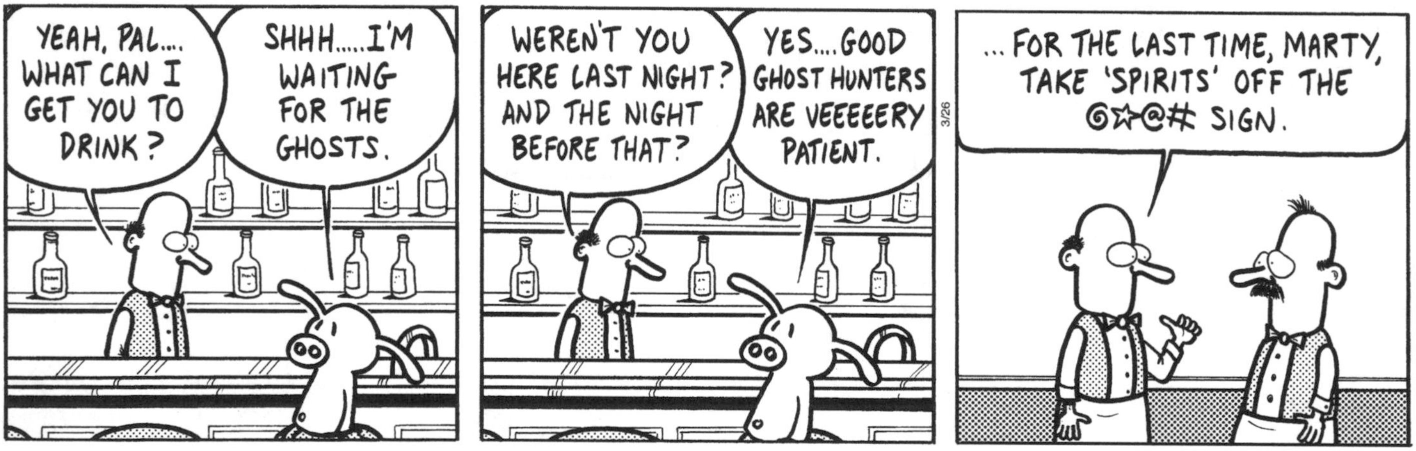
YEAH, PAL.... WHAT CAN I GET YOU TO DRINK?
SHHH.....I'M WAITING FOR THE GHOSTS.
WEREN'T YOU HERE LAST NIGHT? AND THE NIGHT BEFORE THAT?
YES....GOOD GHOST HUNTERS ARE VEEEEERY PATIENT.
3/26
...FOR THE LAST TIME, MARTY, TAKE 'SPIRITS' OFF THE @☆@# SIGN.

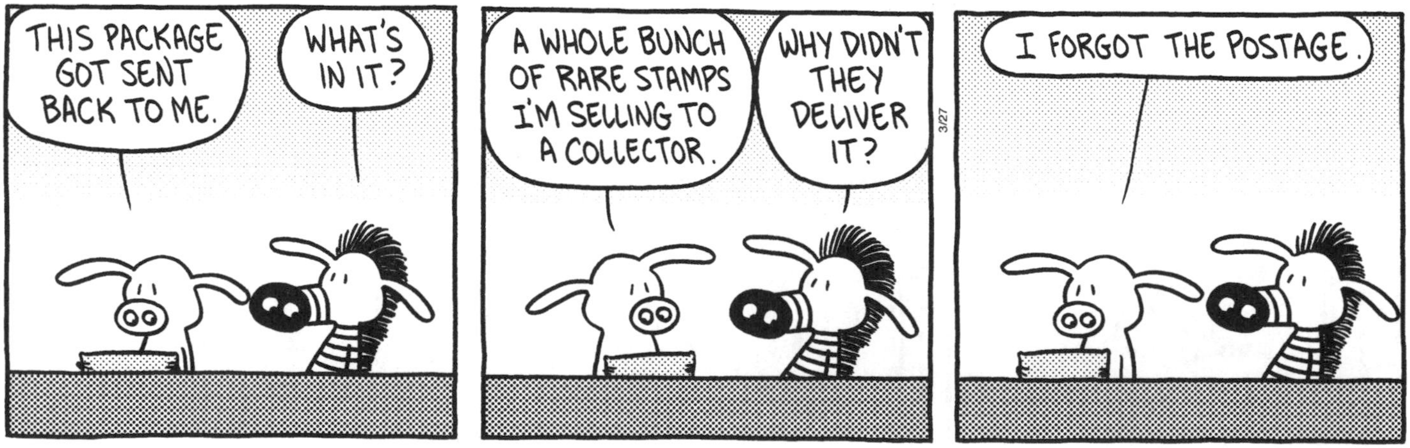
THIS PACKAGE GOT SENT BACK TO ME.
WHAT'S IN IT?
A WHOLE BUNCH OF RARE STAMPS I'M SELLING TO A COLLECTOR.
WHY DIDN'T THEY DELIVER IT?
3/27
I FORGOT THE POSTAGE.

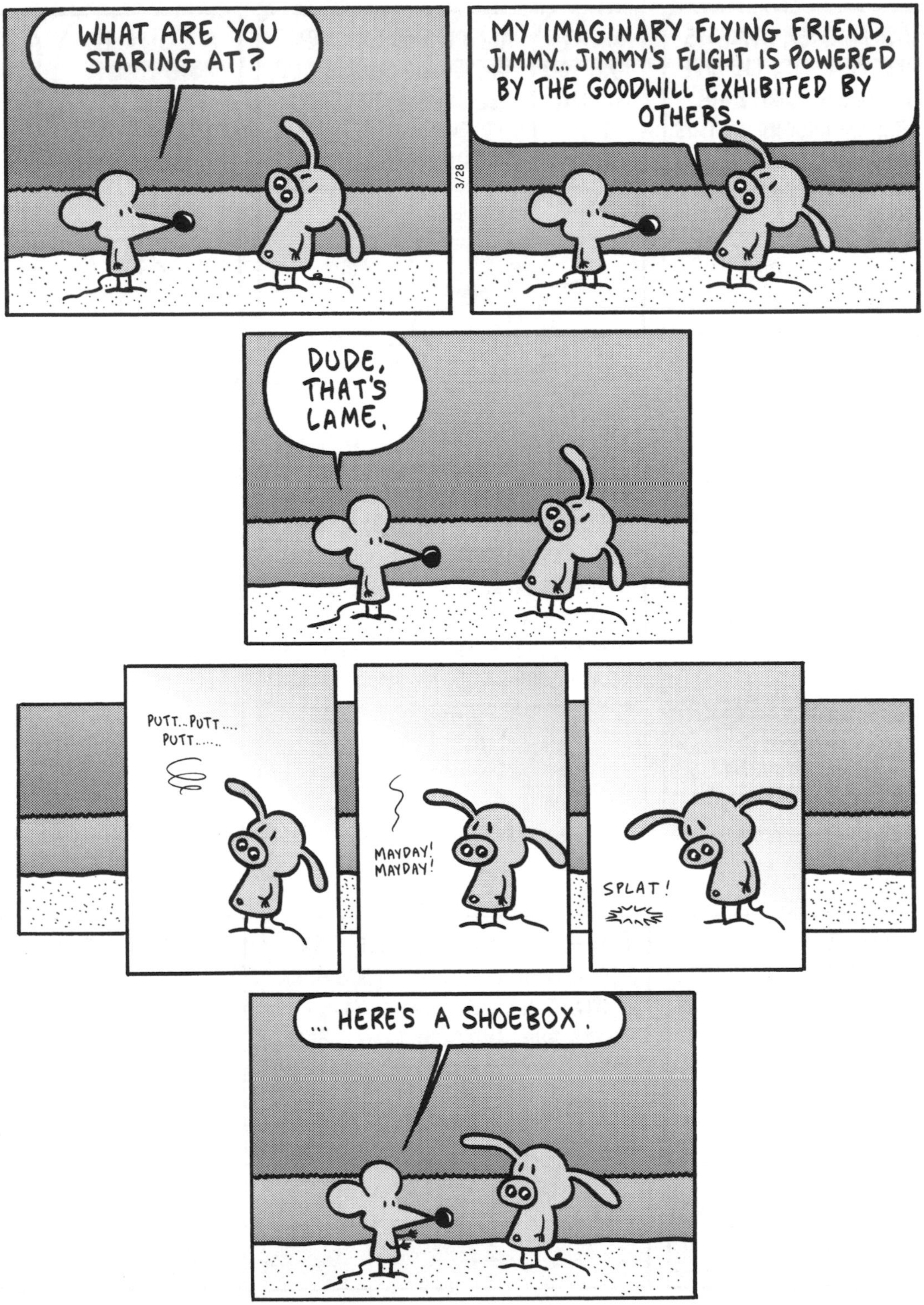
WHAT ARE YOU STARING AT?
3/28
MY IMAGINARY FLYING FRIEND, JIMMY... JIMMY'S FLIGHT IS POWERED BY THE GOODWILL EXHIBITED BY OTHERS.
DUDE, THAT'S LAME.
PUTT..PUTT.... PUTT......
MAYDAY! MAYDAY!
SPLAT!
... HERE'S A SHOEBOX.

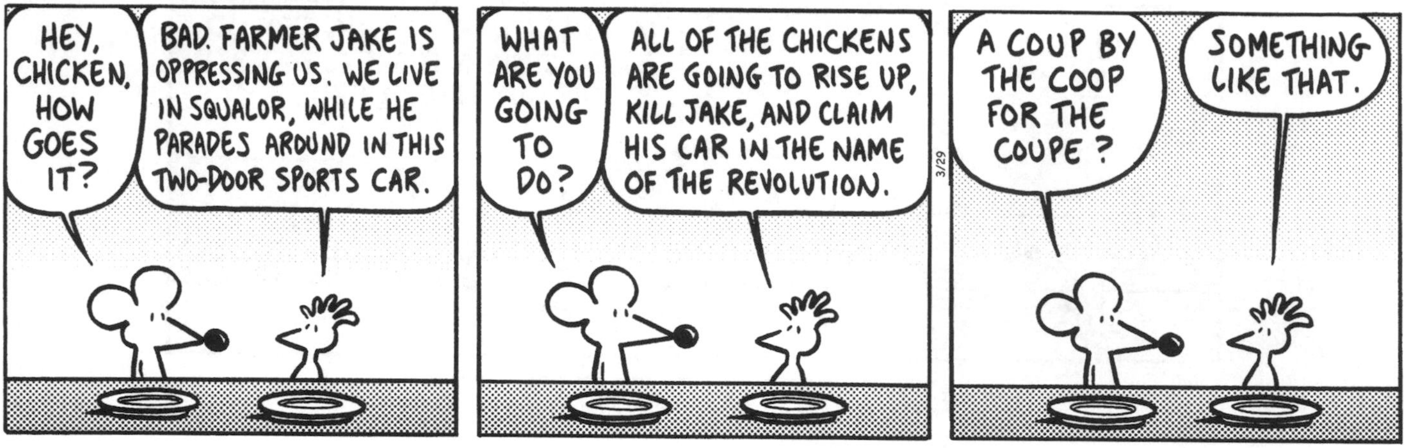
HEY, CHICKEN, HOW GOES IT?
BAD. FARMER JAKE IS OPPRESSING US. WE LIVE IN SQUALOR, WHILE HE PARADES AROUND IN THIS TWO-DOOR SPORTS CAR.
WHAT ARE YOU GOING TO DO?
ALL OF THE CHICKENS ARE GOING TO RISE UP, KILL JAKE, AND CLAIM HIS CAR IN THE NAME OF THE REVOLUTION.
3/29
A COUP BY THE COOP FOR THE COUPE?
SOMETHING LIKE THAT.

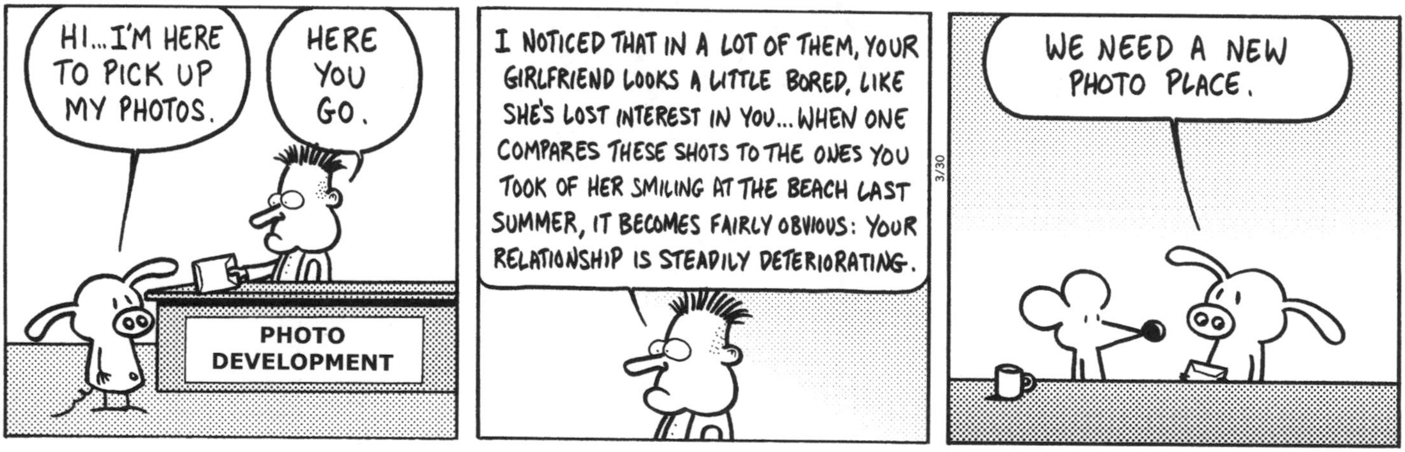
HI... I'M HERE TO PICK UP MY PHOTOS.
HERE YOU GO.
PHOTO DEVELOPMENT
I NOTICED THAT IN A LOT OF THEM, YOUR GIRLFRIEND LOOKS A LITTLE BORED, LIKE SHE'S LOST INTEREST IN YOU... WHEN ONE COMPARES THESE SHOTS TO THE ONES YOU TOOK OF HER SMILING AT THE BEACH LAST SUMMER, IT BECOMES FAIRLY OBVIOUS: YOUR RELATIONSHIP IS STEADILY DETERIORATING.
3/30
WE NEED A NEW PHOTO PLACE.

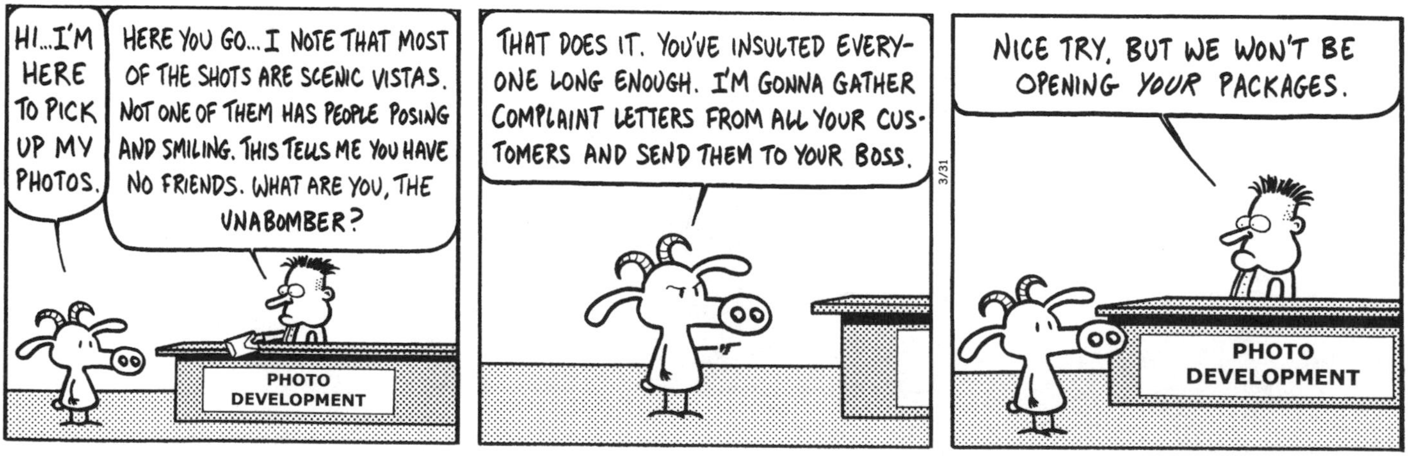
HI... I'M HERE TO PICK UP MY PHOTOS.
HERE YOU GO... I NOTE THAT MOST OF THE SHOTS ARE SCENIC VISTAS. NOT ONE OF THEM HAS PEOPLE POSING AND SMILING. THIS TELLS ME YOU HAVE NO FRIENDS. WHAT ARE YOU, THE UNABOMBER?
PHOTO DEVELOPMENT
THAT DOES IT. YOU'VE INSULTED EVERYONE LONG ENOUGH. I'M GONNA GATHER COMPLAINT LETTERS FROM ALL YOUR CUSTOMERS AND SEND THEM TO YOUR BOSS.
3/31
NICE TRY, BUT WE WON'T BE OPENING *YOUR* PACKAGES.
PHOTO DEVELOPMENT

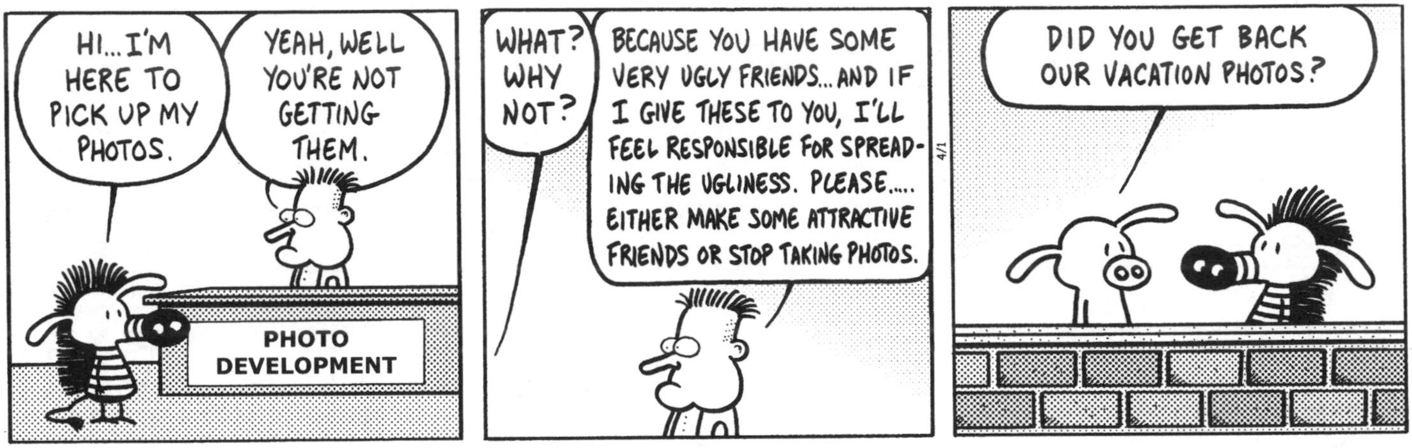
HI... I'M HERE TO PICK UP MY PHOTOS.
YEAH, WELL YOU'RE NOT GETTING THEM.
PHOTO DEVELOPMENT
WHAT? WHY NOT?
BECAUSE YOU HAVE SOME VERY UGLY FRIENDS... AND IF I GIVE THESE TO YOU, I'LL FEEL RESPONSIBLE FOR SPREADING THE UGLINESS. PLEASE..... EITHER MAKE SOME ATTRACTIVE FRIENDS OR STOP TAKING PHOTOS.
4/1
DID YOU GET BACK OUR VACATION PHOTOS?

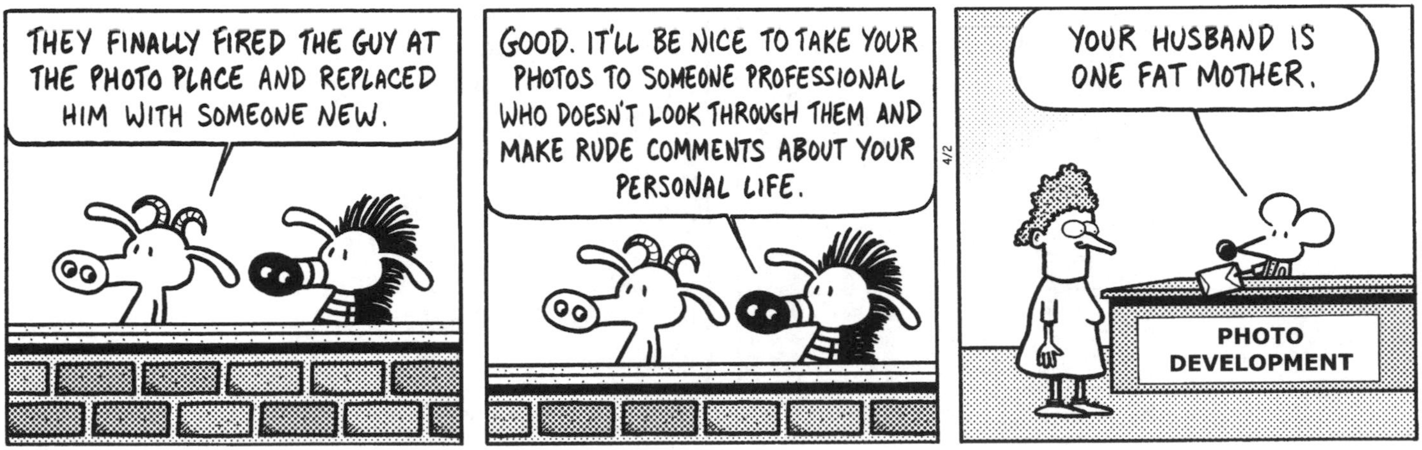
THEY FINALLY FIRED THE GUY AT THE PHOTO PLACE AND REPLACED HIM WITH SOMEONE NEW.
GOOD. IT'LL BE NICE TO TAKE YOUR PHOTOS TO SOMEONE PROFESSIONAL WHO DOESN'T LOOK THROUGH THEM AND MAKE RUDE COMMENTS ABOUT YOUR PERSONAL LIFE.
4/2
YOUR HUSBAND IS ONE FAT MOTHER.
PHOTO DEVELOPMENT

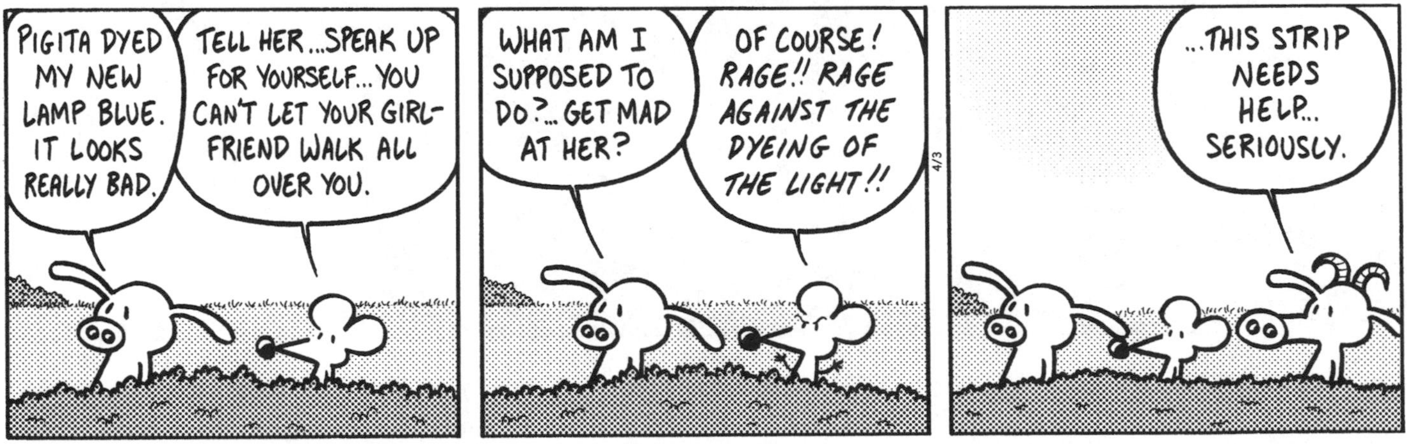
PIGITA DYED MY NEW LAMP BLUE. IT LOOKS REALLY BAD.
TELL HER... SPEAK UP FOR YOURSELF... YOU CAN'T LET YOUR GIRLFRIEND WALK ALL OVER YOU.
WHAT AM I SUPPOSED TO DO?... GET MAD AT HER?
OF COURSE! RAGE!! RAGE AGAINST THE DYEING OF THE LIGHT!!
4/3
...THIS STRIP NEEDS HELP.. SERIOUSLY.

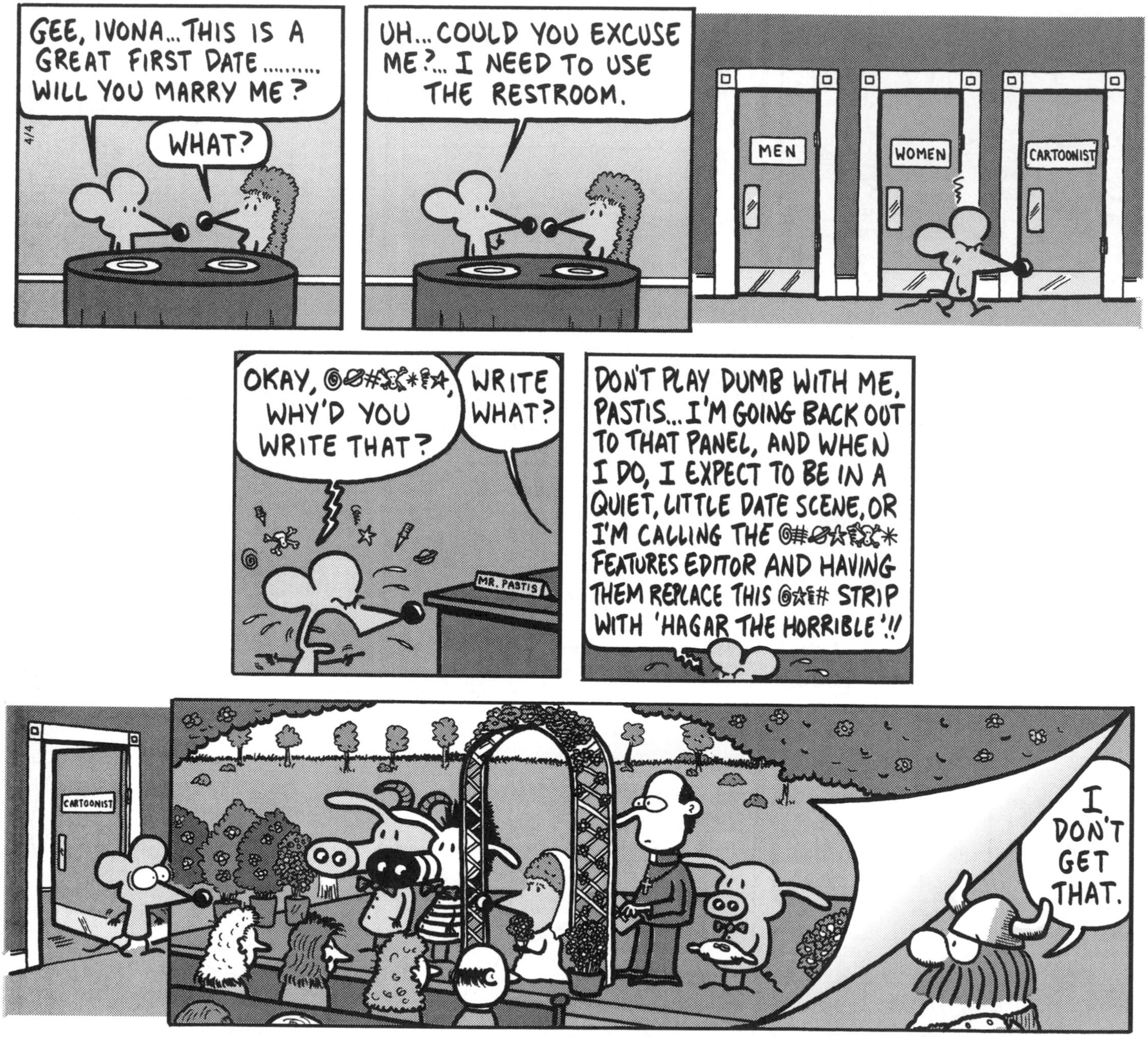
4/4
GEE, IVONA... THIS IS A GREAT FIRST DATE .... WILL YOU MARRY ME?
WHAT?
UH... COULD YOU EXCUSE ME?... I NEED TO USE THE RESTROOM.
MEN
WOMEN
CARTOONIST
OKAY, @@#☠*$☆, WHY'D YOU WRITE THAT?
WRITE WHAT?
MR. PASTIS
DON'T PLAY DUMB WITH ME, PASTIS... I'M GOING BACK OUT TO THAT PANEL, AND WHEN I DO, I EXPECT TO BE IN A QUIET, LITTLE DATE SCENE, OR I'M CALLING THE @#@☆☠* FEATURES EDITOR AND HAVING THEM REPLACE THIS @☆$# STRIP WITH 'HAGAR THE HORRIBLE'!!
CARTOONIST
I DON'T GET THAT.

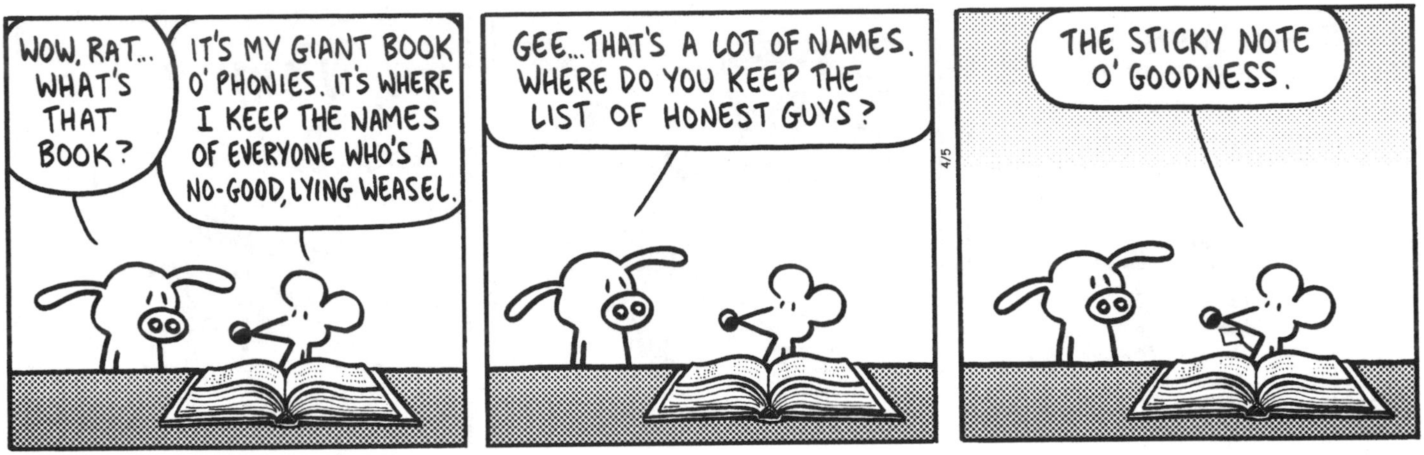
WOW, RAT... WHAT'S THAT BOOK?
IT'S MY GIANT BOOK O' PHONIES. IT'S WHERE I KEEP THE NAMES OF EVERYONE WHO'S A NO-GOOD, LYING WEASEL.
GEE...THAT'S A LOT OF NAMES. WHERE DO YOU KEEP THE LIST OF HONEST GUYS?
4/5
THE STICKY NOTE O' GOODNESS.

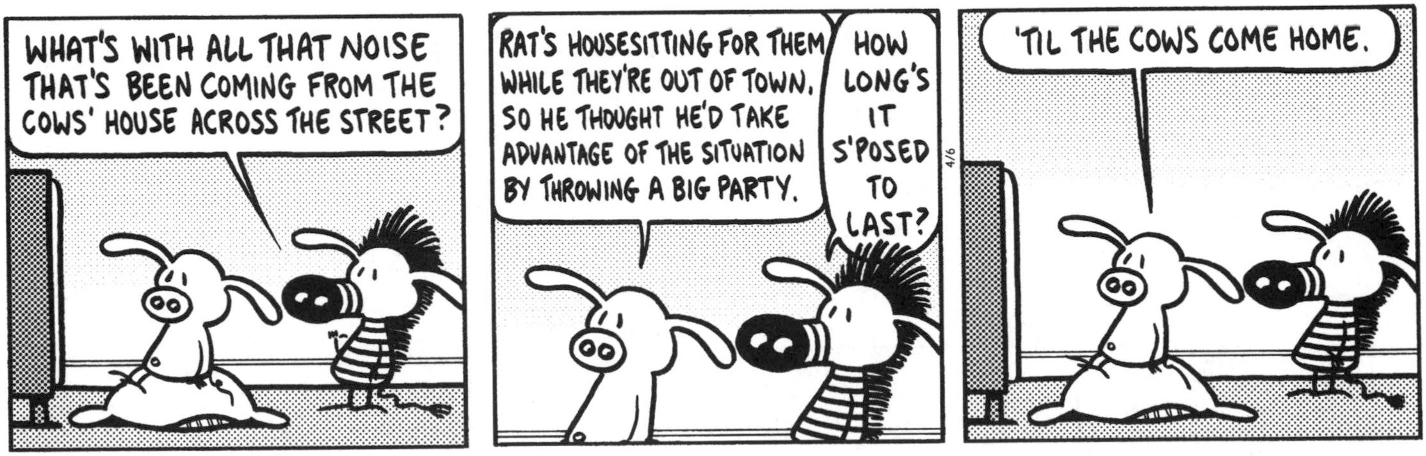
WHAT'S WITH ALL THAT NOISE THAT'S BEEN COMING FROM THE COWS' HOUSE ACROSS THE STREET?
RAT'S HOUSESITTING FOR THEM WHILE THEY'RE OUT OF TOWN, SO HE THOUGHT HE'D TAKE ADVANTAGE OF THE SITUATION BY THROWING A BIG PARTY.
HOW LONG'S IT S'POSED TO LAST?
4/6
'TIL THE COWS COME HOME.

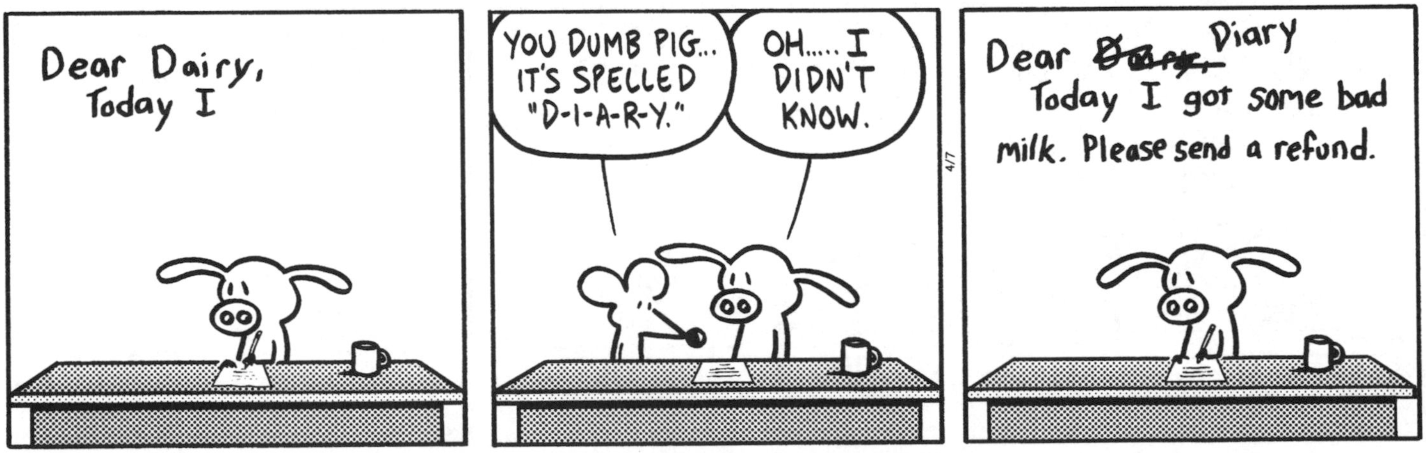
Dear Dairy,
Today I
YOU DUMB PIG... IT'S SPELLED "D-I-A-R-Y."
OH..... I DIDN'T KNOW.
4/7
Dear ~~Dairy,~~ Diary
Today I got some bad milk. Please send a refund.

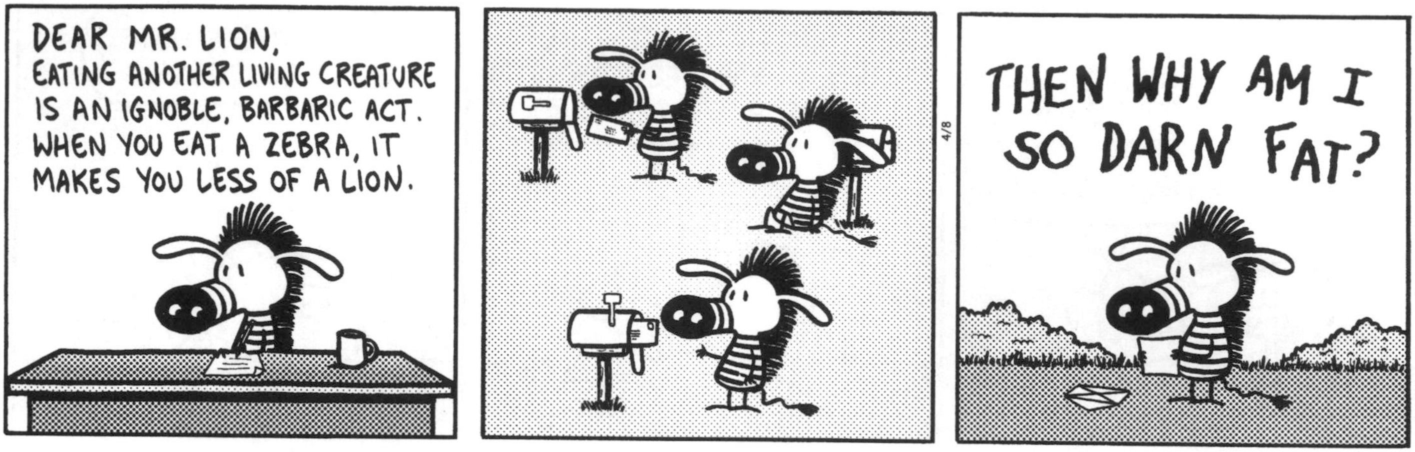
DEAR MR. LION,
EATING ANOTHER LIVING CREATURE IS AN IGNOBLE, BARBARIC ACT. WHEN YOU EAT A ZEBRA, IT MAKES YOU LESS OF A LION.
4/8
THEN WHY AM I SO DARN FAT?

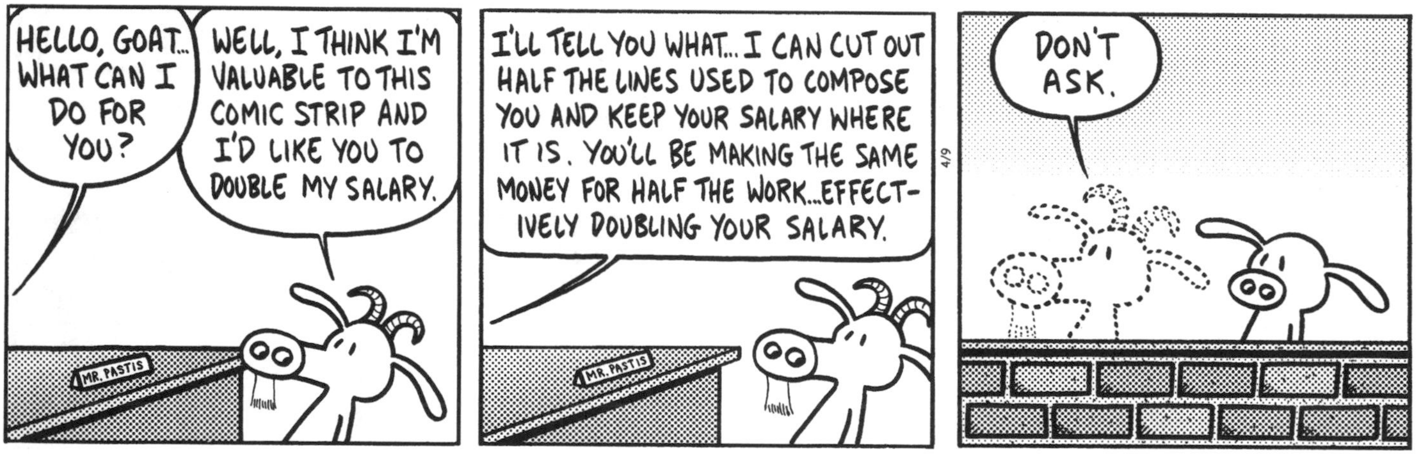
MR. PASTIS
HELLO, GOAT... WHAT CAN I DO FOR YOU?
WELL, I THINK I'M VALUABLE TO THIS COMIC STRIP AND I'D LIKE YOU TO DOUBLE MY SALARY.
MR. PASTIS
I'LL TELL YOU WHAT... I CAN CUT OUT HALF THE LINES USED TO COMPOSE YOU AND KEEP YOUR SALARY WHERE IT IS. YOU'LL BE MAKING THE SAME MONEY FOR HALF THE WORK... EFFECTIVELY DOUBLING YOUR SALARY.
4/9
DON'T ASK.

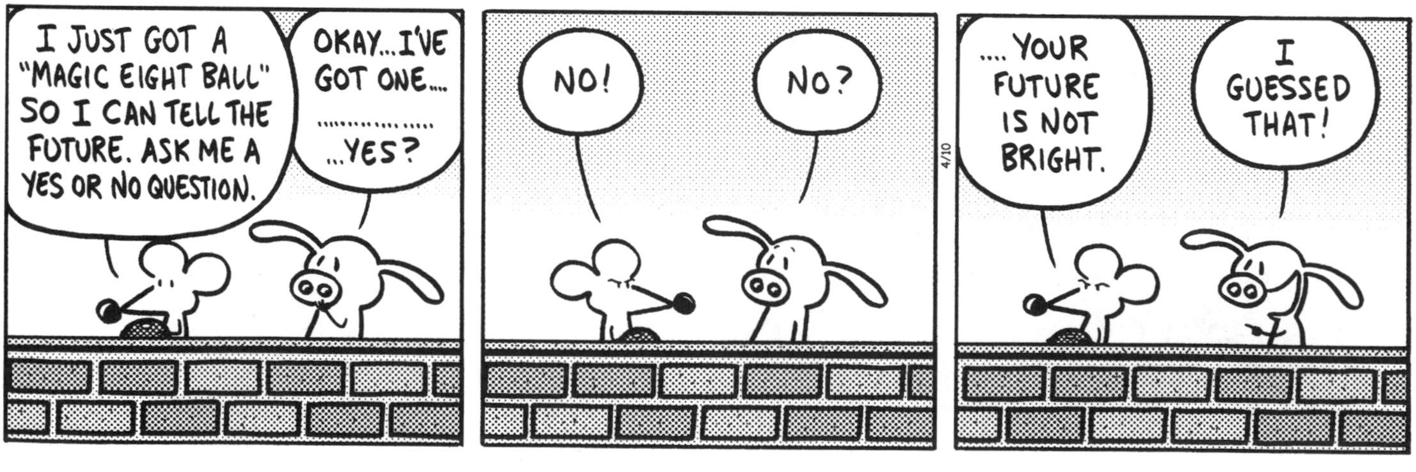
I JUST GOT A "MAGIC EIGHT BALL" SO I CAN TELL THE FUTURE. ASK ME A YES OR NO QUESTION.
OKAY... I'VE GOT ONE.... ....YES?
NO!
NO?
4/10
.... YOUR FUTURE IS NOT BRIGHT.
I GUESSED THAT!

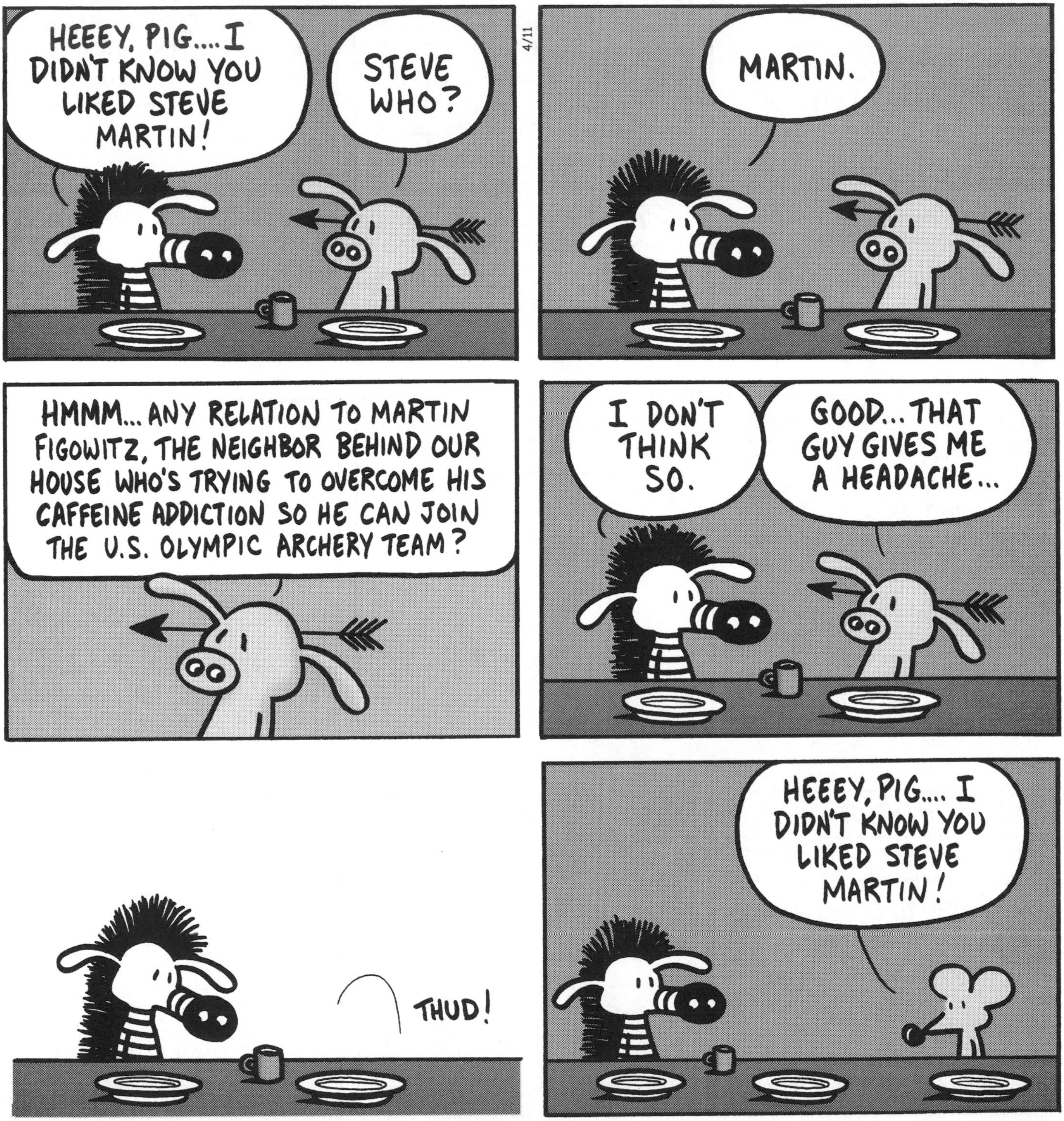
HEEEY, PIG.... I DIDN'T KNOW YOU LIKED STEVE MARTIN!
STEVE WHO?
4/11
MARTIN.
HMMM... ANY RELATION TO MARTIN FIGOWITZ, THE NEIGHBOR BEHIND OUR HOUSE WHO'S TRYING TO OVERCOME HIS CAFFEINE ADDICTION SO HE CAN JOIN THE U.S. OLYMPIC ARCHERY TEAM?
I DON'T THINK SO.
GOOD... THAT GUY GIVES ME A HEADACHE...
THUD!
HEEEY, PIG.... I DIDN'T KNOW YOU LIKED STEVE MARTIN!

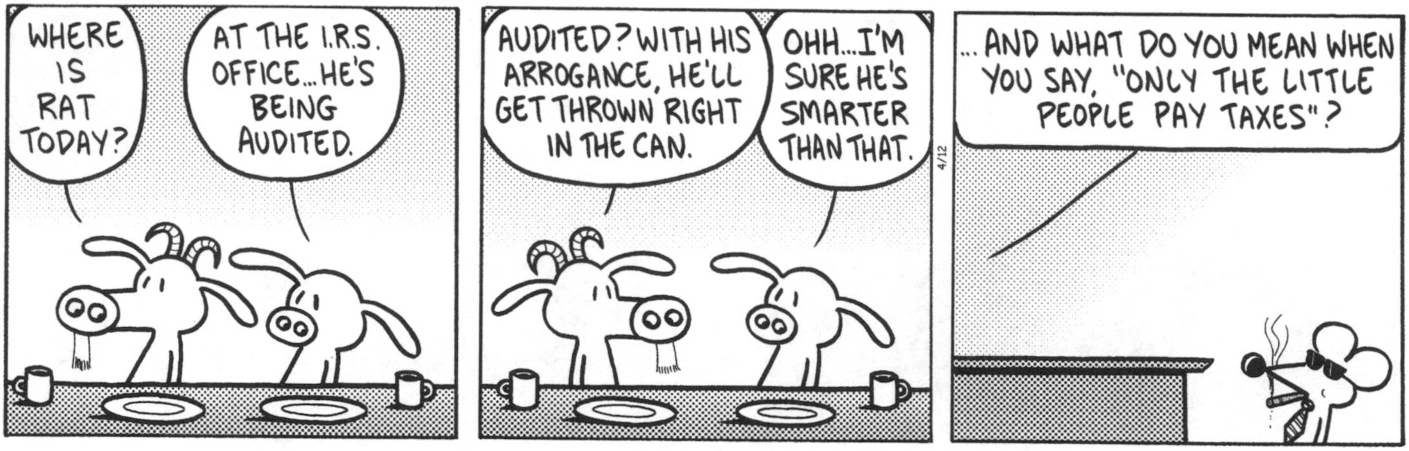
WHERE IS RAT TODAY?
AT THE I.R.S. OFFICE... HE'S BEING AUDITED.
AUDITED? WITH HIS ARROGANCE, HE'LL GET THROWN RIGHT IN THE CAN.
OHH... I'M SURE HE'S SMARTER THAN THAT.
4/12
... AND WHAT DO YOU MEAN WHEN YOU SAY, "ONLY THE LITTLE PEOPLE PAY TAXES"?

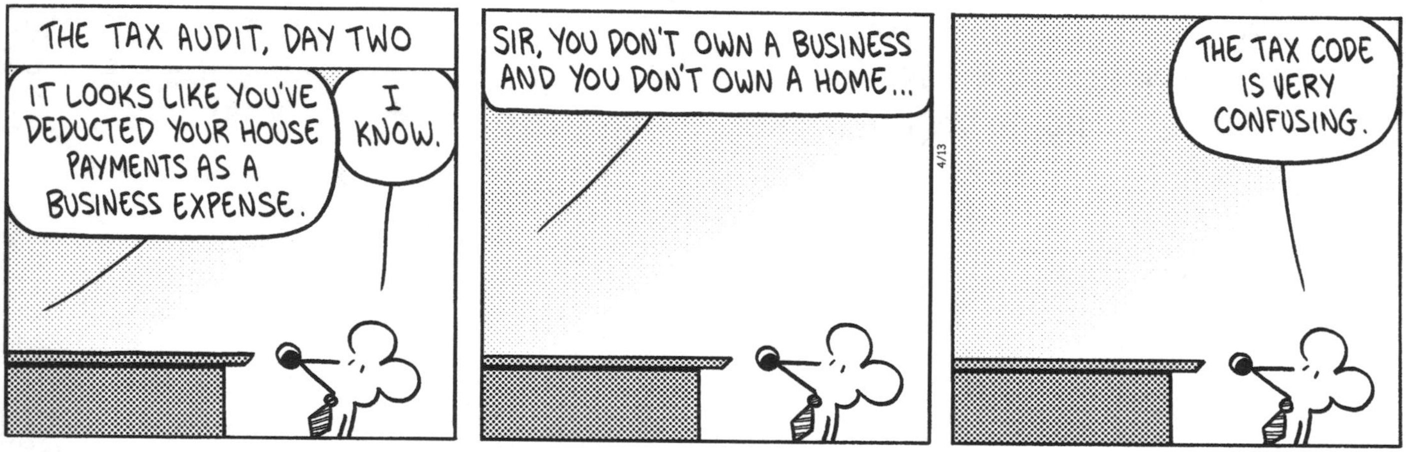
THE TAX AUDIT, DAY TWO
IT LOOKS LIKE YOU'VE DEDUCTED YOUR HOUSE PAYMENTS AS A BUSINESS EXPENSE.
I KNOW.
SIR, YOU DON'T OWN A BUSINESS AND YOU DON'T OWN A HOME...
4/13
THE TAX CODE IS VERY CONFUSING.

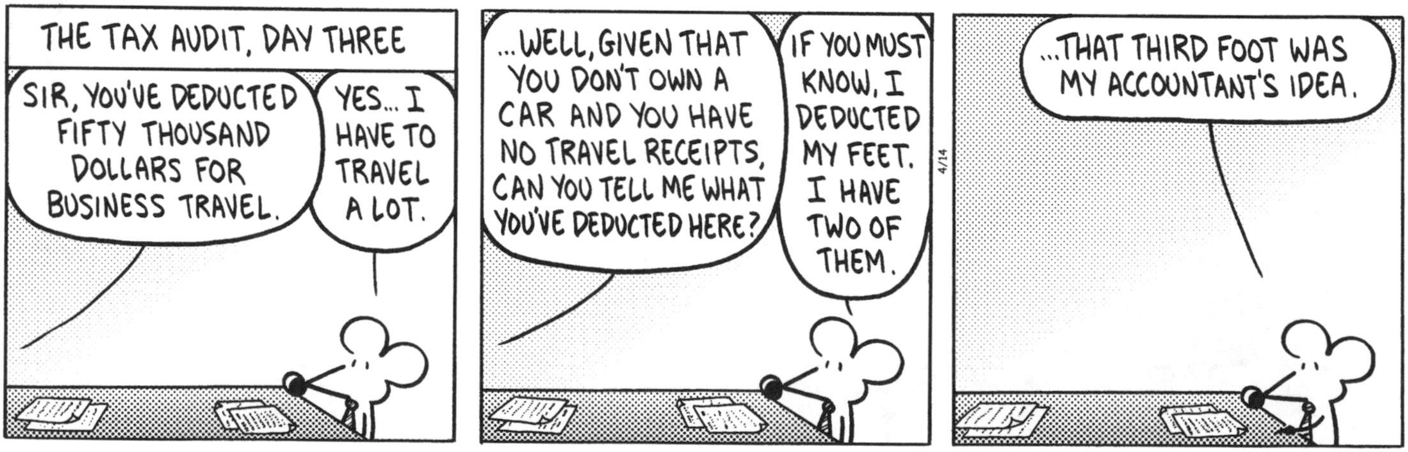
THE TAX AUDIT, DAY THREE
SIR, YOU'VE DEDUCTED FIFTY THOUSAND DOLLARS FOR BUSINESS TRAVEL.
YES... I HAVE TO TRAVEL A LOT.
... WELL, GIVEN THAT YOU DON'T OWN A CAR AND YOU HAVE NO TRAVEL RECEIPTS, CAN YOU TELL ME WHAT YOU'VE DEDUCTED HERE?
IF YOU MUST KNOW, I DEDUCTED MY FEET. I HAVE TWO OF THEM.
4/14
... THAT THIRD FOOT WAS MY ACCOUNTANT'S IDEA.

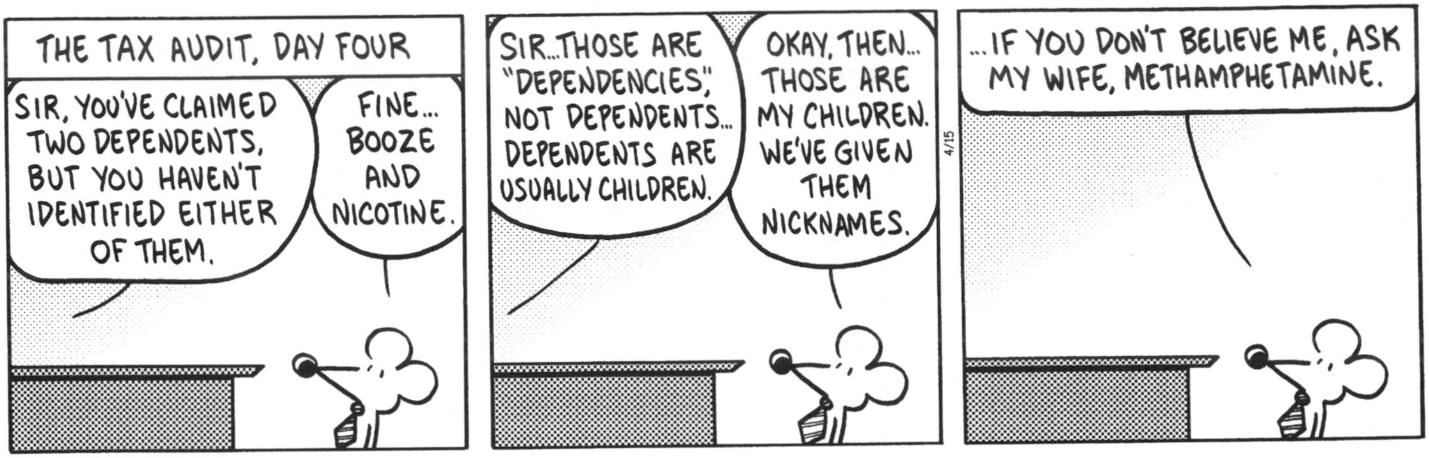
THE TAX AUDIT, DAY FOUR
SIR, YOU'VE CLAIMED TWO DEPENDENTS, BUT YOU HAVEN'T IDENTIFIED EITHER OF THEM.
FINE... BOOZE AND NICOTINE.
SIR...THOSE ARE "DEPENDENCIES," NOT DEPENDENTS... DEPENDENTS ARE USUALLY CHILDREN.
OKAY, THEN... THOSE ARE MY CHILDREN. WE'VE GIVEN THEM NICKNAMES.
4/15
...IF YOU DON'T BELIEVE ME, ASK MY WIFE, METHAMPHETAMINE.

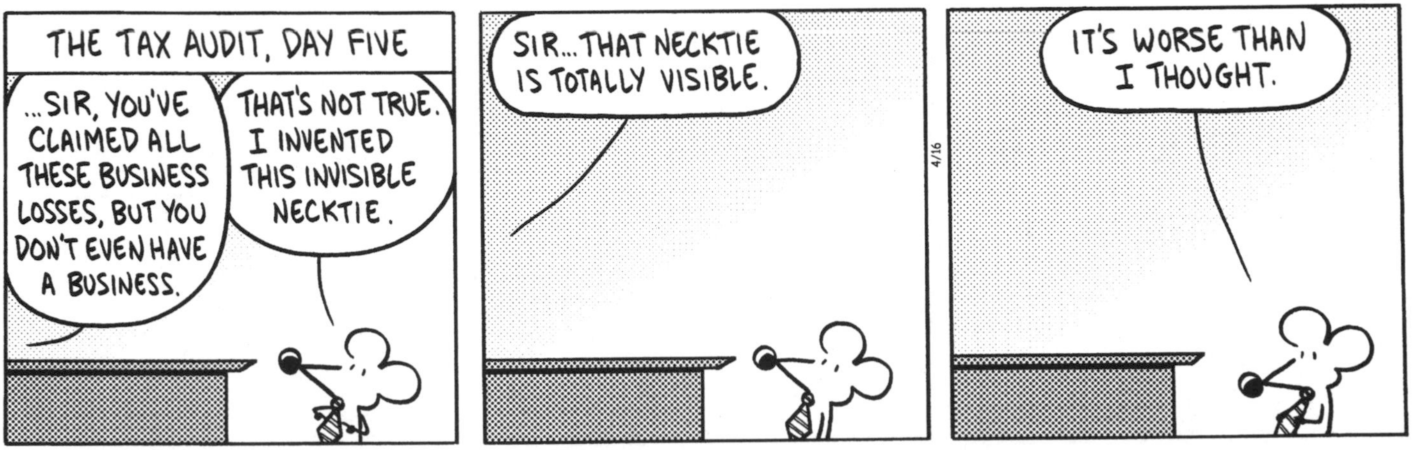
THE TAX AUDIT, DAY FIVE
...SIR, YOU'VE CLAIMED ALL THESE BUSINESS LOSSES, BUT YOU DON'T EVEN HAVE A BUSINESS.
THAT'S NOT TRUE. I INVENTED THIS INVISIBLE NECKTIE.
SIR...THAT NECKTIE IS TOTALLY VISIBLE.
4/16
IT'S WORSE THAN I THOUGHT.

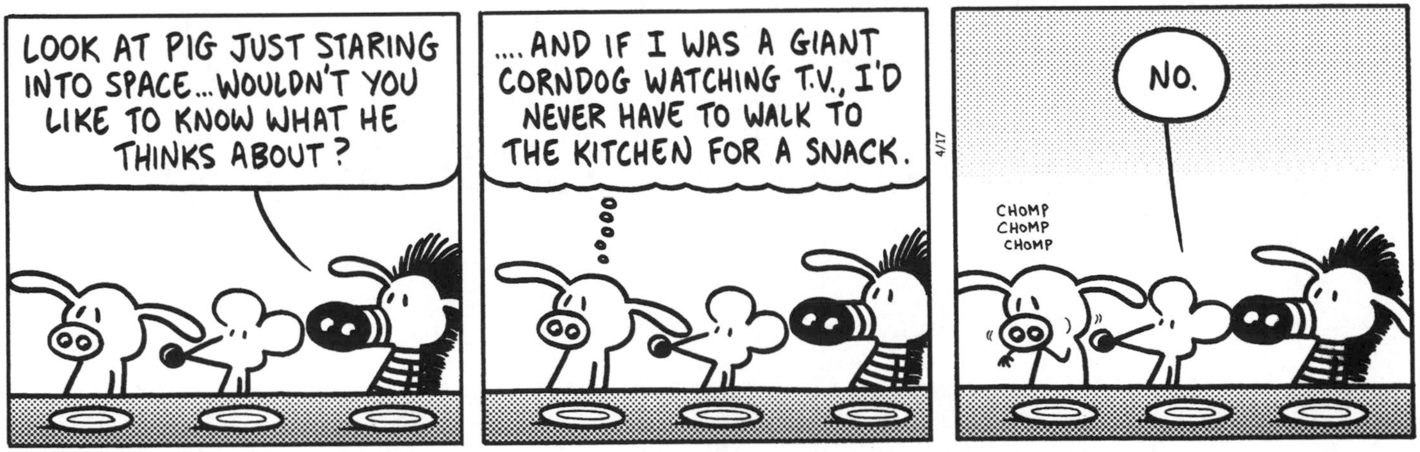
LOOK AT PIG JUST STARING INTO SPACE...WOULDN'T YOU LIKE TO KNOW WHAT HE THINKS ABOUT?
....AND IF I WAS A GIANT CORNDOG WATCHING T.V., I'D NEVER HAVE TO WALK TO THE KITCHEN FOR A SNACK.
4/17
CHOMP CHOMP CHOMP
NO.

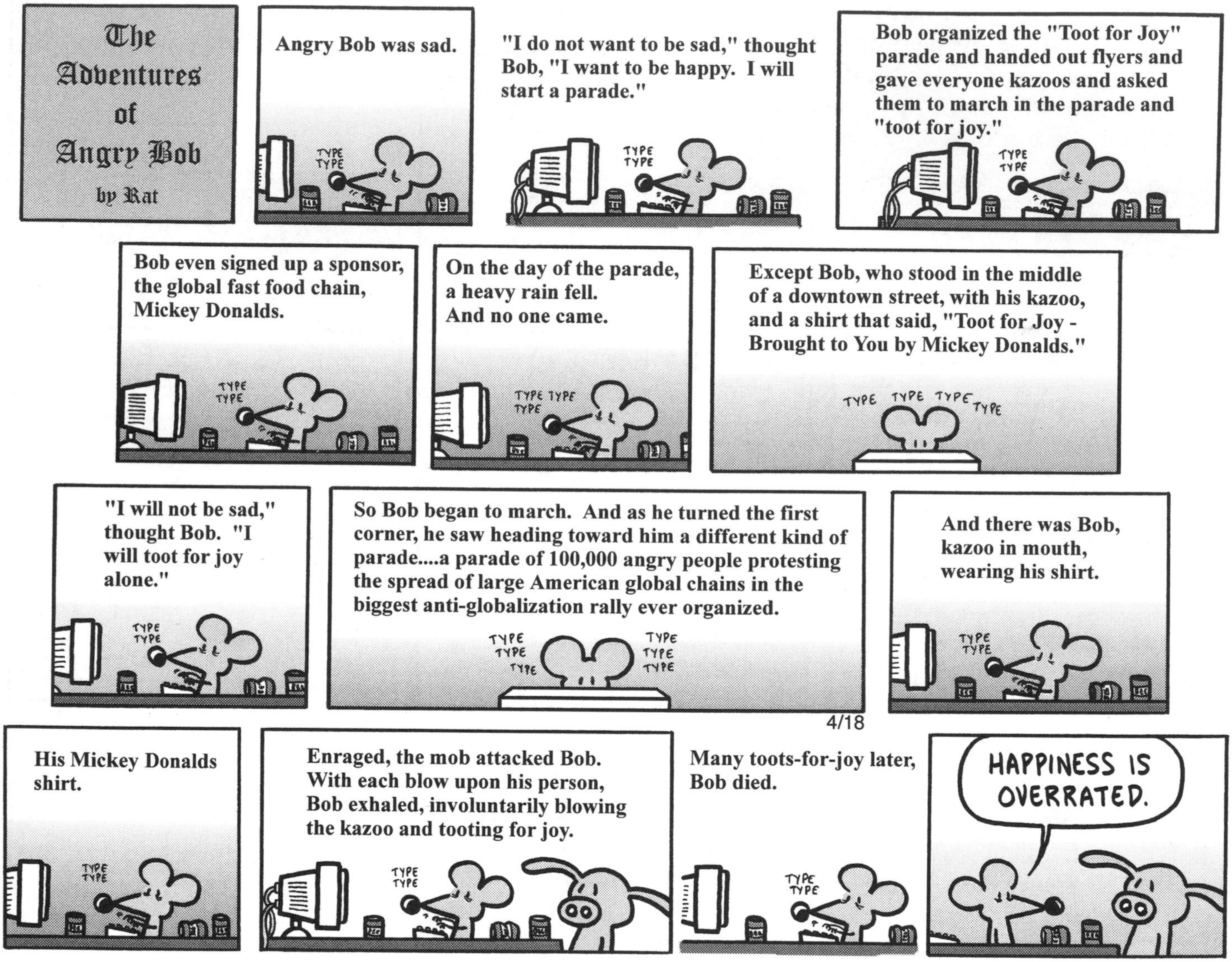
The Adventures of Angry Bob
by Rat
Angry Bob was sad.
TYPE TYPE
"I do not want to be sad," thought Bob, "I want to be happy. I will start a parade."
TYPE TYPE
Bob organized the "Toot for Joy" parade and handed out flyers and gave everyone kazoos and asked them to march in the parade and "toot for joy."
TYPE TYPE
Bob even signed up a sponsor, the global fast food chain, Mickey Donalds.
TYPE TYPE
On the day of the parade, a heavy rain fell. And no one came.
TYPE TYPE TYPE
Except Bob, who stood in the middle of a downtown street, with his kazoo, and a shirt that said, "Toot for Joy - Brought to You by Mickey Donalds."
TYPE TYPE TYPE TYPE
"I will not be sad," thought Bob. "I will toot for joy alone."
TYPE TYPE
So Bob began to march. And as he turned the first corner, he saw heading toward him a different kind of parade....a parade of 100,000 angry people protesting the spread of large American global chains in the biggest anti-globalization rally ever organized.
TYPE TYPE TYPE TYPE TYPE TYPE
And there was Bob, kazoo in mouth, wearing his shirt.
TYPE TYPE
4/18
His Mickey Donalds shirt.
TYPE TYPE
Enraged, the mob attacked Bob. With each blow upon his person, Bob exhaled, involuntarily blowing the kazoo and tooting for joy.
TYPE TYPE
Many toots-for-joy later, Bob died.
TYPE TYPE
HAPPINESS IS OVERRATED.